Arendt, Camus, and Mode.

MW01492794

Jeffrey C. Isaac

ARENDT, CAMUS,
and
MODERN REBELLION

YALE UNIVERSITY PRESS   NEW HAVEN & LONDON

Designed by Nancy Ovedovitz and set in Galliard type by
Rainsford Type. Printed in the United States of America
by Book Crafters, Inc., Chelsea, Michigan.

Library of Congress Cataloging-in-Publication Data
Isaac, Jeffrey C., 1957–
    Arendt, Camus, and modern rebellion / Jeffrey C.
    Isaac.
    p.   cm.
    Includes bibliographical references and index.
    ISBN 0-300-05203-0 (cloth)
          0-300-06054-8 (pbk.)
    1. Arendt, Hannah—Contributions in political science.
    2. Camus, Albert, 1913–1960—Contributions in
    political science. 3. Democracy. 4. Political science. I.
    Title.
JC251.A74I83   1992   92-8593
320.5—dc20   CIP

A catalogue record for this book is available from the
British Library. The paper in this book meets the
guidelines for permanence and durability of the
Committee on Production Guidelines for Book Longevity
of the Council on Library Resources.

10 9 8 7 6 5 4 3 2

For Debra, Adam, and Annelise
And for Mom and Dad

Contents

Acknowledgments

In the course of my research for this book, I have incurred many debts of gratitude, and it is with great pleasure that I acknowledge them. David Spritzen has been a truly inspirational friend and colleague. It was David who first opened my eyes to Camus, an invaluable gift. His own book *(Camus: A Critical Examination)* is more than a model of scholarship; it is a life's work, a labor of love, and I have benefited greatly from its insights. I have learned no less from David's tireless and dedicated activism. Like Camus's Dr. Rieux, David lives on the plane of his ideas—a model for us all.

As a teacher, I have come to appreciate the often subtle ways in which one makes an impact on others. In working on this project I have often found myself engaged in an imaginary dialogue with many of those who have taught me: Robert Dahl, Ray Franklin, Michael Harrington, Mike Krasner, Peter Manicas, and Lennie Markovitz. While none of these fine teachers can be held accountable for what I have imagined them to say, it is nevertheless my pleasure to acknowledge their contribution to my thinking.

Three colleagues have been especially helpful. Jean Elshtain gave an exceptionally careful and scrupulous reading of my manuscript, from which I have profited greatly. Ian Shapiro, my good friend and colleague since graduate school, offered a relentless critique of the manuscript when I needed it most. I have no doubt that he will find much in this book too "postmodern" to suit his taste; and yet I am sure he will agree that our arguments about these matters have been fruitful ones. In the past few years I have learned much from my conversations and exchanges with Michael Walzer, whose work on twentieth-century intellectuals has inspired my own.

I have also had the pleasure of presenting sections of the book, on two occasions, to the Political Science Department at the University of Minnesota. It is with gratitude that I acknowledge the support and probing criticism offered by faculty and graduate students, and thank Terence Ball, Mary Dietz, Jim Farr, Ed Fogelman, and John Freeman for their hospitality. Many other scholars in the field have also commented on various parts of the work that went into this book, including Seyla Benhabib, Marshall Berman, Mitchell Cohen, William Connolly, Peter Euben, Bonnie Honig, Judith Shklar, Svetozar Stojanovic, Mike Wrecszin, Elisabeth Young-Bruehl, and Burt Zweibach.

I am fortunate to have exceptional colleagues at Indiana University. Casey Blake and Bob Orsi both read parts of this book, and their incisive comments and political good sense are always highly valued. Jack Bielasiak, Freddy Diamant, Norm Furniss, C. R. D. Halisi, Russ Hanson, Kevin Middlebrook, Mike Morgan, Derek Penslar, Jean Robinson, Alvin Rosenfeld, Dina Spechler, Marty Spechler, and Tim Tilton have all offered insight and support. I have also learned from the graduate students I have taught over the past few years, especially Jacek Dalecki, Krista Gardner, Mike Malloy, Rob Martin, Eric Olive, and Christiane Olivo. Greg Sumner, whose dissertation on Dwight Macdonald I have had the privilege of reading, deserves special mention, both because of the amount I have learned from him and because he has so faithfully sent me articles on the New York Knicks, Celtics fan though he may be.

I also thank Ted Carmines, Chair of the Political Science Department, Morton Lowengrub, Dean of the College of Arts and Sciences, George Walker, Dean of Research and Graduate Development, and Anya Royce, Dean of the Faculty, for the leave time and financial assistance they have provided me during the writing of this book. This support, along with the NEH Summer Fellowship I received in 1990, has been materially and emotionally indispensable.

I have been graced by the exceptional professionalism and intellectual integrity of my editors at Yale University Press. John Covell has from the beginning treated me with the kind of seriousness and attentiveness every author dreams of. Richard Miller has scrupulously and generously reviewed the manuscript, helping me to turn it into a much better book than it was before he got his hands on it. Both editors have satisfied my highest expectations about publishing a scholarly book that seeks a general readership.

No book is written in a vacuum. I have been blessed with wonderful friends and family, whose support and love have been a constant source of inspiration. I would like to thank Richard Balaban, Julie Bloom, Andy Mallor, Jane Mallor, Carolyn Lipson-Walker, and George Walker, whose friendship has enriched my life and that of my family during the writing of this book. Our common pursuit of a meaningul Jewish life has shown me that the solidarities we create are as vital as those we inherit. My brother, Gary Isaac, and sister-in-law, Toni Gilpin, have engaged me in many a stimulating political argument. My parents, Sylvia and Hyman Isaac, have always sacrificed so that I could follow my dreams. Even when they have had no idea what I was doing, they have been behind me because I was doing it. My father, a printer, has helped with the proofreading of this book. His collaboration has been very special to me.

Finally, I express my deep gratitude to my wife, Debra Kent, and our children, Adam and Annelise, whose love and laughter have kept me honest. They have reproached me for my grandest conceits and indulged me my more tolerable ones. There is nothing like one's family to bring a theorist down to earth, and to teach one how limiting, and how marvelous, the world really is.

Arendt, Camus, and Modern Rebellion

Introduction

Say what you will—the Communists were more intelligent. They had a grandiose program, a plan for a brand-new world in which everyone would find his place.... People have always aspired to an idyll, a garden where nightingales sing, a realm of harmony where the world does not rise up as a stranger against man nor man against other men, where the world and all its people are molded from a single stock and the fire lighting up the heavens is a fire burning in the hearts of men, where every man is a note in a magnificent Bach fugue and anyone who refuses his note is a mere black dot, useless and meaningless, easily caught and squashed between the fingers like an insect.

From the start there were people who realized they lacked the proper temperament for the idyll and wished to leave the country. But since by definition an idyll is one world for all, the people who wished to emigrate were implicitly denying its validity. Instead of going abroad, they went behind bars.

They were soon joined by thousands and tens of thousands more.... And suddenly those young, intelligent radicals had the strange feeling of having sent something into the world, a deed of their own making, which had taken on a life of its own, lost all resemblance to the original idea, and totally ignored the originators of the idea. So these young, intelligent radicals started shouting to their deed, calling it back, chasing it, hunting it down. If I were to write a novel about that generation of talented radical thinkers, I would call it Stalking a Lost Deed.

—*Milan Kundera*

There are many ways of reading the history of the twentieth century. Unabashed modernists may see it as a history of enormous and unprecedented progress, represented by the development of science and technology, the expansion of the wealth of nations, and the growth of statehood as an instrument of national self-determination—human empowerment triumphant. To antimodernists it may appear as a history of ceaseless and purposeless change, of restless destruction of cultural and natural environments, an example of the dangerous Promethean spirit unleashed at the dawn of modernity. Neither of these readings is without foundation, and yet both are ultimately unsatisfactory. Each, in a different way, fails to acknowledge the striking discontinuity of the twentieth century, which in both its dramatic accomplishments and its horrendous atrocities has defied the expectations established by previous eras. Each is indiscriminate—the first in its embrace, the second in its condemnation; the first in its naive optimism, the second in its pessimism. Both fail to capture what Charles Taylor has called "the unique combination of greatness and danger, *grandeur et misère,* which characterizes the modern age."[1]

The twentieth century was born of some of the noblest aspirations of the modern world—progress, enlightenment, human emancipation. Kundera gives a sense of the genuine appeal of envisioning a realm "where the world does not rise up as a stranger against man nor man against other men." And yet at its most evocative his prose turns dark and foreboding, and clues us in to the danger of such a vision, to the recalcitrance of the world and of other human beings, and the limits of even our best-considered historical projects. The tragedy of this century is the tragedy of intelligence gone awry and rebellion run amok.

This book is about the effort to stalk the lost deeds of the twentieth century, to identify the original ideas from which they sprung, to examine how they took on a life of their own and lost touch with their origins, and to inquire as to how we might scold them, chase them, and hunt them down. The perspectives of Hannah Arendt and Albert Camus are the lenses through which I shall explore these concerns. As major political intellectuals of their generation they offer penetrating insight into the problem of rebellion and community in the modern world. Is it possible to imagine any limits on human power in a secular age that has witnessed the brutal exercise of totalitarian power? Is it possible to struggle for new forms of political community in the name of human dignity without erecting new prisons in place of the old ones? Can we, "without the help either of the eternal or rationalistic thought," create for ourselves our own values?[2] These questions, which preoccupied an earlier generation, continue to force themselves on us.

This remains true even in the moment of great liberal enthusiasm that seems to have overtaken us. As communism has collapsed in the former lands of the Soviet Union and Eastern Europe, many liberals have proclaimed the triumph of reason and the end of history.[3] Political scientists, political consultants, and so-called constitutional specialists hurry eastward to offer their wisdom. They have seen the future, and it is the West. And yet there is a strange disjunction between this enthusiasm and the intellectual foundations upon which it rests. Although ideologues celebrate the triumph of liberalism, they can offer no principled defense of the liberalism they trumpet. In a strange reversal indeed, it seems that we have all become Hegelians; and that very German philosopher of history who seemed only a few years ago to epitomize what threatened the intellectual foundations of "the open society" has now become the philosophical herald of the conquest of liberty. Like the Hegelians of earlier eras, our liberal Hegelians pray (and prey) before the altar of history, turning the present into "a sheer gaping at success, into an idolatry of the actual."[4] And yet beneath the triumph of reason there lurks the spectre of uncertainty and disillusion.

Contemporary political thinking is clearly at an impasse. Prevailing modes of thought are increasingly subject to suspicion, and the Enlightenment project of seeking to ground freedom on first principles, universal truths about human nature, is in disrepair if not disrepute. This disenchantment was anticipated by C. Wright Mills thirty years ago: "Our major orientations—liberalism and socialism—have virtually collapsed as adequate explanations of the world and of ourselves. These two ideologies came out of the Enlightenment, and they have had in common many assumptions and values. In both, increased rationality is held to be the prime condition of increased freedom. The liberating notion of progress by reason, the faith in science as an unmixed good, the demand for popular education and the faith in its political meaning for democracy—all these ideas of the Enlightenment have rested upon the happy assumption of the inherent relation of reason and freedom."[5]

In recent times this "happy assumption" has given way to a generalized crisis of confidence in reason. The vanguard of this movement has been largely philosophical. Philosophers of science like Thomas Kuhn, Imre Lakatos, and Paul Feyerabend have undermined belief in such notions as scientific truth and progress in understanding reality, and thereby have helped to inspire a deep epistemological skepticism.[6] Pragmatic philosophers like Richard Rorty have built upon this skepticism, calling into question two ideas central to modern political thought: that we can have grounded knowledge of ourselves, and that the institutions of modern politics are based on real progress in such knowledge.[7] Post-structuralist writers like Michel Foucault and Jacques Derrida have gone even further, emphasizing the discursive constitution of human identity and challenging the very notion of human nature as a possible object of knowledge, thus casting suspicion on the theoretical and practical achievements of modernity.[8] These philosophical currents have converged to form an intellectual tidal wave commonly referred to as postmodernism. Jean-François Lyotard, in *The Postmodern Condition*, has formulated an influential statement of the postmodernist view: "I will use the term *modern* to designate any science that legitimates itself with reference to a metadiscourse . . . making an explicit appeal to some grand narrative, such as he dialectics of Spirit, the hermeneutics of meaning, the emancipation of the rational or working subject, or the creation of wealth. . . . Simplifying in the extreme, I define *postmodern* as incredulity toward metanarratives."[9] Such incredulity is not confined, however, to an intellectual avant-garde of Continental philosophers and literary critics. It is an enduring feature of our cultural landscape.

This crisis of confidence is reflected in the most influential idioms of academic political theory. The decidedly "antifoundational" impulse of contemporary liberal political philosophy is strikingly at variance with the extreme confidence, indeed hubris, with which many liberal politicians and ideologists now present their views.[10] With some historical oversimplification it can be argued that modern liberal theory has typically relied on some grand narrative, whether it be a conception of the rights-bearing subject of contractarianism, the rational maximizer of utilitarianism, or the noumenal self of Kantian ethics. The efforts of John Rawls in *A Theory of Justice* and Robert Nozick in *Anarchy, State, and Utopia* are but the most recent attempts to derive a theory of justice from a grand philosophical conception of the individual.[11] These efforts have spawned a cottage industry of critiques, and it is notable that the most current attempts of liberals to justify their commitments disavow any philosophical intention. Judith Shklar, for example, has endorsed a "liberalism of fear," which she defends in terms of the aversion to cruelty expressed by moralists like Montaigne and Montesquieu, an aversion supposedly implicit in the morality of liberal society, which emerged out of the ruins of the European religious wars of the sixteenth and early seventeenth centuries.[12] Rawls himself, in a number of recent articles, has disavowed metaphysical readings of his theory of justice, insisting that in his book he sought to do no more than articulate the sense of fairness presupposed by liberal practice, and not to offer any grand justification of this sense of fairness.[13] Perhaps the most ambitious, and most influential, version of this liberalism has been enunciated by Richard Rorty, who has explicitly endorsed a "post-modern bourgeois liberalism."[14] Rorty repudiates any philosophical or principled justification and identifies with liberalism for no other reason than because it is the prevailing tradition in the West. What he calls the liberal belief that cruelty is evil is for him nothing more than what liberals have come to believe: "We cannot look back behind the processes of socialization which convinced us twentieth-century liberals of the validity of this claim and appeal to something which is more 'real' or less ephemeral than the historical contingencies which brought those processes into existence."[15] Rorty cheerily interprets this liberalism as an inherently inclusive way of life that "is dedicated to enlarging itself," exaggerating its concern with the sufferings of others and saying little about its less benign forms of enlargement.[16] To be sure, Rorty endorses a kind of liberal humanitarianism. But he refuses to provide a principled defense of this endorsement; indeed, he denies that such a defense is necessary or even possible. Liberals may have what he calls a solidarity with the suffering; but this solidarity has nothing to do with a common humanity or human condition, and it requires no further justification than itself. Presumably for Rorty such solidarity is so compelling to liberal citizens that there is no need to argue on its behalf. Contemporary liberalism has thus become "postmodern" in its suspicion of grand narratives about universal truths or freedoms, a suspicion which has done little to temper the enthusiasms of many of its triumphant supporters.

The same suspicion of foundational arguments characterizes the various forms of communitarianism that have gained currency among political theorists by purporting to criticize liberalism. Here too any reliance on a theory of truth or human nature is disavowed, and claims about politics are relativized to the concerns of "embodied selves" inhabiting particular, local traditions.[17] This postmodern suspicion has, ironically, even infected the writings of those more conservative thinkers who criticize modernity for its value relativism. Alasdair MacIntyre, for example, whose *After Virtue* indicted modernity for its lack of a firm ethical foundation, argues in *Whose Justice, Which Rationality?* that there is no principled way to adjudicate moral disagreements between traditions, including the disagreement between the neo-Aristotelianism he endorses and liberalism.[18] Similarly, Allan Bloom, in his neo-Platonic *The Closing of the American Mind,* rehearses all of the expected charges against modern value relativism without providing any account of what values one should adopt and how they might be justified.[19] While endorsing the "Great Conversation" of Western intellectual history, he nowhere indicates the kind of answers such a conversation might furnish. Such criticisms of the egoism and nihilism of modernity are thus highly formalistic and abstract; they gesture at a moral stance without providing any reasonable warrant for one.

Contemporary Marxist theory also exhibits many of the symptoms of this postmodern condition. In the postwar period its grand narrative of "the emancipation of the rational or working subject" has been substantially revised if not repudiated, largely as a consequence of the critical interventions of such thinkers as Sartre, Althusser, Adorno, and Marcuse, but also owing to the political obstacles confronting Marxism to which these theorists addressed themselves.[20] And yet, as I have argued elsewhere, even this more sophisticated and pluralistic Marxism remains wedded to certain core beliefs about the primacy of production and the historical dynamic of class struggle, which it has become increasingly difficult to justify in the light of contemporary experience.[21] As MacIntyre has observed, those Marxists who have disavowed Marx's materialist philosophy of history "have characteristically become unable to offer any account of their reasons for adopting the moral and political allegiance that they do."[22] As a result, contemporary Marxism is riven by controversy about such questions as what it means to be a Marxist in the late twentieth century, what the morality of Marxism is, and how the traditional understanding of class struggle needs to be modified in the light of "new social movements." Current arguments among Marxists about "post-Marxism" parallel broader intellectual debates about postmodernism. Marxism, like liberalism, has substantially abandoned the metaphysics that has traditionally underwritten its historical perspective and political practice. And as with liberalism, although this repudiation of metaphysics has not driven all of its practitioners to abandon ship, it has led to a similar crisis of justification. There is, of course, one major difference: whereas the resounding collapse of communism in the East has dealt a harsh blow to Marxist class politics throughout the world, further dispiriting the Marxist vision, the liberal ascendancy that is its most obvious product has provided liberalism with a consolation that its own theoretical defenders are unable to offer—the consolation of seeming success.

Across the political spectrum political theory seems to have lost its nerve, experiencing a disenchanting skepticism and possessing little sense of the possibilities of creative historical agency. While such a malaise is no doubt due in part to the powerful influence of developments in philosophy, literary criticism, and historiography, just as important is the disarray of Western politics. While Western leaders display boundless enthusiasm for democracy abroad, they seem allergic to its more local expressions, and show little inclination to tackle the serious social, economic, and environmental problems that confront their fellow citizens. Self-congratulatory rhetoric is a cheap substitute for serious political vision.

In the Eastern half of Europe the victories of democratic oppositions and the crash of communism have given way to increasingly acrimonious and divisive forms of political conflict. The "triumph of democracy" in the East has generated enormous enthusiasm and opportunity, but also grave danger and uncertainty. If democracy is to succeed, it must confront a series of issues—religious, ethnic, ecological, and economic—that pose fundamental challenges to the liberalism being celebrated as the wave of the future. While the foundations of postwar politics in both East and West decay, the superstructural "baroque arsenals" of the United States and the former Soviet Union remain poised for global annihilation—a vivid reminder of the dead weight of history. Meanwhile, the Third World remains the site of untold misery, political violence, and ecological devastation. It is telling indeed that one of the fastest-growing Third World industries is the dumping of the refuse of advanced industrial societies.[23]

The Persian Gulf war to "liberate" Kuwait epitomizes the exhaustion of the political ideologies that have long held sway in the West. Bolstered by its own empty rhetoric about "just war" and "human rights," the Bush administration wasted no time in transforming Saddam Hussein, a leader whose brutality had never deterred American support, into Hitler reincarnate. Rushing to employ force, it mobilized an overwhelming military response to Iraqi aggression. The outcome of the war—the deliverance of the Kuwaitis and Saudis into the hands of their own dictatorial monarchies, the environmental devastation of Kuwait, the creation of hundreds of thousands of refugees, the indifference to Kurdish self-determination, the death of thousands of Iraqi civilians and the ruin of Iraqi civilian infrastructure—may have demonstrated the might of the United States, but it also demonstrated the profound cynicism of a politics whose worship of "smart bombs" and "precision missiles" renders it indifferent to human rights and human needs. Yet if supporters of the war displayed chilling cynicism and hypocrisy, the response of its opponents was often no less cynical. Often relying on the rhetoric of anti-imperialism and anti-Zionism, much of the left was content to condemn the American military response while remaining silent about what the United States was responding *to*. Nostalgic for the seeming simplicity of the Vietnam antiwar movement, and cynically recalling the examples of Panama and Nicaragua, many in opposition to the war refused to confront the barbarity of the Iraqi Ba'ath regime or ask what measures they would be willing to support in order to halt its aggression. Mirroring the nihilism of the battlefield, the political debate over the war became little more than a battle of appalling slogans and images. Neither side appeared to care about the real human consequences of the war. Both were content to ideologize it. Neither the stale Marxian rhetoric of anti-imperialism nor the selective, hypocritical liberal invocations of human rights seemed relevant to the matters at hand. And yet our political language offered us few alternatives within which to articulate our despair.

In the light of this failure of our language it is hard to avoid the "postmodern" suspicion of which Lyotard has written, and which seems to have permeated the enterprise of political theory. We live in the midst of a profound and undeniable crisis of the "discourses of legitimation" that have animated the modern world. Yet however sound the skepticism about such discourses, the call to abandon them—to cease inquiring into human nature, attempting to articulate epistemological criteria, and trying to provide reasons for political obligation or rebellion and visions of the good society—is troubling.

One reason is the suspicion that such legitimations are necessary for both our theoretical and our practical activities. It is true, as self-styled postmodernists assert, that there are no incorrigible foundations or innocent premises of political argument. But as Ian Shapiro has remarked, rejecting foundational argument on account of this "makes about as much sense as saying that because there is no single type of foundation on which all buildings . . . can be built to last forever, we should henceforth build all buildings with no foundations at all. They would, then, of course, all quickly fall over."[24] Our choice is not between absolute foundations or no foundations, between overblown metanarratives or just plain narratives, but between convictions resting on warranted but contingent principles and those based on ungrounded assertions or prejudices. Foundational commitments are indispensable. Questions about human nature and the human good are central to politics, even if they can never be answered once and for all, nor in a theoretically neutral way. The effort to avoid them is disingenuous, for if we do not take them up explicitly we are likely simply to smuggle them into our arguments through the back door.

The postmodernist suspicion of foundations leads to the effacement, if not abandonment, of *criticism* as a guiding ideal of theory. If there are no metanarratives, no underlying reasons for us to do what we should do, then the theorist or political writer is under no obligation to offer such reasons in support of his or her proposals. Theory then becomes rhetoric, or poetry, or perhaps a game, in which the writer's will to power or self-expression becomes his or her primary motivation. This tendency is most clearly exemplified in Rorty's philosophy of edification, which invites the theorist to become a "private ironist," constantly creating himself or herself like a Nietzschean work of art without any sense of seriousness about the common world.[25] For Rorty the writing is its own justification; no more need be said or done, and whatever is done in the broader public world needs no help from the writer. This spirit of levity is also exhibited in the generally precocious way in which writers like Derrida and Feyerabend—and even more so their American admirers—write about the world, and in their explicit efforts to subvert the notions of freedom and truth. The abandonment of critique, however, is not limited to those postmodern writers who boldly celebrate the utter contingency of all meanings and realities. It is also characteristic of those many more conventional political theorists who choose to rely on intuitions or cultural conventions rather than to offer principled justifications of their political preferences. Echoing Edmund Burke's critique of the metaphysics of modern rights theory, "this barbarous philosophy, which is the offspring of cold hearts and muddy understandings," such writers value embodied traditions or contextual judgments over the effort to articulate universal truths and critical standards.[26]

Further, the antifoundational turn in political theory is disturbingly apolitical. It is certainly influenced by political events, and its participants make political arguments, defending kinds of liberalism or Thomism or anarchism. These arguments undeniably have political intent and political consequence. Both Rorty's criticism of cruelty and MacIntyre's Thomist communitarianism, for example, envision, however abstractly, a model of political community, whether it be the liberal *rechstaat* or the enclosures of the church. Yet ironically, in spite of all their talk of context and concreteness, these writers fail to address contemporary political realities in anything like a substantive manner. Although Rorty writes with sensitivity about cruelty, discussing passages from Nabokov and Orwell, there is very little discussion of contemporary cruelty and its complex causes, or the complicity of "liberal" regimes like the United States, to be found in his book. MacIntyre writes about the virtues of Thomism, but he says nothing about the world of power in which religious institutions and movements operate, about such things as the papacy, liberation theology, economic justice, or gender inequality within the

Catholic tradition. And though Derrida writes with intelligence about "racism's last word," he says little about the system of apartheid that the word justifies, about how to change that system, or indeed why it should be changed, what *values* would be advanced by changing it.[27] To make such observations is less to criticize the political leanings of these authors than to question their refusal as theorists to meaningfully address the real political world. There is a disembodied quality to even the best political theory that makes it possible for such theory to function as academic currency or rhetoric, but renders it ill-suited to rational argument about real political questions whose answers have real human consequence and not simply a metaphoric effect.

There is, finally, the force of current events themselves. While political theorists go on about the pointlessness of talk about foundations, the democrats of Central Europe have set about the task of establishing new foundations for their politics. While political theorists insist that there is no common humanity, and that talk of such a humanity is a category mistake, a transcendental illusion, these democrats have long maintained that there is a common humanity—what Camus calls a "solidarity of chains"—that binds us together, that enjoins us to support one another in the struggle for democracy, and that suggests that we ought to be cautious and self-critical in our efforts. The astonishing events of the past three years offer eloquent testimony that there might well be a human nature, a recalcitrance of the human spirit which defies ideological illusions as well as disillusioned rhetoric about the end of ideology, and that there are certain universal standards we can ignore only at our peril.

This book is about modern rebellion. The current antifoundational turn in political theory is closely linked, in my view, with a profound distrust of architectonic systems and grand ideological visions. There is no doubt that much of this distrust derives from the miserable experience of revolutionary politics in the twentieth century. The imagery of "historical breaks," "social transformations," and "conscious mastery of the historical process" has born rotten fruit in political practice. Metaphysical confidence in collective political agency has thus given way to a more chastened sense of the limits of political knowledge and practice. And yet the modern conception of freedom, of humans as makers of their own destinies, is a powerful one. As Charles Taylor has eloquently argued, the sense of rebelliousness, of pushing up against existing limits, of envisioning and constructing new worlds, is inextricably woven into the fabric of modern life. This seems true whether we like it or not, though I believe, along with Taylor, that on balance it is a good thing.

In my view the current suspicion of grand philosophical narratives and Promethean political projects is essential for thinking clearly about our recent history and our current predicament. But for many contemporary theorists this sensibility is not simply an inescapable element of our historical experience but an absolute given of political inquiry. For them it is not a starting point of critical inquiry so much as a terminus. Thus they playfully or earnestly, subversively or conservatively, embrace this suspicion rather than accept it as an attitude that must be constructively and—at the risk of inviting Nietzschean scorn—seriously built upon.

The writings of Hannah Arendt and Albert Camus are important because they point the way toward a more satisfactory political orientation. As Norman Jacobson has put it, they offer us a political theory without solace, without the guarantees that modern ideologies have typically purported to provide.[28] Like the postmodernists, both writers criticized the Enlightenment faith that science and reason could be the unproblematic agents of human empowerment. Yet for Arendt and Camus this critique is based on a serious and sustained interrogation of historical experience as much as it is on a deconstruction of metaphysical philosophy. Although both writers were suspicious of the justifications and programs entailed by liberal and Marxist versions of universalism, neither was willing to abandon the idea that there is a common human condition, and they steadfastly insisted that this made a politics of human rights imperative. Further, despite their deep aversion to the typical agencies of modern politics—bureaucratic states and political parties—both refused to abandon politics as a specific practice of effecting public power. Instead they envisioned other, more spontaneous and anarchistic forms of political activity and organization. In short, their common vision, far from being edifying, agonistic, or blandly conventional, sought to reappropriate the historical themes of modern rebellion and to revitalize public life. Both sought to stalk lost deeds, but not to shoot them down. Neither was content to articulate a negative dialectic, however profound, and both sought to build on the ruins of the twentieth-century crisis of modernity that they experienced. As Camus put it, "It is essential for us to know whether men, without the help of either the eternal or rationalistic thought, can unaided create his own values. . . the uneasiness that concerns us belongs to a whole epoch from which we do not want to dissociate ourselves. . . . No, everything is not summed up in negation and absurdity. But we must first posit negation and absurdity because they are what our generation has encountered and what we must take into account."[29]

I shall seek here to retrieve the political vision articulated by Arendt and Camus, and to explore the historical contexts that illuminate it. My aim is not to present these thinkers as saints or authorities, only as exemplary theorists and political actors, who point the way toward a rebellious politics that is alive to many of the concerns of postmodern writing and yet is self-assuredly normative and humanistic.

But why Arendt and Camus? There are a number of reasons for considering them to be exemplary. The first is that they belong to the generation of European and American intellectuals who experienced firsthand the traumas of the twentieth century—two world wars, failed revolutions, the Holocaust, and the Cold War.[30] Both Arendt and Camus were profoundly influenced by these events, which they believed made necessary new ways of thinking about political life. It is a striking if incredible fact that the historical experience of the twentieth century has largely been erased from the institutional memory of academic political theory.[31] The traditional canon of political philosophy, divided as it is into "classical" and "modern," excludes many important twentieth-century thinkers and is, more importantly, constitutionally incapable of appreciating the significance of the issues that they address. Thus while Camus, Simone Weil, Ignazio Silone, George Orwell, Walter Benjamin, and many others are excluded from this canon altogether, Arendt is considered an adjunct member, along with Sheldon Wolin, Leo Strauss, and Eric Voegelin, as recent commentators on "the tradition."[32] This is of course a complicated and controversial matter, but it is notable that the Arendt who figures in this discussion is not really Hannah Arendt but a caricature of the original, someone who is introduced in order to expatiate on Descartes or Marx or Jefferson or Augustine (and, more recently, such current academic favorites as Habermas or Foucault) but who, it would seem, has little if anything to say about such mundane topics as warfare, totalitarianism, Hitler, Stalin, political Marxism, postcolonialism, or twentieth-century revolutions. Theodor Adorno, another sometime favorite among the more avant-garde political theorists, once wrote that "after Auschwitz to write a poem is barbaric."[33] Whether this is true, and indeed what it means, is a matter of some controversy, but the academic discipline of political theory has found it possible to produce thousands upon thousands of pages about justice and morality written as if Auschwitz had never existed and the complex events preceding and following it had never occurred. There is a gap in our historical consciousness that needs to be filled, and doing so is not only of historiographical interest. For it will reveal that many of our current intellectual concerns and political problems have been around for some time, and have been addressed in profound, if often forgotten, ways.

The wide circle of Resistance intellectuals (so-called because of their participation in the Resistance to the Nazis during World War II) to which Arendt and Camus belonged was a special group. In one respect these writers typified what Foucault has called the postmodern "specific" intellectual, suspicious of grand projects—"intellectual freelances," in Camus's phrase, refusing to consider themselves "organic intellectuals" of any particular group or party and denying World-Historical significance to any movement or cause.[34] But they were deeply engaged public intellectuals. Regardless of whether they had university degrees or affiliations—many did not—they addressed public issues of war and peace, freedom and justice, in a variety of idioms, participating in a broader culture of political discussion and debate. They thus epitomized what Michael Walzer has called "connected social critics."[35] For Walzer the critic, unlike the armchair philosopher, disavows a posture of theoretical detachment, preferring instead to identify with and engage the historical experience and culture of his or her time. Occupying the contested terrain of social life, avoiding the temptations of both pious, Archimedean detachment and boorish, blind loyalty to the status quo, the social critic sees political argument as a way of resolving pressing practical problems of human living.

Arendt and Camus were intellectuals of this type. Whereas Arendt, trained as a systematic philosopher, is most famous for her philosophical treatises, Camus, a Nobel Prize–winning author, is best known for his journalism and fiction. But both authors wrote in a variety of idioms—books, essays, journalism—and both sought to get to the bottom of the civilizational crisis of the twentieth century through the sensitive but bold use of reason. Both expressed an aversion to what Camus called "rationalistic thinking" and Arendt called "ideologies"—grand systems, inflexible orthodoxies purporting to explain everything and indifferent to the finely textured character of experienced reality. But neither was averse to the critical use of reason, and both were, in their own ways, profoundly *theoretical* writers engaged with other important twentieth-century literary and political intellectuals and with a variety of important political groupings.

Both were, in different ways, intellectuals of the left sympathetic toward the modern revolutionary experience. Though neither was a fallen Communist, both were acutely aware of the shattering significance of totalitarianism. Both Arendt and Camus were iconoclastic thinkers, but this did not deter them from identifying, in a nondoctrinaire fashion, with contemporary movements for political empowerment. One of the themes of this book is their participatation in the aborted effort to find a "third way" between liberalism and Marxism, especially as these had become incarnated in the Cold War antagonism between American and Soviet imperialisms.

In all of these respects Arendt and Camus were representative of a generation of intellectuals whose insights need to be recovered. But it is my belief they also stand out among this generation. This judgment is admittedly at least in part a matter of personal taste, as I have found the work of both thinkers to be unusually insightful and compelling. In no way do I mean to suggest that an analysis of the work of Weil or Silone or Merleau-Ponty would be any less valuable.[36] But there are, I believe, certain things about my subjects which warrant their treatment together in a book of political theory. Unlike many of their colleagues, though Arendt and Camus were sharply critical of Marxism, they retained many left-wing commitments, especially an affinity with anarchist politics. Both drew nourishment from a pagan appreciation of the ancient Greeks, which they brought to bear on current events in a way at odds with the Hegelian spirit of much twentieth-century radical thinking, and yet also at odds with any kind of nostalgia. And both shared a tragic sensibility that was influenced by Nietzsche—a characteristic that makes them especially relevant to contemporary postmodernists—yet both sought to join this appreciation of ambiguity to a distinctively democratic politics, one centered not on the institutions of mass politics but on the voluntary associations of civil society.

But perhaps the best reason to consider Arendt and Camus together is their complementarity. In Arendt one finds some of the most powerful theoretical diagnoses of the crisis of this century, diagnoses written in systematic, expository prose yet laced with a sardonic wit and a profound sense of tragic drama. In Camus one encounters equally deep insights, usually developed in novelistic or dramatic form and yet grounded in an incisive, if often elusive, theoretical analysis. By reading these figures against one another I believe it is possible to provide new and revealing interpretations of them both.

Viewing Arendt against the backdrop of the Camusian notions of absurdity and revolt allows us to situate her within the intellectual culture of disenchanted mid-twentieth-century radical politics and to better appreciate her thoroughly contemporary concerns. The Arendt discussed below is thus a rather different figure than the Grecophile philosopher one frequently meets in the academic literature. It would of course be sheer folly to deny the more classical elements of her work. But I believe that these have been vastly exaggerated out of an inattention to her own historical concerns. Such attention, however, forces us to relegate these elements to a more marginal role. This move will disturb many academic political philosophers whose interpretations have tended to focus on these classical elements. This is not the place to rebut such interpretations. The present book has other, more political and thematic concerns. But I believe that the interpretation I offer illuminates central aspects of Arendt's thought that have been marginalized if not suppressed by the fixation with her classicism.

Similarly, viewing Camus against the backdrop of the Arendtian conceptions of praxis, representative thinking, and political community reveals his profound preoccupation with the revitalization of public life. My Camus is thus far removed from the solitary, moralistic "noble soul" familiar to admirers and critics alike. Again, it would be foolish to deny this aspect of his thought. Camus himself confided in his *Notebooks* that "I am not made for politics because I am incapable of wanting or accepting the death of the adversary." There was something about the closures attached to political action that discomforted Camus. And yet he refused the role of noble soul, maintaining that "modern man is obliged to become concerned with politics. I am concerned with it, in spite of myself and because, through my defects rather than through my virtues, I have never been able to refuse any of the obligations I encountered."[37] As we shall see, Camus is a political creature and indeed a political *theorist,* one for whom our defects and our culpabilities as human beings define our existence. He presents a coherent view of the human condition and of politics, even if his writing defies conventional theoretical labels and methods, and displays an ethical sensitivity—at times even anguish—uncharacteristic of most political writers.

It is important, however, to issue a caveat. I argue that Arendt and Camus arrive at a similar vision of a democratic "rebellious politics," one that refuses to privilege any form of human authority and that values chronic contestation in political life. Yet I do not wish to attribute to their respective intellectual projects a substantive unity. There is no evidence that either writer understood himself or herself to be participating in a common project with the other, beyond the general sense in which both saw themselves as helping to reconstitute political thought in a nihilistic age. There is no evidence of which I am aware that Camus even read any of Arendt's work. It is certain that Arendt read some of Camus's writings, but it is equally certain that she misunderstood his work in the fashion typical of many of his readers.

In an early essay on French existentialism, for example, Arendt, reviewing Camus's *The Stranger* and Sartre's *Nausea* for the *Nation*, lumps Camus together with Sartre as writers who "deny the possibility of a genuine fellowship between men, of any relationship which would be direct, innocent, free of pretense." Arendt acknowledges that "the good thing about Sartre and Camus is that they apparently suffer no longer from nostalgia for the good old days," that they possess "a definite modernity of attitude which does not try to hide the depth of the break in Western tradition." This comment reveals a great deal, both about Arendt's own conception of the tasks of theory and about her sense of a point of contact with the thought of Camus. Yet she also maintains that the existentialist valuation of solitude contains dangerous "nihilistic elements."[38] This same interpretation of Camus is also presented, in passing, in a much later essay, "Civil Disobedience," in which she criticizes traditional conceptions of conscientious civil disobedience because "the rules of conscience hinge on interest in the self" rather than in the larger political world. The example she offers of a conception of resistance preoccupied with the self is that of Camus. Yet the evidence she offers for such an interpretation is not a text from Camus but rather a text from Christian Bay that refers to "Camus's . . . stress on the necessity of resistance to injustice for the resisting individual's own health and welfare."[39]

These references indicate that Arendt had little familiarity with Camus's political writing. It appears she was unaware that Camus explicitly distinguished himself from existentialism because, in his words, in the existentialist universe "man is free of the shackles of his prejudices, sometimes from his own nature, and reduced to self-contemplation, becomes aware of his profound indifference to everything that is not himself. He is alone, enclosed in this liberty."[40] As I shall argue, Camus's thinking was far removed from the Cartesian individualism with which it is normally associated, a point only highlighted by reading it against Arendt. A clue to the real character of his thought is offered in a letter to Roland Barthes, in which he writes, "Compared to *The Stranger*, *The Plague* . . . represent[s] the transition from an attitude of solitary revolt to the recognition of a community whose struggles must be shared. If there is an evolution from *The Stranger* to *The Plague*, it is in the direction of solidarity and participation."[41] Arendt, hardly alone, seems to have failed to note this evolution in Camus's thinking.

Elisabeth Young-Bruehl reports at least two encounters in Paris between Arendt and Camus. The first, in 1946, prompted Arendt to observe favorably that Camus was "a new type of person, who simply and without any 'European nationalism' is a European." The second, in 1952, in the midst of the controversy surrounding *The Rebel,* led her to write her husband, "Yesterday I saw Camus: he is, undoubtedly, the best man now in France. He is head and shoulders above the other intellectuals."[42] There is, then, evidence of some personal relationship and, at least on Arendt's part, of some admiration. There is also the shared connection with Dwight Macdonald, the editor of *politics,* the maverick left-wing journal of the 1940s. Macdonald both translated and published Camus's work, which he credited with having influenced his important essay "The Root Is Man," and referred to Arendt, his friend, as "the most original and profound— and therefore the most valuable—political thinker of our times."[43] This connection is indicative of the similarities in outlook of Camus and Arendt, for Macdonald was at the center of a network of important radical resistance intellectuals that included such notable figures as Camus, Nicola Chiaromante, Mary McCarthy (one of Arendt's closest friends), Andrea Caffi, and Lewis Coser.[44]

Also suggestive of these similarities is Arendt's description of post-Liberation French political culture in the above-mentioned *Nation* review:

> If the Resistance has not achieved the European revolution, it seems to have brought about, at least in France, a genuine rebellion of the intellectuals. . . . This may reflect, of course, a desire to escape from political action into some theory which merely talks about action, that is, into activism; but it may also signify that in the face of the spiritual bankruptcy of the left and the sterility of the old revolutionary elite—which have led to the desperate efforts at restoration of all political parties—more people than we might imagine have a feeling that the responsibility for political action is too heavy to assume until new foundations, ethical as well as political, are laid down, and that the old tradition of philosophy . . . is actually an impediment to new political thought.[45]

It is impossible to read this often-ignored text without picking up the resonances with Arendt's own main theoretical works. The impotence of received political philosophies, the need for new political and ethical foundations, the spiritual bankruptcy of the left—these are main themes of Arendt's writing. It is clear from her comments here that she identifies with postwar Resistance literature, of which Camus was the outstanding figure.

These disparate comments are indicative of some personal and intellectual affinities and connections between Arendt and Camus. But the most powerful connection is the commonality of sensibility, theoretical orientation, and political conviction to be found in their writings. This is best seen, not surprisingly, through a critical exegesis and reconstruction of their arguments, which is the main task of the present work.

This book can most easily be considered a work of normative political theory broadly understood. In it I engage in extensive textual exegesis and conceptual criticism, seeking to elucidate the contributions of Arendt and Camus to contemporary thinking about practical problems of politics. Although the book is primarily about Arendt and Camus, its subtext, never far from the surface, is contemporary thinking about such practical problems as the sources of resistance to oppression, the need to cultivate a healthy sense of limits in politics, and the prospects for democratic alternatives to mass politics. This is what I understand normative theory to be, and the kind of normative theory that I support necessarily requires attention to historical and political concerns, the sorts of things often considered the province of professional historians or political scientists. Only with a sense of history—of limits and opportunities, problems and prospects—is it possible to speak meaningfully about the proper ordering of political life.

Our political condition in the 1990s has a history that continues to bear upon us, however much we choose to ignore it. Part of the way to think about our current problems lies in exploring that history. The works of Arendt and Camus are no panaceas. But, as I hope to show, their insights can make an important contribution to our historical understanding, and to our ability to rethink the imagery appropriate to our politics at the dawn of the twenty-first century. In this sense this book attempts a fusion of horizons, bringing Arendt and Camus into a dialogue with us that is sensitive to the distance that separates them from us but is also aware of their legacy, an unfinished project in which we might take part.

Each chapter of this book addresses distinct thematic questions on the way to retrieving the vision of a rebellious politics. In Chapter 1, I undertake a brief cultural biography of the generation of intellectuals to which Arendt and Camus belonged. I assess the impact of such events as the rise of Stalin, two world wars, and the Holocaust both on that generation as a whole and on Arendt and Camus in particular, suggesting that a novel sensibility based on a unique mixture of pessimism and courage resulted from these experiences. In Chapter 2, I explore Arendt's and Camus's common appreciation of the traumas inflicted by totalitarianism on mod-

ern civilization, an appreciation shared by contemporaries such as George
Orwell and Arthur Koestler.

Chapter 3 examines Arendt's and Camus's critiques of modernity. I
focus on their common aversion to the Prometheanism of modern humanism, discussing their accounts of both liberalism and Marxism. Although much of their insight is drawn from Nietzsche, I maintain that
neither Arendt nor Camus is willing to follow the philosopher of suspicion
all the way down the dark path to an active nihilism. This discussion of
the limits of modernity leads me to the arguments of Chapters 4 and 5,
where I explore the vision of rebellious politics at which Arendt and Camus
converge. I argue that for both writers ethical and political conduct is
constrained by elements of our common human condition. I examine the
importance of human finitude, dialogue, and political judgment for both
thinkers, exploring their affinities with and divergences from the views of
liberals like Raymond Aron, libertarian Marxists like Rosa Luxemburg,
and democratic theorists like John Dewey. Although sensitive to the question of limits that is acutely posed by liberalism, both Arendt and Camus
supported a robustly democratic politics that is perpetually open to disagreement, contestation and revision. I conclude that Arendt and Camus
are best thought of as democrats of an anarchist stripe, providing that we
understand this term accurately and that we underscore the limits of any
conventional labels in capturing their unconventional visions.

Chapters 2 through 5 constitute the core of my interpretation of the
political theories of Arendt and Camus. In the remaining chapters I seek
to give life to these theories by treating them as skeletons which might
support a flesh-and-blood politics. In Chapter 6, I explore the practical
commitments of Arendt and Camus, seeking to show how these commitments exemplified their political principles. I discuss their common
interest in a "third way" that rejects both Soviet-style commmunism and
American-style capitalism. I also demonstrate the similarities between
Arendt's views regarding Israel and Palestine, and Camus's regarding Algeria, showing how both thinkers arrived at a conception of moderation
and peaceful coexistence based on confederational arrangements.

Finally, in Chapter 7, I critically assess the contributions of Arendt and
Camus. I emphasize in particular their influence on contemporary Eastern
European democratic theorists of civil society. But I also discuss a number
of areas in which their thinking can be found wanting—their blindness
to questions of gender and sexuality, their underappreciation of the potential role of a critical social science, and their syndicalist devaluation of
representative government and social democratic politics.

Though Arendt and Camus have much to offer us, there are limits to their vision. The problem of reconstituting our political thinking and action still stands before us. But that is as it should be. For no analysis of the writings of other theorists can substitute for our own inquiries and engagements.

Chapter 1

HUMANITY AT ZERO HOUR

We were born at the beginning of the First World War. As adolescents we had the crisis of 1929; at twenty, Hitler. Then came the Ethiopian War, the Civil War in Spain, and Munich. These were the foundations of our education. Next came the Second World War, the defeat, and Hitler in our homes and cities. Born and bred in such a world, what did we believe in? Nothing. Nothing except the obstinate negation in which we were forced to close ourselves from the very beginning. The world in which we were called to exist was an absurd world, and there was no other in which we could take refuge. . . . If the problem had been the bankruptcy of a political ideology, or a system of government, it would have been simple enough. But what happened came from the very root of man and society. There was no doubt about this, and it was confirmed day after day not so much by the behavior of the criminals but by that of the average man. . . .

Now that Hitler has gone, we know a certain number of things. The first is that the poison which impregnated Hitlerism has not been eliminated; it is present in each of us. . . . Another thing we have learned is that we cannot accept any optimistic conception of existence, any happy ending whatsoever. But if we believe that optimism is silly, we also know that pessimism about the action of man among his fellows is cowardly.

Albert Camus spoke these words in 1946 at Columbia University in New York.[1] Though highly personal, they offer a cogent precis of the experience of a generation of political intellectuals. Caught in a maelstrom of unpredictable and bloody events set off by the First World War, these individuals were subjected to a particularly brutal form of intellectual shock therapy. As Nichola Chiaromante recalled, "I remember being totally obsessed by a single thought: we had arrived at humanity's zero hour and history was senseless; the one thing that made sense was that part of man which remained outside of history, alien and impervious to the whirlwind of events."[2] Even conservative and religious thinkers, who had long expatiated on the dangers of modern secularism and the original sinfulness of human initiative, were not immune to the feeling that all bets were off, that traditional understandings—of class, community, nation, church, God—were somehow inadequate to the task of coping with the world.[3] But particularly vulnerable were intellectuals, liberal and socialist alike, who had been reared on the modernist imagery of human rationality and historical progress, whose intellectual optimism left them ill-prepared for the abyss into which European civilization had fallen.

Sheldon Wolin has argued that "most of the great statements of political philosophy have been put forward in times of crisis," that the classic political philosopher typically "must reconstruct a shattered world of meanings and their accompanying institutional expressions; he must, in short, fashion a political cosmos out of political chaos."[4] For Wolin such epic writers as Plato, Machiavelli, and Hobbes seek to "encompass" disorder, to respond to the challenge of political crisis by fashioning an "architectonic" vision of political reconstruction. Though not without its problems, this has proven a fruitful way to think about political theory and, if true, it would suggest that Hannah Arendt and Albert Camus simply follow in a long tradition of political inquiry.[5] Their sense of a break in history would then be but another instance of a sense of crisis experienced by most political theorists since the ancient Greeks. Whatever the merits of Wolin's scheme, however, there are two reasons why it will not do as an account of the political theory under consideration.

First, the events of the twentieth century, well summed up in Camus's speech, are in their scrupulous barbarity different in character from the sorts of disorder and destruction experienced in previous ages. Though the world has certainly seen its share of chaos and destruction, until recently these have been limited both by the technologies available and by the aspirations of political leaders. The disorder of 1914–1945, by contrast, was made possible by the transcendence of such limitations. Global in scope, it was animated by grandiose schemes of world historical transformation, and implemented by highly "civilized" technologies of death and destruction. Second, if the crisis to which Camus and Arendt respond is novel, so too are the sorts of "solutions" both present to this crisis. Both writers seek to offer a new vision of politics, but both resolutely oppose architectonic systems. There is a self-conscious skepticism, and modesty, to the vision of politics shared by Arendt and Camus, which distinguishes them from the more "epic" writers discussed by Wolin. In my view it is just this modesty of vision that makes them more appropriate models for contemporary political theory. Yet if the modesty of their writings was due to their common horror and disillusionment, its *visionary* character stemmed from their shared inspiration by the practices of resistance to totalitarianism.

The Century of Total War

The nineteenth century has often been called the century of progress.[6] Inaugurated by a wave of republican revolutions and succored by optimistic philosophies of history, the political theory of the nineteenth century was circumscribed by the competing logics of revolution and reaction. "Progressives" and "conservatives" agreed on little, but they agreed that democratic revolutions were the wave of the future. Conservatives, to be sure, looked upon this prospect with fear, and sometimes with apocalyptic horror, equating the demise of traditional authorities with the demise of civilization itself.[7] Progressives as well often acknowledged the underside of historical change; Marx was not alone in considering force a midwife of progress. And yet I think it is fair to say that neither progressives nor reactionaries anticipated the death, devastation and disillusionment produced by twentieth-century politics.

These realities, of course, in no way exhaust the record of twentieth-century history, which has also seen its share of liberation and empowerment. But the achievements of the twentieth century have come at a heavy price. Camus spoke for many when he wrote that the history of his generation was convulsive, nihilistic, and "absolutely insane."[8] No doubt the most obvious example of insanity was the sheer destructiveness of twentieth-century politics. In the early months of the First World War, Rosa Luxemburg observed that "this world war means a reversion to barbarism . . . either the triumph of imperialism and the destruction of all culture . . . de-population, desolation, degeneration, a vast cemetery; or the victory of socialism."[9] Where Luxemburg was wrong was in the dualism of her alternatives. The war brought barbarism *and* socialism, in a dangerous, explosive combination that eventually helped fuel a second, even more destructive, world war. From the perspective of the late twentieth century it is easy to take this destructiveness for granted. But though history has long known violence and brutality, the twentieth century is unique in being, in the words of Raymond Aron, "the century of total war."[10]

The two world wars saw unprecedented destruction and violence on a global scale. Millions of people were killed, and millions more wounded, in the First World War. In the wake of this wreckage the Russian, Prussian, Hapsburg, and Ottoman monarchies fell. The resulting breakup of long-standing empires in Europe, Asia, and the Middle East began a protracted and convulsive process of decolonialization.[11]

The consequences of the Second World War were still more shattering. The death toll even exceeded that of the earlier war. The Nazi genocide took more than 11 million civilian lives, including 6 million Jews, over three-quarters of the Jewish population of Europe. As did its predecessor, this war left vast numbers of people homeless.[12]

Twentieth-century politics demonstrated that, *pace* Marx, it was the modern war machine as much as the bourgeoisie that ceaselessly conjured up new and improved technologies, designed less for production than for demolition. If the First World War brought the invention of mustard gas and the tank, the Second World War inaugurated even more potent means of destruction—saturation aerial bombing and the atomic bomb. One of the most significant ethical and political consequences of the two world wars was the effacement of any practical distinction between combatants and civilians.[13] On the single night of 13 February 1945, the firebombing of Dresden killed 135,000 people. When the delayed effects of irradiation, destruction, and disease are considered, there is no doubt that the atomic bombs dropped by the United States on Hiroshima and Nagasaki took an even greater toll.[14]

As devastating as the loss of life was the loss of humanity, as peoples and cultures were swept away in a tidal wave of barbarism. The two world wars saw the development of propaganda into a science and an art, as governments strove to vilify the enemy and to mobilize entire populations behind the war efforts.[15] The language of a "poisoned" world, to borrow Edmund Wilson's phrase, became commonplace. Echoing Camus, Wilson suggested that this poison could not simply be identified with abstract political forces, that it was "present in each of us."[16] It is difficult to appreciate the cultural and historical significance of such a pollution of the spirit. It was not simply a question of the murder of individuals and the destruction of the peoples of Europe; the very fabric of Europe as a civilization, a repository of art, music, and religion, was torn asunder by the war. As Dwight Macdonald noted, "One of the many things I cannot get accustomed to in this war is the fact that the most ancient, beautiful buildings of Europe may be blasted to bits in a few hours. Rome, Paris, Assisi . . . who knows when they will join Warsaw, Bath, Coventry, Nuremburg, Frankfort, Kiev, Cologne, Palermo, Naples, Rotterdam, Cracow, London, and Berlin? It is like living in a house with a maniac who may rip up the pictures, burn the books, slash up the rugs and furniture at any moment."[17]

The sheer destructiveness of twentieth-century politics was a symptom of its irrationality and unpredictability. One of the most frightening features of the war years was the extent to which political instrumentalities had taken on a life of their own, producing extraordinary reversals and monstrous unintended consequences. As Orwell wrote, "we live in a lunatic world in which opposites are constantly changing into one another."[18] Dwight Macdonald echoed the feelings of many intellectuals terrified by the extent to which the war had overcome natural sympathy and common sense and replaced them with politically induced bellicosity: "As it grinds on, as it spreads and becomes more violent, the conflict becomes less and less meaningful, a vast nightmare in which we are all involved and from which whatever hopes and illusions we may have had have by now leaked out."[19] The war epitomized a more general reality of the time—the sheer scale of political conflict, the enormity of its stakes, placing whole continents, indeed the globe itself, up for grabs and jeopardizing entire peoples and cultures. As Simone Weil put it, "We seem to have lost the very rudiments of intelligence, the notions of measure, standard, and degree; of proportion and relation; of affinity and consequence . . . we people our political world with monsters and myths; we recognize nothing but entities, absolutes, finalities."[20]

The First World War was but the inaugural episode in a series of traumatic political events—the transformation of revolutionary dictatorship in Russia into Stalinist totalitarianism; the implosion of the Weimar Republic and the rise of fascism; the fratricidal suppression of revolution by the Communists in Spain leading to the victory of Franco; the Hitler-Stalin pact of 1939; World War II itself, and the Nazi genocide in Europe; the Soviet massacres at Katyn and Warsaw, and the deliverance of Eastern Europe from Nazism to Stalinism; the bombings of Hiroshima and Nagasaki. These distinctive, complex events shared a monstrous disjunction between word and deed, between stated intention and consequence. Each was the occasion of extraordinary propaganda and deceit; each was produced by the actions of political leaders blind to their own limits, intoxicated by their sense of power and their faith that history would vindicate them. These disturbing events followed one upon the next with a disorienting rapidity that only exacerbated the sense that history was out of control, a suspicion all the more frightening to those nourished upon the typically modern faith in the progressive unfolding of the human power to control.[21] These events defined the political landscape for the generation to which Arendt and Camus belonged. They signified a frightening centralization of power in the hands of political organizations, a profound corruption of the human spirit by the instruments of deceit and destruction. As George Orwell put it, modern man, a "quite irresponsible rebel" confident in his capacities, had torn away what Edmund Burke once called "the decent drapery" of tradition, only to discover that "the thing at the bottom was not a bed of roses at all, it was a cesspool of barbed wire."[22]

Perhaps the most cogent statement of disillusionment with the modern faith in history is Walter Benjamin's "Theses on the Philosophy of History." Benjamin, a German Jewish refugee from Nazism who in 1940 took his own life to avoid capture by the Nazis, sought to chastise those leftists—liberals, Social Democrats, and Communists alike— whose "dogmatic" conception of progress rendered them incapable of anticipating or combatting the rise of Nazi totalitarianism. Conceiving fascism as the final stage of capitalism, and considering its grossest barbarities to be superstructural aberrations, the left had disarmed itself intellectually long before it was disarmed by the fascists: "One reason why Fascism has a chance is that in the name of progress its opponents treat it as a historical norm. The current amazement that the things we are experiencing are 'still' possible in the twentieth century is not philosophical. This amazement is not the beginning of knowledge—unless it is the knowledge that the view of history which gives rise to it is untenable."[23] Benjamin calls this view of history a "snare," which had entrapped its proponents in an unwarranted and unrealistic "faith in progress" and "confidence in their 'mass basis.' " He remonstrates that instead of undertaking creative analysis of and strategic responses to the novel historical moment, the left takes solace from the notion that it is "moving with the current."[24]

Echoing Machiavelli, Benjamin chastises those who associate the passage of time with the triumph of virtue. In place of this confident, Promethean vision of historical progress, Benjamin suggests a more disturbing image:

> A Klee painting named "Angelus Novus" shows an angel looking as though he is about to move away from something he is fixedly contemplating. His eyes are staring, his mouth is open, his wings are spread. This is how one pictures the angel of history. His face is turned toward the past. Where we perceive a

chain of events, he sees one single catastrophe which keeps piling wreckage upon wreckage and hurls it in front of his feet. The angel would like to stay, awaken the dead, and make whole what has been smashed. But a storm is blowing from Paradise; it has got caught in his wings with such violence that the angel can no longer close them. This storm irresistibly propels him into the future to which his back is turned, while the pile of debris before him grows skyward. This storm is what we call progress.[25]

These lines were written in 1940, by all accounts before the official plans for the Nazi "final solution" were even considered. But it is impossible to read them without thinking of the piles upon piles of corpses produced by the Nazi death machine. In this terrifying vision, history is a supra-human process, hurtling forward, out of control, with its back toward the future, destroying everything in its wake. The vivid imagery of extraordinary power and utter uncontrollability is sobering. Equally telling is the portrait of the angel itself, agape at what passes before his eyes, seeking to "make whole what has been smashed" yet unable to do so, propelled forward not by malign forces but by a violent storm "blowing from Paradise." Benjamin's account of historical progress deliberately controverts the optimistic schema that had long prevailed among the "progressive" intelligentsia.[26]

Arthur Koestler spoke for many when he observed that the modern world seemed caught in the terrifying "spasms of its death struggle."[27] The empowering agencies of modernity had turned in on themselves, changing from means of freedom into means of domination and destruction. From the perspective of the 1940s the promise of modernity seemed to have issued in nihilism and despair. Reason had been eclipsed, freedom driven "from the streets and broad places once open to all."[28] Far from riding a rising tide of history, the world was pitching headlong into an abyss.

The War Years for Arendt and Camus

Both Arendt and Camus experienced the traumas of mid-century firsthand. For Arendt this meant exile, internment, and homelessness. Born in 1906 in Königsberg, the city of Kant, she was raised as an assimilated German Jew. She was educated at the top German universities (Marburg, Frieburg, and Heidelberg) and instructed by the triumvirate of twentieth-century German idealism—Edmund Husserl, Martin Heidegger, and Karl Jaspers. As Elisabeth Young-Bruehl reports, the security Arendt felt in this tradition of German academic philosophy was shattered by the rise of Nazism.[29]Arendt was politicized by Kurt Blumenfeld, chief spokesman for the Zionist Organization of Germany, who heightened her awareness of Jewish identity, and her life was thrown into turmoil by Hitler's rise to power in 1933.

Her first husband, Günther Stern, a Communist, was forced to flee Berlin after the Nazi burning of the Reichstag on February 27, 1933, and the crackdown on the left that followed. Arendt remained, offering her apartment as a way station in an underground railroad for Hitler's enemies. She also worked for the Zionist Organization of Germany to document anti-Semitic conduct as part of its effort to raise international consciousness about the plight of German Jews. In this capacity she was arrested and held for eight days, prompting her to leave Germany clandestinely, making her way from Prague to Geneva to Paris, where she arrived in the autumn of 1933. There she worked with various Zionist organizations, including Agriculture et Artisanat, an organization providing young Jewish émigrés with vocational and agricultural training to prepare them for a future in Palestine, and Youth Aliyah, an association aiding the emigration of Jewish youth to Palestine. In 1935 Arendt personally brought a group of French-Jewish children to Palestine. She continued these activities until 1940, when, after war broke out between France and Germany, she was interned as a German refugee. Of this experience she later wrote, sardonically: "Apparently nobody wants to know that contemporary history has created a new kind of human beings—the kind that are put into concentration camps by their foes and internment camps by their friends."[30] Unlike many German Jews, who were later turned over to the Nazis by the Vichy government, she and her second husband, Heinrich Blucher, managed to obtain their release, whereupon they set sail for New York. America was to be the final destination for this self-described "Ulysses wanderer," who suffered "desperate confusion" about her identity.[31]

Arendt later reflected on this experience in a moving essay, "We Refugees": "We lost our home, which means familiarity of daily life. We lost our occupations, which means the confidence that we are of some use in this world. We lost our language, which means the naturalness of reactions, the simplicity of gestures, the unaffected expression of feelings. We left our relatives in the Polish ghettos and our best friends have been killed in concentration camps, and that means the rupture of our private lives. . . . We were once somebodies about whom people cared, we were loved by friends, and even known by landlords as paying our rent regularly."[32] It is impossible to understand Arendt's deep concern with the problem of modern worldlessness without appreciating the force of this deracinating experience. The exile forced upon her by the rise of totalitarianism made her painfully aware of the fragility, and the importance, of places of shelter, spaces in which people could feel personal security and common belonging. For her this problem was inextricably human *and* political, requiring collective rather than individualistic solutions. She reflected on the political situation of the Jewish refugee, foreshadowing her later conception of politics as a space of public appearance: "Today the truth has come home: there is no protection in heaven or earth against bare murder, and a man can be driven at any moment from the streets and broad places once open to all."[33] Arendt's belief that human rights were a fragile political achievement jeopardized by the principle of national sovereignty was rooted in this personal ordeal.

Homelessness and statelessness were bad enough but, as Young-Bruehl reports, Arendt was shattered by the knowledge of Hitler's "final solution." As she recounted years later "At first we did not believe it. . . . A half a year later, when it was proven to us, we finally believed it. Before that, one would say to oneself—so, we all have enemies. That's quite natural. Why should a people have no enemies. But this was different. This was really as though the abyss had opened. . . . This should never have been allowed to happen. I don't mean the number of victims, but the method, the fabrication of corpses. . . . This . . . was something that none of us could reconcile ourselves to."[34]

Arendt's theoretical writings bear the imprint of these terrible events. She remained preoccupied with the problem of historical understanding, with how her contemporaries might "reconcile themselves" to the awful things that had happened—how they might comprehend them so that they might not give up on the meaning of their acts. And yet she refused to shy away from the gravity of this problem and the difficulty of such understanding.[35] This is clear, for example, in Arendt's first political work, *The Origins of Totalitarianism,* where she writes:

> Two world wars in one generation, separated by an uninterrupted chain of local wars and revolutions, followed by no peace treaty for the vanquished and no respite for the victor, have ended in the anticipation of a third World War between the two remaining world powers. . . . Never have we depended so much on political forces that cannot be trusted to follow the rules of common sense and self-interest—forces that look like sheer insanity, if judged by the standards of other centuries. . . . On the level of historical insight and political thought there prevails an ill-defined, general agreement that the essential structure of all civilizations is at the breaking point. Although it may seem better preserved

in some parts of the world than in others, it can nowhere provide the guidance to the possibilities of this century, or an adequate response to its horrors.[36]

This sensibility pervades her work. Arendt insists that we can take no comfort in traditional concepts or expectations, that the radical novelty—the radical evil—of contemporary events requires a new kind of thinking.[37]

This deeply pessimistic sense that history has been shattered is perhaps most poignantly expressed in Arendt's early essay, "Organized Guilt and Universal Responsibility": "How great a burden mankind is for man.... [We have] in fear and trembling...finally realized of what man is capable—and this indeed is the precondition of any modern political thinking. ...upon them and only them, who are filled with a genuine fear of the inescapable guilt of the human race, can there be any reliance when it comes to fighting fearlessly, uncompromisingly, against the incalculable evil that men are capable of bringing about."[38] Guilt, evil, fear and trembling—the imagery is stark and powerful, and offers little solace to her readers.[39] The events of the mid-twentieth century leave Arendt with a profound sense that the political world is in shambles. Far from the spirit of optimism, she suggests that perhaps the most appropriate response to the wreckage produced by the angel of history is humble repentance.

Camus's experience was no less intense or traumatic. Born in 1913 in Mondovi, Algeria, he was first introduced to the horrors of war by the death of his father, who was killed at the battle of the Marne in 1914. Camus's early childhood was marked by economic deprivation and bouts of tuberculosis, both of which prepared him for the experience of "exile" to follow. As a French-Algerian philosophy student at the University of Algiers, Camus was first drawn to political affairs in the 1930s. Joining the Communist Party of Algeria (PCA) in 1934, he was active in campus politics and the cultural politics of such Communist-inspired theater groups as the Theatre du Travail.[40] He was expelled from the PCA in 1937. As a vocal critic of the party's drastic move toward French nationalism in 1936 as part of its Popular Front strategy, its complacent attitude toward the claims of native Algerian Arabs, and its authoritarianism and hypocrisy, Camus was not cut out for the ideological discipline the party demanded.[41] Camus's first political experiences were thus grounded in the fateful developments of Stalinism.

His disenchantment and eventual break with Communism in no way diminished his left-wing attachments. Indeed, as his leftism was inspired by his identification with the plight of the common man rather than by any Marxist orthodoxy, the break only strengthened his radicalism. When the Spanish Civil War broke out in 1936, Camus co-wrote and produced a play, *Revolte dans les Asturies,* celebrating the rebelliousness of the Spanish working class. Disturbed by the mendaciousness of Communist Popular Frontism, he was horrified by the triumph of Franco. As he later recalled, the defeat of the Republic "for the first time, in the face of a world still sunk in its comfort, gave Hitler, Mussolini, and Franco a chance to show even children the meaning of totalitarian technique.... For the first time men of my age came face to face with injustice triumphing in history. At that time the blood of innocence flowed amid a chatter of pharisees."[42] An entry in his *Notebooks* accurately articulates his sense of politics during this period: "Every time I hear a political speech or read those of our leaders, I am horrified at having, for years, heard nothing which sounded human. It is always the same words telling the same lies."[43]

After the break with the Communist Party, Camus worked as a jour-nalist for the socialist *Alger-Républicain,* where he subjected the French colonial regime to harsh criticism. The rise of war fever frightened him. Two 1939 entries in his *Notebooks* articulate his growing despondency:

> They have all betrayed us, those who preached resistance and those who talked of peace.... Never before has the individual stood so alone before the lie-making machine.... We used to wonder where war lived, what it was that made us so vile. And now we realize that we know where it lives, that it is inside ourselves. ... It is in this terrible loneliness both of the combatants and of the noncom-batants, in this humiliated despair that we all feel, in the baseness that we feel growing in our faces as the days go by. The reign of beasts has begun.
>
> The hatred and violence that you can already feel rising up in people. Nothing pure left in them. Nothing unique. They think together. You meet only beasts, bestial European faces. The world makes us feel sick, like this universal wave of cowardice, this mockery of courage, this parody of greatness, and this with-ering away of honor.[44]

Camus believed that the collective passions produced by war propaganda and fanatical nationalism would lead to the eclipse of all individuality. He also feared the closure of political possibilities that war might bring. As he put it in a September 1939 editorial in *Le Soir Républicain,* "Never perhaps have left-wing militants had so many reasons to despair."[45] And yet, despite his aversion to war, he saw that "it is always useless to try to cut oneself off, even from other people's cruelty and stupidity": "There is nothing less excusable than war, and the appeal to national hatreds. But once war has come, it is both cowardly and useless to try to stand on one side under the pretext that one is not responsible. Ivory towers are down.

Indulgence is forbidden—for oneself as well as for other people."[46] This insistence on "remaining inside" the "absurd misfortunes" of his time was a hallmark of Camus's political writing. Although he refused to "take sides" if that required him to ignore the complexities of the situation and to identify what is justifiable with what is absolutely virtuous or good, he also recognized that it is often necessary to choose, even if choice is difficult.

Thus in September 1939, after the Nazi invasion of Poland and Hitler's declaration of war against France, he attempted to enlist in the French army. Turned down because of his tuberculosis, he went to Paris, where he worked as a journalist and wrote fiction. As the war progressed he found himself cut off from his wife and family in Algeria, experiencing a profound sense of "exile."[47] Camus reflects on the rupture caused by the war and the German occupation in his 1944 "Letters to a German Friend": "Death strikes everywhere and at random. . . . For five years it was no longer possible to enjoy the call of birds in the cool of evening. We were forced to despair. We were cut off from the world because to each moment of the world clung a whole mass of mortal images. For five years the earth has not seen a single morning without death agonies, a single evening without prisons, a single noon without slaughters."[48] Like most of his contemporaries, Camus incorporated this experience of danger and sep-aration into his reflections on ethics and politics, perhaps most powerfully in a defense of existential philosophy, "Pessimism and Courage." Re-sponding to the criticism that existentialism is a philosophy of despair whose negativism renders it unsuited to problems of human life, Camus maintained that "it is essential for us to know whether man, without the help of either the eternal or rationalistic thought, can unaided create his own values. . . . The uneasiness that concerns us belongs to a whole epoch from which we do not want to dissociate ourselves. . . . No, everything is not summed up in negation and absurdity. But we must first posit negation and absurdity because they are what our generation has encountered and what we must take into account."[49]

The encounter with absurdity is an encounter with the terrifying elu-siveness of human power, and with the deafening silence of a universe that can provide no ethical moorings, no defense against what Arendt called "the incalculable evil that men are capable of bringing about." This belief that political values must emerge from the eye of the historical storm animates Camus's most important political work, *The Rebel*, which begins in much the same tone as Arendt's *The Origins of Totalitarianism*:

> The purpose of this essay . . . is to understand the times in which we live. One might think that a period which, in a space of fifty years, uproots, enslaves, or kills seventy million human beings should be condemned out of hand. But its culpability must be understood. In more ingenuous times . . . when the slave chained to the conqueror's chariot was dragged through the rejoicing streets . . . the mind did not reel before such unabashed crimes, and judgment remained unclouded. But slave camps under the flag of freedom, massacres justified by philanthropy or by a taste for the superhuman, in one sense cripple judgment. On the day when crime dons the apparel of innocence—through a curious transposition peculiar to our times—it is innocence that is called upon to justify itself.[50]

For Camus too modern man is on the edge of an historical abyss. Criminality, in the guise of philanthropy, has shaken settled norms of justice, crippling ethical judgment, which is ill-prepared for such a transposition of innocence and guilt.

Although this sense of crisis was engendered by the similar political experiences of Camus and Arendt, these were passed through the filter of the genre of phenomenological or "existential" philosophy which both of them engaged. As political creatures both Arendt and Camus were most active as *writers,* and as such their engagement with events was always mediated through their engagement with texts. Both writers were drawn to the works of Augustine, whose appreciation for the fragility of the human world resonated with their own experience. Both were deeply influenced by their readings of the writings of Melville and Kafka, and the philosophy of Kierkegaard, Nietzsche, Heidegger, and Jaspers. From these they drew insights into the estrangement and violence of modern civilization that were affirmed by the nihilism of twentieth-century politics. Contrary to the more buoyant attitude to be found in political perspectives like utilitarian liberalism or scientific socialism, these texts offered probing insights into the monstrousness and absurdity of modern forms of mastery and self-mastery. Going beyond good and evil as these are conventionally understood, they helped identify a pathos of modernity that corresponded to the experience of exile that Arendt and Camus shared. And though neither writer was an existentialist, the common view of the human condition on which they converged was based in part on a critical appropriation of the themes present in this quite variegated literary and philosophical genre.

Yet if both writers agreed that "optimism is silly," they also agreed that "pessimism about the action of man among his fellows is cowardly." For both writers the events surrounding the rise of totalitarianism represented a crucible of modern civilization, an "extreme situation" in which the ethical resources of modernity were put to the test.[51] The structure of civilization was pushed "to the breaking point," but it was not yet completely broken. If political events were cause for despondency, they also offered some basis, however slim, for hope. For as well as the rise of brutal totalitarian regimes and bloody world war, they also witnessed the resistance to totalitarian aggression and the struggle for a more just and peaceful world. Alan Megill has suggested that the idea of crisis articulated by such "prophets of extremity" as Nietzsche and Heidegger is indiscriminate, and that it focuses on grandiose metaphysical concerns at the expense of the more immediate political sources of our ills.[52] The same cannot be said of Arendt and Camus, whose concern with metaphysical themes was grounded in an engagement in the politics of their time. Both writers discerned danger *and* possibility in the present.

Although both Arendt and Camus endured displacement and hardship because of the rise of totalitarianism, both refused to resign themselves to the role of passive victim. Both were, in their own ways, resistants. In addition to her Zionist work in France from 1933 to 1940, Arendt supported the boycott of German goods, activities of the Ligue contre l'Antisemitisme to publicize anti-Semitic laws and practices in Germany, and efforts to provide legal defense for two Jews, David Frankfurter and Hermann Grynzpan, each of whom had assassinated a Nazi official, in Switzerland and France respectively. Upon emigrating to the United States she continued her Zionist activities and also worked actively in support of the effort to establish a Jewish army to fight Hitler.[53] Camus too was active in the resistance to fascism, first in the mid–1930s through his support for the Spanish Republic and then, from 1943 onward, as chief editor of *Combat*, the influential organ of the French Resistance.[54]

The importance of the legacy of resistance is clear in the writings of both Arendt and Camus. Arendt begins *Between Past and Future* with the aphorism of René Char, French poet and resistant, that "our heritage was left to us by no testament."[55] Char's reflection, Arendt asserts, underscores both the enduring significance and the ephemerality of the French Resistance. The collapse of France had shocked Char and his contemporaries, highlighting the bankruptcy of French politics and the knavery of its leadership. Arendt's description of these French intellectuals could well be a description of herself: as a consequence of defeat and occupation they "were sucked into politics as though with the force of a vacuum." The heavy weight of moral responsibility was a form of liberation from "the weightless irrelevance of their personal affairs." Thus "without premonition and probably against their conscious inclinations, they had come to constitute willy-nilly a public realm where—without the paraphernalia of officialdom and hidden from the eyes of friend and foe—all relevant business in the affairs of the country was transacted in deed and word." The heroes of the Resistance had discovered the public realm and the value of political praxis. As she notes, quoting Char, they "found themselves." Ceasing to be suspicious of their own insincerity, they experienced themselves as authentic and free, "not, to be sure, because they acted against tyranny and things worse than tyranny—this was true for every soldier in the Allied armies—but because they had become 'challengers,' had taken the initiative upon themselves and therefore, without knowing it or even noticing it, had begun to create that public space between themselves where freedom could appear."[56] The resistants had become rebels, and in expanding the space for freedom they hoped to liberate their country from oppression.[57]

Camus's *Combat* essays, especially those written on the eve of the Liberation, reveal a similar appreciation for the Resistance. He recognizes that resistance involved enormous sacrifice, that "it had all the weight of blood and the dreadful heaviness of prisons."[58] Yet like Arendt, he celebrates that "we have lived the years of fraternity,"[59] that out of this abyss has come a vital and fertile experience. And, like her, he insists that this experience not be squandered, that it be continued, and that it hold out against the forces of Restoration: "No one can think that a freedom torn from such convulsions will have the calm, tame aspect that some enjoy imagining. This dreadful travail will give birth to a revolution."[60] Profoundly shaken by the traumatic experiences of the war, Camus is perhaps even more disturbed by the possibility that his compatriots might learn nothing from these experiences, either from their sense of horror or from the exhilaration of their resistance. It would be a cruel irony indeed were totalitarianism to have succeeded even in its defeat, inducing pervasive forgetfulness and disillusion among its victims and its conquerors.

For both Camus and Arendt the resistance to Nazism represented a beacon of hope in the darkness of war, destruction, and death. It offered some testimony that the ability to initiate, as Arendt put it, "is the supreme capacity of man."[61] It provided the "force of evidence" that in the midst of the rubble of modernity there remained something on which to pin the hope of reconstruction.[62] In the words of René Char, the wartime experience of revolt demonstrated that "as soon as truth finds an enemy to its measure, it lays aside the armor of ubiquity and fights with the very resources of its condition. It is indescribable, the sensation of that depth which becomes volatile even as it becomes concrete."[63] The armor of ubiquity, the common sense of modern politics, was for both Camus and Arendt clearly insufficient if one was to comprehend how the world had arrived at this moment of crisis and envision what might be done to repair the damage to human dignity.

Chapter 2

TOTALITARIANISM AND THE INTOXICATION OF POWER

In their effort to understand the horrors of their age, Arendt and Camus, like so many intellectuals of their generation, converged on the concept of totalitarianism—a concept that, curiously, has disappeared from the lexicon of political theory. This is unfortunate both for political theory and for political understanding in general. Arendt and Camus believed that the horrors of the mid-twentieth century constituted a break in civilization, which disclosed novel and horrifying human possibilities, implicated crucial features of modern civilization, and required new political concepts to repair it. The concept of totalitarianism, at once theoretical and dramatic, provided them with the key with which to unlock these new mysteries. Their analyses are strikingly similar, and at the same time are complementary. Arendt's work supplies some of the most probing philosophical and historical insights into these new realities, whereas Camus's work explores their shocking and dramatic character. Yet Arendt's is laced with a dramatic sensibility, and Camus's is informed by a keen theoretical understanding.

A Genealogy of Totalitarianism

Political ideas never step innocently onto the historical scene. This is supremely true of the concept of totalitarianism, which has been used and abused in a variety of ways. Having become a major weapon in the ideological armory of the West in the wake of the Second World War, it is neither surprising nor disturbing that it should have become subject to attack by more critically minded intellectuals.

Yet in one of the cruel ironies of history, the critics of the concept of totalitarianism had more in common with their adversaries than they thought. Both groups saw the term as being a piece of Cold War ideology; they merely differed about whether they liked it or not. Neither group believed that the idea of totalitarianism had any deeper historical or moral significance. In this regard the entire debate about totalitarianism mirrored the normalization of the postwar world.[1] It became identified with the East-West struggle and detached from any concern with the catastrophes of the recent past. Even the critics of the idea, those most intent on challenging prevailing orthodoxy, failed to see its radical implications.

Thus Benjamin Barber focused on the Cold War use of the term, insisting that it is moribund if not intellectually "dead" and deadening, an "emotivist" and "ideological perspective": "The mood of political crisis and ideological urgency that surrounded such studies naturally gave totalitarianism a controversial, sometimes polemical aura from which the term has never been satisfactorily emancipated. . . . The vision of political reality upon which the idea of totalitarianism is founded not only is unreflective of modern political experience but was antiquated at the time the idea was first employed."[2] Barber proceeded to castigate the "nefarious" semantic imprecision and the rhetorical, subjective character of the concept, challenging its scholarly appropriateness for an objective, analytic political science. He concluded that "it is difficult to find a convincing justification for the presence of totalitarianism in the vocabulary of comparative political analysis. . . . [It] has no specific meaning at all and is thus, for the purposes of analysis, quite useless."[3] Likewise, in a 1968 essay, Herbert Spiro hazarded a hopeful projection that "as the social sciences develop more discriminating concepts of comparison . . . the use of the term 'totalitarianism' may also become less frequent."[4]

These repudiations of the concept of totalitarianism rested in part on a critique of what Spiro and Barber called the "counter-ideological uses of 'totalitarianism'" in providing an ideological rationale for postwar American Cold War liberalism.[5] This theme has more recently been taken up by the German historian Hans Mommsen, who argues that "the theory of totalitarianism . . . has assumed the features of an ideological syndrome." Unlike Spiro and Barber, Mommsen sees the theory as "a heuristic model, originally fruitful in terms of the historical insights it yielded, [which] was intellectually impoverished and transformed into an indirectly assertive ideology designed to preserve existing, liberal-parliamentary structures."[6] But, like them, he too maintains that it has become no more than an "ideological slogan," concluding that "the theory of totalitarianism, regressing—quite contrary to the intentions of Franz Neumann, Ernst Fraenkel, and Hannah Arendt—to its historical point of departure, threatens to obstruct the view of the actual perils to democratically constituted societies."[7]

These writers are partially correct; as Spiro and Barber put it, "totalitarianism" was "an essentialist concept serving as a cornerstone of American counter-ideology in the cold war."[8] But that is not all it was. Indeed, as used by writers like Arendt and Camus, it was not simply a heuristic device but a concept with historical, even metaphysical significance, implicating a set of foundational questions about modernity and its possibilities. Seen in this light, its appropriation by Cold Warriors should serve as an impetus for uncovering the original critical intention. The idea of totalitarianism as it emerged from the debacle of the 1930s was born of a context quite different from that of the Cold War. And its proponents were in no way connected, either intellectually or politically, to any establishment that they sought to rationalize. In fact, the idea was designed to comprehend nothing less than the unanticipated crisis of Western civilization.

The context for the emergence of totalitarianism as a political and theoretical concept was the unprecedented mass mobilization of World War I and the political upheaval in central and southern Europe that followed its uncertain conclusion.[9] The term seems first to have been employed by the Italian fascists as an honorific description of their movement. Coined by Giovanni Gentile, it was used by Mussolini in a 1932 article for the *Enciclopedia Italiana*, in which he declared, "The armed party leads to the totalitarian regime. . . . A party that governs totalitarianly a new nation is a new fact in history."[10] The Italian Marxist Antonio Gramsci also wrote approvingly of the Communist party as the vanguard of a "totalitarian movement" incorporating the national will and extending beyond the state into virtually all realms of social life.[11] Most commentators agree that these uses of the term antedate the full emergence of totalitarianism in Nazi Germany and Stalinist Russia and that, whatever political aspirations they express, they do not fully anticipate the extreme concentration of power and its nihilistic exercise on which writers like Arendt and Camus later focused. The same could probably be said of the term's German origins, although German writers endowed it with a more activist, and sometimes racialist, character. Carl Schmitt's *Die Wendung zum totalen*

Staat (1931), Ernest Junger's *Die totale Mobilmachung* (1934), and General Erich Ludendorff's *Der totale Krieg* (1935) all articulated antiparliamentarist and neofascist themes; yet if Mommsen is correct, these works reflected more the hopes of Hitler's conservative allies seeking an authoritarian state than they did the aims of the National Socialist movement.[12]

The idea of totalitarianism was soon appropriated by European intellectuals, many forced into exile by the rise of Nazism, who were revolted by the growth of anti-liberal and anti-democratic movements. Reeling from a rapid succession of traumatic events—the Moscow trials of 1934–36, the betrayal of revolution in Spain, the Nuremburg laws—that seemed to upset commonplaces about the polarity of communism and fascism, these figures converged on the idea of totalitarianism in order to identify theoretically the unprecedented and frightening political realities before their eyes.[13]

Hans Kohn and Sigmund Neumann made early efforts to note the similarities between Nazism and Stalinism, focusing on the mobilizational and total character of state power in these regimes and locating the origins of this new political formation in the interwar years.[14] Elie Halévy's "L'Ere des tyrannies" (1936) also emphasized the influence of war mobilization on the rise of totalitarianism, maintaining that as a consequence, "on the one hand, a complete socialism is moving towards a kind of nationalism. On the other hand, an integral nationalism is moving towards a kind of socialism."[15] Raymond Aron took up similar themes, supporting Halévy's thesis regarding the symmetries between Stalinism and fascism:

> Political freedom: the plebiscites only represent the derisory symbol of the delegation by the people of its sovereignty to absolute masters. Personal freedom: against abuses of power, neither the German citizen, nor the Italian citizen, nor the Russian citizen, have any means of recourse; the bureaucrat and the member of the Communist Party, the local *führer* and the secretary of the *fascio*, are the slaves of their superiors, but objects of fear to private individuals. Intellectual freedom, freedom of the press, freedom of speech and scientific freedom—all the freedoms have disappeared. If, in English democratic practice, opposition is, as an admirable phrase has it, a public service, in the totalitarian states opposition is a crime.[16]

These early efforts were accompanied by a spate of books on the dangers posed by the totalitarian regimes.[17] These books do not share a common political perspective, although virtually all of their authors thought of themselves as antitotalitarian. Some, like Karl Mannheim and Emil Lederer, articulated a Tocquevillean liberalism, while others, like Ludwig von Mises and Friedrich von Hayek, advocated a straightforward market libertarianism based on neoclassical economic conceptions. On the independent left were such writers as Ignazio Silone, George Orwell, and Arthur Koestler. These activist writers produced some of the most influential portraits of totalitarianism, texts distinguished by their starkly dramatic depiction of the absurdities of totalitarian ideology—Silone's novel *Bread and Wine* (1937) and his essay *The School for Dictators* (1939), Koestler's *Darkness at Noon* (1941) and his collection *The Yogi and the Commissar* (1945), and Orwell's journalistic *Homage to Catalonia* (1939) and his novels *Animal Farm* (1945) and *1984* (1949).[18]

On the non-Communist Marxist left, too, a good deal of theoretical argument concerned itself with totalitarianism. This is clear in the writings of the Frankfurt school, which sought in the 1940s to blend elements of the official Marxist theory of monopoly state capitalism with a more innovative approach. Herbert Marcuse's "The Struggle Against Liberalism in the Totalitarian View of the State" (1934) was an early such effort, though it focused only on emergent Nazism and relied for much of its explanatory force on Nazism's correspondence "to the monopoly stage of capitalism." Max Horkheimer's "The Authoritarian State" (1940) emphasized the parallels between Nazism and Soviet "state socialism," labeling both "authoritarian" and "repressive" and identifying the "permanent mobilization" and "arbitrariness" of concentration camps characteristic of Nazism and Stalinism. Friedrich Pollock's "State Capitalism: Its Possibilities and Limitations" (1941) developed similar arguments, distinguishing between the attenuated "democratic state capitalism" characteristic of the United States and Western Europe and the "totalitarian state capitalism" characteristic of Nazism and the Soviet Union, which "offers the solution of economic problems at the price of totalitarian oppression." And Franz Neumann's *Behemoth* (1942) was among the most formidable and systematic scholarly efforts to understand "the structure and practice of national socialism."[19]

One can discern similar developments within the Trotskyist movement despite the fact that Trotsky and those most loyal to him never abandoned their Leninist commitments nor their view of the Soviet Union as a "deformed workers' state." In 1937 Trotsky himself observed that "Stalinism and fascism, in spite of a deep difference in social foundations, are symmetrical phenomena."[20] Trotsky's own work during this period exhibits a creative effort to develop new theoretical categories within Marxism in order to explain this "deadly similarity." In his 1939 essay

"The USSR in War" he went so far as to suggest that the coming war, if it did not bring about a world revolution, would lead to the emergence in the Soviet Union of "a totalitarian regime" heralding "the eclipse of civilization." Should this occur, Trotsky maintained, "a new minimum program would be required—for the defense of the interests of the slaves of the totalitarian bureaucratic society."[21] His followers, most notably the American Max Schactman, took this line of inquiry even further, arguing that the Soviet Union, like Nazi Germany, was a "bureaucratic collectivist" regime in which a new ruling class had emerged and a wholesale social revolution had become necessary. Whereas Trotsky's position professed to be based on support of the Soviet "socialist" system but opposition to its political elite, Schactman's entailed an attitude of unequivocal opposition to the Soviet system.[22] Similar arguments were also developed by Victor Serge, the French Marxist who had been imprisoned by Stalin and went on to become one of the most influential European critics of Stalinism.[23]

André Liebich has recently suggested that perhaps the most innovative Marxist thinking on this subject was Rudolph Hilferding's "State Capitalism or Totalitarian State Economy" (1940), published in the Paris-based Russian Menshevik journal *Sotsialisticheskii Vestnik*.[24] In this essay Hilferding, one of the outstanding Marxist theorists of the twentieth century, insisted that "the controversy as to whether the economic system of the Soviet Union is 'capitalist' or 'socialist' seems to me rather pointless. It is neither. It represents a *totalitarian state* economy, i.e., a system to which the economies of Germany and Italy are drawing closer and closer." Liebich argues that Hilferding's analysis represented "the first time . . . that a major Marxist theorist posed in such clear-cut terms the problem of the relation between Marxism and totalitarianism," and that it "was the culmination of a prolonged debate within Italian, German, and Russian emigré socialist circles about the applicability of Marxist categories to the historical processes they were witnessing."[25]

So *totalitarianism* was part of the common currency of critical intellectuals trying to comprehend and face the challenges posed by both Nazism and Stalinism. As George Orwell saw, the efforts of these intellectuals were far from academic, and even farther from any sort of apologetics: "One development of the last ten years has been the appearance of the 'political book', a sort of enlarged pamphlet combining history with political criticism, as an important literary form. . . . [Of] the best writers in this line . . . nearly all of them have been renegades from one or another extremist party, who have seen totalitarianism at close quarters and known the meaning of exile and persecution."[26] Most of these writers recognized that the reality of totalitarianism posed a challenge to foundational modern political beliefs about truth, freedom, and human nature. As Orwell put it, "We are moving into an age of totalitarian dictatorships, an age in which freedom of thought will be at first a deadly sin and later on a meaningless abstraction. The autonomous individual is going to be stamped out of existence."[27] For this reason he resists the standard liberal optimism that right will triumph in the end: "The peculiar horror of the present moment is that we cannot be sure that this is so. It is quite possible that we are descending into an age when two and two will make five when the Leader says so."[28] Such a world would be "phantasmagoric," the living nightmare that he later depicted in *1984*. But such a nightmare could not be written off as unrealizable; indeed, totalitarianism posed a challenge to cherished convictions inherited from the Enlightenment:

> The terrifying thing about the modern dictatorships is that they are something entirely unprecedented. Their end cannot be foreseen. In the past every tyranny was sooner or later overthrown, or at least resisted, because of 'human nature', which as a matter of course desired liberty. But we cannot be at all certain that 'human nature' is a constant. It may be just as possible to produce a breed of men who do not wish for liberty as to produce a breed of hornless cows. The Inquisition failed, but then the Inquisition had not the resources of the modern state. The radio, press-censorship, standardised education and the secret police have altered everything.[29]

For writers like Orwell and Hilferding, totalitarianism evidenced an organized and complicitous practice of barbarity beyond all previous expectations. The systematic and successful employment of deceit, and the frightening gullibility and acquiescence of large numbers of people, flew in the face of Enlightenment faith in the triumph of human reason and truth. The seemingly unproblematic identification of individuals with totalitarian regimes, and their willing performance of genocidal acts, undermined any belief in a necessary human inclination toward freedom. The perverse technologies of death and the bureaucratic administration of their use simply mocked the characteristically modern dictum of Sir Francis Bacon: "Human knowledge and human power meet in one. Nature to be commanded must be obeyed; and that which in contemplation is as the cause is in operation as the rule."[30] There is no more apt description of the intellectual operations of the Nazi scientists, for whom contemplation of the various "causes" of mass death was one with their murderous operationalization. As Arendt put it, "The concentration camps are the laboratories where changes in human nature are tested."[31] If for Adam Smith the paradigm of human technique was the pin factory and for Karl Marx the textile mill, for the critics of totalitarianism it was the corpse factory.

Yet not only did totalitarianism stand as a reproach to Enlightenment optimism. More disturbing yet was the possibility that it represented the apotheosis of this optimism. For if in many ways totalitarianism appeared as a regression to a savage state, driven by base tribal animosities and cruelties long surpassed by modern civilization, in other ways it epitomized this civilization in its exaltation of technique, in its vision of a world rendered transparent to human discernment and wholly subject to human will—in short, in its unbridled faith in human power.

Because of its profound evil, totalitarianism seemed literally to defy comprehension, confusing not only its protagonists but its victims and potential victims as well. Undermining any faith in the link between reason and freedom, it also challenged Enlightenment beliefs about natural sympathy and moral sense. For as shocking as the brutality of totalitarianism was the moral indifference with which it was received.[32] The tendency to discount stories of totalitarian atrocities was no doubt reinforced by the experience of unrelenting propaganda during World War I, much of which turned out to have been patently false. And yet among the most disconcerting aspects of the history of totalitarianism is the fact that although its horrors were real, and there were eyewitnesses to testify to them, they were ignored. Arthur Koestler's moving 1944 essay "On Disbelieving Atrocities" makes this frustratingly clear:

> We, the screamers, have been at it now for about ten years. We started on the night when the epileptic van der Lubbe set fire to the German parliament; we said that if you don't quench those flames at once, they will spread all over the world; you thought we were maniacs. At present we have the mania of trying to tell you about the killing, by hot steam, mass-electrocution, and live burial of the total Jewish population of Europe. So far only three million have died. It is the greatest mass-killing in recorded history; and it goes on daily, hourly, as regularly as the ticking of your watch. . . . [People] don't believe in concentration camps, they don't believe in the starved children of Greece, in the shot hostages in France, in the mass-graves in Poland; they have never heard of Lidice, Treblinka, or Belzec; you can convince them for an hour, then they shake themselves, their mental self-defence begins to work and in a week the shrug of incredulity has returned like a reflex temporarily weakened by a shock.[33]

In such circumstances to speak the truth is to give the appearance of insanity, to have lost "contact with reality and live in a phantasy world." And yet, Koestler suggests, "perhaps it is we, the screamers, who react in a sound and healthy way to the reality which surrounds us, whereas you are the neurotics who totter about in a screened phantasy world because you lack the faculty to face the facts?"[34] What, in other words, if the nightmare is real, and settled convictions are like narcotics, preventing the dreamers from awakening?

This was the challenge of totalitarianism. The analyses of this new mode of corpse production provided by Arendt and Camus are remarkably similar. Both focused less on what political scientists might call regime characteristics and more on the metaphysics of totalitarianism. While rooting themselves in a knowledge of totalitarianism as a political formation, both sought to identify and explore the respects in which totalitarianism represented an unanticipated and thought-defying transmogrification of the human condition, disclosing new and horrifying human possibilities on a mass scale. For both writers this was evidenced in four ways: the bureaucratization of murder, the radical subversion of language, the destruction of subjectivity through enforced "loneliness," and ideological fanaticism. Further, for both writers these attributes of the totalitarian plague cannot easily be quarantined, nor can the disease be identified with some external, aberrational force. The poison, as Camus once put it, is in us and in our civilization. This being the case, the possibilities disclosed by totalitarianism implicate modern civilization itself and require a thoroughgoing rethinking of modern life.

The Manufacture of Corpses

For both Camus and Arendt the most obvious characteristic of totalitarianism is its systematic, bureaucratic murderousness. In *The Rebel* Camus acknowledges the ubiquity of murder and oppression throughout history, and yet he insists that there is something novel about the current forms these inhumanities have taken: "There are crimes of passion and crimes of logic. The boundary between them is not clearly defined. But the Penal Code makes the convenient distinction of premeditation. We are living in the era of premeditation and the perfect crime."[35] For Arendt too it is the murderous logic of totalitarianism that marks its distinctiveness. As she writes of the genocidal universe of the Nazi death camps, "Suffering, of which there has always been too much on earth, is not the issue, nor is the number of victims. Human nature as such is at stake. . . . even though it seems that these experiments succeed not in changing man but only in destroying him, by creating a society in which the nihilistic banality of *homo homini lupus* is consistently realized."[36]

Whereas much of the political-science literature on totalitarianism either ignored or minimized the importance of the Nazi program of genocide, the dark shadow of this atrocity falls on the entirety of *The Origins of Totalitarianism*, in which Arendt devotes over thirty pages to the "total domination" practiced in the Nazi concentration and extermination camps. This final section of the book, punctuating Arendt's analysis, indicates that for her it is the genocide that constitutes "the true central institution of totalitarian organizational power."[37] Arendt writes that "the concentration and extermination camps of totalitarian regimes serve as the laboratories in which the fundamental belief of totalitarianism that everything is possible is verified.... The camps are meant not only to exterminate people and degrade human beings, but also to serve the ghastly experiment of eliminating, under scientifically controlled conditions, spontaneity itself as an expression of human behavior and of transforming the human personality into a mere thing, into something that even animals are not."[38] She acknowledges that "there have almost always been wars of aggression," that "slavery is one of the oldest institutions of mankind," and that "not even concentration camps are an invention of totalitarian movements."[39] But totalitarianism is unique in its radically anti-utilitarian character; its brutality transcends any kind of economic or political calculus other than that of brutality itself. Its principle is that "everything is possible," that all, including humanity, is superfluous, manipulable, dispensable, destructible. It is this principle, and the systematic way in which it is carried out, that distinguishes totalitarianism from other forms of organized violence and oppression. The scale and organization of mass murder practiced by the Stalinist and Nazi regimes, for Arendt, can be understood in no other way. Neither can the fact that in the cases of both systems these practices were institutionalized *after* the regimes had consolidated themselves and all political opposition had been suppressed.

Thus, in discussing the extent to which both Stalin and Hitler "threw overboard all utilitarian considerations" during World War II, she observes of the latter that "neither military, nor economic, nor political considerations were allowed to interfere with the costly and troublesome program of mass exterminations and deportations."[40] And in discussing the operations of the Nazi death camps, she observes that whereas in the early years of the regime the SA had practiced rather nasty torture and brutality, "the real horror began . . . when the ss took over the administration of the camps. . . . The old spontaneous bestiality gave way to an absolutely cold and systematic destruction of human bodies, calculated to destroy human dignity; death was avoided or postponed indefinitely. The camps were no longer amusement parks for beasts in human form, that is, for men who really belonged in mental institutions and prisons; the reverse became true: they were turned into 'drill grounds,' on which perfectly normal men were trained to be full-fledged members of the ss."[41] Murder was simply the terminus of a prolonged and systematic process of mortification and degradation, an exercise of power based on the nihilistic premise that everything is possible, that there is no end to what humans are capable of doing and of enduring. Arendt asks, "What meaning has the concept of murder when we are confronted with the mass production of corpses?"[42] Indeed, it is this feature of totalitarianism that seems most to distinguish it from other forms of genocide, like the Turkish slaughter of the Armenians in 1915 or the European annihilation of the American Indians. The totalitarian project of mastery seems more total, and less explicable in terms of any "normal" political calculus, whether it be a desire for land or the fear of a perceived enemy in time of war. In this sense, relentless destructiveness seems to have been the raison d'être of the totalitarian regimes.[43]

Perhaps the starkest description of this machinery of death and destruction is Arendt's *Eichmann in Jerusalem*. Arendt recounts Eichmann's position in a vast bureaucratic hierarchy of repression and death, detailing the various overlapping authorities responsible for dealing with the "Jewish question" and the role that Eichmann played in their activities:

> Eichmann's position was that of the most important conveyor belt in the whole operation, because it was always up to him and his men how many Jews could or should be transported from any given area, and it was through his office that the ultimate destination of the shipment was cleared, though that destination was not determined by him. But the difficulty in synchronizing the departures and arrivals, the endless worry over wrangling enough rolling stock from the railroad authorities and the Ministry of Transport, over fixing timetables and directing trains to centers with sufficient "absorptive capacity," over having enough Jews on hand at the proper time so that no trains would be "wasted," over enlisting the help of the authorities in occupied or allied countries to carry out arrests, over following the rules and directives with respect to the various categories of Jews, which were laid down separately for each country and constantly changing—all this became a routine.[44]

A daunting task, this handling of the "Jewish question," but certainly no crime of passion, and Arendt, through the brilliant understatement of her prose, conveys its unprecedented horribleness.

In this light, possibly the most telling incident in Eichmann's career regards his attitude toward the Romanians, who had managed, within a matter of months, to kill close to 300,000 Jews with hardly any German help. Arendt reports that "even the S.S. were taken aback, and occasionally frightened, by the horrors of old-fashioned, spontaneous pogroms on a gigantic scale; they often intervened to save Jews from sheer butchery, so that the killing could be done in what, according to them, was a civilized way."[45] Here Arendt, who herself describes in detail the Einsatzgruppen, the Nazi mobile killing units responsible for many mass murders on the eastern front, employs overstatement about ss sensitivity in order to underscore the difference between ad hoc, vicious brutality and brutality of a more organized, indeed "civilized" sort. She reports that Eichmann implored the Nazi Foreign Office to stop the Romanians, who had an insufficient appreciation of the proper timetable of the final solution.

Arendt thus concludes that the crime was unprecedented, not simply because of its enormity, but also because of its logic and its modus operandi. In making this judgment she reproached the Jerusalem court, and the Jewish community more generally, for whom the Nazi atrocities were simply an extreme form of the anti-Semitic persecution that Jews had experienced throughout history. This conclusion, she argued, was based on a failure to understand "that the supreme crime it [the court] was confronted with, the physical extermination of the Jewish people, was a crime against humanity, perpetrated on the body of the Jewish people, and that only the choice of victims, not the nature of the crime, could be derived from the long history of Jew-hatred and anti-Semitism."[46] For Arendt such a crime, and such a criminal—the "law-abiding citizen of a criminal state"—defied prevailing conceptions of guilt and innocence. If murder has, in various ways, long been considered by the Western tradition an aberration, a crime punishable by constituted authority, the totalitarian regimes reveal the reality of murder and murderousness as a civilizational norm, if not a categorical imperative of virtuous citizenship. This insight lies at the heart of Arendt's famous argument about the banality of evil. For her the profundity of totalitarian evil lies precisely in its ordinariness. Not explicable as a burst of malevolent passion or even a deeply motivated set of political convictions, totalitarian mass murder was routinized and normalized until it came to define the very character of Russian and German societies. To speak of the banality of evil in no way mitigates the fact that totalitarianism was evil; on the contrary, it points up how this evil was so ingrained in the social fabric that it could be performed routinely, with little thought.[47]

Camus also focuses on the novel character of totalitarian murderousness. Echoing Arendt, he notes of Nazism that "all problems are . . . militarized and posed in terms of power and efficiency. . . . Man, if he is a member of the party, is no more than a tool in the hands of the Führer, a cog in the apparatus, or, if he is the enemy of the Führer, a waste product of the machine."[48] Camus maintains that the sheer nihilism governing the exercise of power distinguishes totalitarian violence from other kinds, however malignant: "The crimes of the Hitler regime, among them the massacre of the Jews, are without precedent in history because history gives no other example of a doctrine of such total destruction being able to seize the levers of command of a civilized nation. But above all, for the first time in history, the rulers of a country have used their immense power to establish a *mystique* beyond the bounds of any ethical considerations. This first attempt to establish a Church on nihilism was paid for by complete annihilation."[49] As evidence of this he points to the Nazi destruction, exceeding all military precedents, of the Polish village of Lidice. The Nazis were not satisfied to vandalize the city and seek reprisals against its inhabitants. Instead they burned every house, murdered every man, deported every woman and, separately, every child. As Camus reports, special teams were dispatched to level the terrain with dynamite, and "to make assurance doubly sure, the cemetery was emptied of its dead, who might have been a perpetual reminder that once something existed in this place."[50]

Such scrupulous brutality was not, however, the exclusive province of the Nazis. In parallel fashion the Soviet concentration camp system had in fact "accomplished the dialectical transition from the government of people to the administration of objects, but by identifying people with objects." Soviet totalitarianism aspires to universal power, an "Empire of objects" in which "men are united by mutual accusation," a state of siege in which the reconciliation of the wolf and the lamb is overseen by the executioner.[51]

The totalitarian state of siege is vividly depicted in Camus's fiction. Thus in *The Plague*, described by Camus as an allegorical tale of "the struggle of the European resistance movements against Nazism,"[52] mass death suddenly and unexpectedly overtakes the city of Oran, transforming it into "a huge necropolis." The city government quarantines all of those suspected of being "infected," registers all deaths ("which showed the distinction that can be made between men, for example, and dogs; men's deaths are checked and entered up"), and organizes the flinging of the dead "into the death pits indiscriminately." Eventually more space is needed for the dead, and so a streetcar line is employed to transport the bodies to a crematorium on the outskirts of town for mass burning. The plague is described by Rieux, the narrator, as a "monotonous abstraction" which regularly and systematically takes its toll on the city, leveling all distinctions, working to annihilate all values, all traces of human dignity.[53]

The uniquely abstract character of the totalitarian pestilence is also explored in Camus's drama. Thus in *Caligula* the brilliantly insane tyrant seeks to "exploit the impossible," placing everything "on an equal footing," sentencing all to death "without a hearing."[54] Camus wants us to see that this tyrant is no ordinary despot but something more deadly, and more serious. Thus when the corrupt patricians conspire against Caligula, considering him a bully, a buffoon, and a crazy tyrant who threatens their prerogatives, Cherea, the voice of reason and moderation, retorts: "You haven't taken your enemy's measure; that's obvious, since you attribute petty motives to him. But there's nothing petty about Caligula. . . . And what I loathe in him is this: that he knows what he wants. . . . Our deaths are only a side issue. He's putting his power at the service of a loftier, deadlier passion; and it imperils everything we hold most sacred. True, it's not the first time Rome has seen a tyrant wielding unlimited power; but it's the first time he sets no limit to his use of it, and counts mankind, and the world we know, for nothing."[55]

This is even more clearly developed in *State of Seige,* where the totalitarian Plague appears, decreeing "eliminations." The Plague is accompanied by "the perfect Secretary," an Eichmann-like character who administers his commands, "sure that everything can always be put right; that there's no muddle in the accounts that can't be straightened up in time, and no missed appointment that can't be made again." [56] The Secretary proceeds to issue a series of edicts that sound frighteningly familiar to those acquainted with the totalitarian regimes: the houses of the "infected" are to be marked with a black star; all essential foodstuffs are to be requisitioned by the state, to be distributed only to those who can prove their loyalty to the new social order; a strict curfew is to be enforced; aiding those afflicted with the disease is forbidden "except by reporting the case to the authorities"; informing on one's family is to be rewarded with a Good Citizenship Ration; and everyone is ordered to keep a vinegar pad in their mouth at all times to tutor "discretion and the art of silence."[57] These edicts are presented coldly and candidly, their form and their content taking the citizens of Cadiz aback. As if to clarify matters, the Plague plainly declares his intentions:

> I am the ruler here.... When I say I rule you, I rule in a rather special way—it would be more correct to say I function.... I'm sure you'd like to see me as a sort of black king or some monstrous, gaudy insect. That would satisfy your dramatic instincts.... Well, they won't be satisfied this time. I don't wield a scepter or anything like that; in fact I prefer to look like a quite ordinary person, let's say a sergeant or a corporal.... So now your king has black nails and a drab uniform. He doesn't sit on a throne but in an office chair. His palace is a barracks and his hunting-lodge a courthouse. You are living in a state of siege.
>
> So take good notice, sentiment is banned, and so are other imbecilities.... Instead of these I give you organization.... As from today you are going to learn to die in an orderly manner.... There will be no more dying as the fancy takes you. Lists will be kept up—what admirable things lists are!—and we shall fix the order of your going. Fate has learned wisdom and will keep its records.
>
> So line up for a decent death, that's your first duty.... From this day on you are going to be rational and tidy. The wearing of badges will be compulsory. Besides the mark on your groins you will have the plague star under your armpits, for all to see—meaning that you are marked down for elimination.... I bring you order, silence, total justice.... My administration has begun.[58]

There is an unreality to this scene, but its rudiments were real enough. As Orwell's O'Brien puts it in *1984,* the totalitarian regime defies all traditional terms of political discourse, the first for which "power is not a means; it is an end."[59] Never before had political power been organized and exercised with such scrupulousness, and for the purpose of destroying the bodies and souls of masses of people—indeed, entire nations. Most disturbing, perhaps, is the possibility that such nihilism represents simply an extreme case of the modern tendency to reduce problems of human living to matters of technique. Totalitarianism in this sense symbolizes the triumph of functional reason, which has emptied the universe of any transcendent meaning, leaving a world where the only value is the value of human mastery and organizational power for its own sake.

The Decentering of the Subject

The terminus of totalitarian domination was death. But, as Arendt indicated, the structure and process of totalitarian society destroyed the soul as well as the body, working to extinguish all vestiges of autonomy and independent selfhood.[60] This program was nowhere implemented with complete success. But if the cynicism of the totalitarian regimes was not horrifying enough, the gap between intention and result was often even more terrifyingly narrow. Political-science treatments of this process, including Arendt's, focus on the "atomization" of the populace, the suppression of all independent organizations, the penetration of the regime into all aspects of public and private life, the functioning of propaganda, mass hysteria, and mobilization, and the effects of terror itself in accomplishing this figurative and literal deconstruction of the subject.[61]

But for Arendt and Camus these institutional features of totalitarianism were less important than its phenomenology. Although both were fully aware of the political realities of totalitarianism and struggled against them, even more disturbing was the universe of experience constructed by those realities, as well as the kind of person, whom Arendt called a virtual "nobody," that they typically produced. For both, the concept of loneliness captures this experience, and for both the construction of loneliness was not simply a negative but also a positive process. Like many contemporary social theorists, Arendt and Camus saw that, at least in the case of totalitarianism, socialization begins from the ground up. And for both thinkers that ground is language.[62]

In their view a hallmark of totalitarianism is its radical subversion of language. Both consider language to be a decisive human faculty, a potential means of individual lucidity, public disclosure, and interpersonal communication and understanding. The notion that language is a uniquely human attribute making civilized behavior and human community possible goes back at least as far as Aristotle, and it is a view with wide currency throughout most of the history of Western political thought. Even Hobbes, who saw the connection between language and freedom as problematic and who sought to empower the state as the creator of meanings, never imagined that the link between language and some kind of autonomy could be severed; his Leviathan constitutes a common language so as to make civil freedom possible.[63] And yet totalitarianism seems to sever this link, destroying any kind of lucidity, disclosure, or understanding, indeed placing the notion of self-interest itself in question.

As Camus writes, "Dialogue and personal relations have been replaced by propaganda or polemic, which are two kinds of monologue. . . . The gospel preached by totalitarian regimes in the form of a monologue [is] dictated from the top of a lonely mountain. On stage, as in reality, the monologue precedes death." [64] Camus makes this vividly clear in *Caligula*, where the monologues of the tyrant, the products of "the god-like enlightenment of the solitary," do quite literally precede death.[65] In *State of Siege*, too, only the words of the Plague and his functionaries have any validity—thus the vinegar pads on the tongues of all citizens, which help to advance what the Plague calls "the august silence of all perfect social orders."[66] As Nada, the Plague's collaborator, puts it. "We want to fix things up in such a way that nobody understands a word of what his neighbor says. And, let me tell you, we are steadily nearing that perfect moment when nothing anybody says will rouse the least echo in another's mind.... [Then] we shall be well on the way to that ideal consummation— the triumph of death and silence."[67]

This aspiration to omnipotence, seeking absolutely to control not simply expression but even thinking, and equating such control with perfection, is paralleled in Orwell's *1984,* where "the whole aim of Newspeak is to narrow the range of thought.... The Revolution will be complete when the language is perfect." And, of course, the language will only be perfect when it has been rendered wholly consistent with officially sanctioned meanings. Only then will the revolution have achieved its ideal—"three hundred million people all with the same face."[68] Koestler, in reflecting on his experience as a Communist, gives some sense of how deeply this linguistic transubstantiation extended, beyond the Soviet regime to the Communist movement itself:

> Not only our thinking, but our vocabulary was re-conditioned. Certain words were taboo—for instance "lesser evil" or "spontaneous"; the latter because "spontaneous" manifestations of the revolutionary class-consciousness were part of Trotsky's theory of Permanent Revolution. Other words and turns of phrase became favorite stock-in-trade. I mean not only the obvious words of Communist jargon, like "toiling masses"; but words like "concrete" or "sectarian" ("You must put your question into a more concrete form, Comrade"; "you are adopting a Left-sectarian attitude, Comrade").... Repetitiveness of diction, the catechism of technique of asking a rhetorical question and repeating the full question in the answer; the use of stereotyped adjectives and the dismissal of an attitude or fact by the simple expedient of putting words in inverted commas and giving them an ironic reflection (the "revolutionary" past of Trotsky, the "humanistic" bleatings of the "liberal" press, etc.); all these are essential parts of a style, of which Josef Djugashwili [Stalin] is the uncontested master, and which through its very medium produced a dull, hypnotic effect. Two hours of this dialectical tom-tom and you didn't really know whether you were a boy or a girl, and were ready to believe either as soon as the reflected alternative appeared in inverted commas.[69]

As Koestler indicates, such language games cut to the very soul of their practitioners, affecting not simply what could be said but what could be thought and even felt.

Arendt too explores this subversion of language and atrophy of thought, describing the various bureaucratic "language rules" governing the classification of Nazi operations: "The prescribed code names for killing were 'final solution,' 'evacuation'. . . and 'special treatment.'. . . Deportation— unless it involved Jews directed to Theresienstadt, the 'old people's ghetto,' for privileged Jews, in which case it was called 'change of residence'— received the names of 'resettlement' and 'labor in the East.' "[70] She argues that Eichmann, as a product of these rules, was the paradigmatic totalitarian individual. "Officialese is my only language," she quotes him as testifying, and observes that "officialese became his only language because he was genuinely incapable of uttering a single sentence that was not a cliché." Even for Eichmann, she asserts, slogans, code words, and platitudes were not a completely effective insulation from the cold realities of Nazism. She recounts that he was sickened by some of the murder he witnessed in the camps—but only temporarily, and he never let it interfere with the performance of his duties as "a law-abiding citizen" of the genocidal Third Reich. As Arendt observed of his conduct during his trial, "The longer one listened to him, the more obvious it became that his inability to speak was closely connected with an inability to think, namely, to think from the standpoint of somebody else. No communication was possible with him, not because he lied but because he was surrounded by the most reliable of all safeguards against the words and presence of others, and hence against reality as such."[71]

Eichmann was completely bereft of what Arendt would later call the power of judgment, which rests on "an anticipated communication with others with whom I know I must finally come to some agreement."[72] So lacking, he could not be considered an authentic moral agent. As Arendt writes in *The Human Condition,* with Eichmann in mind, "The disclosure of who somebody is, is implicit in both his words and his deed. . . . Without the accompaniment of speech, at any rate, action would not only lose its revelatory character but, by the same token, it would lose its subject, as it were; not acting men but performing robots would achieve what, humanly speaking, would remain incomprehensible."[73]

The totalitarian individual, a product of terror and the manipulation of language, is just such a nobody, not simply prevented from associating freely, but deprived of the means of any human solidarity. The totalitarian regime extends the project of mastery beyond behavior to the very constitution of subjectivity. Controlling and manipulating language, it treats individuals not as originators of meanings but as transmission belts of official directives. Depriving people of the spontaneity associated with the use of their natural languages and colloquial expressions, totalitarianism undermines the familiarity and security of their lifeworlds.[74] Perhaps most important, it deprives individuals of a central medium of human solidarity, the medium of shared language and communication. This is what Camus means in saying that the ideal-typical language of totalitarianism is monologue: the rulers speak and command, and the subjects are silent and obey. Even friendship must be negated, for its principles—selectivity and particularity—run counter to the general loyalties totalitarian power demands. In its place Camus discerns a new "Empire of friendship," which is the "befriending of objects":

> The friendship of objects is friendship in general, friendship with everything, which supposes—when it is a question of self-preservation—mutual denunciation. He who loves his friend loves him in the present, and the revolution wants to love only a man who has not yet appeared. To love is, in a certain way, to kill the perfect man who is going to be born of the revolution. In order that one day he may live, he should now on be preferred to anyone else. In the kingdom of humanity, men are bound by ties of affection; in the Empire of objects, men are united by mutual accusation. The city that planned to be the city of fraternity becomes an ant-heap of solitary men.[75]

Arendt calls this the experience of loneliness, "the experience of not belonging to the world at all, which is among the most radical and desperate experience of man."[76] The totalitarian individual is thus cut off from all the particular ties that bind, from all that distinguishes his or her identity as an individual, cut off, like the citizens of Oran, from the sea, from the world, from each other. This is not simply a political or social but a metaphysical experience, involving much more than social isolation and cutting to the core of humanness. As Arendt writes, "What makes loneliness so unbearable is the loss of one's own self which can be realized in solitude, but confirmed in its identity only by the trusting and trustworthy company of my equals. In this situation, man loses trust in himself as the partner of his thoughts and that elementary confidence in the world which is necessary to make experiences at all. Self and world, capacity for thought and experience are lost at the same time.[77]

Such loneliness would seem to bring us full circle. We are back to the beginnings of modern philosophy—to Descartes' *cogito*, radical inwardness, self-subsistent subjectivity. But it only seems this way, for the totalitarian individual, according to Camus and Arendt, lacks any firm anchoring and is virtually deprived of self, thoroughly deconstructed, if not destroyed, by totalitarian domination. Bereft of reason, autonomy, and conscience, ready and willing to destroy what exists, be it traditions or entire peoples, the totalitarian individual would seem to give the lie to the Enlightenment and leave us, at the dusk of modernity, adrift in the morass of a hopeless nihilism.

The Supersense of Totalitarianism

How is the emptying of the world of meaning, the ruthless destruction of everything that exists, possible? It seems to defy common sense and run contrary to all previously evidenced modes and rationales of human conduct. As strange and as troubling as it may be, this is a fact about totalitarianism from which neither Arendt nor Camus shied away. They thus both emphasized its relentlessly ideological character. For both writers totalitarian ideologies, Nazi and Communist, offer totalizing interpretations of human history and society and propose grandiose programs of historical transformation in accordance with these interpretations. These ideologies are secular versions of traditional religion in their faith in the future; but they are profoundly unlike traditional religions in their unalloyed faith in human capacities.[78] Recognizing no limits to their understanding or their power, such ideologies underwrite the effort to remake the world, to establish a vision of perfect, final justice, and to eliminate all obstacles to this vision.[79]

For Camus, the murderous systems of Stalinism and Nazism are both rooted in a kind of cowardice typical of the ideological mentality: "As soon as man, through lack of character, takes refuge in a doctrine, as soon as crime reasons about itself, it multiplies like reason itself and assumes all the aspects of the syllogism.... Ideology today is concerned only with the denial of other human beings.... It is then that we kill."[80] Far from being driven by petty greed or even profound animosity, totalitarian murder is fueled by a grand vision of a future world in which even the most barbarous cruelties will be redeemed. In this vision cruelty is not really cruelty at all, nor is murder really murder. Rather, they are necessary and virtuous deeds hastening the arrival of a world where there will no longer be any need for them. This is the cowardice of ideology—that it offers comfort and consolation, rationalizing criminality and effacing any reliable boundary between innocence and guilt. Motivated by "nothing other than the ancient dream of unity common to both believers and rebels, but projected horizontally onto an earth deprived of God," totalitarianism is a form of perfectionist politics, seeking to suppress any and all human

differences and dedicated with a homicidal logic to the pursuit of a uni-
form, homogeneous, *final* social order:

> [Totalitarianism] supposes a negation and a certainty: the certainty of the
> infinite malleability of man and the negation of human nature. Propaganda
> techniques serve to measure the degree of this malleability and try to make
> reflection and conditioned reflex coincide. Propaganda makes it possible to sign
> a pact with those who for years have been designated as the mortal enemy.
> Even more, it allows the psychological effect thus obtained to be reversed and
> the people, once again, to be aligned against this same enemy. The experiment
> has not yet been brought to an end, but its principle is logical. If there is no
> human nature, then the malleability of man is, in fact, infinite. Political realism,
> on this level, is nothing but unbridled romanticism, a romanticism of expe-
> diency.[81]

Ideology, purporting to articulate cosmic necessity, whether of World
History or Aryan destiny, demands the unequivocal submission of concrete
human beings, who "are hostile to it insofar as human nature, to date,
has never been able to live by history alone and has always escaped from
it by some means."[82] Totalitarian ideology is thus both figuratively and
literally terroristic, refusing to tolerate the particularities and differences
that comprise the existing world. It is figuratively terroristic insofar as it
entails a perpetual uncertainty regarding what is "necessary" that affects
all but the sanctum sanctorum of the party elite. They alone can claim to
speak for necessity and to maintain innocence; all others are under suspicion, potentially if not actually to be considered "objectively guilty." As
in *State of Siege,* they are at best candidates for official "certificates of
existence" attesting to their validity. As the Secretary says, "We start with
the premise that you are guilty. But that's not enough; you must learn to
feel yourselves that you are guilty."[83] And ideology is literally terroristic
insofar as it licenses systematic murder.

Arendt highlights these same features in the appendix to her *Origins,*
"Ideology and Terror: A New Form of Government." Here she argues
that the essence of totalitarianism is the rejection of all legality. Denying
all fixed standards of right and orderly conduct, "totalitarian policy claims
to transform the human species into an active unfailing carrier of a law
to which human beings otherwise would only passively and reluctantly be
subjected." Totalitarianism is premised upon a "refusal to accept anything
as it is." Whether the driving force of this development is called nature
or history is relatively unimportant. "In these ideologies, the term 'law'
itself changed its meaning: from expressing the framework of stability

58

within which human actions and motions can take place, it became the expression of the motion itself."[84] For Arendt, as for Camus, because there is no rest, no order on which to base one's expectations and one's conduct, totalitarianism is terroristic. Life under such conditions becomes subject to radical insecurity and uncertainty. Law here becomes but the execution, usually quite literal, of historical necessity as discerned by the elite. Moreover, this law is executed with what Arendt calls a "stringent logicality"

> While the totalitarian regimes are thus resolutely and cynically emptying the world of the only thing that makes sense to the utilitarian expectations of common sense, they impose upon it at the same time a kind of supersense which the ideologies actually always meant when they pretended to have found the key to history or the solution to the riddles of the universe. . . . The insanity of such systems lies not only in their first premise but in the very logicality with which they are constructed. The curious logicality of all isms, their simple-minded trust in the salvation value of stubborn devotion without regard for specific, varying factors, already harbors the first germs of totalitarian contempt for reality and factuality.[85]

Such contempt for the given Camus calls an "insensate passion for nothingness."[86] For both writers totalitarian ideology licenses the performance and rationalization of the most barbarous deeds, the denial of the most obvious experiences, the willful fabrication of the most preposterous truths—all in the name of a higher truth. Thus totalitarian regimes are organized into what Arendt calls a "hierarchy of contempt," where at the lower levels extraordinary gullibility and unquestioned obedience are demanded, and at the higher levels an extreme but paradoxically sincere form of cynicism obtains: the leadership possesses almost sacred power to interpret doctrine and determine truth.[87] At this level ideology is almost pure form, devoid of virtually all content. Although Arendt acknowledges differences in the rhetoric and stated goals of Nazism and Stalinism, she insists that these differences are effaced by the formal similarities between the two ideologies in practice. The ideologies of totalitarian regimes are infinitely manipulable to meet the needs of the moment, and totalitarian leaders recognize the constraints of neither veracity nor factuality: "In distinction to the mass membership which, for instance, needs some demonstration of the inferiority of the Jewish race before it can safely be asked to kill Jews, elite formations understand that the statement, all Jews are inferior, means, all Jews should be killed; they know that when they are told that only Moscow has a subway, the real meaning of the statement is that all subways should be destroyed, and are not unduly surprised when they discover the subway in Paris."[88]

This way of thinking is a deadly form of casuistry. On it the Paris subway cannot be a *real* subway, but at the same time it cannot be permitted to continue to exist. Once destroyed, the "truth" that only Moscow has a subway is secured; but of course this truth was never in doubt. Arendt furnishes other examples—the bourgeoisie and kulaks are the "dying classes" of Russia and thus must be killed; the Jews are a "diseased," "dirty" a subhuman race polluting the German people and need to be eliminated; they therefore must be dehumanized, subjected to filth and disease, and, ergo, eliminated. A term that comes up frequently in the writings of Arendt and Camus, and Koestler and Orwell as well, is the "dreamy unreality" of political events and official claims in totalitarian societies. For these regimes, as O'Brien (the interrogator in *1984*) puts it baldly, reality "exists in the human mind, and nowhere else . . . only in the mind of the Party, which is collective and immortal."[89]

Thus the most astonishing and phantasmogoric reversals are possible. As Camus observed, thinking of the Hitler-Stalin pact of 1939, it is possible to claim at one moment that the most hated enemy is now an ally and the most beloved ally an enemy. This is vividly depicted in Orwell's *1984*. Winston is momentarily taken aback by the events of Hate Week when, after days of hysterical mass demonstrations against Eurasia, it is announced "that Oceania was not after all at war with Eurasia. Oceania was at war with Eastasia. Eurasia was an ally." At that moment Winston is taking part in a rally, listening to a party orator who, "contorted with hatred . . . boomed forth an endless catalogue of atrocities, massacres, deportations, lootings, rapings, torture of prisoners, bombing of civilians, lying propaganda, unjust aggressions, broken treaties. . . . The speech had been proceeding for perhaps twenty minutes when a messenger hurried onto the platform and a scrap of paper was slipped into the speaker's hand. He unrolled it and read it without pausing in his speech. Nothing altered in his voice or manner, but suddenly the names were different."[90]

It is also possible, as Koestler depicts with brilliance in *Darkness at Noon,* to submit to a kind of logicality that requires you to deny your very self. Rubashov, the skeptical old Bolshevik modeled on Trotsky and Bukharin, is confronted with a series of accusations by the party—that he belonged to oppositional groupings, that he performed industrial sabotage against the Soviet state, that he conspired with hostile foreign powers, that he plotted the assassination of No. 1 (Stalin). At first he pleads innocent, having done none of these things. But his accusers, party members well trained in dialectics, insist that if he had entertained doubts about the party, as he had, then he would have done anything to change the regime; thus he was an enemy, and thus "the essence" of the charges is true. As his first accuser, Ivanov, puts it, "The methods follow by logical deduction. We can't afford to lose ourselves in judicial subtleties." For a long time Rubashov resists. At one point, after the brutal Gletkin reads charges in which the word "devilish" appears frequently, he is taken aback, and "for a few seconds Rubashov entertained the hypothesis that Gletkin had gone mad; this mixture of logic and absurdity recalled the methodical lunacy of schizophrenia." But eventually he relents, "lost in the labyrinth of calculated lies and dialectic pretences, in the twilight between truth and illusion." If he had entertained oppositional attitudes then he *must* have gone to any lengths to undermine the regime. In any case, the specifics "made no difference to his guilt." Rubashov confesses and is executed.[91]

How central this mad logicality was to the many confessions will remain a subject of controversy.[92] Undoubtedly matters were quite complex, and there is a bizarre unreality to the action of Koestler's novel, as there is to much that is depicted in the literature on totalitarianism. Some critics have suggested that this unreality impeaches the literature itself. Thus Robert Burrowes has written that Arendt's *Origins* "contains an exotic or fantastic bias," that "her conception of totalitarianism has taken on the character of a demonic construct," and that it "can only be described at best as caricature and at worst as fantasy. It is perhaps ironic that a person who sees totalitarianism as an attempt to translate reality into fiction should herself produce a fictitious theory."[93] Stephen Whitfield also argues that Arendt fails to capture much that is important, asserting that "her terrifying series of illuminations of the fantastic was not always rectified by an awareness of the obvious."[94] Both Isaac Deutscher and Raymond Williams have criticized Orwell's *1984* for an obsession with a "mysticism of cruelty" that obscures the complexity of Stalinist and Nazi societies.[95] Roland Barthes, Jean-Paul Sartre, and François Jeanson made similar criticisms of Camus's *The Plague,* claiming that in failing to present totalitarianism as the work of human protagonists Camus attributes to it an illusory mystique.[96]

It would be a mistake to dismiss these criticisms. Both Arendt and Camus often sacrifice scientific understanding to metaphysical insight. But this, I think, is precisely their strength as writers. What their critics often fail to see is that writers like Arendt and Camus identified realities of the twentieth century that were difficult to accept, much less comprehend. When Deutscher declares that the Marxist "may feel upset or mortified" by the cruelties of our century "but he need not feel shaken in his *Weltanschauung*" because "the class struggle, as Marx describes it, is anything but a rational process,"[97] it is hard to know where to begin to respond, just as it is hard to know what to say to those, like Burrowes, who assert that more scholarly "detachment" and "objectivity" is needed in order to develop appropriately rigorous comparative concepts. Deutscher does not tell us what class struggle has to do with the Nazi death camps or Soviet gulags, nor does Burrowes explain to us how to assimilate the systematic mass murder of civilians, and the fanaticism that attended such murder, into the vocabulary of "value-free" political science.[98]

The challenge, in short, is that the events and processes that Arendt and Camus sought to describe *were* fantastic and, in comparison to other events and processes, unprecedentedly horrible. This does not necessarily render constitutional analysis or class analysis irrelevant; but it does render them incapable of fully comprehending the terrible politics of our century. For it is notable that these modes of analyses are conspicuously silent about the most distinguishing features of the totalitarian regimes—the camps—and that they fail to ask the most obvious, but no less important, question: *how could these things have happened?* As Arendt put it, quite bitter that while her people were gassed and burned in Auschwitz and Treblinka the world was silent: "The reason why the totalitarian regimes can get so far toward realizing a fictitious, topsy-turvy world is that the outside non-totalitarian world. . . . indulges also in wishful thinking and shirks reality in the face of real insanity." What such people refuse to acknowledge is "the utter lunacy" of the totalitarian world.[99] She thus contends that "only the fearful imagination," which insists on "dwelling on horrors," is capable of grasping such realities; and she proceeds to apply such an imagination in order to convey the reality of the concentration camps and shake up settled convictions about the human possibilities of evil:

This atmosphere of madness and unreality, created by an apparent lack of purpose, is the real iron curtain which hides all forms of concentration camps from the eyes of the world. Seen from outside, they and the things that happen in them can be described only in images drawn from a life after death, that is, a life removed from earthly purposes. Concentration camps can very aptly be divided into three types corresponding to three basic Western conceptions of a life after death: Hades, Purgatory, and Hell. To Hades correspond those relatively mild forms, once popular even in non-totalitarian countries, for getting undesirable elements of all sorts—refugees, stateless persons, the asocial and the unemployed—out of the way. . . . Purgatory is represented by the Soviet Union's labor camps, where neglect is combined with chaotic forced labor;

Hell in the most literal sense was embodied by those types of camp perfected by the Nazis, in which the whole of life was thoroughly and systematically organized with a view to the greatest possible torment. . . . Suddenly it becomes evident that things which for thousands of years the human imagination had banished to a realm beyond human competence can be manufactured right here on earth.[100]

Contemporary philosophers have argued that scientific understanding, like all human understanding, proceeds by way of providing metaphorical redescriptions of phenomena.[101] What better redescriptions have been provided by academic political science, Marxist or liberal, than this one? The problem is not simply how to understand the subjective experiences of those who lived through the realities of totalitarian mass murder; it is how to grasp the political realities that made such experiences possible. This is, to be sure, a matter fit for causal analysis, but it also raises deeper metaphysical questions about the extent and limits of human power.[102] Totalitarianism, in short, seems to defy standard frameworks of interpretation, presenting novel forms of human exertion and debasement, and Camus and Arendt refuse the complacency of such frameworks. But they also reject the position most forcefully articulated by Elie Wiesel, who has argued paradoxically about the Holocaust that "whoever has not lived through it can never know it. And whoever has lived through it can never fully reveal it."[103] Although it may well be that it is impossible to reproduce the awful experience of having lived through the death camps, both writers insist that it is possible, and indeed necessary, to incorporate these events into our experience and to come to an understanding of their significance.

An appreciation of the difficulties involved in interpreting totalitarianism should clear up some of the confusion about what otherwise seems a major inconsistency of Arendt's argument in *The Origins of Totalitarianism*. This is the fact that although she persistently attributes intentionality to totalitarian rulers and regimes, asserting for example that the camps "serve as the laboratories in which the fundamental belief of totalitarianism that everything is possible is verified," she also repeatedly insists that "totalitarian dictators do not consciously embark upon the road to insanity."[104] Arendt is emphatic that the reality of totalitarianism defies all expectations and shatters all precedents. If this is so, then it would seem foolish to explain it as the product of evil design. In the course of her analysis Arendt raises deep philosophical questions about the applicability of categories like intentionality to the kind of thoughtless and irresponsible, almost robotic behavior characteristic of totalitarian individuals.[105] Why, then, does she persistently treat totalitarianism as an agent, at times even a juggernaut? The answer, I think, is because this is how it appears. Totalitarian regimes, whatever their complexity, present themselves on the stage of history as divinely inspired agents if not divinities themselves. Much like the commodities that Marx describes in the early chapters of volume 1 of *Capital*, they seem more real than the humans whose behavior produces them. Arendt's point is not that totalitarian regimes are governed by a single, conscious intention to exercise power nihilistically. It is that these regimes present themselves, and are experienced by their supporters and their victims, as animated by power for its own sake. This is the structural logic of totalitarianism, that its complex social machinery is so relentlessly focused on its destructive and murderous policies. The unity, indeed the anthropomorphism she thus often attributes to totalitarian regimes is a reflection of the unprecedented power they possess and claims they make.

This also helps us understand the power of Camus's literary depictions of totalitarianism. It is true, as Sartre and others pointed out, that there is an unreality to Camus's treatment of totalitarianism as a natural epidemic. But there is an unreality about totalitarianism itself. The totalitarian regime claims to do what only god was previously believed to have done— to decide the lives and deaths of everyone, to compel men to justify themselves, and to subject them to ultimate judgment. The ahistorical and inhuman character of the plague corresponds to the inhuman character of totalitarianism itself. Of course it is a reality in history, produced by humans. But its abrupt and unforeseen character, its vicious barbarity, and its utter absurdity make it difficult to understand or depict in conventional terms. Irving Howe and Mark Crispin Miller have suggested that we understand the world of Orwell's *1984* as a "perfect nightmare," a stylized world of pure nihilism one step beyond the realities of totalitarianism. According to Miller, it presents "a relentless evocation of a world in which there is, will always be, no difference,"[106] where all is governed by the imperatives of pure power. Camus's fictional accounts are more relenting, but they too are stylized nightmares designed to capture the brutal absurdity of totalitarianism. This is why, for instance, the characters of both Caligula and the Plague speak so candidly, why their words are commands instantaneously carried out. Like O'Brien in *1984*, who declares that "power is not a means, it is an end," these characters express not necessarily what any actual person, even Hitler or Stalin, has ever wholly believed. Rather, they express those beliefs which alone might render intelligible the nihilistic practices of totalitarianism. If a totalitarian system could speak, it would say what Caligula or O'Brien says.

Both Camus and Arendt considered totalitarianism to be nothing less than a political and cultural trauma, an intoxication with power comprehensible only to those willing to open their eyes and stare in the face a nightmare made real. And what made this nightmare of destruction most frightening was the fact that it was the product of a monstrous construction of the human mind.

Modernity and the Origins of Totalitarianism

If both writers saw totalitarianism as a plague on Western civilization, neither sought to dismiss it as an aberration or to minimize its significance for understanding not only the Other but also ourselves. After World War II and the defeat of Nazism, only the Soviet Union remained as an example of some version of totalitarianism. Amidst the climate of the emerging Cold War, the theory of totalitarianism was seized upon as an ideological justification for the foreign policies of the United States and its various alliances, who had identified the source of the totalitarian threat—the Soviet Union—and its ideological and military antithesis—"pragmatic," liberal democracy. Thus a literary and political genre, in many ways quite different from the literature of the 1930s and 1940s, was established, a genre with a fairly clear genealogy from such books as Friedrich and Brzezinski's *Totalitarian Dictatorship and Autocracy* (1956) to more recent accounts like Kirkpatrick's *Dictatorships and Double Standards* and Revel's *The Totalitarian Temptation*.[107] Whereas this genre tends to treat totalitarianism primarily in terms of the threat Soviet imperialism poses to "Western freedom," the analyses of totalitarianism presented by Arendt and Camus indict modern civilization as a whole and in no way serve to furnish "the West" with a clear conscience.

Thus Camus, in *The Rebel*, indicts the bourgeoisie for laying the groundwork for the barbarism of the twentieth century, insisting that "by its essential corruption and disheartening hypocrisy, it helped to discredit, for good and all, the principles it proclaimed. Its culpability in this regard is infinite." As he describes totalitarianism later in the text, "such a plant could, in fact, thrive only in the soil of accumulated inequalities."[108] Camus considers the injustices of capitalism to be a fertile source of indignity, suffering, and resentment. He also views the bourgeois language of human freedom as deeply hypocritical, often masking an indifference to the plight of those lacking in wealth and privilege. This indifference to the suffering of others is accompanied by an attenuated sense of moral responsibility and a lack of concern with public affairs. In both *The Plague* and *State of Siege* bourgeois society proceeds apace, "discussing shipments, bills of lading, discounts," unaware of the pestilence that is germinating in its midst.[109] There are probably no less admirable characters in *Caligula* than the patricians, who are concerned only with their "petty humiliations" and are oblivious to the true measure of the tyrant in their midst. In *State of Siege* the rulers of Cadiz are conspicuously absent throughout much of the action of the play, having emigrated to safer shores and having left resistance in the hands of the common people. As the Plague ominously declares in parting, discerning the trumpets heralding the return of the ruling class, "Listen! My star's in the ascendant once again. Those are your former masters returning, and you will find them blind as ever to the wounds of others, sodden with inertia and forgetfulness of the lessons of the past.... They are my hope and strength."[110] Upon their arrival Nada, the nihilist, for once clearly articulates Camus's own sense of things: "Here they are, the old gang! They are all coming back: the men of the past, the fossils, the dead-enders, the triflers, smooth-tongued, comfortable.... Instead of shutting the mouths of those who air their grievances, they shut their own ears.... Look! Do you see what they're up to? Conferring decorations on each other! .... The blood of those you call the just ones still glistens on the walls—and what are those fine fellows up to? Giving each other medals!"[111]

This dialogue echoes the passions of postwar French society, still reeling from the traumas of occupation, resistance, and collaboration. But it also articulates Camus's refusal to allow the struggle against totalitarianism to be conscripted for the Cold War. This is made clear in Camus's response to the criticism of Gabriel Marcel, who had "expressed surprise that a play about totalitarian tyranny would be laid in Spain" rather than the Soviet Union:

> May I confess that I am somewhat ashamed to ask the question for you? Why Guernica, Gabriel Marcel? Why that event which for the first time, in the face of a world still sunk in its comfort, gave Hitler, Mussolini, and Franco a chance to show even children the meaning of totalitarian technique? Yes, why that even, which concerned us too? For the first time men of my age came face to face with injustice triumphing in history. At that time the blood of innocence flowed amidst the chatter of pharisees, which, alas, is still going on. Because there are some of us who will never wash our hands of that blood.[112]

Camus maintained that the traumas of totalitarianism implicate European civilization as a whole, and that its origins are deeply embedded in the structures of modern society. Thus Dr. Rieux reflects that "the plague bacillus never dies or disappears for good; that it can lie dormant for years and years in furniture and linen-chests; that it bides its time in bedrooms, cellars, trunks, and bookshelves; and that perhaps the day would come when, for the bane and enlightening of men, it would rouse up its rats again and send them forth to die in a happy city."[113]

Arendt's analysis in *The Origins of Totalitarianism* is more scholarly and historical, but it sounds similar themes:

> If it is true that the elements of totalitarianism can be found by retracing the history and analyzing the political implications of what we usually call the crisis of our century, then the conclusion is unavoidable that this crisis is no mere threat from the outside, no mere result of some aggressive foreign policy of either Germany or Russia, and that it will no more disappear with the death of Stalin than it disappeared with the fall of Nazi Germany. It may even be that the true predicaments of our time will assume their authentic form—though not necessarily the cruelest—only when totalitarianism has become a thing of the past.[114]

Arendt makes three crucial points in this passage. The first is that totalitarianism is the culmination of "the crisis of our century," a crisis with a traceable history and definite political consequences. This is in fact the major thesis of her book, only the last third of which discusses totalitarianism itself. The first third discusses the modern history of anti-Semitism and its close ties to the political economy of the modern nation-state. The second third discusses the processes of European imperialism—economic expansionism, colonial bureaucracy, the decline of parliaments and of the bourgeois public in general, culminating in the "explosion" of August 4, 1914, a "catastrophe" that "seems to have touched off a chain reaction in which we have been caught ever since"—inflation, unemployment, civil wars, mass migrations, expulsions, displacements. Arendt argues that even before the rise of totalitarianism the catastrophe of 1914 had "shattered the facade" of European politics, exposing the anguish of vast numbers of people for whom legality and propriety had ceased to offer any comfort.[115] Like Camus, Arendt believes that totalitarianism was fueled by a long history of indifference to hidden suffering.

Arendt's second point follows from this: totalitarianism is not simply something "out there," nor can it be explained in terms of the evil machinations, ideological agendas, or "organizational weapons" of Communist "subversives." It is a historically specific kind of regime made possible by a type of crisis that may or may not be repeated but many of whose conditions persist, and it must be understood soberly. Arendt is clear that the issues she raises go much deeper than anticommunism and in fact defy any such orthodoxy, warning in her in her 1966 preface that "we have inherited from the cold-war period an official 'counter-ideology,' anti-Communism, which also tends to become global in aspiration and tempts us into constructing a fiction of our own," blinding us to the political realities confronting us.[116]

This leads to her third point: the soil from which totalitarianism sprang, the political terrain that we still occupy, poses problems that are no less disturbing for their being nontotalitarian. One problem seems particularly to disturb her, no doubt for partially autobiographical reasons: namely, "the decline of the nation-state and the end of the rights of man." A central subtext of her book is that the theory and practice of state sovereignty, whatever its virtues once were, is incapable of handling the problems and resolving the conflicts that threaten to overwhelm our world. As she puts it, in words that can give comfort to no reigning ideology, in the age of imperialism and world war "the very phrase 'human rights' became for all concerned—victims, persecutors, and onlookers alike—the evidence of hopeless idealism or fumbling feeble-minded hypocrisy."[117] This is of course a major problem of contemporary political theory, but even more so a problem of politics itself, testing our ability to sustain even a minimal standard of human dignity. Arendt thus concludes that any adequate response to the horrors of totalitarianism must include a new conception of human justice and solidarity, that "human dignity needs a new guarantee which can be found only in a new political principle."[118]

Such a diagnosis hardly serves the recuperative purposes of the Cold War "counter-ideological uses of totalitarianism." For both Arendt and Camus the dangers posed by totalitarianism were not restricted to the Nazi and Stalin regimes. They required a much more thoroughgoing critique of modern politics, a task that both writers set for themselves.

Chapter 3

THE AMBIGUITIES OF HUMANISM

For both Arendt and Camus the crisis of civilization in the twentieth century was no mere aberration. Shattering long-standing assumptions about human empowerment and progress, it demanded a determined effort to rethink the reigning political imagery of modernity. And for both writers this meant a critique of modern humanism and its culmination in twentieth-century Marxism. Both agreed that Nazism, terrifying as it was, was the product of "subterranean currents" in Western politics. As Camus put it, the fascist ideologies "chose to deify the irrational, and the irrational alone, instead of deifying reason. In this way they renounced their claim to universality." True, fascism was part of the moral and political crisis of interwar European civilization. In its militarism, its ideological grandiosity, and its pioneering techniques for the mastery of the world, it was not far removed from the main currents of modern history. As Arendt saw, in many ways fascism gave expression to nihilistic impulses just beneath the surface of civilized European society. And yet despite its seriousness, and indeed despite the fact that Nazism posed perhaps a more potent threat to freedom than did Stalinism, it did not present the same challenge to political thought. As Camus noted, "Despite appearances, the German revolution . . . was only a primitive impulse whose ravages have been greater than its real ambitions. . . . Russian communism, on the contrary, has appropriated [a] metaphysical ambition . . . the erection, after the death of God, of a city of man finally deified." Hitlerism represented "the ethics of the gang"; communism, on the other hand, "has behind it a respectable tradition."[1] As Arendt put it, one cannot understand it "without taking into account the whole tradition of political philosophy."[2] Both writers sought to excavate this tradition and to understand how and why it went wrong.

In their writings Camus and Arendt exhibit a metaphysical strain deeply influenced by the work of Friedrich Nietzsche and Martin Heidegger, both of whom sought to trace the experience of nihilism to its roots in modern humanism.[3] Like Nietzsche, Arendt and Camus view the condition of modernity as one of homelessness and estrangement in which men, having dethroned God, hopelessly and dangerously seek through their own efforts the certainty and solidity that only a God can provide. Like Heidegger, they see modern subjectivity as engendering an unbridled, Promethean will to power. In many ways their critique of modernity can be read as a gloss on Heidegger's claim that "the more extensively and the more effectually the world stands at man's disposal as conquered, and the more objectively the object appears, all the more subjectively, i.e., the more importunately, does the subjiectum rise up, and all the more impetuously too, do observation of and teaching about the world change into a doctrine of man, into anthropology."[4] In exploring this dangerous rising up of the modern subject, Arendt and Camus articulate themes also sounded by such antimodernist contemporaries as Leo Strauss and Eric Voegelin, who assert that nihilistic value relativism is at the heart of modern consciousness, and such "critical theorists" as Max Horkheimer and Theodor Adorno, who associate modernity with the triumph of a rampant instrumental reason.[5] Like all of these writers, Arendt and Camus see the modern world, wholly disenchanted, as driven by the principle of human self-assertion and empowerment. As William Connolly has put it, "In modernity, the insistence upon taking charge of the world comes into its own."[6] For both writers this insistence on taking charge has involved noble efforts to humanize the world, to appropriate nature productively, and to create new forms of individual and collective autonomy. But it has also too often involved an ignoble forgetfulness of human finitude. In some instances this obliviousness has licensed monstrous projects of political transformation, just as the Communist faith in history licensed Stalinism. In other instances it has proven itself incapable of discerning such monstrosities and guarding against them, in the way that so many liberals and "progressives" failed to take seriously the possibility that Nazism was not an aberration but a dangerous reality. In either case, whether by commission or omission, humanism would seem culpable of some of the most profound evils of our time.

Yet although Camus and Arendt can be seen as metaphysical thinkers, their analyses are distinctively historical and anti-essentialist. Both writers believe that the discursive frame of modern humanism has played an important role in politics, and they seek to criticize the modern faith in human accomplishment; but both refuse to view political history as the mere working out of a metaphysical construct, whether it be Nietzsche's "will to power," Heidegger's "modern world picture," Strauss's "historicism," Voegelin's "gnosticism," or Horkheimer and Adorno's "instrumental reason." Unlike these writers, neither Arendt nor Camus offer a totalizing critique of modernity; their discriminating explorations of modern hubris also discern central aspects of humanism worthy of retrieval.[7] Both have a profound sense of the contingency of the modern humanistic discourse and of the diverse forms of politics that it makes possible. In this regard both are distinctly non-apocalyptic thinkers, who refuse to paint their picture of modernity with too wide a brush.[8] Although they share a revulsion from a Hegelian philosophy of history, they avoid the historicism that ironically informs so much post-Nietzschean thought, for which history is a story of regress rather than progress, servitude rather than freedom—most clear in Heidegger's claim that modern suffering is due to an instrumental reason forgetful of its primeval origins in Being.[9] Both Arendt and Camus remain sensitive to those possibilities excluded or marginalized by the modern impulse to take charge of the world. But they reject wholesale condemnations of modernity and reductive accounts that attribute the horrors of the century to the unrelenting triumph of a villainous, demiurgic humanism.[10]

This is clear, for instance, in Arendt's insistence that we must distinguish between "the modern age—rising with the climax in the revolutions in the eighteenth, and unfolding its general implications after the Industrial Revolution of the nineteenth—and the world of the twentieth century, which came into existence through the chain of catastrophes touched off by the First World War. To hold the thinkers of the modern age ... responsible for the structure and conditions of the twentieth century is even more dangerous than it is unjust. The implications apparent in the actual event of totalitarian domination go far beyond the most radical or most adventurous ideas of any of these thinkers."[11] For Arendt any view of twentieth-century history as the mere expression of a "modern world view" is unjust because it glosses over important historical discontinuities in its effort to render simplistic, overgeneralized judgments about the

sweep of modern history. And it is dangerous because it relies on a ne-
cessitarian logic and denies the concreteness and open-endedness of human
history. Arendt's political theory is designed to criticize precisely such a
way of thinking.

This is evident in her exchange with Eric Voegelin about *The Origins
of Totalitarianism*. Voegelin, strangely reading Arendt as a "liberal progressive," insists that "the true dividing line in the contemporary crisis
does not run between liberals and totalitarians but between the religious
and philosophical transcendentalists on the one side, and the liberal and
totalitarian immanentist sectarians on the other side."[12] Thus concrete
political events become read against a global narrative of metaphysical
struggle with its roots in the decay of Hellenism, a narrative according to
which modernity is equated with the advent of "spiritual disease." Arendt's
response strikes at the heart of Voegelin's approach:

> Mr. Voegelin seems to think that totalitarianism is only the other side of
> liberalism, positivism and pragmatism. But whether one agrees with liberalism
> or not . . . the point is that liberals are clearly not totalitarians. This, of course,
> does not exclude the fact that liberal or positivistic elements also lend themselves
> to totalitarian thinking; but such affinities would only mean that one has to
> draw even sharper distinctions because of the *fact* that liberals are not totali-
> tarians. . . . I think that what separates my approach from Professor Voegelin's
> is that I proceed from facts and events instead of intellectual affinities and
> influences. This is perhaps a bit difficult to perceive because I am of course
> much concerned with philosophical implications and changes in spiritual self-
> interpretation. But this certainly does not mean that I described "a gradual
> revelation of the essence of totalitarianism from its inchoate forms in the eight-
> eenth century to the fully developed," because this essence, in my opinion, did
> not exist before it had not come into being. I therefore talk only of "elements,"
> which eventually crystallize into totalitarianism, some of which are traceable to
> the eighteenth century, some perhaps even farther back. . . . Under no circum-
> stances would I call any of them totalitarian.[13]

For Arendt, Voegelin's brand of political theory represents the worst
kind of essentialism, treating real historical phenomena as the surface
expressions of seemingly deeper but in fact vaguer realities. In the process,
political reality is distorted and, what is more dangerous, contemporary
readers are offered false comfort in reified metaphysical categories. Arendt's
The Human Condition is more focused on philosophical self-interpretations
and implications than is *The Origins of Totalitarianism*. But both proceed
from a sober sense of historical concreteness, and if they concern themselves
with metaphysical "elements" this is not because they would reduce history

to them but rather because Arendt believes that such elements have played an important and often neglected role in history. And because she is intent on thinking beyond the crisis in which she finds herself, she is particularly concerned with identifying those elements of modern thought that are implicated in this crisis.

Camus, whose emphasis on metaphysical elements was also often misconstrued, had a similar view of the importance of modern political ideologies. Ironically, if the conservative Voegelin took Arendt to task for her "materialism," the radical Francis Jeanson, in his famous attack on *The Rebel,* upbraided Camus for his "idealism," claiming that in Camus's writing "formulas tirelessly succeed formulas, all equally perfect and pure, reduced to essentials, free of the slightest trace or smudge of mere existence. . . . One can see that this strange conception of history comes down to a suppression of history as such. In fact, it amounts to the elimination of all concrete situations, in order to obtain a pure dialogue of ideas."[14] Camus's response (which has not been translated into English, and tends to be ignored by commentators on his work) clarifies the specific intent of *The Rebel* and explains why he thinks it pressing to concentrate on discursive realities:

> If I were to devote a study exclusively to the influence of Greek comedy on Moliere's genius this would not mean that I was denying the Italian sources of his work. In *The Rebel* I have undertaken a study of the ideological dimension of revolutions. This was not only my right in the strictest sense; perhaps there is a certain urgency to this task at a time . . . in which a rather patient public is subjected to hundreds of volumes and publications on the economic foundations of history and the influence of electricity on philosophy. . . . I have argued only . . . that one can discern in the revolutions of the twentieth century, among other elements, an effort to deify man; and I have specifically chosen to illuminate this theme. *And in this I was justified, provided only that I clearly announced my intention—which I did*: "The purpose of this analysis is not to provide, for the hundredth time, a description of the revolutionary phenomenon, nor once more to register the historical or economic causes of the great revolutions. It is to discover in certain facts of the revolution the logical implications, the explanations, and the enduring themes of metaphysical revolt."[15]

The views of Arendt and Camus on the question of historical interpretation are remarkably similar. For them, as for Heidegger, "metaphysics grounds an age"; it constitutes the psychic subsoil of a civilization, providing a general foundation of cultural understandings and inflections— regarding human being and historical possibility—on which social and political practices are constructed and reconstructed.[16] Yet both thinkers are resolutely historical in their treatments of such foundations, viewing them as similarly subject to historical construction and reconstruction. Although they seek to delineate broad contours of the history of ideas, their judgments are tempered by a keen sense of historical specificity. Both thus seek to delineate a certain logic to modern political discourse while emphatically repudiating any myth—Hegelian, Heideggerian or otherwise—of the necessary unfolding of ideas. And both treat such a logic as an enabling, indeed activating condition, but not as a deux ex machina. It is to such a logic that I now turn.

The Prison House of Humanism

"The astonishing history evoked here is the history of European pride."[17] So Camus begins *The Rebel*. For Camus rebellion is at the heart of the Western experience. It is a demand on the part of man for recognition, a refusal of indignity and a "passionate affirmation" of human value. Camus's rebellion refers to the exercise of human freedom, to the fact that humans are agents always capable of surpassing or at least distancing themselves from their existing circumstances. Rebellion can be seen as the practical embodiment of humanism, a vigorous expression of human powers; humanism, then, is the practical awareness of the rebellious potential that is latent in all human conduct. It is only in the modern world that such a humanism, foreshadowed in the premodern period, comes into its own.

Camus argues that rebellion is first registered in philosophical understanding by the ancient Greeks, and he traces it back to the myth of Prometheus, "the most perfect myth of intelligence in revolt." *The Rebel* can be read as an extended reflection on the archetypical power of this ancient myth. Yet although Camus links rebellion with the Promethean conquest of fire, he argues that for the Greeks rebellion against nature was like "butting one's head against a wall."[18] He thus insists, in a passage reminiscent of Nietzsche's *The Birth of Tragedy*, that "metaphysical rebellion presupposes a simplified view of creation—which was inconceivable to the Greeks. . . . The idea of innocence opposed to guilt, the concept of all of history summed up in the struggle between good and evil, was foreign to them. . . . The Greeks never made the human mind into an armed camp, and in this respect we are inferior to them."[19] Like Nietzsche, for Camus the turning point in Western philosophy is the ascendancy of a Platonic metaphysical dualism, a "will to truth" that heralds the death of the Greek way of life and culminates in the the emergence of Christianity.[20]

The Christian worldview, centering around a narrative of sin, powerlessness, and redemption, is marked by a profound sense of rupture that Camus believes it neither possible nor desirable to dismiss. For this reason he admires in Augustine "the uneasiness of his sensibility."[21] But he also argues that "Christianity in its essence . . . is a doctrine of injustice. It is founded on the sacrifice of the innocent and the acceptance of this sacrifice. Justice on the contrary does not proceed without revolt."[22] In this respect Christianity is founded upon a humbling of the human spirit, a repression of rebellious impulses. Yet ironically, if Christianity tends to preach worldly passivity, Camus also believes that it articulates a dangerously messianic ideal: "What constitutes the irreducible originality of Christianity is the theme of the Incarnation. . . . The problems [of the world] themselves are incarnated and the philosophy of history is born. . . . And Christianity will only give body to this idea, so foreign to the Greeks, that man's problem is not to perfect his nature, but to escape from it."[23] Thus the theme of transcendence becomes established, and a redemptive ideal, an end of history, is introduced as a horizon of Western thought.

This ideal, however, is for Christianity beyond history itself, a promissory note for human suffering, grounded ultimately upon faith rather than reason and projecting a transcendent rather than mundane fulfillment. In this sense true metaphysical rebellion awaits the dawn of modernity. While in the early modern era Christianity is "submitted to the critical eye of reason. . . [whereby] the ground will be prepared for the great offensive against a hostile heaven," only in 1789 does that authentic rebellion appear in coherent and vigorous form, "when modern times begin to the accompaniment of the crash of falling ramparts."[24] The French Revolution inaugurates the age of a distinctively modern politics, propelled by the belief in the integrity and freedom of man, liberated from the constraints of church, superstition, and privilege, to create his own destiny. As Hegel wrote: "The greatness of our time rests in the fact that freedom, the peculiar possession of mind where it is at home with itself in itself, is recognized."[25] For Camus this self-assurance poses the possibility of a world in which human dignity and freedom are advanced. But the universal aspiration to bring the world wholly into accord with human purpose, to lay claim to ownership of "treasures formerly squandered on heaven," is also dangerous. For in banishing God, humans assume a heavy burden. Camus's description of humanism in the age of Enlightenment prefigures the more recent writings of Foucault on the modern subject and its disciplines:

> From this moment, man decides to exclude himself from grace and to live by his own means. Progress, from the time of Sade up to the present day, has

consisted in gradually enlarging the stronghold where, according to his own rules, man without God brutally wields power. In defiance of the divinity, the frontiers of this stronghold have been gradually extended, to the point of making the entire universe into a fortress erected against the fallen and exiled deity. Man, at the culmination of his rebellion, incarcerated himself; from Sade's lurid castle to the concentration camps, man's greatest liberty consisted only in building the prison of his crimes.[26]

For Camus modern politics is thus founded on what Lyotard has called a "grand narrative" of human progress.[27] Originating in an authentic effort to cast off the fetters of oppression and affirm the dignity of ordinary people, humanism, a liberatory idea, has ensnared modern man in prisons of his own creation, where he has become both victim and executioner. Seeking to destroy external forms of authority, it has unintentionally created its own church, complete with priests, dogma, rites of passage, and heavenly aspirations—a universal will to power framed in terms of the rights of man or the movement of history. These churches are diverse—nation-state, proletarian dictatorship, modern technology—but they all worship before the same divinity, human empowerment itself. Like Camus's Caligula, modern man commands the heavens, subjecting everything to his purposes, seeking to prove "to imaginary gods that any man, without previous training, if he applies his mind to it, can play their absurd parts to perfection."[28] Of course this is not all that Camus discerns in modern humanism. To be precise, he calls it a contradiction. But he refuses to dismiss one ominous pole of this contradiction as an aberration, insisting that it expresses an impulse deeply embedded in modernity.

The Rebel offers a sketch of the hubris of modern man. Prefiguring writers like François Furet, Camus locates this arrogance in Rousseau's sacred body politic and in the French revolutionary Reign of Terror.[29] Echoing Hegel's critique of abstract right, he remarks that "morality, when it is formal, devours."[30] Camus observes that "the condemnation of the king is at the crux of our contemporary history. It symbolizes the secularization of our history and the disincarnation of the Christian God." As a consequence there is no longer anything "but a semblance of God, relegated to the heaven of principles."[31] Transcending the uncertainties and ambivalences of the mundane world, such categorical imperatives of human morality enjoin humans to divest themselves of their passion in the name of universal reason, to envision a kingdom of ends in which their differences will be eclipsed by their common humanity. Thus begins the transformation of the intellectual from a voice of the church into a legislator of reason.[32] For Camus, as for Arendt, this tendency is abetted by two of the "evil geniuses" of the nineteenth century, Hegel and Marx, and only partially mitigated by the third, Nietzsche.[33]

Arendt's account develops similar themes. Like Camus, she identifies the pre-Socratic Greek world with a more balanced and moderate conception of human living, one that is reflected in the public rituals of tragic drama.[34] Drawing from Nietzsche and Heidegger, Arendt argues that this balance is undermined by the Socratic valorization of the *vita contemplativa*, which drives a wedge between worldly experience and truth, between experienced relationships and justice, and devalues the political realm, discovered by the Greeks, where men subsist and act uniquely as self-disclosing beings.[35] The central argument of *The Human Condition* is that the core tradition of Western political thought, from Plato through Marx, conceives of politics on the metaphors of subsistence and fabrication rather than action in common with others.[36] Even Plato and Aristotle, who seek to restore the *polis* and its uniquely public values, consistently think of political life in terms of craft analogies, whereby the craftsman, possessed of expert knowledge, shapes nature to his purposes. As Arendt writes, "the Platonic identification of knowledge with command and rulership and of action with obedience and execution overruled all earlier experiences and articulations in the political realm and became authoritarian for the whole tradition of political thought ... [substituting] making for acting in order to bestow upon the realm of human affairs the solidity inherent in work and fabrication."[37] Political philosophy is thus founded on a quest for certainty, a fear of unpredictability and difference, and an interest in control.[38]

Arendt is ambivalent about early Christianity. On the one hand, she believes that it emerged in "dark times," much like the present, and articulated a sense of dissonance and exile that might afford insight into current efforts to constitute free political communities. On the other hand, she believes that Christian metaphysics marginalizes questions of worldly living and is thus profoundly antipolitical.

Like Camus, Arendt wrote her doctoral dissertation on Augustinian philosophy and drew inspiration from certain early Christian themes. She praises Augustine's sense of the strangeness of the universe, his insight into the limits of human reason, and his grim vision of the political world.[39] She claims that Augustine saw, as most political philosophers have not, that the ultimate "nature of man" is not accessible to human reason, and that such a knowledge of the human essence and destiny—which "would be like jumping over our own shadows"—is capable of being possessed only by a God.[40] As a consequence he had unique insight into the ambiguous and limited character of human agency, which was contained in his dual conception of *libertas* or freedom. Augustine, true to Pauline theology, posits a conception of free will as subjective discipline or command, a view that reinforces the Platonic identification of politics with control and prefigures the modern Cartesian dualism of subject and object.[41] But Augustine also presents "an entirely differently conceived notion" of freedom viewed "not as an inner human disposition but as a character of human existence in the world."[42] This is his notion of natality. In Arendt's reading of this notion, freedom—the capacity to begin anew, to transvalue the world—is a property not of individual wills but of historically situated humans. People possess such freedom by virtue of their embeddedness in an intersubjective world of shared meanings and experiences, and exercise it in ways that always might escape their original intentions. For Arendt this almost existentialist dimension of early Christian thought is contrary to any metaphysical dualism and amenable to a more adequate conception of politics, one that takes into account the pluralistic character of political agency and the limited and partial character of political life.[43]

But if certain elements of Christianity expressed genuinely rebellious impulses, Arendt also believed that these impulses were eclipsed by the flight from reality underwritten by Christian theology. In this respect Christian doctrine represents a form of worldlessness and political withdrawal more powerful even than that articulated by classical Greek political philosophy. Thus she writes in *The Human Condition* of the "un-public," "un-political" character of Christianity, observing that its "worldlessness . . . is possible only on the assumption that the world will not last," an assumption supported by the doctrine of the immortality of the soul. For Arendt, as for Camus, the redemptive vision of Christianity, and all visions of a final imperative of right or end of history derived from it, are hostile to the actual arts of living.[44] She thus insists that "unlike the common good as Christianity understood it—the salvation of one's soul as a concern common to all—the common world is what we enter when we are born and what we leave behind when we die. It transcends our lifespan into past and future alike; it was there before we came and will outlast our brief sojourn in it."[45] Like Camus, Arendt believes that the Christian metaphysic lessens the significance of human mortality and slanders life. The consolation it offers relieves us of the responsibility and the anguish of living our own lives and making our own consequential, and all too human, decisions. In this context she favorably invokes Machiavelli's critique of Christianity, insisting that the Christian concern with the soul and with goodwill is "ruinous" to politics—not because she wished to repudiate the possibility of a political morality, but because she wished to repudiate political *moralizing*. Politics for her deals with differences, ambiguities, imperfections, and in this sense is necessarily resistant to the imperatives of pure goodness and to all expectations of ultimate judgment (an idea similar in her mind to the idea of a Final Solution).[46]

Christianity, then, is responsible for introducing into the Western tradition the discourse of human subjectivity and transcendence, valuing the soul at the expense of the body and eternal redemption at the expense of precarious human community. But for her, as for Camus, Christianity is an otherworldly discourse in which "every word is an act of grace."[47] Human subjectivity, however estranged from the world, is both established and ultimately redeemed by a deus ex machina—God. The Christian sense of the tension of existence is thus relieved by the leap of faith upon which Christianity depends. It is thus only in the modern, secular world that a pure philosophy of subjectivity, only hinted at in Neoplatonism and Christianity, can be realized.[48]

This is a major argument of *The Human Condition*. With the rise of what Arendt calls "the social," commercial conduct and capital accumulation become the central preoccupations of the modern world. Coincident with the advent of capitalism is the destruction of medieval cosmic certainties and the development of modern science, heralded by Gallileo's invention of the telescope. Modern man thus experiences what Arendt, following Heidegger, calls radical "world alienation."[49] With the explosion of a geocentric conception of the universe and the undermining of many of the central tenets of medieval Christian metaphysics, "modern men were not thrown back upon this world but upon themselves. One of the most persistent trends in modern philosophy since Descartes . . . has been an exclusive concern with the self." Arendt argues that the other side of modern philosophy's concern with isolated subjectivity is its conception of otherness as objectivity, as material to be measured and transformed:

> Only the modern age's conviction that man can know only what he makes, and that he therefore is primarily *homo faber* and not an *animal rationale*, brought forth the much older implications of violence inherent in all interpretations of the realm of human affairs as a sphere of making. . . . Marx's dictum that "violence is the midwife of every old society pregnant with a new one," that is, of all change in history and politics, only sums up the conviction of the whole modern age and draws the consequences of its innermost belief that history is "made" by men as nature is "made" by God.[50]

Like Camus, for Arendt modern politics is characterized by successive attempts to "storm the heavens," replacing God with man and constructing new churches to replace the old. Hobbes's *Leviathan* is clearly the most vivid illustration of this trend, but for Arendt not simply monarchical absolutism but all forms of modern state are founded upon such violence.[51] In the beginning, man made the commonwealth; this metaphor itself bespeaks of violence, of a working and acting upon others as if they were natural objects, if not artifacts of one's own creation. As Max Weber proclaimed, "one can define the modern state sociologically only in terms of the specific means peculiar to it, as to every political association, namely, the use of physical force."[52] For Arendt, Weber expresses the common sense of modern politics, according to which the state is an entirely constructed concentration of force designed to secure civil order. Such a conception of politics is perpetually liable to an "ethic of efficacy" that refuses the recalcitrance of the world and is insensitive to the problems of judgment that attend all political action, but especially the employment of violence.[53] As she writes, "The very substance of violent action is ruled by the means-end category, whose chief characteristic, if applied to human affairs, has always been that the end is in danger of being overwhelmed by the means which it justifies and which are needed to reach it. Since the end of human action, as distinct from the end products of fabrication, can never be reliably predicted, the means used to achieve political goals are more often than not of greater relevance to the future world than the intended goals."[54] The problem with modern ways of thinking about politics is that their confidence in human powers makes them blind to the limits and ambiguities of human agency. Further, as they come up against these limits and ambiguities, they tend to respond with a redoubled effort to surmount them. As Heidegger put it, the more objectively the object appears, the more imperious does the modern subject rise up against it. In this regard modern thought has an authoritarian propensity.

Arendt too discerns such an authoritarian propensity in Rousseau's *volunté général*, which proposes to surpass inequality through the sheer willfulness of a unanimous collective élan that brooks no difference.[55] She levels a similar charge against Kant's more liberal theory of natural right: "The categorical imperative is postulated as absolute and in its absoluteness introduces into the interhuman realm—which by its nature consists of relationships—something that runs counter to its fundamental relativity. The inhumanity which is bound up with the concept of one single truth emerges with particular clarity in Kant's work. . . . It is as though he who had so inexorably pointed out man's cognitive limits could not bear to think that in action too, man cannot behave like a god."[56] Anticipating the arguments of theorists like Jürgen Habermas, Arendt insists that Kant's conception of autonomy posits a single sovereign subject whose practical reason can discern laws of universal validity. The danger here is that such a form of monologic reasoning—"act so that the maxim of my conduct can be a universal law"—ignores the irreducible plurality of the human world.[57] That all ethical subjects might divest themselves of their specific attachments and reason in similar ways, and that the outcome of such reasoning might produce categorical principles that are universally binding, strike her as heroic and indeed horrifying assumptions. In Kant's practical reason there seems little room for the otherness of actual moral agents and little sense of the limits of moral reason in coming up against this otherness. As we shall see, by the idea of "representative thinking" Arendt tries to preserve the Kantian idea of the dignity of each individual without viewing ethical judgment as an abstractive process of practical reason issuing in absolute imperatives.

Like Camus, she believes that such absolutes are dangerous, however well-intentioned their motivations. For they draw their nourishment from a confidence about the intrinsic autonomy of the will or power of the mind which it is no longer possible to share. Equally disturbing is the typically modern agency of such visions—the sovereign state. Whether viewed as the repository of the general will of the citizenry or a guarantor of the rights of man, such an agency rests, as Weber saw, on a concentration of violent powers that have been exercised with great frequency and destructiveness in the modern era.

The Critique of the Hegelian-Marxist Tradition

For both Camus and Arendt the deification of man characteristic of Enlightenment thinking reaches its culmination in the writings of Hegel and Marx. In an important sense their efforts are directed against the Hegelian-Marxist legacy, which for them unites a modernizing historicism with a dangerous faith in reason. Whereas their modern predecessors, from Hobbes through Kant, present an ahistorical conception of a human subject that is transparent to itself and wholly capable of self-legislation, Hegel and Marx treat such a unified, sovereign subjectivity as the outcome of a long, progressive historical development. For Hegel this development is understood as the triumph of a World Spirit which after many conflicts finds itself "at home with itself in itself." For Marx it is understood as the triumph of man as laborer when, under communism, "the practical relations of everyday life offer to man none but perfectly intelligible relations with his fellows and to nature. The life process of society . . . is treated as production for freely associated men, and is consciously regulated by them in accordance with a settled plan."[58] Both Arendt and Camus recoil from the credulous faith in history that Hegel and Marx seem to have shared.

In this reaction they follow Nietzsche, who observed that Hegel "has implanted in a generation that he has thoroughly penetrated the worship of the 'power of history' that turns practically every moment into a sheer gaping at success, into an idolatry of the actual. . . . If each success is comprised by a 'rational necessity,' and every event is the victory of logic or the 'Idea,' then—down on your knees quickly, and let every step in the ladder of 'successes' be revered! What? There are no more ruling mythologies? What? Religions are becoming extinct? Look at the religion of the power of history, and the priests of the mythology of Ideas with their scarred knees!"[59] For Nietzsche the Hegelian "idolatry of the actual" is an elaborate form of worldlessness that is anathema to human creativity and agency. Because all human actions and encounters can be explained, *rationalized*, in terms of their insertion in a supramundane narrative of progress, Hegel's philosophy of history relieves the anxieties and challenges of life. It offers metaphysical comfort and skirts the real ethical challenges of historical existence. Camus certainly shared this view, insisting that however accurate Hegel's critique of the "terrorism" of Jacobin "abstract reason," Hegel's own "concrete reason" was no less terrifying: "Truth, reason, and justice were abruptly incarnated in the progress of the world. . . . These values have ceased to be guides in order to become goals. . . . Reason has embraced the future and aspired to conquest . . . From this moment on dates the idea . . . that man has not been endowed with a definitive human nature, that he is not a finished creation but an experiment, of which he can be partly the creator. With Napoleon and the Napoleonic philosopher Hegel the period of efficacy begins."[60] For Camus Hegel's philosophy of history inserts man into a cosmic drama in which freedom progressively, and necessarily, unfolds. Authentic value is thus to be found only at the end of history; "until then there is no suitable criterion on which to base a judgment of value. One must act and live in terms of the future. All morality becomes provisional."[61] In this regard Hegel's thought is a form of nihilism, embracing the destructive march of reason through human history and claiming a privileged standpoint—the "end" of history—from which, like Minerva's owl, to judge it after the fact.[62]

This is also Arendt's view. She writes that "Hegel's truly revolutionary idea was that the old absolute of the philosophers revealed itself in the realm of human affairs, that is, precisely that domain of human experiences which the philosophers unanimously had ruled out as the source or birthplace of absolute standards." [63] This was, of course, Hegel's own intention, stated most forcefully in the introduction to *The Phenomenology of Mind*— to transcend the dualisms of Western philosophy since Socrates, to comprehend and complete this philosophy by rendering reason concrete.[64] The price of this concreteness is for Arendt a view of history as "at once dialectical and driven by necessity . . . [it] bears men on its irresistible flow, like a powerful undercurrent, to which they must surrender the very moment they attempt to establish their freedom on earth." [65] For her, such a philosophy of history lends itself to an ethic in which success is the only standard of value. Her concluding appendix to *The Origins of Totalitarianism*, "Ideology and Terror: A Novel Form of Government," is among the most vivid accounts in political theory of the practical nihilism such a faith in history can support.[66]

For both Arendt and Camus the danger of such a philosophy of history is only partly based in its quasi-mystical idealism, reifying concepts and positing the transubstantiation of ideas in an ascending spiral of apparently self-generated motion.[67] Even more important is the philosophical anthropology that it supports—a metanarrative of the estrangement and eventual recuperation of an essential subject, whether this subject be Spirit or Man as collective laborer. In this regard there is little difference between Hegelian idealism and Marxist materialism. Indeed for both writers more troubling than the vulgar materialism of orthodox communism was the more humanistic version of Hegelian-Marxism defended by such writers as George Lukacs, Jean-Paul Sartre, and Maurice Merleau-Ponty, who offered nuanced, qualified defenses of communism based on their readings of the dialectical currents of history.[68] Rather than associate Marx's thought with a crass positivism, they both consider Marx "the greatest pupil Hegel ever had."[69]

For both writers Marx's greatness resided in his conscious rebellion against all prior political philosophy, expressed most clearly in his concern with action: "The philosophers have only interpreted the world; the point, however, is to change it."[70] And yet if Marx promises a new, more worldly vision of political agency, his overturning of Hegelian idealism still draws its nourishment from Hegel's philosophy of the subject. Man replaces Spirit, and revolutionary praxis replaces speculative metaphysics. But the modernist aspiration to transform the world in the name of truth, to establish a universal empire of reason, remains.

In this regard, Arendt insisted, Hegel's philosophy was politically innocuous precisely because of its excessively speculative character: "For Hegel, the importance of the concept of history was primarily theoretical. It never occurred to [him] . . . to apply this concept directly by using it as a principle of action." This move was left to Marx, who viewed the end of history as an end of human action, a state of affairs toward which political praxis is directed. In Arendt's estimation, this vision, especially when tied to a utilitarian concern with the production of wealth, was bound to result in an eviscerated and portentous model of politics:

> In this version of deriving politics from history, or rather political conscience from historical consciousness . . . we can easily detect the age-old attempt to escape from the frustrations and fragility of human action by construing it in the image of making. What distinguishes Marx's own theory from all the others in which the notion of "making history" has found a place is only that he alone realized that . . . if one imagines that one can make history, one cannot escape the consequence that there will be an end to history. Whenever we hear of grandiose aims in politics, such as establishing a new society in which justice will be guaranteed forever, or fighting a war to end all wars or to make the whole world safe for democracy, we are moving in the realm of this kind of thinking.[71]

It is useful read Arendt's famous criticisms of Marx in *The Human Condition* against the backdrop of this remark. Arendt objects to Marx above all because for him politics is an instrumental activity undertaken in the service of labor, an effort radically to transform the world in the name of an end, the "free association of producers," that is immanent within history. Giving short shrift to questions of intersubjectivity, Marx places the problem of objectification, the conquest of nature, at the center of his political vision. And blind to the difficult responsibilities of political judgment, his class analysis of politics pretends to derive "political conscience from historical consciousness."[72]

Arendt argues that Marx's labor-centered view of politics promotes domination if not outright physical violence, because its strategic concern places a premium on acting on others rather than in concert with them. Arendt remarks on "the faithfulness of his descriptions to phenomenal reality," observing that the pride of place given to labor and production in Marx's theory corresponds to their real primacy in modern society.[73] But in this respect, she argues, Marx practices an "idolatry of the actual," mirroring rather than criticizing the forms of modern social life. He employs a "consistent naturalism" in his understanding of the centrality of labor and in his wish, shared with Locke, "to see the process of growing wealth as a natural process, automatically following its own laws and beyond wilful process and purposes."[74] Marxism is of a piece "with the evolution and development theories of the nineteenth century," all of which were process-oriented and glorified historical movement and modernization.[75]

The criticisms that follow from this reasoning seem rather obscure when considered in isolation from Arendt's analyses of twentieth-century politics, but when read in that light they become clearer and more compelling. The first is that Marx's labor metaphysic fatefully confuses labor and work, appropriation and property. It epitomizes the "worldlessness" of modernity, celebrating the ceaseless transformation of the world rather than the construction and preservation of secure, relatively permanent things, spaces, and relationships. Arendt's claim that Marx conceives labor as biological metabolism may be profoundly flawed, but her insight into the relentless modernism of Marx's theory is harder to criticize.[76] The end of production for Marx, she argues, is and can only be consumption; history is a process whose justification resides in the transcending of scarcity, which its growing productivity makes possible.[77] This may not be all that there is to Marx's vision, but it is most certainly a pervasive theme.[78] The most powerful statement of it in Marx's work is his famous paean to the "uncertainty," "agitation," and "disturbance" caused by capitalism, whereby "all that is solid melts into air, all that is holy is profaned, and man at last is forced to face his real conditions of life and his relations with his fellow men."[79]

There is, to be sure, something faintly damning about such praise, and Marx certainly wished to criticize the suffering caused by the relentless development of the productive forces under capitalism.[80] But it is notable that such a critique, itself often marginalized by Marx's "mature" posture of "scientific" antimoralism, was articulated almost exclusively in terms of an economic exploitation of labor whose alleviation could only be achieved through *further* appropriations of the world and more relentless technological change. Thus Marx's moral condemnation of this suffering did not prevent him from valuing the changes that frequently contributed to it.

Furthermore, Arendt suggests, the nobility of Marx's criticisms is undermined by the philosophy of history in which they are embedded, a philosophy that is silent about questions of political judgment, responsibility, and freedom.[81] In this respect the Marxist project of "making history" is marked by a deep strand of nihilism. Despite the "fanatical zeal for justice" that clearly animates his writing, like Hegel he endorses a "sheer gaping at success."[82]

Arendt's second criticism is that that there is a "fundamental and flagrant contradiction" at the heart of Marx's analysis:

> Marx's attitude toward labor, and that is toward the very center of his thought, has never ceased to be equivocal. While it was an "eternal necessity imposed by nature" and the most human and productive of man's activities, the revolution, according to Marx, has not the task of emancipating the laboring classes but of emancipating man from labor; only when labor is abolished can the "realm of freedom" supplant the "realm of necessity."[83]

Here again, Arendt's reading of Marx is dubious. After all, Marx envisioned not the abolition of labor but the abolition of labor as a servile and burdensome activity; indeed, the principle of communism, "from each according to his ability, to each according to his need," itself suggests the continued need for some kinds of labor. Yet at a deeper level Arendt's point is a powerful one—that Marx's vision of communism, the horizon against which all of his historical and moral judgments are made, is invidiously utopian. Marx's language about the realms of necessity and freedom, and indeed a whole series of images, metaphors, and claims that he presents, all suggest an apocalyptic break in history, one whose future contours are left disturbingly unspecified.[84] Whatever the complexities of Marx's moral vision, it is at least paradoxical that one for whom laboring is a central ontological and historical category should speak of casual hunting, fishing, and criticism when describing his ideal (postindustrial) society.[85]

Arendt not only objects to Marx's underspecification of important ideals, especially the ideal of freedom itself. She also takes issue with the almost willful optimism implicit in the very idea of the emancipation from necessity. For however much the reorganization of society might foster more empowering and gratifying labor, "not even this utopia could change the essential worldly futility of the life process."[86] There are, then, limits to even the best forms of social life, an insight toward which Marx often seemed blind.[87]

Camus's criticisms of Marxism parallel those of Arendt. He too admired Marx's passion for justice and his engagement with politics. But Camus also believed that Marx's theory undermined the noble ideals that animated his work. Marxian socialism, Camus writes in *The Rebel*, seeks "to reinstate the supreme being on the level of humanity. . . . From this angle, socialism is therefore an enterprise for the deification of man and has assumed some the the the characteristics of traditional religions."[88] These include a "scientific messianism" of bourgeois origin, characterized by a buoyancy about the development of industry and technology. Here Camus draws heavily from the writings of Simone Weil on the degradation of modern laborers, insisting that socialists have in practice proved no better than capitalists in addressing the existential problem of meaningful, dignified work.[89] Another is the historicism that Marx draws from Hegel, which for Camus means that "values are only to be found at the end of history . . . [and] all morality becomes provisional." Camus is only half-facetious when he observes that "Marx is only anticapitalist in so far as capitalism is out of date," suggesting that Marx's philosophy of history undermines the possibility of a fully worked out ethic of socialist ends and socialist means.[90]

For Camus this historicism is joined with a prophetic vision of communism as "the riddle of history solved," the "reconciliation of the wolf and the lamb," the end of human alienation. And it is here that Marx's theory prefigures the atrocities of Stalinism: "In the perspective of Marxist prophesy, nothing matters. In any event, when the bourgeois class has disappeared, the proletariat will establish the rule of universal man at the summit of production, by the very logic of productive development. What does it matter that this should be accompanied by dictatorship and violence? In this New Jerusalem, echoing with the roar of miraculous machinery, who will still remember the cry of the victim?"[91] Marx, Camus writes, blends "the most valid critical method with a Utopian Messianism of highly dubious value."[92] As a "method of criticism of contemporary society" Marxism has profound validity, revealing the reality of suffering and hypocrisy "that is hidden beneath the formal values" of bourgeois freedom.[93] Marx's moral concern is a point to which Camus continually returns: "The ethical demands that form the basis of the Marxist dream . . . [constitute] the real greatness of Marx. By demanding for the worker real riches, which are not riches of money but of leisure and creation, he has reclaimed, despite all appearance to the contrary, the dignity of man. In doing so, and this can be said with conviction, he never wanted the additional degradation that has been imposed on man in his name."[94]

And yet even if Marx sought human dignity, this commitment was undermined by the utopian messianism that he derived from Hegel. Camus does not absolve Marx of historical responsibility for the way in which his ideas have lent themselves to abuses, but his comments suggest that the question of Marx's responsibility is an enormously difficult one. Indeed these tensions, both within Marx's thought and within the Marxist tradition, are explicitly acknowledged by Camus.

Neither Arendt nor Camus conflates Stalinism with Marxism. And while both argue that Marxism as an ideology has fettered the rebellious impulses that gave rise to it, both also insist that it is precisely because of these noble impulses that criticism of Marxist movements must be discriminating. Thus Camus asserts that "Russian communism is forgetful of its real principles," that Marxism has value as one of the legitimate heirs of the modern rebellious impulse, and that Stalinism has travestied this value. Indeed, he goes so far as to declare that even in the twentieth century this value persists and needs to be rescued from those, on the right and the left, who simply equate Marxism with despotism: "There is undoubtedly in Russia today, even in its Communist doctrines, a truth that denies Stalinist ideology. But this ideology has its logic, which must be isolated and exposed if we wish the revolutionary spirit to escape final disgrace." Camus's subtlety, then, does not end with Marx. Stalinism, he asserts, was something "Marx never dreamed of. . . Nor indeed did Lenin, though he took a decisive step toward establishing a military empire."[95] In Camus's view Lenin is Marx's disciple and, as such, he helps to turn Marx's theory into a doctrine and erects a church—the party-state—to incarnate and spread its truth. Camus's discussion of Lenin's doctrines of vanguard party and revolutionary dictatorship is sharply critical, but even here he emphasizes the unintended and contingent character of the Bolshevik Revolution's culmination in Stalinism.

It would be an error to overemphasize Camus's sympathy for Bolshevism, but his understanding of the Russian Revolution is notably judicious. He observes of the Bolshevik seizure of power, "From this moment on, the history of the interior struggles of the party, from Lenin to Stalin, is summed up in the struggle between the workers' democracy and military and bureaucratic dictatorship; in other words, between justice and expediency."[96] Camus does not elaborate, but his comments seem to acknowledge the authentic aspirations to which the Revolution gave voice and to view Soviet history as a process where different outcomes were possible, and none was preordained.

Here too his analysis is close to that provided by Arendt, especially in her 1966 preface to *The Origins of Totalitarianism*, where she criticizes deterministic analyses of Stalin's rise to power. Agreeing with Merle Fainsod's claim that by the mid–1920s the Bolshevik regime was politically floundering, she nonetheless maintains, "What he fails to see . . . is that there existed an obvious alternative to Stalin's seizure of power and transformation of the one-party dictatorship into total domination, and this was the pursuance of the NEP policy as it was initiated by Lenin." Her footnote to this remark is even more emphatic: "This alternative is usually overlooked in the literature because of the understandable, but historically untenable, conviction of a more or less smooth development from Lenin to Stalin. It is true that Stalin almost always talked in Leninist terms. . . [but] Stalin filled these old Leninist concepts with a new, distinctively Stalinist content."[97]

These historiographical comments make clear that the criticisms of Marxism offered by Arendt and Camus were nuanced and highly contextualized. Stressing both the "logic" of Marxism as an ideology and the contingency of twentieth-century history, both thinkers refused to blame Marx for the rise of Soviet totalitarianism. Furthermore, for both of them the metaphysical flaws of Marxism were linked not simply to the brutalities of Soviet communism, especially under Stalin, but to the failure of twentieth-century socialism more generally. Especially important here was the failure of either Bolshevism or social democracy to deal prudently and effectively with the onset of the First World War and the subsequent rise of fascism. This is a subtext of Arendt's *Origins,* littered as it is with citations from Luxemburg, Hilferding, and Trotsky.[98] Those commenting on Arendt's criticisms of Marxism in *The Human Condition* and *Between Past and Future* often fail to see that her philosophical objections rest on an acute historical awareness. Crucial for her was the inability of European socialists to comprehend the roots of imperialism in nationalism, racism, and militarism or to appreciate the gravity of imminent world war:

> In Marxist terms the new phenomenon of an alliance between mob and capital seemed so unnatural, so obviously in conflict with the doctrine of class struggle, that the actual dangers of the imperialist attempt—to divide mankind into master races and slave races . . . to unify the people on the basis of the mob— were completely overlooked. Even the breakdown of international solidarity at the outbreak of the first World War did not disturb the complacency of the socialists and their faith in the proletariat as such. Socialists were still probing the economic laws of imperialism when imperialists had long since stopped obeying them.[99]

Her unambiguously negative comments about European parliamentary politics in the aftermath of the war also indicate that Arendt's criticism of socialist complacency in the face of imperialism was not limited to the Bolsheviks but extended to social democrats as well.[100]

Ironically, Arendt's opinion of Lenin seems much higher than her view of social democratic leaders or of the other Bolsheviks. She praises many of his policies immediately following the Revolution, observing that "it seems clear that in these purely practical political matters Lenin followed his great instincts for statesmanship rather than his Marxist convictions."

Indeed she maintains that "there is no doubt that Lenin suffered his greatest defeat when, with the outbreak of the civil war, the supreme power that he originally planned to concentrate in the Soviets definitely passed into the hands of the party bureaucracy," calling this a "tragic development."[101] It is hard to avoid the impression that Arendt found Lenin's Machiavellian *virtu* appealing and certainly considered it a refreshing invigoration of Marxist historicism. For Lenin the Marxist philosophy of history was no longer a strategic guide, only a source of metaphysical comfort and confidence. Lenin's "instinct for statesmanship" alerted him to the contingencies of history and to the importance of creative political agency. Yet it is also clear that Arendt believes that his "Marxist convictions"—about class struggle and economic modernization and, more important, about the laws of history—played an important role in the Bolshevik regime's eventual crushing of revolutionary aspirations.[102] As Arendt noted, with the Civil War pronouncements of Lenin and Trotsky in mind, "the belief in history which teaches certain procedures by which one can bring about the end" is likely to produce barbarous results. Contrary to expectations, "the breaking of eggs in action never leads to anything more interesting than the breaking of eggs. The result is identical with the activity itself: it is a breaking, not an omelet."[103]

Perhaps Arendt's most subtle analysis of Marxism was her essay on Rosa Luxemburg. Luxemburg was clearly a heroine for Arendt, largely by virtue of her views about revolutionary spontaneity and political participation, but also because of her status as a female Jewish pariah. Arendt's essay presents an interesting diagnosis of European Marxism at the turn of the century. She argues that in spite of furious disagreements, both Luxemburg and Eduard Bernstein shared an aversion to the position of Karl Kautsky, prevalent within the German Social Democratic Party (SPD) and the Second International, for whom " 'the iron law of necessity' was . . . the best possible excuse for doing nothing."[104] Echoing her friend Walter Benjamin's insistence that "nothing has corrupted the German working class so much as the notion that it was moving with the current,"[105] Arendt believed that this "excuse for doing nothing" fatefully contributed both to the weakening of revolutionary radicalism and to the eventual rise of fascism.

Luxemburg's own brand of revolutionary Marxism, epitomized by her critique of the Bolshevik dictatorship, is one with which Arendt expresses much sympathy.[106] But she is also highly critical, especially of Luxemburg's misreading of the national question. She concedes that the course of events bore out Luxemburg's aversion to nationalism, but holds nonetheless that nothing "contributed more to the catastrophic decline of Europe" and that Luxemburg was "unable to gauge correctly the enormous force of nationalist feeling in a decaying body politic."[107] Like Lenin, in spite of her commitment to an activist conception of revolutionary politics Luxemburg's residual "Marxist convictions" about the primacy of class struggle and the progressive movement of history returned to haunt her. Because she considered nationalist identity to be regressive, anachronistic, and thus aberrational, she was unable to appreciate fully the need to grapple with it in politically creative ways. In this respect she indeed compares poorly with Lenin, who made a real effort creatively to incorporate the nationalities question into a Marxist framework. But Arendt also suggests that this is an issue that defies the Marxist worldview. Whatever Lenin's strategic insights into the proximate consequences of the First World War, neither he nor any other Marxist was able to anticipate the maelstrom of bloody events that followed or to gauge the significance of nationalism for these events.[108]

In the Luxemburg essay Arendt insists on the openness of history and the contingencies of politics, something that was essential to Luxemburg's brand of Marxism. Arendt's account of the significance of the assassination of Luxemburg and Karl Liebknecht in January 1919 (in a review of a book by Peter Nettl) illustrates her keen sense of the fateful ironies of historical contingency: "With the murder . . . the split of the European Left into Socialist and Communist parties became irrevocable; 'the abyss which the Communists had pictured in theory became . . . the abyss of the grave.' And since this early crime had been aided and abetted by the [Social Democratic] government, it initiated the death dance in postwar Germany. . . . Thus Rosa Luxemburg's death became the watershed between two eras in Germany; and it became the point of no return for the German Left."[109]

Camus offers a similar view of the fissures within the international socialist movement. He too believed that the events surrounding the First World War cruelly undermined Marx's hopes of proletarian internationalism, and that geopolitical pressures frustrated whatever slight possibilities there were for a creative revolutionary politics, demonstrating that "war and nationalism were realities in the same category as the class struggle. Without an [automatic] international solidarity of the working classes . . . no interior revolution could be considered likely to survive unless an international order was created . . . either by almost simultaneous revolutions in every big country, or by the liquidation, through war, of the bourgeois nations; permanent revolution or permanent war." While revolutionary upsurges in Germany, Italy, and France marked the high point in revolutionary hopes and aspirations, he continues, "the crushing of these revolutions and the ensuing reinforcement of capitalist regimes have made war the reality of revolution. Thus the philosophy of enlightenment finally led to the Europe of the black-out."[110]

This analysis has obvious affinities with the Trotskyist view that the failure of proletarian internationalism led to the containment of the Russian Revolution and its ultimate betrayal of revolutionary aspirations. And yet Camus lodges this account within a broader analysis of the role of Marxist assumptions in helping to bring about this unfortunate outcome.[111] Had the Marxist parties not so credulously believed in "a solidarity that would come into play automatically," and had they been more alive to the ambiguities of political identity and the complexities of political agency, they may have been able to present a more compelling and effective response to the onset of war.

Thus for both Camus and Arendt, Marxist socialism is a form of rebellion against injustice whose underlying metaphysical currents—a labor metaphysic, a modernizing optimism, a faith in history— have helped to undermine, indeed devour, its own rebellious impulses. Marxism, giving voice to the noblest aspirations of modern humanism, seeks to storm the heavens, but its own intellectual foundations prevent it from figuring out how to live in a world without God. The humanism of the Hegelian-Marxist tradition nobly articulates a vision of historical agency and transcendence. Its secular insistence on worldly action and justice exemplifies the progress achieved through modernity. But its Promethean aspirations are incompatible with any sense of the limits of human conduct, the partial nature of even the most emancipatory politics, and the need to treat nature, and humans, with care. Camus, writing from the vantage point of the military division of Europe at the height of the Cold War, eloquently articulates the sense that noble dreams had been transformed into nightmares:

> Here ends Prometheus' itinerary. Proclaiming his hatred of the gods and his love of mankind, he turns away from Zeus with scorn and approaches mortal men in order to lead them in an assault against the heavens. But men are weak and cowardly; they must be organized. They love pleasure and immediate happiness; they must be taught to refuse . . . immediate rewards. Thus Prometheus, in his turn, becomes a master who first teaches and then commands. Men doubt that they can safely attack the city of light and are even uncertain whether the city exists. They must be saved from themselves. The hero then tells them that he, and he alone, knows the city. Those who doubt his word will be thrown into the desert, chained to a rock, offered to the vultures. The

others will march henceforth in darkness, behind the pensive and solitary master. Prometheus alone has become god and reigns over the solitude of men. But from Zeus he has gained only solitude and cruelty. He is no longer Prometheus, he is Caesar. The real, eternal Prometheus has now assumed the aspect of one of his victims. The same cry, springing from the depths of the past, rings forever from the Scythian desert.[112]

For both writers this Promethean betrayal has assumed political significance in the context of a maelstrom of historical forces, over only some of which Marxists had any control. Indeed, as the previous chapter made clear, for Arendt and Camus these events implicate above all the system of imperialist states constructed by the European bourgeoisie, and the corrupt and unjust societies upon which these states were built. And if the rebellious impulses of Marxism have been devoured in part by its hunger for power, the same can be said of the impulses of European liberalism, whose utopia had become hypocritical ideology long before the turn of the century. Neither of these traditions is above reproach for the catastrophes that culminated in the rise of totalitarianism. The special concern of both writers with the failures of Marxism may well be due to their attraction to its passionate zeal for justice and dignity. The failure of Marxism represents the tragic apotheosis of modern humanism, giving way to even more disturbing forms of unadulterated nihilism.

The Critique of Pure Nihilism

"The most universal sign of the modern age: man has lost dignity in his own eyes to an incredible extent. . . . We are losing the center of gravity that allowed us to live."[113] Nietzsche's insight anticipates the widespread sense of despair that disturbs Camus and Arendt. For both thinkers modern politics can be viewed as an incomplete rebellion against God, a profound identity crisis, a kind of spiritual adolescence in which modern man rebels in vain against the authority of his father only to internalize it more thoroughly. But the father has died, and so the life of modern man loses its grounding. As Camus put it, "It happens that the stage set collapses . . . in a universe suddenly divested of illusions and lights, man feels an alien, a stranger. His exile is without remedy, since he is deprived of the memory of a lost home or the hope of a promised land. This divorce between man and his life, the actor and his setting, is properly the feeling of absurdity."[114]

For both Camus and Arendt this sense of absurdity signals the exhaustion of the vital energies of modern culture. Both writers recognized its intellectual roots in modern society and its increasing plausibility in a century of total war.[115] Far removed from Hegel's nineteenth-century vision of a human spirit "at home with itself in itself," the twentieth century had witnessed a monstrous disjuncture between human purpose and outcome that could only invite an intense feeling of unredeemable exile, a sense that the world was emptied of all meaning and that human living was pointless.

Perhaps Camus's most moving discussion of nihilism is his four-part essay "Letters to a German Friend," written in 1944 on the eve of the liberation of France. Here he associates fascism with a European "tragedy of the intelligence," chastising his fictional interlocutor for believing that "everything was equivalent and that good and evil could be defined according to one's wishes. You supposed that in the absence of any human or divine code the only values were those of the animal."[116] Camus acknowledges the genuine intellectual attractions of nihilism. He is quite aware that many of his contemporaries, especially modernist intellectuals, are drawn toward nihilism, toward its mystique of cruelty and its contempt for hypocrisy. Articulating a pervasive sense of the failures of reason, nihilism's absolute "metaphysical revolt" symbolizes a crisis of value in the modern world. But Camus makes clear how dangerous and irresponsible he considers such a cynical leveling out of all distinctions.

The Rebel offers a brief genealogy of this nihilism. Its forerunner is the Marquis de Sade, who "pursued a monstrous dream of revenge" against modern rationalism and whose "inordinate thirst for a form of life he could never attain was assuaged in the successive frenzies of a dream of universal destruction." Camus is not dismissive of Sade's accomplishment. "He rejects," Camus writes, "with exceptional perspicacity for his times, the presumptuous alliance of freedom with virtue." Indeed, he continues sardonically, Sade's "total submission to evil leads to an appalling penitence, which cannot fail to horrify the Republic of enlightenment and of natural goodness." And yet Sade's program is a program of domination, of "the total subjection of the majority," expressing a "thirst for blood" whose logic must lead to "universal annihilation."[117] While Camus rejects the dangerous alliance of freedom and self-righteous virtue that culminated in Jacobin terror, he sees that its remedy is not an equally dangerous alliance of hedonism and Machiavellian *virtu*. He is just as critical of the "dandies" of the Romantic movement—figures like Lermontov and Baudelaire whose "cry of outraged innocence" against the corruptions of modernity abjures any "positive content." For these intellectuals "the apocalypse becomes an absolute value in which everything is confounded—love and death, conscience and culpability." Camus argues that the dandy is an inauthentic rebel, a *poseur* whose revolt against convention is entirely self-absorbed:

> The dandy creates his own unity by aesthetic means. But it is an aesthetic of singularity and of negation. . . . The dandy can only play a part by setting himself up in opposition. He can only be sure of his own existence by finding it in the expression of others' faces. . . The dandy, therefore, is always compelled to astonish. Singularity is his vocation, excess his way to perfection. Perpetually incomplete, always on the fringe of things, he compels others to create him, while denying their values.[118]

Camus does not wish to reinstate the virtues of rationalism, for he agrees with the Romantics that modern forms of rationality are often hopelessly naive and dangerously imperious, and that the orders they institute often produce new forms of suffering. But he insists that the Romantic revolt against the iron cage of modernity is "sterile," that it takes place in "a make-believe world" and does little to inscribe real value in the world.[119] Indeed its nostalgia, far from resisting the sufferings of modernity, mirrors the modern faith in human empowerment, substituting the myth of a pastoral past for the myth of a redemptive future.[120] He has a similar view of twentieth-century surrealists and dadaists, whose criticisms are "invaluable": "while reason embarks on action and sets its armies marching on the world, the splendid night in which Breton delights announces dawns that have not yet broken."[121] And yet the surrealist vision of revolt is "an absolute and consolatory myth" that is epitomized by the infamous statement of André Breton, which he "must have regretted ever since 1933—that the simplest surrealist act consisted in going out into the street, revolver in hand, and shooting at random into the crowd." Camus does not criticize surrealism as an aesthetic; indeed he acknowledges its artistic creativity and power.[122] Yet he sees its militant antipolitics as a dangerous politics in spite of itself, an audacious "mixture of Machiavellianism and Augustinism." Surrealists thus delighted in the breakdown of European civilization, indifferent to the likely political consequences to follow: "these frenetics wanted 'any sort of revolution,' no matter what as long as it rescued them from the world of shop-keepers and compromise in which they were forced to live. In that they could not have the best, they still preferred the worst. In this respect they were nihilists."[123]

Camus shares the surrealist sense of the absurd, of the disjunctures of experience, the strangeness and often grotesqueness of the familiar. *The*

Stranger is a vivid fictional account of this, as Merseault goes through the motions of bourgeois daily life in complete estrangement, experiencing his existence as entirely without meaning.[124] Yet Camus refuses to turn this sensitivity into an absolute. For him it can only be a "point of departure," a stimulus to a more satisfying way of reconstituting the world.[125]

On this score his views are again echoed by Arendt, in a brilliant and often overlooked section of *The Origins* on "the temporary alliance between the mob and the elite." The elite to which she refers here is the intellectual elite of the "front generation" of World War I, the literary avant-garde that gave voice to the pervasive sense of civilizational crisis that accompanied that war. Arendt notes their "antihumanist, antiliberal, anti-individualist, and anticultural instincts ... their brilliant and witty praise of violence, power and cruelty." This elite, who rejected the pseudo-scientific justifications for the imperialism and racism of the bourgeoisie ("They read not Darwin but the Marquis de Sade"), was distinguished by "their high literary standard and great depth of passion." Arendt observes that "if we compare this generation with the nineteenth-century ideologists ... their chief distinction is their greater authenticity and passion."[126] Like Camus, she suggests that the nihilism of this generation expressed the nihilism of bourgeois society (indeed, a major theme of Arendt's writing is the "superfluousness" engendered by modern mass society):

> What the spokesmen of humanism and liberalism usually overlook ... is that an atmosphere in which all traditional values and propositions had evaporated (after the nineteenth-century ideologies had refuted each other and exhausted their vital appeal) in a sense made it easier to accept patently absurd propositions than the old truths which had become pious banalities. ... Since the bourgeoisie claimed to be the guardian of Western traditions and confounded all moral issues by parading publicly virtues which it ... actually held in contempt, it seemed revolutionary to admit cruelty, disregard of human values, and general amorality, because this at least destroyed the duplicity upon which the existing society seemed to rest.[127]

But the apparent rebelliousness and seeming brilliance of such a contempt for authority notwithstanding, its "vulgarity, with its cynical dismissal of respected standards and accepted theories carried with it a frank admission of the worst and a disregard for all pretenses which were easily mistaken for courage and a new style of life." Arendt deplores the nihilism of these intellectuals, who "did not know they were running their heads not against the walls but against open doors," whose fascination with destruction and whose cynical repudiation of humanism played right into the hands of the nascent totalitarian movements.[128] Such an elite lacked any "sense of reality," and in their fascination with the rhetoric of anti-humanism they remained oblivious to the terrible practical consequences of their nihilistic impulses.[129] In the sheer delight with which they welcomed the destruction of bourgeois respectability they self-indulgently flaunted all standards and irresponsibly added fuel to the fires that were to consume Europe.

In the face of these intellectual currents, which in different ways remained stuck in their negativity, Camus and Arendt sought some reliable basis upon which to defend positive values. And yet if both rejected nihilism, they also refused to dismiss it. It is above all this refusal that drew them both to Nietzsche, the "evil genius" who, more than any other thinker, stared unflinchingly into this cultural abyss. In this sense both are heirs to his "lucid intelligence," which sought "to transform passive nihilism into active nihilism."[130] Yet both also believed that his thought, as the highest consciousness of nihilism, failed to move sufficiently beyond it.

In her essay "Tradition and the Modern Age" Arendt links Nietzsche with Kierkegaard and Marx as "conscious rebels" against the tradition of political thought who yet remain entrapped within it. According to Arendt, "Nietzsche's inverted Platonism, his insistence on life and the sensuously and materially given as against the suprasensuous and transcendent ideas which, since Plato, had been supposed to measure, judge, and give meaning to the given, ended in what is commonly called nihilism." Yet, she continues, "Nietzsche was no nihilist"; indeed his writing probes the meaninglessness of the world because he "wanted to assert the dignity of human life against the impotence of modern man."[131] Arendt sympathizes with Nietzsche's writing, which in its radicalness prefigures the actual break in history symbolized by totalitarianism; Nietzsche saw that we were at a civilizational watershed, that conventional standards of good and evil had expired. And yet Arendt also insists that "the opposition between the transcendent and the sensuously given took its revenge upon Nietzsche." She suggests that "he was the first to fall prey to the delusions which he himself had helped to destroy," reinstating metaphysics "in its newest and most hideous form" and thereby introducing a radical relativism "into the very matters whose absolute dignity he had wanted to assert—power and life and man's love of his earthly existence."[132]

Arendt's comments on Nietzsche's "repudiation of the will" in *The Life of The Mind* are equally ambivalent. On the one hand she invokes his critique of modern subjectivity, quoting his famous aphorism in *Beyond*

Good and Evil about the "multiple phenomenon" of willing.[133] Nietzsche's appreciation of the ambiguities of intentionality, and of the psychological and intersubjective limitations of selfhood, seem shared by Arendt. For her too the world is a place of mental and political dissonance.[134] And yet Arendt is unwilling to adopt the doctrines of the will to power, eternal recurrence, and *übermensch* that Nietzsche offers as responses to this dissonance. Their consequence is that: "with the elimination of intent and purpose, of somebody who can 'be held responsible,' causality itself is eliminated."[135] Arendt does not here explicitly condemn this consequence; but it would be extraordinary indeed if she, a thinker for whom the awful irresponsibilities of totalitarianism constituted the horizon of her writing, could wholeheartedly embrace it. It is evident from what she says about Nietzsche here that she believes the problem of responsibility to be a complex and ambiguous one; acknowledging the psychological and intersubjective constituents of human conduct, she clearly rejects the notion of an ethically sovereign self. She does not believe that people are characterized by an unproblematic personal identity and unity of purpose. Her own experiences of marginality, displacement, and exile made that belief impossible. But this does not mean that she rejects the idea of ethical responsibility—the idea that people ought to act with an awareness of their own limits, and that they ought to be held accountable for their actions through social forms of constraint. Nietzsche's *übermensch* seems quite literally "above" such concerns; this is what makes him unsuitable as a model for human living. Indeed, his will to power incarnates, as Arendt herself says, "the most hideous form" of essentialism and, ironically, represents the culmination of modern subjectivism. Arendt's references to Nietzsche in *The Human Condition* and "On Violence" consistently refer to him as a philosopher of violence rather than power, exalting a uniquely modern form of destructiveness.[136] This may also be the meaning of Arendt's assertion that Nietzsche's inverted Platonism "ended in what is commonly called nihilism" though "Nietzsche was no nihilist"—in other words, that Nietzsche was a nihilist in spite of himself.

On this score Arendt seems to be following Heidegger, who writes: "With the consciousness that "God is Dead" . . . the self-consciousness in which modern humanism has its essence completes its last step. It wills itself as the executor of the unconditional will to power. . . . The name for this form of man's essence that surpasses the race of men up to now is 'overman.' . . . The name "overman" designates the essence of humanity, which, as modern humanity, is beginning to enter into the consummation belonging to the essence of its age."[137] Heidegger proceeds to argue that

Nietzsche, in his "active nihilism," expresses the deepest and darkest tendencies of modern humanism, going so far as to assert that "the value-thinking of the metaphysics of the will to power is murderous in a most extreme sense, because it absolutely does not let Being itself take its rise"[138]—namely, it represents an unconditional metaphysical assault on the world. This is undoubtedly what Arendt means when she observes that Nietzsche inserts a radical relativity into those values of human dignity that he seeks in vain to secure. It is not that the logical consequence of Nietzsche's thought is murder; it is that Nietzsche's indiscriminate embrace of the entirety of human experience, and his glorification of an active will to power that abjures good and evil, recognizes no limit to what "superior" creatures might do.

Camus's view of Nietzsche is quite similar. Like Arendt he identifies with Nietzsche's critique of the self-assured, modern sovereign self. This affinity with Nietzsche is clearest in Camus's first cycle on the absurd—his novel *The Stranger,* his play *Caligula,* and particularly his essay *The Myth of Sisyphus.* Much of Camus's sense of the metaphysical absurdity of the universe derives from Nietzsche. So does the intense individualism of his "absurd man," who "can only drain everything to the bitter end, and deplete himself. The absurd is his extreme tension, which he maintains constantly by solitary effort, for he knows that in that consciousness and in that day-to-day revolt he gives proof of his only truth, which is defiance." Such a man disavows all "ethical codes," wishing to live "without appeal." What follows from this is what Camus calls in *The Myth of Sisyphus* an "ethics of quantity": "What counts is not the best living but the most living. . . . A man's rule of conduct and his scale of values have no meaning except through the quantity and variety of experiences he has been in a position to accumulate. . . . The present and the succession of presents before a constantly conscious soul is the ideal of the absurd man."[139] For Camus such an attitude is exemplified in the Greek myth of Sisyphus, who is eternally condemned by the gods to the "futile and hopeless labor" of rolling a boulder to the top of the mountain, and whose lucidity and courage in the face of this absurd experience constitutes his joy and his victory, which "silences all the idols." The parallel between this myth and Nietzsche's eternal recurrence is quite clear: in both cases character involves a forbearing refusal to be crushed as "the eternal hourglass of existence is turned upside down again and again, and you with it, a speck of dust."[140]

Even here Camus is not fully Nietzschean; his absurd man is more ordinary and certainly less aristocratic. He is also more possessed of a sense of limits and of human responsibility: "The absurd does not liberate; it binds. It does not authorize all actions.... All systems of morality are based on the idea that an action has consequences that legitimize or cancel it. A mind imbued with the absurd merely judges that those consequences must be considered calmly. In other words, there may be responsible persons, but there are no guilty ones."[141] With Nietzsche, Camus rejects religiously inspired moral absolutes; there are no guilty persons in the sense of ultimate guilt attributed by theologies or philosophies of history. That is, the present is not a corrupt or incomplete moment that necessarily points beyond itself to a moment of redemption and completion, and there is no standpoint from which ultimate judgments can be delivered. Yet there *are* responsible persons, who behave rightly or wrongly, and such persons must be judged, albeit "calmly." For this reason Camus became a vociferous opponent of capital punishment—but not of a judicial process based on standards of criminal guilt and innocence.[142] Such a humane sensibility seems far removed from that of Nietzsche, and it is hard to imagine Camus writing, for example, that "no act of violence, rape, exploitation is intrinsically 'unjust,' since life is violent, rapacious, exploitative, and destructive and cannot be conceived otherwise."[143] Indeed even Camus's "conquerors," his archetypes of courage, "never leave the human crucible.... There they find the creature mutilated, but they also encounter there only the values they like and admire, man and his silence.... Taut faces, threatened fraternity, such strong and chaste friendship among men—these are the true riches because they are transitory."[144]

As Camus's thinking matured it moved even farther from Nietzsche. In his own words this involved a "transition from an attitude of solitary revolt to the recognition of a community whose struggles must be shared ... in the direction of solidarity and participation."[145] While *The Plague* expresses this evolution in its fictional depiction of the solidarity between the characters of Rieux and Tarrou, it is even more clearly articulated in *The Rebel*. Here Nietzsche is presented as the lucid consciousness of European nihilism, who is first and foremost a "diagnostician" of European cultural malaise. Unless we recognize this at the outset, Camus insists, "we can draw no conclusions from Nietzsche except the base and mediocre cruelty that he hated with all his strength." Nietzsche saw Christianity and its modern humanistic denouement as a "slander upon life," and he sought a "renaissance" in the arts of living. His great insight, according to Camus, is that "from the moment that man believes neither in God nor in important life, he becomes 'responsible for everything alive, for everything that, born of suffering, is condemned to suffer from life.' It is he, and he alone, who must discover law and order. Then the time of exile begins, the endless search for justification, the aimless nostalgia, 'the most painful, the most heartbreaking question, that of the heart which asks itself: where can I feel at home?' "[146] Camus believes that Nietzsche fully appreciated the painfulness of this question. He saw that there must be values in the world and yet that there is no eternal or universal law to ground them; that in a world without order nothing is forbidden, but nothing is authorized either. Nietzsche's solution—heroism, "the asceticism of the great man, 'the bow bent to the breaking point,' " the *übermensch*—is, according to Camus, a noble one, exalting human creativity and power in all of its tragic ambiguity.[147] But it is also deeply flawed as a human ethic.

First, it "ends in a deification of fate." Nietzsche's doctrine of *amor fati* ultimately involves "an absolute submission to the inevitable." Like Arendt, Camus claims that Nietzsche's doctrine of the will to power, by endorsing a virtually superhuman exaltation, involves a withdrawal from the world, a radical anticonsequentialism, of which the myth of eternal recurrence is an extreme expression. Camus writes that for Nietzsche "the world is divine because the world is inconsequential. That is why art alone, by being equally inconsequential, is capable of grasping it." Thus, paradoxically, Nietzsche's "active nihilism" results in a kind of passivity, a disengaged aestheticism with troubling political overtones. Nietzsche, Camus continues, "dreamed of tyrants who were artists. But tyranny comes more naturally than art to mediocre men."[148] It is Nietzsche's failure to speak to the more mundane forms of tyranny, and to imagine healthier outlets for the sense of powerlessness experienced by ordinary people, that thus constitutes his greatest failing. If Nietzsche's artistic tyranny is not intended to justify cruelty and oppression, it is nonetheless true that it refuses any principled criticism of cruelty and oppression, disdaining politics in favor of an aesthetic elitism.

Unlike Nietzsche, Camus is revolted by tyranny in any of its forms. He thus is forced to address the authoritarian political consequences of Nietzsche's philosophy. He insists that Nietzsche's thought is itself far removed from Nazism. Although "he confused freedom and solitude, as do all proud spirits, his 'profound solitude at midday and at midnight' was lost in the mechanized hordes that finally invaded Europe." Indeed, Camus continues, with the exception of Marx there is no thinker who has been more despoiled by his putative heirs than Nietzsche. But, he asks, is there anything in Nietzsche's work that can be used in support of oppression and murder? "The answer must be yes. From the moment that the methodical aspect of Nietzschean thought is neglected (and it is not certain that he himself always observed it), his rebellious logic knows no bounds."[149] Nietzsche seeks a transvaluation of values; but he fails, says Camus, to authorize or prescribe, and his philosophy thus licenses everything:

> "When the ends are great," Nietzsche wrote to his own detriment, "humanity employs other standards and no longer judges crime as such even if it resorts to the most frightful means." He died in 1900, at the beginning of the century in which that pretension was to become fatal. It was in vain that he exclaimed in his hour of lucidity, "It is easy to talk about all sorts of immoral acts; but . . . I could not bear to break my word or to kill; I should languish, and eventually I should die as a result—that would be my fate." From the moment that assent was given to the totality of human experience, the way was open to others who, far from languishing, would rather gather strength from lies and murder.[150]

Nietzsche, Camus holds, is indirectly responsible for having legitimized the unconstrained exercise of power. Indeed, Camus continues, his responsibility goes even further, for Nietzsche's ideal of "a superior type of humanity" instantiates, however unintentionally, a philosophy of history no less than does Marxism: "Nietzsche laid claim to the direction of the future of the human race. 'The task of governing the world is going to fall to our lot.' And elsewhere: 'The time is approaching when we shall have to struggle for the domination of the world, and this struggle will be fought in the name of philosophical principles.'"[151] In this respect Nietzsche's philosophy represents an extreme form of nihilism. This is the evil of his genius. And if it stands steadfastly against any "base or mediocre cruelty," its glorification of a "nobler" sort of cruelty is no less troubling. Camus's own description of Caligula can be read as an account of Nietzsche's *übermensch*: "He challenges friendship and love, common human solidarity, good and evil. He takes those about him at their word and forces them to be logical; he levels everything around him by the strength of his rejection and the destructive fury to which his passion for life leads him. But, if his truth is to rebel against fate, his error lies in negating what binds him to mankind. . . . *Caligula* is the story of a superior suicide. . . . Consequently it is a tragedy of the intelligence."[152]

Camus never denied the relevance of Nietzsche's writings or their influence on his thought. But as his writing became more deeply concerned with ethics and politics he came to appreciate Nietzsche's profound insufficiency. Camus's opinion on this score was not simply a philosophical one; it was deeply colored by his assessment of the historical moment as one in need of some anchoring for humane values:

> On the frontiers of intelligence we know most certainly that there is truth in any theory and that none of the great experiences of humanity . . . is *a priori* insignificant. But the occasion forces us to a choice. In this way it seems essential to Nietzsche to attack Socrates and Christianity with forceful arguments. But in this way on the other hand it is essential for us to defend Socrates today, or at least what he represents, because the era threatens to put in their place values that are the negation of all culture and because Nietzsche might here achieve a victory that he would not want.[153]

What Socrates represents, what we desperately need, is a principled commitment to truth and freedom in a world overcome with cynicism. What Nietzsche offers instead is a deconstruction of the very idea of principles. For this reason his genealogical method, however profound, is not enough. It fails constructively to address real human problems and gives short shrift to our abilities, as humans, to construct meaningful and beneficial, if limited, solutions to them.

Between Past and Future

As critics of modernity both Arendt and Camus find themselves in something of a political no-man's-land. They recognize that it is very difficult to live with modernity, but they see that it is equally difficult to live without it. Both seek to lay bare a dangerous, Promethean humanism at the heart of modern political discourse. But having done so, they are left with a question—where do we go from here? Their efforts to answer this question constitute the most interesting and enduring legacy of their writing.

Both Arendt and Camus have often been seen as thinkers who, in different ways, disengaged from the political life of modernity, Arendt through a retreat to nostalgic visions of ancient Greece and Rome, Camus through a pious and overly aesthetic moralism. This is the dominant way of reading them in both academic and political circles, and it is not without support.[154] The classical world exercised a powerful hold on Arendt's mind, undoubtedly in part a residue of her training in German idealist philosophy, but also a consequence of her understanding of the importance of the Greek and Roman political experiences.[155] And Camus's writings on political themes were at times marked by an overblown prose style that threatened to muddle his lucid philosophical judgments. The fact that both writers, in different ways, fit uneasily into postwar intellectual and

political categories lends credence to the charges of esotericism and withdrawal. But I believe that such charges are nonetheless deeply mistaken.
We have seen that Arendt and Camus were exceptional members of an
exceptional generation of political writers deeply touched by the atrocious
events of the twentieth century, that the horizon of their thinking was the
problem of totalitarianism, and that their respective criticisms of modern
philosophy were marked by a deep historical sensitivity. They were critical
of modernity and quite unsettled by the historical epoch in which they
lived. But they in no way sought to disavow or take flight from that epoch.
Both sought to understand it and to engage it. As Camus wrote, "Nothing
authorizes me to pass judgment upon an epoch with which I feel in
complete solidarity. I judge it from within, blending myself with it. But
I reserve the right, henceforth, to say what I know about myself and about
others . . . in order to locate, among the obscure walls against which we
are blindly stumbling, the still invisible places where doors may open."[156]

If it is possible to view Arendt and Camus through the lenses of postmodernism, it is necessary to be quite careful about how this should be
done. Both saw the limits of characteristically modern, humanistic ways
of thinking about politics. Both rejected an anthropocentrism that too
often ignored the fragility of all human projects in a recalcitrant world.
But both sought to remedy these limits through a critical reappropriation
of that very humanism. The thinking of each represents something of a
culmination of the modern effort to storm the heavens. Yet unlike many
other modern thinkers, who have worshiped before the altars of various
idols, they both seek to learn how to live in a world without God, in a
disenchanted, absurd universe. Arendt insists that "I am not homesick
enough . . . because I do not believe in a world . . . in which man's mind,
equipped for withdrawing from the world of appearances, could or should
ever be comfortably at home."[157] Camus too insists that "the important
thing . . . is not to be cured, but to live with one's ailments."[158] Thus he
rejects any escape from his absurd predicament, choosing instead to "stake
everything on the renaissance." Both thinkers are resolutely at odds with
any sentimental or Romantic effort to restore the world to some essential
unity; indeed, for both it is such an aspiration, at the heart of modern
ideological thinking, that nourishes the worst forms of political nihilism,
devaluing the present at the expense of some mythical, archetypical future.[159]

Both Arendt and Camus defend a political ethic that draws heavily on
the accomplishments of modernity. This is clearer in the case of Camus,
whose *The Rebel* is an explicit effort to inquire whether and how it is

possible for rebellion, an achievement of modernity, to remain "faithful
to its first noble promise."[160] But it is no less true for Arendt, in spite of
her pronounced classicism. If one focuses only on her more philosophical
texts, like *The Human Condition, Between Past and Future,* and *The Life of
the Mind,* as many academic political philosophers have done, it is possible
to lose sight of her engagement with modern politics and her modernist
sensibilities. But if one reads these important texts against the backdrop
of her early political essays on Europe and Zionism, which culminated in
The Origins of Totalitarianism, and her later essays on American politics,
then she is cast in a different light. In this context a book like *On Revolution*
loses some of its esoteric character and appears as strikingly similar to
Camus's *The Rebel.* Both works are magnetically drawn to that consum-
mately modern political phenomenon, revolution, and both seek to address
that phenomenon from the perspective of the prospects for peaceful and
dignified political community in the late twentieth century. Both Camus
and Arendt develop what might be called a political ethic of revolt, one
that seeks to resuscitate the modern, universalist ideals of human autonomy
and democratic self-governance by embedding them in an ethic of limits.
Both, in other words, seek new intellectual foundations for a reconstruction of contemporary political life, foundations capable of addressing distinctively contemporary political problems. It is to these foundations that
I now turn.

Chapter 4

REVOLT AND THE FOUNDATIONS OF POLITICS

It is common these days to acclaim that we are without political foundations. With Rorty and Lyotard we are wary of grand narratives, suspicious of public power and indeed of politics altogether. As Camus put it, the question before us is clear: "Can one transform the world without believing in the absolute power of reason?"[1] The history of the twentieth century invites a skeptical response, leading many to conclude that we ought to abandon alternative visions of politics. At its most political, in the writing of Foucault and Lyotard, contemporary postmodern theory proposes what Lyotard calls an "agonistics"—a celebration of the heterogeneity of local political struggles and an emphatic refusal to propose any overarching criteria of legitimacy: politics without public life.[2] At its least political, in the work of Rorty, it proposes an ironic self-creation that equally abandons any concern with reconstituting public life.[3]

For Arendt and Camus the moral impasse, and the human suffering attending it, is much too serious to allow either of these options. As heirs of Nietzsche they welcome the demise of the props and crutches that have long sustained political orders unable to stand without such supports. Yet both writers also recognize the need for some anchoring for human freedom. As Camus writes:

I do not have enough faith in reason to subscribe to any belief in progress or to any philosophy of history. I do believe at least the man's awareness of his destiny has never ceased to advance. We have not overcome our condition, and yet we know it better. We know that we live in a contradiction, but we also know that we must refuse this contradiction and do what is necessary to reduce it. Our task as men is to find the few principles that will calm the infinite anguish of free souls. We must mend what has been torn apart, make justice imaginable again in a world so obviously unjust, give happiness a meaning once more to peoples poisoned by the misery of the century.[4]

Arendt too sees that the decline of tradition offers "the great chance to look upon the past with eyes undistracted by any tradition, with a directness which has disappeared" since the demise of the ancient Greeks.[5] Yet she also recognizes that "with the world as it is, it is difficult to enjoy this advantage. For . . . the pillars of the truths have also been the pillars of the political order, and the world . . . needs such pillars in order to guarantee continuity and permanence, without which it cannot offer mortal men the relatively secure, relatively imperishable home that they need."[6] It is thus necessary to furnish some new principles, to draw upon the fragments of outmoded idioms and forge them into a new way of thinking about ethics and politics.[7]

For both Arendt and Camus the chance to think and act "without banisters" is an extraordinary yet perilous opportunity. While refusing false comforts, both recognized the pressing need for positive values. All the same, both appreciated the limited and partial character of all ethical principles. This is the "contradiction" to which Camus refers. Yet neither sought to escape this contradiction. Because both writers had a deep sense of solidarity with their world, they saw that some kind of normality, no matter how partial, was necessary if people were to live free and secure lives. For this reason they sought to articulate new foundations for political life.

Foundations without Foundationalism

It is fashionable to suspect any effort to speak about ethical foundations as a new form of essentialism. While such suspicion is not without merit, it is a mistake to conflate foundations with foundationalism. As Joseph Margolis puts it, foundationalism is "the belief that we possess a privileged basis for cognitive certainty." In the history of philosophy this belief has often been attached to the doctrine of essentialism, "the belief that, conceding whatever difficulty and self-correction may obtain, the structure of the actual world *is* cognitively transparent to, or representable by, us."[8] It is commonly acknowledged that these are naive philosophical doctrines and there are no good reasons to accept them.[9] We need forthrightly to recognize that the world is irremediably elusive and that there is no necessary correspondence between it and our representations of it. But this does not require us to abandon the search for foundations in political life, only to rethink what such an inquiry can hope to accomplish. In Margolis's words, "Human inquiry pursues universal conditions without universalism, foundations without foundationalism, essentials without essentialism."[10] We need to ground and legitimate our activities, but also to recognize the tentative and limited character of such grounds and legitimations—that is, to be conscious of the historically relative and fallible nature of even our best considered theoretical judgments.[11]

Arendt and Camus shared a similar view of the importance of foundational inquiry. How else can one understand the role of ideas like "the human condition" and "absurd universe" in their work? And yet both thinkers developed their theories with great circumspection, rejecting any form of essentialism. In this regard their writings offer an important corrective to what has by now become a fruitless academic debate between so-called foundationalists and antifoundationalists.[12]

That Arendt shared such a view is perhaps most clearly demonstrated in her exchange with Eric Voegelin over her book *The Origins of Totalitarianism*. Charging Arendt with philosophical confusion for calling concentration camps "laboratories for experiments in transforming human nature," Voegelin presents a good example of the kind of foundationalism Arendt opposed: " 'Nature' is a philosophical concept; it denotes that which identifies a thing as a thing of this kind and not of another one. A 'nature' cannot be changed or transformed; a 'change of nature' is a contradiction of terms; tampering with the 'nature' of a thing means destroying the thing. To conceive the idea of 'changing the nature' of man (or of anything) is a symptom of the intellectual breakdown of Western civilization."[13] Voegelin is an essentialist—he has no doubt that the world is composed of fixed essences that it is possible for philosophy to represent in an unproblematic, privileged manner. Yet in his exaggerated attack on Arendt he rightly sees that Arendt's approach to this matter is radical, that it registers both the intellectual and the political "breakdown of Western civilization." Refusing the solace of Voegelin's recourse to an unchanging nature, Arendt presses on at the edge of the abyss: "The success of totalitarianism is identical with a much more radical liquidation of freedom as a political and as a human reality than anything we have ever witnessed before. Under these conditions, it will be hardly consoling to cling to an unchangeable nature of man.... Historically we know of man's nature only insofar as it has existence, and no realm of eternal essences will ever console us if man loses his essential capabilities."[14]

Arendt here makes two points. First she insists, against Voegelin, on the limits of philosophical knowledge. We know about human nature historically only if it has existence; as Margolis puts it, our "truths" about such matters are but "reasonable posits in accord with empirical inferences."[15] Second, she insists on an historical ontology. For her the properties of human beings may be changeable and indeed have evidenced such change, and there is nothing in God, natural law, or history that can be assumed to offset or remedy this. Whatever claims we can make about human nature, Arendt insists, must be judged pragmatically in the light of the evidence of history. In this sense there can be no privileged, ultimate knowledge of the human essence.

This insight lies at the root of Arendt's distinction between human nature and the human condition, one of the most important distinctions in her corpus. Arendt argues that although human beings are "conditioned beings," their common condition "does not constitute anything like human nature."[16] She clearly wants to maintain, against those for whom nothing meaningful can be said about the boundary conditions governing human conduct, that human existence does have distinguishing, limiting features. Yet she just as clearly wants to avoid the kind of essentialism epitomized by Voegelin, for whom such limiting features are unchanging and unambiguous. Arendt's explanation of her distinction is reminiscent of her exchange with Voegelin. The conditions to which she refers, she writes, do not "constitute essential characteristics of human existence in the sense that without them this existence would no longer be human." In other words, these conditions are not essences, and because they are historically emergent there is no way for philosophy to fix them once and for all. Drawing on Augustine, she claims that "the problem of human nature ... seems unanswerable," because to possess such ultimate knowledge about ourselves "would be like jumping over our own shadows.... If we have a nature or essence, then surely only a god could know and define it.... The question about the nature of man is no less a theological question than the question about the nature of God; both can be settled only within the framework of a divinely revealed answer."[17]

The metaphor of jumping over our own shadows vividly captures the problem with seeking to define conclusively human nature in Arendt's terms: it is an effort to foretell the ending of a story that is not yet complete and is inherently open-ended. To be human is to live and act with imperfect knowledge, without knowing the ultimate causes or consequences of our activity. Our essences could only be known to us once the story of humanity had been brought to an end. Of course, in the event of that all-too-terrifying—and all-to-real—possibility, we would not exist, and thus we would be in no position to know anything. But, according to Arendt, this does *not* mean that we can know nothing about ourselves. Reasoned inferences from human history and experience can tell us about those conditions that frame our existence, that enable and constrain us but "never condition us absolutely."[18] Such conditions can be understood as constituting what it is to be a human being without ultimately or unalterably defining it. They make up what we might call a human nature but in a less demanding sense than that required by Voegelin or presupposed by previous traditions of political thought.

Commenting on Karl Jaspers, Camus articulates a remarkably similar view: "In reality, the purely historical absolute is not even conceivable ... since he lives in the midst of this totality [man cannot grasp it]. History, as an entirety, could exist only in the eyes of an observer outside it and outside the world. History only exists, in the final analysis, for God."[19] Like Arendt, Camus rejects the discredited idea that it is possible for human reason to apprehend "the historical Absolute." Because we are irremediably historical beings, stuck between past and future, it is impossible to "grasp"—a term that signifies both knowledge and mastery—our condition in any ultimate sense.

But Camus's call for a more modest conception of human knowledge in no way involves an abdication of human reason. In *The Myth of Sisyphus,* an essay devoted to exploring the "denseness and strangeness of the world," Camus does not abjure knowledge about the human condition:

> We must despair of ever reconstructing the familiar, calm surface which would give us peace of heart. . . . Of whom and of what indeed can I say: "I know that!" . . . Between the certainty I have of my existence and the content I try to give that assurance, the gap will never be filled. Forever I shall be a stranger to myself. In psychology as in logic, there are truths but no truth. Socrates' "Know thyself" has as much value as the "Be virtuous" of our confessionals. They reveal a nostalgia at the same time as an ignorance. They are sterile exercises on great subjects. They are legitimate only in precisely so far as they are approximate.[20]

Lucidity, Camus asserts, requires us squarely to recognize that the human adventure takes place in an "unintelligible" and "measureless universe," one that we can never fully apprehend or make our own. In such a world the only truths we are capable of are approximate. Perhaps the surest of such truths is our finitude itself. "The absurd is born of this confrontation between the human need and the unreasonable silence of the world."[21] But plain "decency" requires that this confrontation not be abandoned. It is wrong to seek to conquer the world, and equally wrong to flee from it; it is wrong to seek a rationalistic system that explains everything, and equally mistaken to dismiss the demands and powers of human reason. We thus need to seek approximate truths as a means of forging a more just and meaningful life.

We need, in short, to ground, and thus to limit, our conduct, seeking foundations at the same time that we acknowledge their provisional character: "Rebellion is born of the spectacle of irrationality, confronting an unjust and incomprehensible condition. But its blind impulse is to demand order in the midst of chaos and unity in the very heart of the ephemeral. It cries out, it demands, it insists that the scandal cease and that what has, up to now, been built upon shifting sands should henceforth be founded upon rock."[22] Camus sees that though we need foundations, to seek the unshakable support of rock represents a flight from responsibility. It is wiser simply to plant our feet on the ground as best we can, frankly acknowledging that we will have to adjust our footing as the soil shifts beneath us.

Power, Frailty, and Freedom

For both Arendt and Camus humans are distinguished by the fruitful and yet tragic interrelation between their enormous creativity and ingenuity and their irredeemable frailty, a connection captured in Arendt's concepts of *natality* and *mortality* and Camus's *rebellion* and *absurdity*. For both writers human beings are creatures capable of grand aspirations and elaborate constructions, and yet also capable of a dangerous forgetfulness of their limitations. This combination of power and limit suggests the values of human autonomy and dignity; and because this noble and yet frail condition is shared by all humans, Arendt and Camus maintain that autonomy and dignity can only be realized in concert.[23]

Neither writer subscribed to the so-called naturalistic fallacy—the claim that ethics is a descriptive account of ideals that are actual properties of existence. Neither saw autonomy or dignity as values inherent in human existence, for they had lived through experiences that showed the barbarity and monstrosity of which human beings are capable. And yet both insist that these values are potentials latent within human existence and necessary for human flourishing. For both writers the alternative to embracing them is insecurity, coercion, bloody conflict, and enormous suffering. For both Arendt and Camus the human condition of power and frailty will either be exploited by ideologies that seek forcibly to transcend human limits and offer false solutions to the unending problems of human living—a recipe for disaster—or it will be sustained by healthy, self-limiting forms of individual and collective autonomy.

Arendt addresses these ontological questions most systematically in *The Human Condition*. Claiming to do "nothing more than to think what we are doing," she centers her discussion around three "fundamental human activities" or dimensions of being—labor, work, and action.[24] Her book is an effort to valorize a distinctive conception of the political that Arendt considers lost to modern political theory. Arendt argues that action is "the only activity that goes on directly between men without the intermediary of things or matter," and that as such it is "*the* condition—not only the condition *sine qua non*, but the *conditio per quam*—of all political life."[25] Whereas the ancient Greeks appreciated the high value of action in relation to labor and work and organized the *polis* around this scale of values, Arendt contends that the tradition of political philosophy beginning with Plato has reversed this scale. In the modern world the activities of "the social" have prevailed, and action has all but been eclipsed. This development is closely linked in her mind to the murderous politics of the twentieth century, and indeed totalitarianism can be seen as the most extreme form of this eclipse.

Arendt's account of the human condition is best understood in terms of her critique of modern humanism. Reacting against modern man's hubristic effort "to become what man cannot be, creator of the world and of himself,"[26] she aims to counteract "the instrumentalization of the whole world and the earth, this limitless devaluation of everything given, this process of growing meaninglessness where every end is transformed into a means and which can be stopped only by making man himself lord and master of all things."[27] For Arendt such nihilism is underwritten by a flawed and shattered metaphysical confidence in human power, and what is needed is a new sense of human limits and possibilities based on an awareness of "a fact over which modern philosophy cannot become tranquil—that man is compelled to assent to a Being which he has never created and to which he is essentially alien."[28]

For Arendt the human condition is an inherently limited condition, since life is bounded by birth and death. Hence she builds her argument on the twin concepts of natality and mortality. *Natality* for Arendt corresponds to the experience of birth and more generally of human initiative or freedom: "The new beginning inherent in birth can make itself felt in the world only because the newcomer possesses the capacity of beginning something anew, that is, of acting."[29] Arendt treats natality largely from the perspective of the agent who by word and deed "inserts" himself into the world and experiences a feeling of spontaneity and freedom in doing so. Yet despite her criticisms of Aristotle's naturalism, Arendt agrees with him that humans are distinguished as a species by their capacity for speech.[30] And it seems to be this capacity that supports both the human freedom to initiate or begin anew and the most important form of this freedom, political praxis, or action in common with others. *Mortality* is for Arendt the ultimate limit of human existence—finitude and eventual death. Mortality poses problems of survival and subsistence, to which work, but preeminently labor, are attempts at solutions. For Arendt there are no ultimate solutions to this problem. All human efforts to deal with the fact of mortality are provisional and, as far as human reason can comprehend, futile. In this respect we must assent to an existence that is "essentially alien," for the worldly constructions we devise in the face of our mortality are inherently fragile. On this point she is perhaps closer to Camus than on any other.

For Arendt humans are limited beings who are endowed with the capacity to infuse reality with meaning and to create a social and political world. Such a "humanized" world is capable of sustaining us as a species and of nourishing our creative and intersubjective propensities. But it has no ultimate grounding or sanction and cannot finally solve the problem of the meaning of our existence, nor can it forestall our own mortality as human beings or the mortality of our fragile solidarities.

Arendt argues that whereas labor is a condition of metabolic interaction with nature common to all biological creatures, *poesis* (work) and *praxis* (action) are the two most important expressions of human agency, the modes whereby we construct and inhabit a distinctively human world. Work is the capacity for human artifice. It confers a stability and solidity on the world. Through work humans appropriate nature in order to construct social and political institutions that anchor and give meaning to our lives. In this sense "the human condition of work is worldliness."[31] Following Hegel, Marx, Lukacs, and Heidegger, Arendt calls work a form of reification. It presupposes a mode of means-ends rationality, whereby humans act upon and seek to transform a world construed as an *object* of our purposes. Such an orientation is indispensable to human flourishing and only becomes problematic for Arendt when it begins to preclude other ways of taking our bearings in the world.

According to Arendt the capacity to act is a political capacity deriving from what Arendt calls *plurality*: "Plurality is the condition of human action because we are all the same, that is, human, in such a way that nobody is ever the same as anyone else who ever lived, lives, or will live."[32] Plurality thus presupposes, first, a generic human equality, a common set of capacities and practical horizons without which free human agency would make no sense, as people "could neither understand each other" nor consider themselves part of a common intersubjective enterprise. Second, it presumes human distinction: if all people were the same "they would need neither speech nor action to make themselves understood." Arendt's view of action is thus deeply at odds with any kind of behaviorism. For her, humans are distinctively hermeneutic beings who sustain their world through various linguistic and practical enactments. To be a human is to possess such interactive skills and to exercise them in relation to others similarly in possession of those skills.[33] Arendt, like Habermas, believes that humans are distinguished by their intersubjectivity.[34]

To act is thus to insert oneself into a public realm whereby one's acts are defined and judged by, and one's character revealed to, others. It is to thrust oneself into an intangible and unpredictable "web of human relationships," a web that both constrains activity and makes it unlikely that one's intentions will be fully realized.[35] Action is thus an inherently relative enterprise, for it engages a world of others with projects and limits of their own. It requires courage, for it involves subjecting oneself to the scrutiny of others in the "harsh light" of the public, and because its unpredictability makes it risky. And it requires sobriety, because it is the consummate expression of "the frailty of human affairs," because it can only take place in a public space in which people are empowered beyond their individual capacities, and because it invariably escapes the intentions of the doer:

> Because the actor always moves among and in relation to other acting beings, he is never merely a "doer" but always at the same time a sufferer. To do and to suffer are like opposite sides of the same coin, and the story that an act starts is composed of its consequent deeds and sufferings. These consequences are boundless, because action . . . acts into a medium where every reaction becomes a chain reaction and where every process is the cause of new processes. . . . The boundlessness of action is only the other side of its tremendous capacity for establishing relationships, that is, its specific productivity; that is why the old virtue of moderation, of keeping within bounds, is indeed one of the political

virtues par excellence, just as the political temptation par excellence is indeed *hubris.*[36]

There is a powerful Kantian strain in this account. Whereas work necessarily objectifies the world, action is intersubjective and involves treating other persons as subjects in their own right, as ends in themselves who thus deserve respect and recognition. In an early essay Arendt refers favorably to Kant's idea that "in every single individual humanity can be debased or exalted," and in the same vein recommends the philosophy of Jaspers, which "sounds the appeal to my freedom [which arises] through communication with others, who as my fellows and through the appeal to our common reason guarantee the universal."[37] And yet Arendt lodges this Kantian concern with human autonomy in a strong conception of intersubjectivity. For her, moral agency is not the province of isolated reasoners, but of communal beings. Man inhabits an "island of freedom" in a "discordant" universe, in which our common condition establishes a common fate: "Existenz itself is never essentially isolated; it exists only in communication and in the knowledge of the Existenz of others. One's fellow men are not (as in Heidegger) an element which, though structurally necessary, nevertheless destroys existence; but, on the contrary, Existenz can develop only in the togetherness of men in the common given world. In the concept of communication there lies embedded, though not fully developed, a new concept of humanity as the condition for man's Existenz."[38] Communication is thus central to Arendt's understanding of political praxis because it is through communicative action that humans sustain a common world. Each individual represents both a complement and a limit to the autonomy of every other individual, and it is by bringing this mutual dependence into common awareness, by articulating common concerns, that genuine freedom is possible. For this reason she admires the Greeks, for they recognized that "to be political, to live in a polis, meant that everything was decided through words and persuasion and not through force and violence . . . a way of life in which speech and only speech made sense and where the central concern of all citizens was to talk with each other."[39] Arendt thus insists that the appropriate model of political life is not command or rulership but *isonomy,* "neither to rule nor to be ruled."[40] In such a circumstance citizens relate to one another as beings equally possessed of needs, wants, and limits, who collectively decide on their common interests through free and open dialogue.

For Arendt the human condition places us together in a recalcitrant world, endowing us with certain needs, like the need for secure, relatively enduring spaces and the need to experience ourselves as active beings, and with certain capacities whose exercise might secure those needs. An aware-ness of this condition suggests to us that we ought to seek to constitute a social world in which we can act securely and freely as different and equal participants in a common life. Such an awareness is in no way necessitated by the conditions of human interaction, but Arendt none-theless considers it an ever-present possibility immanent within ordinary interactions: "These moral precepts are the only ones that are not applied to action from the outside, from some supposedly higher faculty or from experiences outside action's own reach. They arise, on the contrary, directly out of the will to live together with others in the mode of acting and speaking, and thus they are like control mechanisms built into the very faculty to start new and unending processes."[41] It bears repeating that Arendt does not treat such political freedom as a necessary outgrowth of the nature of human existence. She insists throughout her writing that it can only be the result of sober human artifice, of forms of agreement mutually acknowledged and supported, and that human claims and rights have little strength apart from the solidarities and communities in which they might be embedded.[42] And yet although Arendt does not treat po-litical freedom as a "natural right," she does maintain that it is a possibility grounded in the pragmatics of the human condition. In this sense it arises "directly," if never immediately, from the character of human interaction itself.

But here Arendt becomes confusing. She sometimes suggests that these needs and capacities occupy distinct realms of human life, that work is properly thought of as an activity distinct from politics, and that politics by its nature is insulated from the realm of work, let alone labor. Such a view is reinforced by the emphatically anticonsequentialist language that she frequently employs. Thus she categorially distinguishes between power and violence, the latter alone governed by means-ends thinking, the former somehow above such a calculus. In this context she also asserts that the character of true actions is "untouched by any eventual outcome, by their consequences for better or worse," and that such actions "can be judged only by the criterion of greatness."[43]

It would be foolhardy simply to dismiss these formulations, which articulate an esoteric, and probably aristocratic, view of politics of dubious relevance to the modern condition that Arendt herself identifies. But, I would submit, they are best read in the light of the actual political concerns that Arendt expresses in her writing. On this view it is possible to interpret her distinctions less demandingly and to see labor, work, and action as orientations toward the world that are bound up together in every human act rather than as distinct practices.[44] Such a view is not inconsistent with Arendt's text, since her formulations are genuinely ambiguous. Thus while she refers to the "spontaneity and practical purposelessness" of action,[45] she also insists that its boundlessness means that actions always escape agents' intentions—a view which presupposes that they have intentions, that they seek to realize particular objectives. And she also acknowledges that action concerns itself with objective, worldly interests: "These interests constitute, in the word's most literal significance, something which *interests*, which lies between people and therefore can relate and bind them together. Most action and speech is concerned with this in-between, which varies with each group of people, so that most words and deeds are about some worldly objective reality in addition to being a disclosure of the acting and speaking agent." This passage, emphasizing the pragmatic aspects of human agency, is clearly at odds with any esoteric reading of her theory. So is her acknowledgement that "man's capacity to act, and especially to act in concert, is extremely useful for purposes of self-defense or of pursuit of interests," which clearly implies that the category of action has a general application and is not ontologically limited to an esoteric public sphere, as many have argued.[46]

There is a strong anticonsequentialism in Arendt's work, but this tendency may be interpreted more as an aversion to prevailing forms of modern hubris, whether liberal utilitarian or Marxist, than as any deep-seated refusal to admit consequences into the political realm. It is in this light that we should interpret her remarks about the presentness and self-sufficiency of action. When she favorably quotes Plato's contention that "the outcome of action (praxis) should not be treated with great seriousness," the spirit of seriousness she forswears is that decried by Nietzsche, a vain seriousness about our own sovereignty and responsibility that is at odds with the unpredictable, open character of the world. As she continues, "the actions of men appear like the gestures of puppets led by an invisible hand behind the scene, so that man seems to be a kind of plaything of a god."[47] The point here is that the world is absurd, that worldly actions are futile from the perspective of some absolute good, that good intentions and virtues ultimately go unredeemed. But this absurdity is all the more reason to take actions even more seriously, in another, limited sense, for all we can be reasonably assured of is our own agency and the recalcitrance and opacity of the world in which we conduct ourselves.[48] Arendt is not following Plato here, who claims the existence of a transcendent realm of pure forms. All we humans have is ourselves, and our only salvation is

that which we can provide for ourselves. Such cautionary advice offers a
harsh critique of hubris, but it is hardly anticonsequentialist. As Camus
wrote, "All systems of morality are based on the idea that an action has
consequences that legitimize or cancel it. A mind imbued with the absurd
merely judges that those consequences need to be considered calmly"—
but it does not therefore refuse to judge.[49]

Any doubts about the importance of consequences for Arendt are dis-
pelled by a glance back at *The Origins of Totalitarianism,* where a major
theme of Arendt's critique of imperialist politics is its theatricality.[50] This
matter is also clarified by her comments on the student movements of the
1960s. To their credit they exhibited a "sheer joy in action" and a heightened concern with "public happiness." They refused, in other words, to
be bound by the routines and conventions of mass society and exercised
human powers of initiative that have remained too long atrophied. However, Arendt charges, "the trouble with the New Left is that it obviously
cares about nothing less than the eventual consequences of its demonstrations."[51] Here Arendt makes clear the connection between action and
work, politics and consequences. All political action seeks to achieve specific objectives and is in this sense consequential. A politics that is oblivious
to consequences is no less disturbing than one that is guided by considerations of pure expediency. For Arendt the latter tendency has become
prevalent in the modern world, and for this reason in her political theory
she sought to valorize the capacity to act autonomously, a mode of action
unencumbered by the instrumental calculi of liberalism and Marxism. But
this repudiation of a narrow instrumentalism hardly requires for Arendt
that we construe action as an esoteric capacity. Indeed, it is a worldly,
consequential element of being human, one that can exacerbate, or help
alleviate, the ills of the contemporary world.

This reading makes it possible to reinterpret a number of categorial
oppositions that Arendt makes in her theoretical writings—work vs. action,
social vs. political, liberation vs. freedom. In each case the first term is
intended to capture the element of constraint in human agency, the second
term the element of novelty. It is clear that Arendt does wish to recommend
a kind of action that is less assuredly strategic than modern liberalism and
socialism, less concerned with explicable causes and predictable outcomes,
and more concerned with the action itself—its spirit, the values it embodies, and the healthy sense of empowerment it affords. But her shift in
emphasis in no way betokens an indifference to matters of consequence.
Without wishing to defend many of Arendt's dualistic formulations, I
would suggest that they are best seen as the way she poses the dilemma

of ends and means in political life—the problem of balancing normative impulses and concerns with strategic imperatives—a dilemma thrown into relief by the traumatic and disillusioning politics of this century. The non-esoteric and worldly character of Arendt's thinking about politics is illuminated by reading her works in the light of the writings of Camus.

Absurdity and Revolt

Camus's conception of the human condition, like Arendt's, is colored by his understanding of the perilous "history of European pride." While revolting against this vain humanism, he seeks to explore whether humanism might yet remain "faithful to its first noble promise," the promise of human empowerment.[52] This exploration is first pursued in his 1947 essay "Prometheus in the Underworld." What is the meaning of the myth of Prometheus, Camus asks, in a world that worships technology and exalts human mastery? "If Prometheus were to reappear," he suggests, "modern man would treat him as the gods did long ago; they would nail him to the rock in the name of the very humanism he was the first to symbolize." Today's executioners, as Camus put it, are humanists, and today's humanists are likely to be executioners. In the name of their humanism they incarcerate and annihilate human freedom and intelligence. And yet Camus insists that we preserve the myth of Prometheus and the humanistic impulse that it exalts, for it "reminds us that any mutilation of man can only be temporary, and that one serves nothing in man if one does not serve the whole man. . . . In the thunder and lightening of the gods, the chained hero keeps his quiet faith in man. That is how he is harder than his rock and more patient than his vulture."[53]

This quiet faith in man does not involve any optimistic belief in inherent human goodness, much less a faith in progress or history. Camus abjures the "narrow certainties" of humanism "in the sense that it is understood today."[54] But if he concedes that man must assent to an existence in which he is essentially alien, abandoning the vision of human sovereignty, his view is perfectly consistent with a more skeptical form of humanism. At the heart of this view is a conception of humans as agents who, as possessors of interpretive and material powers, seek to sustain value in their world. Humans possess no special privilege, and occupy no special status, in the universe. Pico della Mirandola's famous image of a man created (by God) as the center of the cosmos gives way to a much less exalted image of human beings, born with no special purposes, who find themselves amidst a world of limits and opportunities.[55] There is no telos here, no narrow certainties or guarantees of a happy ending. But there is man as the "force of evidence" of an inclination to inscribe worldly meaning and to assert his own power.[56]

Camus's "absurd universe" is much like Arendt's "human condition." For both writers human existence presents profound limits—what Camus sometimes calls "absurd walls"—but exhilarating challenges and possibilities as well. What is this absurd universe? It is "a universe suddenly divested of illusions and lights, [where] man feels an alien, a stranger. His exile is without remedy since he is deprived of the memory of a lost home or the hope of a promised land. This divorce between man and his life, the actor and his setting, is properly the feeling of absurdity."[57] Camus draws examples from ordinary experience to elucidate this dissonance, an ever-present feature of the human condition that has come into its own—along with rebellion—in the modern world. We live life matter-of-factly, and then one day "the chain of daily gestures is broken" and we wonder why we do what we do; we allow ourselves to be carried by time "yet a day comes when a man notices or says that he is thirty," and then experiences the "revolt of the flesh"; or we glance into a familiar face, which we have long taken for granted without ever clearly examining, and are struck by its strangeness. The experience of nature also calls forth the absurd. The denseness of a stone, the fury of a storm, the harshness of the sun at midday all jar our sense of familiarity and unity with the world. We confront the fact that "at the heart of all beauty lies something inhuman." In all of these examples routine is disturbed, and we come face to face with the elusiveness of experience. For Camus, as for Arendt, the ultimate example of this elusiveness is death itself, which enters without knocking and, reproaching our grandest conceits about human capability, underscores our inescapable finitude. As he writes, "no code of ethics and no effort are justifiable a priori in the face of the cruel mathematics that command our condition."[58] The "cruel mathematics" of human mortality offers the ultimate deconstruction of ethical schemes. An appreciation of our worldliness—our finitude—compels us to acknowledge the fragile, constructed, provisional character of our efforts to sustain meaningful lives and social institutions.

Camus's view of the absurd universe has often been misunderstood. Camus does not to consider life to be pointless; he does not write, as does the young Sartre, that "man is a useless passion."[59] For Camus the world is absurd precisely because of "the wild longing for clarity whose call echoes in the human heart. The absurd depends as much on man as on the world."[60] Absurdity, then, is a product of the human encounter with a world that is "measureless" and "silent" vis-à-vis compelling human needs and purposes.

It may seem that if the world is absurd then there are no grounds for human rights or duties. Camus's writings on ethics seek to refute such reasoning and to demonstrate that there is not "a logic to the point of death."[61] In *The Myth of Sisyphus* Camus takes up the question of suicide, and in *The Rebel* he addresses the question of murder. Both essays ask whether the value of human life can be justified in a silent universe. What, Camus asks, can keep us from mutilating ourselves and others if not God, nature, or history? His answer is that only we can constrain ourselves. But why should we do so? Because although the absurd would seem to license any kind of behavior, upon deeper inquiry it is clear that suicide and murder deny the human value which is itself presupposed by the experience of absurdity. As Camus declares, "to say that the world is absurd, the conscience must be alive":

> The final conclusion of absurdist reasoning is . . . the repudiation of suicide and the acceptance of the desperate encounter between human inquiry and the silence of the universe. Suicide would mean the end of the encounter, and absurdist reasoning considers that it could not consent to this without negating its own premises. . . . Absurdism hereby admits that human life is the only necessary good since it is precisely life that makes this encounter possible and since, without life, the absurdist wager would have no basis. . . . In terms of the encounter between human inquiry and the silence of the universe, murder and suicide are one and the same thing, and must be accepted or rejected together.[62]

Absurdity involves, then, not just the absence of an ultimate answer, but a question, as well as a questioner, whose inquiry attests to the value of human life and to the importance of the freedom to ask elusive questions and dream elusive dreams.

For Camus even the most desperate of experiences attests to the life of the conscience, to the rebellious character of human existence. To be human is to experience and to defy absurdity, to demand that the world be intelligible, that it affirm a sense of meaning, that it offer us security and justice. Rebellion involves "a yes and no simultaneously." It is the act of establishing a borderline, an ethical distinction between permissible and impermissible, good and bad. To rebel is to assert something in oneself that is of value, and to refuse that about the world which denies this value. In rebelling humans implicate "something that transcends the individual insofar as it withdraws him from his supposed solitude and provides him with a reason to act." Rebelliousness "leads at least to the suspicion that, contrary to the postulates of contemporary thought, a human nature does exist, as the Greeks believed."[63]

Like Arendt, Camus believes that humans are distinguished by their need for some enduring, "worldly" creations, and for the continual experience of their own creativity and power—their agency as free beings. Rebellion is for Camus the ground of human ethics. It suggests that there is something in the human spirit that resists the world, that is never exhausted by its embodiment in its absurd natural and social environment. Man, in short, is not useless passion or a figure of discourse but a creative, if tragic, agent of his own destiny. Many commentators have confused Camus's philosophy with that of the young Sartre, interpreting his absurd world as a condition of alienated and solitary individuals.[64] But Camus holds that the experience of rebellion requires at least some common awareness and ideally a genuine solidarity: "The first progressive step for a mind overwhelmed by the strangeness of things is to realize that this feeling of strangeness is shared with all men. . . . The malady experienced by a single man becomes a mass plague. In our daily trials rebellion . . . lures the individual from his solitude. It founds its first value on the whole human race. I rebel—therefore we exist."[65] To rebel, to resist or revalue one's condition, is to move beyond oneself. Every act draws upon a common fund of meanings. Every actor inserts himself or herself, as Arendt puts it, into a complex web of interrelations. Whatever its subjective motivation, rebellion enters into, and invokes, an objective social world and at least potentially shared values.

It was largely in virtue of this belief that Camus insisted that he was "not an existentialist." In a number of essays he accuses Sartre of an excess of individualism and a propensity toward monologue rather than dialogue. Camus observes that Sartre's men "are, in fact, free. But their liberty is of no use to them. . . . For in this universe man is free of the shackles of his prejudices, sometimes from his own nature, and, reduced to self-contemplation, becomes aware of his profound indifference to everything that is not himself. He is alone, enclosed in his liberty."[66] Sartre's characters thus experience nausea and repugnance at the otherness of the world and of their fellows, rather than appreciating that "life can be magnificent and overwhelming—that is its whole tragedy."[67] Camus emphatically rejects the philosophy of "anguish and despair" that he associates with existentialism, insisting that the lesson of his philosophy is "the extreme solidarity of men with one another."[68]

This is not, once again, the organic solidarity of Aristotle's citizen but the elemental commonality of creatures who share certain basic needs and inhabit a common earth and a common world. There is, Camus maintains, "an obvious complicity among men, a common texture, the solidarity of chains, a communication between human being and human being which makes men both similar and united."[69] Camus does not offer a systematic philosophical account of this "solidarity of chains" of the sort to be found in the writings of Merleau-Ponty or the later Sartre.[70] Yet it is clear that he believes that this solidarity derives from the pragmatics of human living. As humans we inhabit common social worlds, share common languages, experience common problems; on a more metaphysical plane we share a common sense of power and limit, of exhilaration and frustration as living creatures inhabiting an absurd world. This "solidarity of chains" recommends certain kinds of conduct and rejects others; it assigns a limit to oppression "within which begins the dignity common to all men."[71] But it presupposes neither that humans were "born" to occupy any particular social form nor that there is anything about the universe that provides any *ultimate* grounds, sanctions, or guarantees of right conduct.

Camus does not offer his interpretation of rebellion as a self-evident truth, much less as a logical deduction from the facts of human existence. It is presented rather as a hypothesis about how we might best organize our social world given our common condition of power and finitude. As David Sprintzen explains:

> If human beings do in fact share certain traits and face a common destiny, is it not possible that making this communality explicit and raising it to the level of common perception could establish . . . a metaphysical base for the elaboration, construction, and development of an ethical frame for the human community? . . . The awareness of our common condition and the minimal evaluative standpoint this may establish—or at least that it would be difficult to deny— would seem to offer the possibility of providing such a foundation.[72]

For Camus an awareness of the human condition makes possible an appreciation of a human solidarity and mutual respect. What follows from this view is the ethical requirement that human communities should nourish such solidarity and respect, values painfully travestied in the twentieth century. "Conquerors on the Right or the Left do not seek unity, which is primarily the harmony of opposites," Camus writes, "but totality, which is the crushing of differences."[73] Like Arendt, Camus contends that freedom involves a recognition of plurality and difference, and a healthy sense of relativity. If the project of totality seeks absolute standards of justice and virtue, the project of unity appreciates the partiality and fragility of all ethical systems. If totality anticipates the erasure of human differences, unity seeks to nourish them. If totality envisions the transcendence of the current social world with its injustices and imperfections, unity suggests that we accept this world as our own and seek to make it better, while remaining wary of all grandiose political projects and idyllic dreams. Unity is a solidaristic yet radically nonconformist ideal of human community. On this view the very idea of a society without differences and antagonisms is dangerous, for it unrealistically anticipates the dissolution of real differences of interest and conviction, and is constitutionally unable to handle them when they persist. However sincere, such an ethical vision is likely to become dismissive and intolerant toward the "inessential" or "anachronistic" and to treat such differences in terms of simple political expediency.[74] Above all, Camus's "unity" is an ideal of civility. As Burton Zweibach writes, "Civility is the subjecting of human action to limits... the reduction of ambiguity to social practice. A civil society may impose boundaries on this conflict. It may confine it.... But it cannot, and should not, eliminate it. Civility is politics without redemption."[75]

For Camus, as for Arendt, the promotion of dialogue is the key to the creation of freer, more satisfying forms of politics. As we have seen, for both writers totalitarianism exhibited a frightening and extreme form of human oppression that sought to suppress all difference through the manipulation of language and the suffocation of dialogue. For Camus this barbarous effort underscored the need for alternative ways of handling human differences:

> There is, in fact, nothing in common between a master and a slave.... Instead of the implicit and untrammeled dialogue through which we come to recognize our similarity and consecrate our destiny, servitude gives way to the most terrible of silences. If injustice is bad for the rebel, it is not because it contradicts an eternal idea of justice, but because it perpetuates the silent hostility that separates the oppressor from the oppressed. It kills the small part of existence that can be realized on this earth through the mutual understanding of men.... The mutual understanding and communication discovered by rebellion can survive only in the free exchange of conversation.[76]

For Camus domination is characterized above all by monologue, by a closure of communication and argument, and a privileging of an official view at the expense of "untrammeled dialogue." This is unjust precisely because it deprives people of the possibility of determining their own principles of relative justice in a world that lacks eternal principles of any kind. Such a silence is a form of contempt for others, who are denied their own voices and treated as objects to be commanded. Dialogue, on the other hand, requires the flourishing of many voices. Such dialogue is an overriding concern of Camus's writings. Indeed, it is the major theme of one of his plays, *The Misunderstanding,* which he describes as "a modern tragedy" of the failure of people to communicate.[77] If for Camus rebellion involves a movement beyond solitude, an exercise of the human power to constitute and reconstitute social life, then dialogue is the distinctive way in which a "solidarity of chains" with one's fellows is forged and common interests are determined and acted upon. Because of the enduring facts of human difference and plurality, dialogue is the only sensible alternative to a politics of coercion.

Arendt and Camus share what Richard Bernstein has called the contemporary concern with "the practical task of furthering the type of solidarity, participation, and mutual recognition that is founded in dialogical communities."[78] In the vein of much contemporary communitarian writing, both authors underscore the importance of intersubjectivity and communication in social life. Rejecting Cartesian individualism, both see that humans are inserted in a web of interrelationships, and that these are the source of both our difficulties and our accomplishments. Recognizing that there is no neat correspondence between our language and nature and that, as Rorty has put it, nature does not speak to us about what we should be or do, both Arendt and Camus view human institutions as the products of our own initiatives and understandings. For this reason human freedom requires that communities establish conditions whereby ethical standards and public policies can be collectively agreed upon rather than arbitrarily imposed.

And yet it is necessary to resist too neat an identification of Arendt and Camus with contemporary communitarians. First, whereas communitarians tend to privilege common understandings and shared norms, Arendt and Camus emphasize the fragility and partiality of all human constructions. For both it is rebelliousness rather than "civic virtue" that is the foundation of human freedom. While communitarians often take comfort in the familiarity of settled ways of life, Arendt and Camus underscore the strangeness and dissonance, the provisionality, of the given. Whereas communitarians often valorize the "embodied" or "encumbered" self, Arendt and Camus maintain that although we can never be wholly disembodied, neither can we ever be wholly embodied. Rather, we are always both in and out; our world is always both familiar and remote. For Camus and Arendt neither our identities nor our affiliations are secure. As Camus put it, "Between the certainty I have of my existence and the content I try to give to that assurance, the gap will never be filled. Forever I shall be a stranger to myself."[79]

Second, the communitarian emphasis on dialogue often privileges the linguistic at the expense of other domains. Bernstein, for example, by treating Arendt primarily in terms of the view of language she shares with such diverse philosophers as Rorty, Gadamer, and Habermas, fails to attach sufficient weight to the institutional forms and ethical ambiguities of Arendtian community. Similarly, Camus's comments about "a harmony of opposites" rather than a "crushing of differences" can easily be misconstrued as recommending a rather inconsequential conversationalism whereby differences are respected, all persons are given a hearing, and nothing is ever accomplished. Yet it is important to avoid such misreadings. For both Arendt and Camus genuine forms of political community require radical changes in the organization of contemporary political life that challenge entrenched bureaucratic structures and forge new spaces of participation. Without such changes effective dialogue is impossible. Yet even with them dialogue is not a purely linguistic phenomenon, but a way of dramatizing, as well as pragmatically articulating, the differences and tensions that define humans as social beings.[80]

Communitarians often present community as an alternative to divisiveness and civic virtue as a counter to partiality. But, as Christopher Lasch has suggested, these oppositions often rely on a nostalgia for a social harmony that has never existed and will never exist.[81] Arendt and Camus, by contrast, present a vision of human community in which conflict plays an important, though never overwhelming, role. Ever sensitive to the discordances and partialities of political life, both are deeply attuned to questions of difference and struggle. For both writers even the most desirable forms of politics are disharmonious. In this respect human rebelliousness or natality furnishes us not only with some first principles of ethical construction, but with an ethic of revolt or struggle as well. Indeed for both Arendt and Camus there is no hiatus between these two problems; the task of construction is always simultaneously a process of criticism and resistance, and the virtue of dialogic forms of politics is that they remain always open and alive to this continuous process of contestation and revision.

An Ethic of Revolt

Arendt and Camus were well acquainted with the dirty, mundane realities of contemporary political life. Neither viewed politics as an esoteric or ethereal activity. While both saw language as a distinctively political capacity and dialogue as a preferred mode of collective decision-making, neither privileged speech or underestimated the importance of less discursive means of interaction. If for both writers persuasion is the ideal form of political action, they recognized that less-than-ideal forms of politics, including violence, were ubiquitous. As Arendt put it, political theory "can only deal with the justification of violence because this justification constitutes its political limits; if, instead, it arrives at a glorification or justification of violence as such, it is no longer political but anti-political."[82] But, as this text makes clear, the problem of violence cannot be dispensed with by political theory—violence lies at its heart. Further, between violence and political persuasion there is a broad range of activities that can only be considered political, including organizing, demonstrating, bringing pressure to bear on others, and engaging in forms of nonviolent conflict in the pursuit of one's objectives. For neither writer is political action innocent, and for both any political theory that imagines it possible to keep one's hands completely clean, including one that treats dialogue as a categorical imperative, is invidiously utopian. The question, as Camus put it, is whether "without laying claim to an innocence that is impossible" we "can discover the principle of reasonable culpability."[83]

For both writers the rebelliousness that grounds the possibility of political freedom is neither an abstract postulate nor an episodic phenomenon. Neither Arendt nor Camus imagines that a single rebellious experience or event can have any particular binding force. The possibility of rebelliousness is latent within interaction itself, and even the best political communities are liable to challenge. For both Arendt and Camus social institutions have what Anthony Giddens has called a "virtual" rather than a substantial reality. Far from being Durkheimian "social facts," they are constituted and sustained by the practical activities of skilled human agents, and are chronically reinterpreted and reconstituted in the course of social life. In this sense all institutions rest on a kind of acceptance or "consent" that is continually being reworked and negotiated and is perpetually liable to contestation and politicization.[84] For both writers politics itself is something of a permanent revolution whereby prior agreements and decisions that have become embodied in laws and institutions have only a pragmatic authority, one that is in principle always open to question.[85] Because both writers place such emphasis on openness and contestation, they are preoccupied with the political ethics of resistance and revolt.

The Rebel, for example, is driven by a distinction between rebellion and

revolution, one that has usually been interpreted to support a liberal reading of Camus. In this view the rebel is someone who quietly, and always
circumspectly, seeks to affirm human dignity while avoiding the fateful
entanglements of political commitment and organizational membership.
The revolutionary, on the other hand, is one who seeks to transform society
in toto, and is willing to license any means in the pursuit of this grandiose
desire. The rebel is a kind of Popperian liberal, and the revolutionary is
a Marxist-Leninist if not an out-and-out Stalinist.[86] This view may seem
plausible, and there is some support for it in *The Rebel.* In the chapter
entitled "Rebellion and Revolution," which punctuates the author's critique of Marxism, Camus criticizes the notion, associated with Sartre, that
the authentic rebel must become a revolutionary. To the contrary, he
asserts that "the revolutionary is simultaneously a rebel or he is not a
revolutionary, but a policeman or a bureaucrat who turns against rebellion.
. . . Every revolutionary ends by becoming either an oppressor or a heretic."
This sounds like a categorical damnation of revolution, which would seem
necessarily to issue in tyranny. And yet the sentence that is sandwiched
between these two claims reads, "So much so that there is absolutely no
progress from one attitude to the other, but coexistence and endlessly
increasing contradiction."[87]

Far from endorsing moral purity, Camus in fact explores the tense
mutual dependence of rebellion and revolution. At the outset he notes
that "the longing for rest and peace must itself be thrust aside; it coincides
with the acceptance of iniquity . . . [and] the silencing of misery. . . . The
future cannot be foreseen and it may be that the historical renaissance is
impossible. . . . [But] this kind of resignation is, quite simply, rejected here;
we must stake everything on the renaissance."[88] The rebel is not a saint
and cannot insulate himself from the political fray. As Doctor Rieux puts
it in *The Plague,* "I feel more fellowship with the defeated than with saints.
Heroism and sanctity don't really appeal to me, I imagine. What interests
me is being a man."[89] Such a man as Rieux refuses to sanctify violence;
but he also refuses a cult of clean hands that would sanctify the injustices
that often call violence forth. He thus acknowledges a "reasonable culpability." The rebellious pole of the contradiction is thus a bit more complicated than it seemed at first.

Camus condemns not revolution per se but what he calls "absolute,"
"historical" or "Caesarian revolution." Whereas the practitioner of the
latter views human beings as infinitely malleable and rejects any limits or
standards, the attitude held by the rebel "is the affirmation of a nature
common to all men, which eludes the world of power."[90] It is only a

particular kind of historical revolution—that associated with the worst features of Bolshevism under Lenin and even more so Stalin—that nihilistically negates the present in the interest of the future.

We seem to confront, Camus observes, an "apparent dilemma" of either "silence or murder—in either case, a surrender. The first case demands a withdrawal from politics, or at least from radical politics, that "consecrates injustice"; the second case embraces a historical necessity that licenses revolutionary destruction. "There is, it would seem, an ineradicable opposition between the movement of rebellion and the attainments of revolution. But these contradictions only exist in the absolute. They suppose a world and a method of thought without mediation." The representatives of these two poles are Koestler's Yogi and Commisar, and Camus repudiates both. "Because both reject the conciliatory value that rebellion, on the contrary, reveals, they offer us only two kinds of impotence, both equally removed from reality, that of good and that of evil."[91]

The posture of absolute moral righteousness accomplishes nothing and consecrates injustice in its refusal to act and take responsibility for the world. And the policy of pure expedience is neither pure nor expedient, consuming first its offspring and then itself in an orgy of destructiveness. Both are forms of absolutism which, in ineradicable conflict, paradoxically achieve the same result—human debasement and injustice. Camus instead proposes that we abandon this cynical dualism: "A revolutionary action which wishes to be coherent in terms of its origins should be embodied in an active consent to the relative."[92] On this view perfect freedom and perfect justice are impossible. The human condition invites us to act in order to humanize our world. In order to act we must develop and sustain practices of resistance and reconstruction, employing political means, organizations, and strategies. We must, in this sense, be revolutionaries. But the human condition also makes the future indeterminate and the ultimate consequences of our acts unknowable. Hence we must act soberly, with commitment and circumspection. "Any historical enterprise can only therefore be a more or less reasonable risk. Insofar as it is a risk it cannot be used to justify any excess or any ruthless and absolutist position."[93]

Camus draws two major conclusions from this argument. The first is the necessity of freedom of speech and, more generally, civil freedom. This conviction is so important that Camus, having just written of the need to "aspire to the relative," contends that authentic revolution "would allow absolute freedom of speech." He argues that given the relativity and indeterminacy of human existence, freedom of expression is a necessary precondition for other freedoms and for justice. His arguments are uncompromising but pragmatic. Suppression of free speech denies from the beginning "that small amount of existence we find in ourselves." It supposes that we cannot trust ourselves and, fatefully, that our present integrity and freedom can be sacrificed to the future, to be retrieved at the proper moment like a bank deposit. Further, freedom of expression is necessary to discover justice, which is not a Platonic form but a fragile human achievement: "Even when justice is not realized, freedom preserves the power to protest and guarantees human communication. Justice in a silent world, justice enslaved and mute, destroys the mutual complicity and finally can no longer be justice. The revolution of the twentieth century has arbitrarily separated . . . two inseparable ideas. Absolute freedom mocks at justice. Absolute justice denies freedom. To be fruitful, the two ideas must find their limits in each other."[94] Rejecting any ethical absolutism, believing that our ideals are only as good as the means by which we seek to achieve and embody them, Camus insists that there can be no justice without the freedom to criticize and to challenge.

Second, Camus rejects the doctrine of absolute nonviolence, which "is the negative basis of slavery and its acts of violence." Violence, he writes, is "a relative risk," which causes "a rupture in communication." It tears the basic fabric of humanity, setting people into irremediable opposition to each other, threatening innocents, and indeed promising to become its own justification. Such a breach is to be avoided whenever possible. Anticipating more recent arguments about structural violence, however, Camus holds that "systematic violence is part of the order of things"; categorical nonviolence is thus itself culpable, because it assents to the status quo in renouncing the exercise of powers necessary to change it. Violence can thus never be ruled out in principle. But

> it must preserve its provisional character . . . [and] can only be an extreme limit which combats another form of violence. . . . The rebel in advance rejects violence in the service of a doctrine or of a reason of State. Every historical crisis, for example, terminates in institutions. If we have no control over the crisis itself, which is pure hazard, we do have control over the institutions, since we can define them, choose the ones for which we will fight, and thus bend our efforts toward their establishment. Authentic arts of rebellion will only consent to take up arms for institutions that limit violence, not for those which codify it.[95]

Hence the kindest words in *The Rebel* are reserved for "the fastidious assassins," the Russian terrorists of 1905, who treated violence with grave circumspection and incarnated its risks in their own lives.[96]

Camus's play *The Just Assassins* is a powerful dramatic presentation of the attitudes of the rebel and the absolute revolutionary. Kaliayev, noble and sensitive, volunteers to assassinate the Russian grand duke. Months are spent in preparation, and yet at the moment of execution he refuses to act because of the presence of the duke's "innocent" young niece and nephew. Stepan, an ideological zealot and the dedicated leader of the group, is apoplectic, and an exchange with Stepan ensues that beautifully articulates the dilemmas of rebellion:

> S: There are no limits! The truth is that you don't believe in the revolution, any of you. . . . If you did believe in it sincerely, with all your hearts; if you felt sure that, by dint of our struggles and sacrifices, some day we shall build up a new Russia, redeemed from despotism, a land that will gradually spread out over the whole earth; and if you felt convinced that then and only then, freed from his masters and his superstitions, man will at last look upward toward the sky, a god in his own right—how, I ask you, could the deaths of two children be weighed in the balance against such a faith?
>
> K: I am ready to shed blood, so as to overthrow the present despotism. But, behind your words, I see the threat of another despotism which, if it ever comes to power, will make of me a murderer—and what I want to be is a doer of justice, not a man of blood.
>
> S: Provided justice is done—even if it's done by assassins—what does it matter what you are? You and I are negligible quantities.
>
> K: We are not, and you know it as well as anyone; in fact it's pride, just pride, that makes you talk as you do now.
>
> S: My pride is my concern alone. . . . I prefer to shut my eyes to it. . . . so that one day it may have a world-wide meaning.
>
> K: Well, you must feel very sure that day is coming if you repudiate everything that makes life worth living today on its account. . . . Those *I* love are the men who are alive today, and walk this same earth. It's they whom I hail, for them I am fighting, for them I am ready to lay down my life. But I shall not strike my brothers in the face for the sake of some far-off city which, for all I know, may not exist. I refuse to add to the living injustice all around me for the sake of a dead justice.[97]

Stepan, articulating the worst sort of Marxist historicism, is motivated by a genuine sense of justice. He is indeed not without virtue,[98] but his faith in history is a form of religious messianism that justifies the sacrifice of the innocent for the sake of an imagined future redemption. By contrast Kaliayev, the authentic rebel, has a more limited view of things. He has concluded that it is necessary to use violence in the name of freedom. But for him this is only a reasonable posit, and it does not rest on any privileged access to truth. Acting in the name of human dignity, he refuses to debase either others or himself in the course of his rebellion. He makes no claims to an impossible innocence, and at the conclusion of the play he kills the duke. But he pays for this murder by sacrificing his own life, and indeed throughout the play his own character reflects and indeed personifies the "laceration" of the world that Camus insists violence, even when justified, represents.[99]

Kaliayev's life embodies the "ceaseless contradiction" between rebellious impulses and revolutionary means of which Camus writes. In his unpublished "In Defense of *The Rebel*" Camus clarifies the intent of his essay, underscoring the disjunction and the necessary connection between these two moments of an authentic political praxis: "In order to reject organized terror and the police, revolution needs to keep intact the spirit of rebellion which has given birth to it, as rebellion needs a revolutionary development in order to find substance and truth. Each, finally, is the limit of the other."[100] Human dignity is thus sustained by an unending and productive tension.

At first glance Arendt's discussion in *On Revolution* seems far removed from the concerns of Camus. It reads like a fable of an authentic revolution, the American Revolution, in which the revolutionaries, inspired by the ancient Greeks and Romans and averse to the instrumentalities of modern politics, engaged in pure, unadulterated action, their hands unsullied by the messiness of which Camus speaks.[101] Yet as James Miller has argued, Arendt is not here practicing conventional history; she is writing history "against the grain." *On Revolution* presents a countermyth to the Bolshevik myth of revolutionary class struggle and the liberal myth of provident, evolutionary economic growth. As Miller writes, Arendt "follows [Walter] Benjamin in constructing revolutionary history as an episodic set of stories needing to be remembered and retold again, lest the true revolutionary spirit . . . be lost 'through failure of thought and remembrance.' "[102] The book's concern with offering exemplary tales instead of analysis has fed the notion that Arendt's view of politics is naively esoteric. And yet *On Revolution* offers a probing consideration of the same problem that motivates *The Rebel,* the problem of how revolution can remain true to its originating spirit, the spirit of freedom.

The "foundation" or "constitution" of a republic—the institutional embodiment of freedom—is the central preoccupation of *On Revolution*. As Arendt makes clear, this kind of project involves a careful equilibration of political means and ends, of instrumental and practical reason—what she calls *poesis* and *praxis*. Because of secularization and the decline of traditional authority, modern revolution—and modern politics more generally—is a problem without an answer; modern man needs some resolution, and yet he cannot rely on any absolute by which to ground himself. This fragility of human constructions is something that all too many modern political agents, in their zeal to emulate God and create a kingdom of ends on earth, have failed to see. And yet it can no longer be ignored. As Arendt argues, the effort "to find a new absolute to replace the absolute of divine power, is insoluble because power under the condition of human plurality can never amount to omnipotence, and laws residing on human power can never be absolute."[103]

The constitution of freedom in the modern world, then, involves a "vicious circle" of legislating.[104] Political agents must often take it upon themselves to fashion new institutions, to give form to their energies and initiatives. And yet they lack the absolute assurance that can only be provided by a transcendent authority, whether it be God, nature, or history. In the course of political life it often becomes necessary to establish some authoritative forms of power. But those who do so would appear to be without any authority themselves. This seems to render the problem of justifying rebellion insoluble. And yet Arendt holds that "there exists a solution for the perplexities of beginning which needs no absolute to break the vicious circle in which all first things seem to be caught. What saves the act of beginning from its own arbitrariness is that *it* carries its own principle within itself . . . that beginning and principle, *principium* and principle, are not only related to each other but coeval."[105] Rebellion must thus, in the course of its conduct, justify itself without appeal to any transcendent being or code. It must self-reflexively acknowledge its own provisionality and fragility. The action must be its own justification by remaining true to the spirit of freedom that animates it.

But recognizing this does not solve the irremediable practical problems involved in such a politics. For a rebellious politics that abjures any claim to transcendent sanction is plagued by its very fragility. On the one hand rebellion is rendered unstable by its "elementary lack of authority."[106] The great virtue of a rebellious politics for Arendt, its provisionality, is also an endemic source of difficulty, because rebellion is always liable to be incapable of inspiring strong convictions—or any convictions for that matter—in the people to whom it appeals. Although rebellious movements and institutions may not suffer a perpetual crisis of legitimacy, they are constitutionally deprived of the sort of transcendent authority invoked by more traditional forms of politics. The inauthoritative authority of rebellious politics places it on what Camus calls "shifting sands" rather than firm soil, much less solid rock. One great danger here is that in the absence of some transcendent grounding, rebellious energies will meet with indifference and give way to frustration and hopelessness.

On the other hand a second, equally serious danger derives from the possibility of a self-devouring zeal, a hubristic faith in a particular revolutionary vision and in the particular means chosen to pursue that vision. This, of course, is the problem that has afflicted twentieth-century revolutionaries. What Arendt says about the American revolutionaries highlights a problem for revolutionaries in general: "They needed a constitution to lay down the boundaries of the new political realm and to define the rules within it . . . they had to found and build a new political space within which the 'passion for public freedom' or the 'pursuit of public happiness' would receive free play for generations to come . . . [they needed] to assure the survival of the spirit out of which the act of foundation sprang."[107] Their problem, in other words, was how to give form to the spirit of rebellion that inspired them to resist oppression, how to constitute institutions that would nurture and not overwhelm the spirit of freedom itself.

Arendt, like Camus, is anguished by this problem. Like him, she finds the need to equilibrate political means and ends inescapable. Though all means are liable to corrupt the ends they are intended to advance, she recognizes that violent means are particularly vulnerable to this failing, because of their potential for irreversible destructiveness and because of the cycle of resentment and revenge that they are likely to produce. Yet in spite of her fears about violence, Arendt presents a nuanced understanding of its role in politics. Recognizing that all political ideals are ambiguous and none is beyond reproach, she sees that violence is an inextricable part of political life. Like Camus, her problem is not how to eliminate it but how to limit it.

Indeed, at the outset of *On Revolution,* a book often noted for its supposedly esoteric conception of politics, Arendt avers that revolution can lay claim to no innocence. Distinguishing between political power and violence, she insists that while the former draws on the power of speech that distinguishes human beings, the latter involves not a communication between subjects but a silence between people viewed as objects. For this reason she holds that "violence is a marginal phenomenon in the political realm," and that "in so far as violence plays a predominant role in wars and revolutions, both occur outside the political realm strictly speaking."[108] But it is clear that Arendt is *not* speaking strictly. For just as the subject of *The Origins of Totalitarianism* was war, the subject of this book is revolution, events which in her view "have thus far determined the phy-

siognomy of the twentieth century."[109] These phenomena may not be
"political" in the strict sense. But an understanding of them forms the
basis of Arendt's political theory—she herself offers revolution as an exemplary form of politics. How can one explain this paradox, whereby
revolution appears both as not strictly political and as supremely political?
The answer, I think, is in the less than strict conception of politics that
Arendt employs in her book.

She acknowledges, for example, that "the problem of beginning" is
central to revolution, and that "such a beginning must be intimately connected with violence." Appealing to the biblical story of Cain and Abel
and the Roman fable of Romulus and Remus, Arendt declares that "whatever brotherhood human beings may be capable of has grown out of
fratricide, whatever political organization men may have achieved has its
origin in crime."[110] These texts suggest that politics cannot be insulated
from questions of violence. But if Arendt recognizes this, she also maintains
that such political violence must always be moderated. In this sense violence is marginal to politics, for it always threatens to overwhelm political
ideals and relationships; but Arendt never says that it is inimical to or
inconsistent with politics. When one reexamines Arendt's key formulation,
one sees that, far from articulating a clear antithesis between politics and
violence, it expresses a rather nuanced view based on a triple qualification:
insofar as violence plays a *predominant* role in wars and revolutions, both
occur outside the political realm *strictly speaking*. In other words, to the
extent that violence is the distinguishing characteristic of these processes,
rendering forms of mutual recognition and conflict resolution ineffectual
and turning organized murder into the principal concern, they are only
marginally political. They represent the limit of politics, the point beyond
which politics ceases to be about positive human relationships and turns
into the codification of destruction.

But although such nihilism may have been the decisive spirit behind
twentieth-century wars, especially the world wars, Arendt is clear that this
is not all that has been involved in twentieth-century revolutions. Unlike
war, the "aim" of revolution is freedom. The problem is that in pursuing
such freedom revolutionaries often must employ means that threaten to
subvert it. Violence is thus central to political theory for Arendt. But
political theory can only be concerned with the problem of limiting violence, never codifying it; "it can only deal with the justification of violence
because this justification constitutes its political limitation; if instead it
arrives at a glorification or justification of violence as such, it is no longer
political but antipolitical.[111] Violence, in other words, must always be

treated with caution, and must always be subordinate to the justifiable political ends it is intended to serve.

This is more clearly developed in "On Violence," Arendt's most sustained discussion of the role of violence in political life. Arendt argues that the vocabulary of modern politics is not sufficiently alive to the important distinction between power and violence, and that this inattention reflects the belief that "the most crucial political issue is, and always has been, the question of Who rules Whom?"[112] Such a belief mistakenly conflates power and violence, viewing politics as a sphere of domination. Power, Arendt maintains, "corresponds to the human ability not just to act but to act in concert." Violence, on the other hand, "is distinguished by its instrumental character" and "is ruled by the means-ends category."[113] These are not so much definitions as they are characterizations, and rather sweeping ones at that. But something of her meaning is clear. Whereas violence is a mode of human conduct vis-à-vis some other construed as object, power is a uniquely and self-consciously intersubjective and reciprocative capacity. Though here again Arendt reveals the influence of Kant, nonetheless a purist understanding of power would be misleading. As Arendt clarifies, "these distinctions, though by no means arbitrary, hardly ever correspond to watertight compartments in the real world, from which they nevertheless are drawn." Further, nothing "is more common than the combination of violence and power, nothing less frequent than to find them in their pure and therefore extreme form."[114] The concepts would thus appear to represent ideal types, designating distinct elements of human conduct that are linked in practice.

Arendt's delineation of such connections casts light on her ethic of revolt. She observes of revolutionary crises that "everything depends upon the power behind the violence."[115] Here collective relationships and projects are seen as underwriting the successful employment of violence. Such interdependence between power and violence cuts both ways; not only does power support violence, but violence is often a necessary means of empowerment:

> Power is indeed the essence of all government, but violence is not. Violence is by nature instrumental; like all means, it always stands in need of guidance and justification through the end it pursues. And what needs justification by something else cannot be the essence of anything.... Power is ... as they say, "an end in itself." ... Power needs no justification, being inherent in the very existence of political communities.... Violence can be justifiable, but it never will be legitimate. Its justification loses in plausibility the farther its intended end recedes into the future. No one questions the use of violence in self-defense,

because the danger is not only clear but also present, and the end justifying the means is immediate.[116]

This text echoes the argument of *The Rebel*. Where Camus's concepts of rebellion and revolution are often seen as opposed but are in fact complementary, the same is true for Arendt's concepts of power and violence. In claiming that power is an "end in itself" Arendt explicitly disavows any Aristotelian teleology. It is not that power *has* a particular end. Such a view of what power requires would "be either question-begging—to enable men to live together—or dangerously utopian—to promote happiness or to realize a classless society or some other nonpolitical ideal, which if tried out in earnest cannot but end in some kind of tyranny."[117] It is that power, the capacity of people to act in concert, is, as we have seen, a preferred mode of relationship, an ideal suggested by the elementary facts of the human condition. In this sense it needs no justification, for it recommends itself not in virtue of its ability to secure some ultimate good but precisely in virtue of the absence of any such ultimate good, the lack of any finality in human affairs beyond the finality of our shared mortality. This does not mean that particular institutional forms of power require no justification. It does mean that their legitimacy derives from their fidelity to the spirit of political freedom itself, and not from their adherence to any good that claims a privileged position secured outside of the political process. Power is thus for Arendt not an ultimate end, only a human, relative good grounded in our condition of being both rebellious and limited creatures.

It is precisely such rebelliousness and imperfection that make violence ever-present in political life. Because of differences between people, and of the partial opacity of efforts at mutual understanding, forms of coercion will always remain available whenever more normal forms of intercourse break down, something that is possible even in the best of societies. We thus need to learn how to limit rather than institutionalize violence. Violence, Arendt insists, has no intrinsic value at all. In the human scale of relative values violence is always subordinate to the human needs and interests that it serves. Like Camus, who asserts that "violence can only be an extreme limit which combats another form of violence, as, for example, in the case of an insurrection,"[118] Arendt too acknowledges that revolutionary acts of liberation and foundation often require coercion and sometimes even murder. But, like Camus, she holds that such violence, however justifiable, can never be legitimate. This view recalls Camus's remark about Kaliayev and the "fastidious assassins of 1905": "necessary and inexcusable—that is how murder appeared to them." Necessary and yet inexcusable—a tragic conjunction from which the just assassins refused to shy away. These men were heroes for Camus because "they lived on the plane of their idea."[119] As revolutionaries, they refused to place themselves above the dangers and risks attached to the use of violence.

It is in this context that one should consider Arendt's remarks about the Eichmann trial. Like Camus, Arendt had wholeheartedly endorsed the use of violence in the struggle against fascism. Whereas Camus, originally supportive of harsh retribution against Nazis and collaborators, eventually revised his opinion, categorically opposing capital punishment as a "cancer upon the body politic,"[120] Arendt endorsed the execution of Eichmann as a criminal against humanity. But she criticized the Israeli uses of the trial for reasons of state.[121] She identifies "one real alternative to what Israel had done: instead of capturing Eichmann and flying him to Israel, the Israeli agents could have killed him right then and there, in the streets of Buenos Aires."[122] There were, she avers, two precedents for this—the cases of Shalom Schwartzbard, who in Paris in 1926 had shot and killed Simon Petlyura, a former Ukrainian hetman responsible for Russian pogroms that had claimed about a hundred thousand victims between 1917 and 1920; and Tehlirian, an Armenian who, in Berlin in 1921, shot to death Talaat Bey, a leader of the Turkish pogroms of 1915 in which an estimated six hundred thousand Armenians were massacred. Both men are reminiscent of Camus's Kaliayev. In both cases the assassin, having performed his deed, immediately gave himself up to the police and insisted on being tried—that is, the killer sought both justice and the public acknowledgement of justice. Arendt is attracted to this alternative for a number of reasons, but mainly because it avoided the instrumentalities of political organizations or state agencies. In both cases, in other words, violence was employed quickly, and proximately, and was thus contained.

For both Arendt and Camus it is not the use of violence so much as its codification that must be categorically opposed. In this respect their views are akin to that of Reinhold Niebuhr, who says that "the realm of politics is a twilight zone where ethical and technical issues meet. A political policy cannot be intrinsically evil if can be proved to be an efficacious instrument for the achievement of a morally approved end. Neither can it be said to be wholly good merely because it seems to make for ultimately good consequences." These questions, he asserts, are irremediably pragmatic and cannot be resolved in an a priori manner. What can be established is that there is an unbridgeable gap separating even the best of human intentions from the world of political consequence. "Nothing is intrinsically immoral except ill-will. Nothing is intrinsically good except good-will."[123] But of course both good- and ill-will are purely subjective phenomena; and the realm of pure will or intention in itself is removed from the world of human affairs. It is only when one acts on such will or intention that one functions as a worldly, political agent; but here one is thrust into a web of unpredictable and uncontrollable relations and consequences and comes up against the purposes and interpretations of others. This is the realm of difference, and of conflict. Niebuhr's formulation underscores the fact that the political world is a world of *relative* values in which being rigidly categorical is the only categorical evil. For, as Niebuhr says, in words that could easily have been written by Arendt or Camus, "Absolutism, in both religious and political idealism, is a splendid incentive to heroic action, but a dangerous guide in immediate and concrete situations. In religion it permits absurdities and in politics...unbearable tyrannies and cruelties."[124]

Although for Niebuhr this sense of human limit and imperfection is underwritten by a neo-Augustinian theology promising ultimate redemption, for Arendt and Camus the tragic character of politics is completely unmitigated. Both writers underscore the necessary tension between the spirit of rebellion and even its most noble achievements. Arendt insists that rebellion presents a genuine "perplexity": "If foundation was the aim and the end of revolution, then the revolutionary spirit was not merely the spirit of beginning something new but of starting something permanent and enduring; a lasting institution, embodying this spirit and encouraging it to new achievements, would be self-defeating. From which it unfortunately seems to follow that nothing threatens the very achievements of revolution more dangerously and more acutely than the spirit which has brought them about."[125] This plaintive observation parallels Camus's claim that "every revolutionary ends by becoming either an oppressor or a heretic."[126] The success of rebellion always threatens to turn into its failure, as its agencies take on an ideological and institutional life of their own, leaving their original rebellious impulse behind. This is not to condemn rebellion, nor to despair of the revolutionary means it inspires. But it is to enjoin political agents to live this contradiction without seeking to sublate it, for it marks a problem without any final solution. The rebel can never feel completely comfortable with the fruits of political engagement. The real issue, then, is whether it is possible to construct institutions that keep the problem open *as* a problem, as opposed to those that seek some kind of closure. Camus's observation acutely captures this sense:

"Does the end justify the means? That is possible. But what will justify the end? To that question, which historical thought leaves pending, rebellion replies: the means."[127] As we shall see below, for both theorists such an insight can only be sustained by a libertarian, anarchist version of democratic politics.

Chapter 5

REBELLION AND DEMOCRATIC POLITICS

The vision of politics shared by Camus and Arendt defies conventional labels. Arendt, once asked about her ideological position, responded, "You know the left think I am conservative, and the conservatives sometimes think I am left.... And I must say I couldn't care less.... So you ask me where I am. I am nowhere. I am really not in the mainstream of present or any other political thought."[1] Camus, who considered himself a "man of the left," is equally difficult to pin down. As he declared, "the lexicons that are proposed to us don't fit."[2]

In this chapter I shall delineate the political vision that I believe both writers shared. Such a politics, I shall suggest, is best thought of as a *rebellious* politics that valorizes political agency and contestation and seeks to create institutions that remain permanently open to such contestation. While such a rebellious politics draws on many sources, including liberalism and socialism, it is best seen as a form of radical democratic politics with a marked anarchist strain, a politics based on the flourishing of spontaneously constituted voluntary associations and oriented primarily toward civil society rather than the state.

As we have seen, for both writers an ethic of revolt is grounded in the absurdity of human existence, the combination of human power and human finitude. Some critics have associated this view with a political existentialism whose celebration of human agency supports an unadulterated and ceaseless refusal of whatever exists. Martin Jay, for example, has argued that Arendt "saw politics . . . as unhampered by all normative or instrumental constraints," that "like the existentialists, she tended to believe in unlimited human malleability with little regard for historical constraints." He thus asserts that for her politics was pure aesthetics, where the only values are glory, heroism, and transvaluation.[3] James Miller, in *Democracy Is in the Streets,* makes clear that this became a common reading of Camus among the leaders of the SDS (Students for a Democratic Society), for whom "authenticity" and existential commitment required a posture of indignant rejection of convention.[4]

Arendt and Camus shared the existentialist belief that the universe was mute, that human freedom could only be forged through human action. It is not hard to see how certain texts—Arendt's discussion of action in parts of *The Human Condition,* Camus's *The Stranger*—could be taken to endorse heroic, defiant action for its own sake. Yet such a reading is entirely at odds with the both writers' project. First, although they were influenced by the absurdism of existential philosophy, both also explicitly rejected that philosophy, and for the same reason. Though they may have agreed that "man must assent to an existence that is essentially alien," they also renounced the Cartesian individualism widely associated with existentialism because of the influence of Sartre. Both held that "existence is never isolated" and that humans shared a "solidarity of chains." Intersubjectivity and difference were thus central to their writings.

More to the point, it is preposterous to claim, as does George McKenna, that for a rebellious politics human freedom "is an unlimited, godlike freedom."[5] Recall, for example, Arendt's insistence, against Kant's categorical imperative, that "in action too, man cannot behave like a god."[6] The cardinal point that both writers hammered home is that humans are not gods, that they are mortal beings whose lives are plagued by suffering and ambiguity, and that their common condition imposes limits on what they can and should do. Neither Arendt nor Camus views human existence as a condition of pure ontological freedom, as does the young Sartre.

While both writers emphasize the innovative potential inherent in human agency, neither supports an attitude of mindless activism or opposition. The rebel is not someone who always says no; he or she is someone who always *can* say no, and who knows this. And a rebellious politics is a politics that is alive to this possibility, that remains tolerant and open to dissent and insurgency, offering manifold opportunities for the revision and reconstitution of social life. Yet at the same time a rebellious politics is self-limiting; rebellious political agency acknowledges its own partiality and provisionality and proceeds with caution, anticipating the opinions, objections, and even opposition of those others with whom the world is shared. It is this ethos of openness, this refusal to privilege existing conventions, rather than any particular institutional arrangement or electoral procedure, that makes rebellious politics supremely democratic.[7]

Toward a Radical Democratic Politics

Camus and Arendt refused to situate themselves clearly within a given political or intellectual tradition. In many ways their intellectual practice is best captured by Arendt's famous metaphor of the pearl diver who searches the depths of the intellectual sea for precious thought fragments that might be brought back to the surface as "new crystallized forms and shapes."[8] Both Arendt and Camus reappropriated the insights ensconced within decaying ideological forms. As a result, their vision of a rebellious politics has affinities with the diverse traditions from which it draws, while resisting any neat incorporation within any one of these traditions.

There are, for example, striking parallels between their vision and the tradition of Continental liberalism that traces its genealogy back to Montesquieu and his concern with liberty and legality, a liberalism whose concern with restraints on despotic power is not tied to "possessive individualism."[9] Camus clearly draws from Alexis de Tocqueville's analysis of American liberty and civil society and Benjamin Constant's critique of revolutionary Jacobinism.[10] Arendt's The Origins of Totalitarianism bears the imprint of Montesquieu and Tocqueville; and, if it can be said to have a hero, it is Clemenceau, who courageously stood behind his principled commitment to equal rights under the law.[11] The influences of Montesquieu and Tocqueville on On Revolution, with its lionization of the American Revolution and its founding principles, are too obvious, and too numerous, to require citation. Neither author makes explicit reference to the influence of Max Weber. But the affinities between their political vision and the arguments of Weber's "Politics as a Vocation" are obvious. Like Weber, both writers concern themselves with the problem of grounding politics in a disenchanted world, and like him they see that the tremendous power ushered in by modern politics also requires an ethic of responsibility, a chastened sense of the limits of the possible and of the often tragic disproportion between intentions and consequences in politics.[12]

Yet neither Arendt nor Camus can be called a liberal. Although they

shared a commitment to civil liberty and an aversion to ideological enthusiasm common among such postwar liberals as Karl Popper or Isaiah
Berlin, both supported a robust ideal of political freedom and participation
that went far beyond the requirements of liberal democracy and representative government. They also articulated uncompromising criticisms of
modern bourgeois society that put them outside the orbit of postwar
liberalism. The decidedly nonliberal cast of their writings is most apparent
when viewed against the work of their closest liberal contemporaries.
Despite a common distaste for political absolutism, it is impossible to read
Arendt as a celebrant of the Cold War liberalism of Arthur Schlesinger's
"vital center."[13] Whereas Schlesinger is concerned with staking out a safe
middle ground from whose vantage point the virtues of the American
party system can be contrasted with the dangers of political radicalism,
Arendt exalts the "lost treasure" of political revolution. Schlesinger supports the process of incremental reform; Arendt endorses popular insurgency. Similarly, while Raymond Aron's conviction that "we have no creed
to teach" could well have been voiced by Camus,[14] one searches Camus's
writing in vain for the call for a renewed European bourgeoisie or
the celebration of a liberal postindustrial "end of ideology," which are at
the heart of Aron's work.[15] Neither Arendt nor Camus dismissed contemporary liberals like Schlesinger or Aron as "bourgeois ideologists." Indeed both writers deplored such gross characterizations, and on occasion
they made common cause with their liberal colleagues. But it is clear
that in crucial respects their beliefs and sensibilities were deeply antiliberal. While they agreed that the age of grandiose ideological conflicts was
passed, they held out for new, creative forms of political resistance to
the statism of totalitarian regimes and, to a lesser extent, liberal regimes
as well.

There are also strong affinities between the views of Arendt and Camus
and the strand of libertarian Marxism developed by figures like Anton
Panneock, the early Antonio Gramsci, and Rosa Luxemburg. Both writers
were clearly inspired by Luxemburg, both quoting a well-known passage
from her critique of Bolshevism, "The Russian Revolution":

> Freedom only for the supporters of the government, only for the members of
> one party . . . is no freedom at all. Freedom is always and exclusively freedom
> for the one who thinks differently. . . . The tacit assumption underlying the
> Lenin-Trotsky theory of the dictatorship is this: that the socialist transformation
> is something for which a ready-made formula lies completed in the pocket of
> the revolutionary party, which needs only to be carried out energetically in

practice. This is, unfortunately—or perhaps fortunately—not the case. . . . The only way to a rebirth is the school of public life itself, the most unlimited, the broadest democracy and public opinion. . . . Without general elections, without unrestricted freedom of press and assembly, without a free struggle of opinion, life dies out in every public institution, becomes a mere semblance of life, in which only the bureaucracy remains an active element.[16]

Luxemburg's political writings articulated a passionate commitment to political freedom and a harsh repudiation of any program of political guardianship or dictatorship. She saw that there were no ready-made formulas for or practical guarantees of a socialist future, and insisted that the instrumentalities of revolution must preserve the revolutionary spirit of freedom. Luxemburg understood that a rebellious politics can take no comfort from a complacent historical determinism, that freedom lies "completely hidden in the midst of the future." Like the early Gramsci, her aversion to party bureaucratism led her to exalt the possibilities of revolutionary spontaneity. Arendt writes that Luxemburg "had learned from the revolutionary workers' councils . . . that 'good organization does not precede action but is the product of it,' and that 'the organization of revolutionary action can and must be learnt in revolution itself, as one can only learn swimming in the water,' that revolutions are 'made' by nobody but break out 'spontaneously,' and that 'the pressure for action' always comes 'from below.' "[17] Luxemburg appreciated what Arendt called the "enormous productivity of action." She thus saw that if revolutionary activity was not self-constituted and self-limiting, it would be undermined by bureaucratic institutions.[18] And yet though both Camus and Arendt were inspired by her revolutionary theory, neither was a Marxist. Both rejected the philosophy of history and the faith in the working class central to even the most libertarian variants of Marxism. As Arendt recognized, although Luxemburg believed that the spontaneous initiative of the people should guide the praxis of the revolutionary party, she still remained committed to the imagery of class struggle and proletarian party politics that distinguished the Marxian world view.[19]

The lexicons of liberalism and socialism do not fit a rebellious politics. The former is too complacent, the latter too credulous, to suit the self-limiting radicalism that both Arendt and Camus endorsed. Although such a politics is vigorously democratic, neither Arendt nor Camus stood within a clearly demarcated tradition of democratic theory. Perhaps this is because no such idiom existed; what came to be called "democratic theory" by postwar academic theorists had for some time consisted of debates between those whose vision of democracy was tied to a liberalism whose moderation defied extensive popular participation, and those whose celebration of popular radicalism was clearly linked to the ideological imagery of class struggle as the motor of history. While both Arendt and Camus were in the broadest sense democratic thinkers, neither could feel comfortable within these idioms of democratic theory. The iconoclastic, quasi-Nietzschean vision of rebellion that they articulated was inspired more by the practical experiences of twentieth-century radicalism than by any democratic theory. And yet although it is doubtful that either writer serious engaged the work of John Dewey, their political vision has striking affinities with his idea of radical democracy.[20]

Like Dewey, Arendt and Camus reject any metaphysical dualism of subject and object, affirm the intersubjective and communicative character of human existence, and emphasize human finitude and the problematic character of even the best human arrangements.[21] Hence they value openness, plurality, and continual inquiry. Dewey's critique of *Their Morals and Ours,* Trotsky's classic Communist defense of revolutionary terror and dictatorship,[22] mirrors the arguments of Camus and Arendt on the need to equilibrate means and ends and the absence of any historical guarantees of political conduct. Dewey, like Camus, contends that "the end in the sense of consequences provides the only basis for moral ideas and action, and therefore provides the only justification that can be found for the means employed."[23] But, he continues, Trotsky's faith in history rendered him unable to assess the real, as opposed to the imagined or intended, consequences of his actions.[24] The Bolshevik leader thus substituted dogma for pragmatic reasoning, sanctifying certain political means, like "proletarian dictatorship," in disregard for the actual, practical consequences they were likely to produce.

This sense of the provisionality of all politics is one of the major themes of Dewey's most important work of political theory, *The Public and its Problems.* Here Dewey argues, against all forms of essentialism, that the real basis of political power lies not its causes or final ends but rather in "what is going on and how it goes on."[25] Much like Arendt, he asserts that politics has no single ultimate good but rather is a relative good that is always in process, practiced in the "in-between spaces" where citizens define and articulate their common concerns. Prefiguring Camus on rebellion and revolution, Dewey distinguishes between the public and its instrumentalities, between groups bound by a shared sense of common interest and conviction and the organizations—including but not limited to the state—whose only value is their ability to advance these concerns and convictions. These instrumentalities may serve public interests, but there are no guarantees that they will, and they will never do so never perfectly. Thus Dewey discerns an unremitting tension at the heart of all politics.

Paralleling Arendt's account of the modern loss of the rebellious spirit, Dewey, writing plaintively about "the eclipse of the public," argues that this distinction between public and instrumentality has been forgotten. The shared understandings of ordinary life and common sense have withered away, people have become confused and indifferent to their public problems, and they have passively acceded to the power of the state, indeed investing it with an almost religious authority.[26] What is but a provisional agency for resolving human problems, sustained and authorized by the legitimacy accorded it by the public, has become an end in itself. Inquiry has ceased, political means having overwhelmed their own original justification. This leads Dewey to his most radical proposal—the establishment of a democratic "Great Community" capable of reinvigorating public life and sustaining empowered citizenship. Dewey's vision of radical democracy nicely underscores many of the leanings of Arendt and Camus:

> From the standpoint of the individual, it consists in having a responsible share according to capacity in forming and directing the activities of the groups to which one belongs and participating according to need in the values which the groups sustain. From the standpoint of the groups, it demands liberation of the potentialities of members of a group in harmony with the interests and goods which are common. Since every individual is a member of many groups, this specification cannot be fulfilled except when different groups interact flexibly and fully in connection with other groups.[27]

According to Dewey public life must be pluralistic and open-ended, encouraging people to recognize mutual interest whenever possible and reach a civil compromise when differences arise.

The democratic principle, Dewey says, is "not an alternative to other principles of associated life. It is the idea of community life itself. It is an ideal in the only intelligible sense of an ideal: namely, the tendency and movement of some thing which exists carried to its final limit, viewed as completed, perfected."[28] Like Arendt and Camus, he believes that such a political principle is not derived from some external source, but rather arises "directly out of the will to live together with others in the mode of acting and speaking."[29] It is the most appropriate principle on which to organize human relationships in which people can flourish in relative freedom and justice. The great virtue of democracy, in this view, is that it alone encourages, indeed requires, civility and public freedom; in other words, it accords with basic human interests in secure and efficacious agency. For Dewey, as for Arendt and Camus, such freedom demands "communication as a prerequisite."[30] Only if there are common meanings and a common vocabulary is it possible for people to have a living, practical consciousness of their common fate and of the importance of dialogue as a preferred means of communal identity and conflict resolution.

According to Dewey, then, the choice facing a society is between democracy and one or another kind of political absolutism seeking to apply "a hard and fast doctrine which follows logically from [its] preconception of the nature of ultimate causes."[31] The latter is a recipe for political irresponsibility. Only a theory of democracy is consistent with a pragmatic view of the human condition. For Dewey such a theory is distinguished by two major attributes. First, it requires that its concepts and general principles be "shaped and tested as tools of inquiry" rather than as ultimate and privileged metaphysical truths. Second, it demands "that policies and proposals for social action be treated as working hypotheses, not as programs to be rigidly adhered to and executed."[32]

It would of course be foolish to claim that either Arendt or Camus was a Deweyan. Whereas Dewey, a New England Protestant reformer, had a deep and abiding faith in the power of reason, science, and education to resolve human problems, Arendt and Camus, products of European catastrophe and students of Nietzsche, shared a profoundly tragic sensibility. There is a certain darkness of vision in these writers that seems absent in Dewey, just as there is a sense of urgency about the need to pick up the pieces of civilization that could only have been felt by people who had experienced at first hand the traumas of World War II in Europe.[33] And yet the three writers shared a profound antipathy to the modern state. In *The Public and its Problems* Dewey asserts that a "Great Community" can only consist of a confederation of local communities:

> Democracy must begin at home, and its home is the neighborly community.
> ... Unless local communal life can be restored, the public cannot adequately resolve its most urgent problem: to find and identify itself. But if it be reestablished, it will manifest a fullness, variety, and freedom of possession and enjoyment of meanings and goods unknown in the contiguous associations of the past. For it will be alive and flexible as well as stable.... While local, it will not be isolated. Its larger relationships will provide an inexhaustible and flowing fund of meanings on which to draw, with assurance that its drafts be honored.[34]

Dewey's commitment to localism was not limited to the American example. In his 1928 eyewitness account of the Russian Revolution, for example, he praises "the sense of a vast human revolution that has brought with it—or rather that consists of—an outburst of vitality, courage, [and] confidence in life," claiming that in spite of the Bolshevik's statist orientation he found at the local level "evidence of the vitality of organized voluntary and cooperative effort."[35]

In these texts Dewey articulates sympathies that are anarchist as well as democratic, envisioning forms of political activity that defy the principle of state sovereignty and the normal institutions—parties, legislatures—of democratic politics.[36] The term *anarchism* is frequently misunderstood. The anarchist advocacy of direct action is often confused with a violent "politics of the deed," and its opposition to authoritarianism is confused with a principled refusal of all authority. Yet as the Russian revolutionary anarchist Voline maintained, anarchism as a political perspective is not averse to authority as such, only to the modern form of rule based on remote centralized states:

> It is not a matter of "organization" or "nonorganization," but of two different principles of organization. . . . Of course, say the anarchists, society must be organized. However, the new organization . . . must be established freely, socially, above all from below. The principle of organization must not issue from a center created in advance to capture the whole and impose itself upon it but, on the contrary, it must come from all sides to create nodes of coordination, natural centers to serve all these points.[37]

As Voline makes clear, anarchism is antipolitical only if the state is considered the *sine qua non* of politics. Yet once this presumption is abandoned it can be seen that anarchism's seeming antipolitics incarnates a different view of social organization, one emphasizing mutualism, solidarity, and voluntary cooperation rather than command and obedience. Such an anarchism celebrates spontaneity but not mindless activism, political participation but not organicism. It is compatible with political authority, but only when such authority is proximate, responsive, and above all provisional. As the Russian anarchist Peter Kropotkin said, "We conceive the structure of society to be something that is never finally constituted."[38]

In this respect both Arendt and Camus can be considered anarchists of a sort—democratic anarchists interested in opening up spaces for political agency that tend to be closed by the modern state, nurturing forms of public identity that defy the boundaries of sovereign nation-states. On many occasions Arendt stated that her model of political community was inspired by the Greek notion of isonomy, "a concept of power and law whose essence did not rely on the command-obedience relationship and which did not identify power and rule or law and command."[39] Political rulership, she declared, was a form of servitude. And the modern concept of sovereignty, concentrating all political power in a centralized, bureaucratic state, was above all else a principle of rule. Camus concurs on this point. "The principle of law," he writes in his *Notebooks,* "is that of the state. Roman principle that 1789 reintroduced into the world through force and against right. We must return to the Greek principle, which is autonomy."[40]

Arendt's and Camus's key texts make clear that twentieth-century anarchist and syndicalist politics inspired their political thinking. Camus, in *The Rebel,* points to "revolutionary trade-unionism" as a prime example of the form rebellious politics might take, because it, "like the commune, is the negation, to the benefit of reality, of bureaucratic and abstract centralism." Whereas "the revolution of the twentieth century"—that is, Bolshevism—"tries to realize itself from top to bottom," revolutionary unionism seeks to accomplish change "from bottom to top."[41] Unfortunately, he claims, "Caesarian revolution [has] triumphed over the syndicalist and libertarian spirit," resulting in a victory of the state over the commune, absolutism over "concrete society," and rational tyranny over freedom.[42] Camus's *Notebooks* make clear that this Mediterranean anarchist spirit, along with its Russian cousin, is a chief source of inspiration.[43] An early essay illustrates his consistency on this score, calling for a Mediterranean socialism inspired by the Spanish revolutionary republic and embodying "a culture that finds life in the trees, the hills, and mankind."[44]

In *On Revolution* Arendt condemns "the revolutionary tradition"—Marxism—for failing "to give any serious thought to the only new form of government born out of revolution." This form—the commune, *Räte, soviet*—represents "a new power structure which owes its existence to nothing but the organizational impulses of the people themselves." The revolutionary council system emerges spontaneously, unanticipated by "revolutionary ideology" which, "anchored in the tradition of the nation-state," considered revolution "a means to seize power" and conflated power "with the monopoly of the means of violence."[45] Such a new political form is foreshadowed, Arendt claims, in Thomas Jefferson's abortive ward system, which sought to divide the United States into a federation of "elementary republics," and in the writings of Proudhon and Bakunin.[46] Yet it has been sustained by no enduring political tradition. Instead, it can be identified only with those moments in which it has fleetingly appeared—the 1871 Paris Commune, the Russian soviets of 1905 and 1917, the German councils of 1918–19, and the Hungarian councils of 1956. Arendt argues that the council system is in direct conflict with the major instrumentalities of modern politics, the centralized nation-state and the parliamentary party system. Not content with being informed about measures taken by parties or assemblies, council members "consciously and explicitly desired the direct participation of every citizen in the public affairs of the country." Echoing Dewey, Arendt holds that under this system " 'every individual found his own sphere of action and could behold, as it were, with his own eyes his own contribution to the events of the day.' " The councils represent nothing less than " 'a direct regeneration of democracy' " valorizing "the average citizen's capacity to act and to form his own opinion."[47] Like Camus, Arendt believes that the beauty of the council system is its rootedness in the direct practical experience of ordinary citizens. As she writes forebodingly, with the forces of modern statism clearly on her mind, "wherever knowing and doing have parted company, the space of freedom is lost."[48]

For Arendt the participatory character of the council system was not its only virtue. Equally important was the fact that it represented, or at least intimated, a new form of global, interregional and international politics. In *The Origins of Totalitarianism* Arendt argues that the modern state's centralized monopoly of violence not only inhibits active citizenship but engenders incessant geopolitical maneuvering and warfare. The principle of national sovereignty is for her incapable of securing either political freedom or peace. Indeed it is incapable of sustaining even the most minimal human rights, privileging dominant nationalities and remaining indifferent to national minorities and stateless persons.[49]

In this light the merit of the council system is that in resisting the forces of military and administrative centralism, it offers an example of a genuinely confederational structure consistent with a cultural and national pluralism as well as a less antagonistic global system. She thus points to "the intimate connection between the spirit of revolution and the principle of federation."[50] The councils prefigure "a new type of republican government" on a global scale: "It took these independent and highly disparate organs no more than a few weeks ... to begin a process of co-ordination and integration through the formation of higher councils of a regional and provincial character, from which finally the delegates to an assembly representing the whole country could be chosen. ... We see here how the federal principle, the principle of league and alliance among separate units, arises out of the elementary conditions of action itself."[51] A major subtext of Arendt's analysis of totalitarianism is the danger of the principle of national sovereignty and the practice of geopolitical imperialism. In her discussion of the Eichmann trial she supports a new system of international jurisprudence capable of regulating and judging human affairs in a truly global world. The advantage of a confederational form of government is thus clear: it promises to mitigate global conflict and establish meaningful connections at every level, especially that of direct citizen participation, between different political communities. In relaxing the centralizing imperatives of the system of sovereign states and in challenging its system of exclusions, confederation allows for multiple forms of identity and inclusion, from the most elementary to the most global.

The council system thus represents a promising alternative to the system of sovereign states and seems to harbor the possibility of embedding human rights in a new framework of meaningful and pluralistic political communities. Arendt writes that "it was nothing more or less than this hope . . . for a new form of government that would permit every member of the modern egalitarian society to become a 'participator' in public affairs, that was buried in the disasters of twentieth-century revolutions."[52] This comment sheds light on Arendt's ambivalence toward modern egalitarianism and the democratic politics that it has inspired. I have already noted that for Arendt laboring seems an almost exclusively biological process, typically involving no agency or subjectivity and based on an elementary human sameness rather than any capacity for distinction. Thus it is deeply antipolitical.[53] According to Arendt the modern political emancipation of labor "was intended to elevate the laboring activity itself."[54] Though justified in terms of a philosophy of the rights of man and citizen, political emancipation in fact brought about a mass society, organized in centralized nation-states in which politics was degraded to the status of a guarantor of the automatic "behavior" of modern society.[55] Arendt is aware that the Greek experience of the *polis* presupposed the exclusion of women and slaves from politics to a private sphere of "darkness," and she is equally clear that the rise of modern mass politics involves the admission of women and laborers into the political realm. There is more than a trace of disdain in Arendt's discussion of this subject. In the light of her explicit criticisms of representative government and party politics, serious questions about her commitment to democracy arise.[56]

Arendt is genuinely ambivalent about democracy. But this ambivalence can be explained without exaggerating her sympathies for Greek slavery and aristocratic politics. As Arendt's treatment of the councils makes clear, she praises them as the embodiment of the "modern egalitarian" idea of democratic participation. And yet she is also critical of modern democracy. How can we make sense of this apparent inconsistency? A remark by Arendt contrasting the party and council systems is revealing here: "both were unknown prior to the revolutions and both are the consequences of the modern and revolutionary tenet that all inhabitants of a given territory are entitled to be admitted to the public, political realm."[57] The council system, the consummate example of her ideal of political community, is a modern and democratic political form, inconceivable for the ancients. And yet so is the system of representative government.

There is undoubtedly an element of Nietzschean elitism in Arendt's writing, most especially in *The Human Condition*. Yet although her tone often displays a condescension that is unsettling to democratic sensibilities, her criticisms seem directed more at the disturbing nihilism of bourgeois mass society than at the modern "revolt of the masses."[58] What Arendt repudiates is not the democratic principle so much as the prevailing form it has taken—a parliamentary statism embedded in a commercial society. She is clearly aware that such a form of government is not without its advantages. At its best "it has achieved a certain control of the rulers by those who are ruled."[59] Arendt's favorable comments on the importance of modern liberty, as well as her frequent insistence on the importance of legality and "fences" protecting individuals, are clear indications that she appreciated the value of liberal democracy.[60] However, Arendt is also clearly aware of its drawbacks. She is convinced that the principle of national sovereignty—a principle accepted by liberal democrats—is inimical to both peace and human rights in an age of imperialism. And she is deeply troubled by the oligarchical character of representative government. Under this system parties serve not as "popular organs" but rather as "the very efficient instruments through which the power of the people is curtailed and controlled," and parliamentary democracy, rather than securing democratic governance, is a "form of government where the few rule, at least supposedly, in the interest of the many."[61]

These comments indicate Arendt's support for egalitarian principles of democratic participation. But Arendt's elaboration on the form they might take is highly qualified and unconventional. Political freedom, she avers, "is possible only among equals, and equality itself is by no means a universally valid principle but, again, applicable only with limitations and even within spatial limits." Citing John Adams, hardly known for his democratic sympathies, she suggests that we think of public spaces as "islands in a sea or as oases in a desert."[62] She further indicates, again following Adams, that such cases might well involve a system of political elites. Her objections to the idea of an elite derive from the oligarchical politics that it usually suggests. It is "profoundly untrue," she proclaims, that "the essence of politics is rulership and that the dominant passion is the passion to rule or to govern." For this reason she adamantly objects to any system that privileges a ruling group, whatever the basis of such privileges. But she lionizes a new kind of elite, one "that is chosen by no one but constitutes itself."[63] Such an elite in fact springs to life during moments of revolutionary upheaval. As she makes clear, the councils were not ruled by such an elite, but rather were themselves constituted by such an elite.

Arendt acknowledges that such a self-constituted elite has the appearance of being deeply undemocratic: "It is not the revolutionary spirit but the democratic mentality of an egalitarian society that tends to deny the obvious inability and conspicuous lack of interest of large parts of the population in political matters as such. The trouble lies in the lack of public spaces to which the people at large would have entrance and from which an elite could be selected, or rather, where it could select itself."[64] Here she acknowledges that such a system of "islands in a sea" is not suited to the kind of mass participation characteristic of liberal democratic politics, for it begins with an awareness of the indifference of most modern citizens to political life and the conformist tendencies of modern society. Its problem, then, is not to include everyone on a large scale, but rather to multiply those "public spaces" available to citizens who are truly interested in participation. These citizens would constitute an elite, but it would be self-selected, consisting of "those few from all walks of life who have a taste for public freedom and cannot be 'happy' without it." Arendt's final comments on this subject are the source of much confusion, undoubtedly fueled by her own lack of precision about a matter of great importance to her theory:

> To be sure, such an 'aristocratic' form of government would spell the end of general suffrage as we understand it today: for only those who as voluntary members of an 'elementary republic' have demonstrated that they care for more than their private happiness and are concerned about the state of the world would have the right to be heard in the conduct of the business of the republic. However, this exclusion from politics should not be derogatory, since a political elite is by no means identical with a social or cultural or professional elite. The exclusion, moreover, would not depend on an outside body; if those who belong are self-chosen, those who do not belong are self-excluded.[65]

What are we to make of this vision? It seems deeply antidemocratic, averse to modern universalist sensibilities and indeed indifferent to the plight of those too caught up in mundane concerns and "private affairs" to engage in public life. And yet I think that another interpretation is possible. Although Arendt holds that such a system of elites is repugnant to "the democratic mentality of an egalitarian society,"[66] she insists that it is required by "the revolutionary spirit." And yet, as we have seen, it is this spirit itself which she describes as the product of modern egalitarianism, claiming that it makes possible "the direct regeneration of democracy."[67] Arendt is clearly operating with two conceptions of democracy, one positive and one negative, the first associated with the modern revolutionary tradition of councils, the second with liberal representative democracy. In underscoring that her political elites would be "self-constituted" she clearly distinguishes them from traditional elites. She does not say much about how such "self-selection" would take place, but she is emphatic that it would *not* rely on a system of legal exclusions. Her examples of such self-constitution—European worker councils, the U.S. civil rights movement, the efforts of Danes to rescue Jews during the Holocaust—all depict political heroism, to be sure; but it is the heroism of ordinary life rather than of a breed of Nietzschean *übermenschen*.

These examples might help us make sense of her cryptic remark that "such an 'aristocratic' form of government would spell the end of general suffrage as we understand it today." Arendt, always ready to shake convention, is being deliberately provocative—note the scare quotes around "aristocratic." She does not repudiate the principle of general suffrage, only general suffrage "as we understand it today." Perhaps it is to Arendt's discredit that she fails to say more about what types of institutions she has in mind. But nowhere does she ever propose that the principle of universal suffrage be abandoned. Indeed, her remarks about self-exclusion suggest to the contrary that in her ideal form of politics the principle would be retained. But it would function differently, no doubt in part because of the confederational structure in which it would operate, in which power would devolve on more local levels of political community, but also because of the existence of these "oases in the desert" upon which she places so much emphasis. Perhaps for her, liberal democracy is best conceived as a political desert in which the rights of participation and contestation are like subterranean currents beneath the sands of a corrupt politics, currents that make possible the flourishing of oases of political agency. Such a desert is, to be sure, less harsh than those in which underground springs have dried up entirely. But its redeeming virtue is less its vast waterless expanses than those oases that it makes possible.

It should come as no surprise that her discussion of the councils offers no grandiose blueprint for the remaking of modern society. While this might seem to be a drawback, Arendt's argument here can be profitably read as making two interconnected points. The first is that we need to rethink the principles and imagery of contemporary politics and organize our societies into more civil and empowered communities. The modern revolutionary tradition, and the confederal structure that it intimates, is here not a blueprint but a model, one that might stimulate and inspire us to consider new, more flexible and pluralistic institutional forms. Arendt's second point is that the complete reorganization of contemporary society is both an unrealistic and probably a dangerous aspiration. Real advances in freedom cannot be accomplished from the top down; they require the political commitment of citizens who are aware of their common interests and empowered to act on them. Therefore, as we seek to reconstitute political life as best and as soberly as we can, we must recognize that both the end and the means of a rejuvenated public life is a robust civil society. This is why her "elites" are so important. Because their political agendas never purport to offer solutions to the riddle of history, and because they never claim to represent the interests of humanity -in toto, they are nothing more than the expressions of a vigorous and rebellious political *pluralism*. Arendt is not claiming that there is only one such elite, nor that those who engage in, and those who disengage from, political life do so forever. Nor is she stipulating in advance how extensive such "oases in the desert" may be. Rather, she is suggesting that they will never include everyone and never terminally resolve the problems of humankind. They will emerge, they may flourish, they may persist or become moribund, only to be replaced by others. Their provisionality is indeed their great virtue. And possibly the best we can hope for from any political system is that it tolerate and indeed encourage the proliferation of those "public spaces" of civil society in which such groups might form.

Such a politics is not necessarily inimical to parliamentary government. It is just not reducible to it. Commenting in an interview on the importance of the council tradition, Arendt recognizes that "there must be something to be found, a completely different principle of organization, which begins from below, continues upward, and finally leads to a parliament." Such a principle, she continues, allows for the reality that "since the country is too big for all of us to come together and determine our fate, we need a number of public spaces within it."[68]

For Arendt it is in civil society rather than in the formal structures of the government that political praxis can best flourish. In the contemporary world a more confederal system of government can allow and indeed promote the praxis of ordinary citizens, but it can never be a substitute for such praxis. Indeed, while enduring institutions are essential to political freedom, the tension between these institutions and the rebellious spirit is equally enduring. This is why spontaneity is central to Arendt's political writing and why, like the revolutionary councils, the student movements and civil disobedience campaigns of the 1960s were so exciting for her. They represented, as she quotes Tocqueville, "the art of associating together" which alone might remedy our political ills.[69] It is above all this art of association that Arendt wishes to promote.

On this point her thinking is again close to that of Camus. He too remained wary of grand schemes and World Historical parties or movements. For Camus rebellious politics must be proximate and concrete; hence the appeal of the "fastidious assassins" to him. This is also the rationale behind the character of Rieux in *The Plague*. In the wake of *The Rebel* many on the left, including Sartre, Barthes, and Jeanson, accused Camus of recommending a "withdrawal from history." For these critics Rieux's localized struggle, against an enemy that was metaphysical rather than political, represents an abandonment of class struggle and a "red cross ethic" of a "noble" but impotent "soul."[70] These critics were right—and profoundly wrong. They correctly saw that the rebellion depicted in *The Plague* is not class struggle, that it involves no political parties or mass movements and has neither grandiose ideological ambitions nor any deep interest in state power. But they were wrong to conclude that it therefore represents a kind of pristine and moralistic political withdrawal. Rather, it depicts a new kind of politics, much like the politics of Arendt's rebellious "elites." As Camus put it in response to Barthes, "it is not legitimate to reproach me or, above all, to accuse me of rejecting history—unless it is proclaimed that the only way of taking part in history is to make tyranny legitimate."[71] Rieux's rebellion, along with that of his comrades, is an "active fraternity" against injustice. In no way does it abandon history. But it refuses any kind of grand historical justification like that found in Marxism, and it also refuses to equate resistance with such "tyrannical" instrumentalities as the revolutionary political party.[72] Rieux is more modest: "I have no more than the pride that's needed to keep me going. I have no idea what's awaiting me, or what will happen when this all ends. For the moment I know this: there are sick people and they need curing."[73]

This comes close to the spontaneity of Arendtian action. Rieux lives

thoroughly in the present. This does not make him indifferent to consequences. It is just that he chooses his ends and his means soberly, and
justifies them not in terms of a grand narrative but in terms of an active
solidarity. His motto repudiates any political praxis bent on thoroughly
transforming the world, but in its modesty it might well be a more apt
idea for our times: "Salvation's much too big a word for me. I don't aim
so high. I'm concerned with man's health; and for me his health comes
first."[74] The agents of Camusian rebellion are deeply committed and never
solitary. But, as in Arendt, they tend to be "self-constituted" members of
a civil society rather than members of parties seeking state power.

Perhaps the most programmatic discussion of Camus's politics is his
essay "Neither Victims nor Executioners." Written in 1946, with the Second World War recently ended and the Cold War about to begin, Camus
criticizes the corruptions of Soviet-style Marxism and American-style liberalism, decrying the "vast conspiracy of silence [that] has spread all about
us." Confronting the debasement of the revolutionary tradition, he says
that we have but two options: "one must either come out for the status
quo—which is a mood of absolute utopia insofar as it assumes the 'freezing'
of history—or else give a new meaning to what might be called relative
Utopia."[75]

In this light he calls for an international democracy and an international
legal code, which together might provide support for human freedom and
dignity. Like Arendt, he calls for a new "style of life" based on the recognition that "little is to be expected from present-day governments, since
these live and act according to a murderous code. Hope remains only in
the most difficult task of all: to reconsider everything from the ground
up, so as to shape a living society inside a dying society. Men must therefore, as individuals, draw up among themselves, within frontiers and across
them, a new social contract, which will unite them according to more
reasonable principles."[76] Such a *civilization du dialogue*, Camus avers, is a
difficult undertaking, but it is only through "the universal communication
of men" that human freedom is possible. For Camus such communication
should be undertaken from the ground up, within and across frontiers,
by self-constituted agents of political renewal.

Drawing their inspiration from a number of political traditions, both
Camus and Arendt support political institutions that are averse to the
modern state. Endorsing a more localized and participatory form of politics, both can be seen as theorists of a robust civil society and as advocates
of a form of global federalism consistent with such a civil society. In some
ways their writings clearly elude the idiom of democratic theory as it is

normally understood, for they are both fairly indifferent to questions of political representation, party organization, and state structure. And yet in their refusal to reduce the problem of democracy to the structuring of the state, both Arendt and Camus can be seen as radical democrats, for they sought to multiply the public spaces through which ordinary citizens might empower themselves. Anticipating the more recent writings of Claude Lefort, they both declared that democratic politics is above all a theater of contestation, in which an egalitarian ethos and a generalized awareness of rights always surpasses the political and legal forms that claim to embody them. Whereas the democratic state professes to represent society as a whole, democratic politics necessarily eludes such representation, always presenting new claims of right that challenge prevailing conceptions of universality and democracy. As Lefort writes, "it is at the heart of civil society, in the name of an indefinite need for a mutual recognition of liberties, a mutual protection of the ability to exercise them, that one may discern a movement antagonistic to that which is propelling state power towards its goal."[77] Although the democratic state is defined primarily by a tendency to homogenize in the name of the universal, civil society is defined by its chronic presentation of differences. There is always, then, a tension between the rebellious impulses actualized by autonomous publics in civil society, and the formal institutions of democratic state power that claim to realize these impulses. For Arendt and Camus it is the cultivation of these impulses, the proximate agencies that might advance them, and the spaces in which they might flourish that constitute the central problem of contemporary politics. For both writers such impulses are probably nowhere better exemplified than in the struggles of the European labor movements. Yet neither writer is willing to identify such struggles with the socialist ideology with which they are often associated.

Bread and Freedom

Although neither Arendt nor Camus displayed a systematic interest in political economy, neither was indifferent to modern political-economic controversies and problems. Both considered capitalism a form of ceaseless appropriation of nature and society which dispossesses laborers from their means of production, undermines enduring communities, and engenders the superfluity of large numbers of people. In this sense both condemned the tendency of bourgeois society to assimilate all values to the exchange values of the market, a nihilistic reduction of the richness of the world. A comment by Arendt nicely sums up this attitude: "The whole modern production process is actually a process of gradual expropriation.... And in this sense Karl Marx was entirely right. He is the only one who really dared to think this new production process through.... Only it is hell. It is not paradise that comes finally out of it... [Marx saw] that capitalism, left to its own devices, has a tendency to raze all laws that are in the way of its cruel progress."[78] Yet in spite of their shared aversion to capitalism Arendt and Camus differ in their criticisms of it. Whereas Arendt provides genuine insight into certain problems of political economy, her general attitude toward the subject is blithely naive and confused. This blitheness opens up an aporia in her thinking, namely, her rigid distinction between the social and the political. This problematic distinction has been discussed at length, and many writers have argued that it empties the political of all significance. Yet although her critics correctly identify the flaws of this distinction, there is nonetheless a certain subtlety and ambivalence to her argument that warrants further discussion.[79]

This quality can best be detected in her treatment of the labor movement in *The Human Condition*, a discussion which stands out in a chapter devoted to insisting on the autonomy of "action" from labor and work, certainly the two concerns most closely associated with the modern labor movement. Arendt begins by commenting on the antipolitical character of labor and thus the seeming unsuitedness of laborers for politics in their capacity as laborers. She proceeds, however, to note a "striking" fact— "the sudden and frequently extraordinarily productive role which the labor movements have played in modern politics. From the revolutions of 1848 to the Hungarian revolution of 1956, the European working class, by virtue of being the only organized and hence the leading section of the people, has written one of the most glorious and probably the most promising chapter of recent history."[80] Arendt contends that these movements were neither driven by economic demands nor led by trade unions, and that they were uniquely and supremely political movements, indeed the *only* true political movements of their time:

> For this political and revolutionary role of the labor movement... it is decisive that the economic activity of its members was incidental and that its force of attraction was never restricted to the ranks of the working class. If for a time it almost looked as if the movement would succeed in founding, at least within its own ranks, a new public space with new political standards, the spring of these attempts was not labor—neither the laboring activity itself nor the always utopian rebellion against life's necessity—but those injustices and hypocrisies

which have disappeared with the transformation of a class society into a mass society.[81]

Arendt's own comments here are as striking as any of the historical realities she discusses. In a book about the distinction between labor and politics she provides but one example of genuine modern political praxis—the labor movement—but asserts that the "spring" of this praxis had nothing to do with labor!

Here Arendt mistakenly conflates two distinct problems. On the one hand she provides a powerful critique of *economism,* the tendency to reduce questions of political principle and organization to matters of economic concern, such as compensation and welfare opportunities. The labor movement, she says, is not driven by purely economic demands, and the trade unions, which "were never revolutionary," are not its only organs. Indeed she maintains that when it is acting in its political and revolutionary capacity (and for her these two are identical), the labor movement, far from being like "any other pressure group," is animated by broader questions of justice and thus exercises a "force of attraction" well beyond the working class.[82] This comment echoes the arguments of such Marxists as Lenin and Gramsci, both of whom argued that the working class needed to transcend a purely "economic-corporate" identity and become truly "hegemonic"—that is, needed to appeal to other constituencies and articulate a compelling vision of the common good.[83] Arendt, of course, departs from them in crucial respects; she rejects their confidence in history, their allegiance to the notion of a working-class party and their project of a total social transformation. But her argument here is particularly striking in the antipathy it exhibits toward workers as such and toward the economic demands they put forth in this capacity. In one respect Arendt seems almost to surpass Lenin in her elitism; after all, Lenin always insisted on the insufficiency of "trade union consciousness," but he never denied its centrality to politics. But Arendt's more general point is that revolutionary politics can never be reduced to economic struggle.

Arendt's rejection of the social as a basis for revolutionary praxis in *On Revolution* can be made sense of as an argument that economism, especially when motivated by a sense of pity for the less fortunate, is not consistent with the need for revolutionary empowerment. This reinforces her other criticisms of Marxism—that it lacks any conception of political judgment and is unable to equilibrate ends and means, and that it is excessively party-oriented and statist in both its revolutionary politics and its revolutionary objectives. As she writes of the Bolsheviks, "They agreed that the end of government was the welfare of the people, and that the substance of politics was not action but administration."[84] This is a criticism of Marxism with which Camus could have agreed. Thus he notes that "our grim philanthropists" of the left are oblivious to the "natural sober pride" of the working class.[85] I think it is fair to say that for both Arendt and Camus an economistic politics often implies a deeply patronizing attitude toward the rebellious capacities of the working class. One of the reasons why Arendt believes that the social question corrupts the revolutionary process is because she believes it is too often tied to a calculus that reduces questions of solidarity and power to questions of utility and consumption. If one accepts this preoccupation it is easy to pass from a view of workers as historical subjects possessed of dignity and power to a view of them as objects of an historical process.[86]

But this is not the only argument Arendt makes, and if on the one hand she criticizes economism, on the other she seems to criticize the economic factor itself as inimical to politics. Thus she claims that the economic interests of the labor movement were merely "incidental" to their revolutionary praxis—not simply that "the spring of these attempts was not labor" but that they were acting as political agents rather than as workers.[87] Here Arendt seems to be asserting a rigid and categorical distinction between the social and the political, viewing the two as mutually exclusive realms. She claims that in spite of their great merits, "the fatal mistake of the councils has always been that they themselves did not distinguish clearly between participation in public affairs and administration or management of things in the public interest. In the form of workers' councils, they have again and again tried to take over the management of the factories, and all these attempts have ended in dismal failure." The councils, she declares, "have always been primarily political." A "lack of interest in social and economic questions . . . was a sign of their political maturity, whereas the workers' wish to run the factories themselves was a sign of the understandable, but politically irrelevant desire of individuals to rise into positions which had then been open only to the middle-class." Not only did the "immaturity" of these workers degrade the praxis of the councils; it also "brought an element of action into the management of things, and this indeed could not but create chaos" for economic life. Arendt in fact claims that it was nothing less than the virtuous "political qualities" of the workers which made them "incapable . . . of rebuilding the economic system of the country."[88]

These categorical claims have generated much-deserved criticism, but it is worth noting Arendt's inconsistency here. She claims both that the fatal error of the councils "has always been" their inability to insulate the political from the economic *and* that they "have always been primarily political." She asserts that the life of the factory involves "the management of things" rather than "action" and that the workers' demand for management was "politically irrelevant"; yet she concedes that what they demanded was nothing less than collective power, not individual access to positions of command over others but "to run the factory themselves."

Here one must frankly acknowledge the undeniably essentialist and obscurantist character of many of Arendt's distinctions. C. B. Macpherson aptly described Arendt's method as "rather a curious practice: of taking a word that has perhaps more than one meaning in the ordinary understanding and giving it a very special meaning and then proceeding from there to reach striking, paradoxical conclusions."[89] Arendt's efforts to clarify this practice at a 1972 conference at York University only add to the confusion. Whereas many of her arguments, including those quoted above, suggest a rigid separation of the social and the political, here she avers that "at all times people living together have affairs that belong in the realm of the public—'are worthy to be talked about in public.' What these matters *are* at any historical *moment* is probably *utterly* different."[90] The example she supplies is that of the medieval cathedral, a public space in which people spoke about matters of common religious concern. This remark takes us in a direction sharply divergent from the main thrust of her categorical distinctions—to the conclusion that the distinction between social and political is a functional rather than a structural one and that, far from demarcating any specific set of concerns or institutions, it designates whatever it is that might be considered subject to political decision. This is a genuine improvement. But Arendt makes no effort to explore its implications or to show how it might be reconciled with her earlier criticisms of the economic concerns of modern revolutions and councils.

Indeed, the comments on economics that follow cast more shadows on the problem. She strangely maintains that while a town meeting might well discuss where to put a bridge, a matter amenable to public deliberation and about which there is no "certainty," many other issues, including the "grave social problems" of contemporary cities, are not thus amenable. Those familiar with the history of the twentieth-century left and sympathetic toward many of Arendt's own insights into this history can only be astonished by her gloss on this claim: "everything which can really be figured out, in the sphere Engels called the administration of things— these are social things in general. That they should then be subject to debate seems to me phony and a plague." When asked by Albrecht Wellmer for "one example in our time of a social problem which is not at the same time a political problem," she falters, and then proceeds to imply that there is none, that all social problems have a political dimension. But she adds that they also have an "administrative" one, and that these need to be insulated from each other in practice.[91] Thus how public housing should be provided and where it should be located are genuine political concerns; but whether people deserve public housing, and questions like "how many square feet every human being needs in order to be able to breath and to live a decent life," are things which can be figured out with certainty and thus can be decided "from above." This is very strange indeed. On the one hand Arendt seems to draw on some Scottish Enlightenment notion about the self-evidence of a natural right to housing, an approach far removed from the body of her political theory. On the other hand she seems to be suggesting that, given such a "moral sense," a great many policy questions are "technical" and unproblematic and should be handled by administrative bureaucracies. How such questions can be decided with "certainty," and how such bureaucracies are consistent with her claims about the importance of decentralized, confederal political structures, are matters about which she says nothing. But it is clear that these are questions about which she has not thought very much. The genuine strength of her distinction between the social and the political derives from her insights into the limits of economism and the importance of solidarity and empowerment. But this insight is overwhelmed by the ill-considered way in which she treats important questions of political economy.

Yet again on this score Arendt is hardly consistent, and one could argue that in her more concrete discussions she does not allow her considered judgments to be constrained by unwieldy distinctions. Even in *The Human Condition* she allows that the labor movement was "the only group on the political scene which not only defended its economic interests but fought a full-fledged political battle,"[92] implying that in practice the economic and the political are interdependent. But this view is even clearer in some of her more concrete political analyses. Her discussion of the Israeli kibbutzim, the system of cooperative work communities, is especially illuminating. She calls these cooperatives "perhaps the most promising of all social experiments made in the 20th century. . . . Here, in complete freedom and unhampered by any government, a new form of ownership, a new type of farmer, a new way of family life and child education, and new approaches to the troublesome conflicts between city and country, between rural and industrial labor have been created."[93] She acknowledges that the kibbutzim have practiced "abstention from politics." But it is clear that she is talking here of partisan politics, and that in fact these cooperatives exemplify the political spirit she idealizes elsewhere: "this enthusiastic concentration on immediate problems, that has enabled the kibbutz pioneers to go ahead with their work, undisturbed by the more noxious ideologies of our times, realizing new laws and new behavior patterns, establishing new customs and new values, and translating and integrating them into new institutions." These pioneers are nothing less than prototypes of those "founders of republics" of which Arendt writes in *On Revolution*.[94] Arendt's final word about them makes clear that at least in this instance the construction of new forms of human community defies any essentialist distinctions between the economic and the political:

> The loss of the kibbutzim, the ruin of the new type of man they have produced, the destruction of their institutions and the oblivion that would swallow the fruit of their experiences—this would be one of the severest blows to the hopes of all those, Jewish and non-Jewish, who have not and never will make their peace with present-day society and its standards. For this Jewish experiment ... [holds promise] for the large mass of men everywhere whose dignity and very humanity are in our time so seriously threatened by the pressures of modern life and its unsolved problems.[95]

This text is a far cry from the cavalier assertions about the "political irrelevance" of the social in *On Revolution*. Arendt's writings on Zionism indicate that she took the kibbutzim, along with the Hebrew University in Jerusalem, to be the heart of the effort to establish a free and politically realistic Zionism in Palestine. She contends that they promised to realize "an age-old Jewish dream of a society based on justice, formed in complete equality, and indifferent to all profit motives."[96] But she also indicates that these achievements were social *and* political, that their cooperative structure of social and economic life made them uniquely suited to ground a confederal, nonstatist, politics.

Arendt draws upon similar insights in her 1970 essay "Thoughts on Politics and Revolution." Here she speaks of "the very inhuman conditions of much of modern economy," arguing that "the alternative between capitalism and socialism is false" because both forms of industrialism have "dispossessed" the masses of their people. She applauds recent efforts in Yugoslavia "to decontrol and decentralize the economy," suggesting that such "experimentation ... with the problem of ownership" holds great promise. Once again she refers to the workers' council system, but here her description has a different coloration. Acknowledging that "none of these experiments redefines legitimate property in a satisfactory way," she notes that the council system promises to do this "by providing job security instead of the security of private property. In [it] . . . individual workers are no longer atomized but belong to a new collective, the co-operative or the factory council, as a kind of compensation for membership in a class."[97] Even here Arendt asserts that such experiments and reforms "have nothing to do with economic systems—except that the economic system should not be used to deprive people of their freedom." But this last clause qualifies the former into oblivion, for her discussion underscores the important ways in which modern forms of economics "deprive people of their freedom" and highlights the interdependence of new economic forms and new political ones. Contrary to *On Revolution* she herself describes the council system as a form of worker "self-management," indicating quite clearly that it involves both a politicization of the workplace and a kind of "elementary republic."

Arendt fails theoretically to register what her own observations establish—that, as Martin Buber put it, decentralized political forms will often "be political and economic units at once."[98] In this respect Camus's thinking is consistent and clear. The modern world, he asserts, degrades people above all by separating creativity and work. The task of the rebel is thus to reunite the two, to nourish "a vast emancipatory movement called culture that is made up of free creation and of free work."[99] Camus, in keeping with his relentless skepticism, denies that human life is governed by essentialist categories or segregated into rigid spheres. Though he is wary of the way in which the economic has been valorized by Marxism, he refuses to dismiss its centrality. This point is made most clearly in Camus's "Bread and Freedom." Like Arendt he associates the European labor movement with the modern struggle for political freedom. Nonetheless, he avers, "the great event of the twentieth century was the forsaking of the values of freedom by the revolutionary movement, the progressive retreat of socialism based on freedom before the attacks of a Caesarian and military socialism."[100]

Camus celebrates the fact that the workers' movements had "assumed responsibility for the double honor of freedom and justice, without ever dreaming of saying that they were incompatible," and he seeks to understand how the betrayal of this "double honor" came about. It was the great insight of Marx, he notes, that "there is no possible freedom for the man tied to his lathe all day long." But thence "it should have been said merely that bourgeois freedom was a hoax, and not all freedom." The great error of Marxism, in Camus's eyes, was that it failed to see that the question of freedom is not reducible to class terms, and the limits of bourgeois freedom indict the adjective, not the noun: "From a justifiable and healthy distrust of the way that bourgeois society prostituted freedom, people came to distrust freedom itself. At best it was postponed to the end of time, with the request that meanwhile it not be talked about." Camus, following Rosa Luxemburg, deplores this postponement. "There is no ideal freedom," he declares, "that will someday be given us all at once, as a pension comes at the end of one's life." Rather, political freedom is something that must be treasured and vigorously protected and exercised. But, he continues, this is no reason to abandon the struggle for economic justice. Between freedom and justice "we cannot choose one without the other. If someone takes away your bread, he suppresses your freedom at the same time. But if someone takes away your freedom, you may be sure that your bread is threatened, for it depends no longer on you and your struggle but on the whim of a master."[101]

For Camus, Arendt's duality of labor and freedom, however well-intentioned and unconventional, can be nothing more than an "infernal" opposition, furthering a "cynical dialectic" between bourgeois and Communist visions. By contrast, Camus stands for a "libertarian socialism." As he puts it, "everything that humiliates labor also humiliates the intelligence, and vice versa. And the revolutionary struggle, the centuries-old straining toward liberation can be defined first of all as a double and constant rejection of humiliation."[102] Both Arendt and Camus saw that capitalism was an important, though not exclusive, source of such humiliation in the modern world. And both writers were drawn to more proximate forms of property, like small proprietorship or worker self-management, as an antidote to this humiliation. Yet while both supported a politics of empowerment, only Camus steadfastly and consistently argued that the reconstruction of political life requires a reconstruction of economic life as well. It is ironic and unfortunate that Arendt, who wrote that "wherever knowing and doing have parted company, the space of freedom is lost," should have failed to place the problem of economic democracy at the center of her political theory.[103]

Judgment and Politics

Despite their differences, both Arendt and Camus believed that economistic reductions of political thinking—whether in the form of liberal technocratic reasoning or Marxian discernments of the contradictions of capitalism and the forward march of labor—are misguided, that they debilitate sober political judgment. In different ways, liberal images of economic growth and Marxian visions of class struggle promote the idea that the political universe can be divided in two, separating those in the vanguard of "progress" and "modernization" and those representing the forces of anachronism. In so doing, both liberal and Marxian political theory posit some ultimate good—increased "welfare" or the transcendence of scarcity—external to the actual processes of political contestation in accordance with which actual politics can be judged good or ill.

Both writers believe that discernments of such immutable economic laws or riddles of history were bankrupt, and that when employed in practice they had produced blindness and barbarity. For both Arendt and Camus a rebellious politics, resting on the fragile foundations of human power and finitude, is most valuable because it allows and indeed promotes continual challenge and contestation and refuses to privilege any conception of an ultimate good. Far from endorsing dualistic conceptions of the political universe, both writers support a politics premised on irreducible plurality, otherness, and difference, and resolutely reject any form of dialectical reasoning that would mitigate such plurality. As witnesses to the horrors of political ideologies seeking to impose a totalistic vision on recalcitrant societies, Arendt and Camus converge on a conception of political judgment as the cardinal virtue of political life. Both writers maintain that political conduct requires extraordinary sobriety and reflexivity, and that it should be based on a healthy appreciation of the limits and ambiguities of all political convictions and choices. There is an amazing similarity between Arendt's theoretical writings on this subject and Camus's journalism and fiction.

Arendt sets forth this idea in a series of essays on the question of judgment. Because this subject has received sustained attention in the scholarly literature, I shall only sketch out the main lines of Arendt's argument.[104] Judgment is for Arendt the way in which we "take our bearings in the world," a "form of cognition . . . by which acting men (and not men who are engaged in contemplating some progressive or doomed course of history) eventually can come to terms with what irrevocably happened and be reconciled with what unavoidably exists."[105] Although in some places Arendt emphasizes the prospective character of judgment and in other places its retrospective character, for the purposes of my discussion it is important to recognize that for her all humans are both agents and patients, that is to say, creatures exercising powers and suffering liabilities, acting upon others and being acted upon in turn.

This sense of power and limit is not normally acknowledged by modern political ideologies. But for Arendt it means that political conduct is best viewed as a form of projection into the future that takes into account the recalcitrant realities of the existing world, including the constraints of the historically given situation and the perspectives of others who may differ. Arendt's text underscores both of these dimensions: she affirms that we are efficacious agents for whom history is not a "progressive or doomed course," yet that we nonetheless face the constraints of "what irrevocably happened" and "what unavoidably exists." Being reconciled with what exists does not mean complacency or mere acceptance. But it does require a healthy sense of our own limits. In this regard judgment is the diametrical opposite of that hubris characteristic of twentieth-century totalitarian movements, which recommends an unwavering confidence in the ability of political agents to remake the world in accordance with an ideological blueprint.

Arendt sees political judgment as a preeminently dialogic orientation. Drawing from Aristotle's conception of *phronesis,* she holds that judgment requires highly contextualized discriminations and a sharp attention to particularity, time, and place. In this sense the exercise of judgment is a form of moderation that acknowledges the importance of situational constraints. Drawing from Kant, she describes judgment as an "enlarged mentality" in which one can "think in the place of everybody else":

> The power of judgment rests on a potential agreement with others, and the thinking process which is active in judging something is not, like the thought process of pure reasoning, a dialogue between me and myself, but finds itself always and primarily, even if I am quite alone in making up my mind, in an anticipated communication with others with whom I know I must finally come to some agreement. From this potential agreement judgment derives its specific validity.... It needs the special presence of others "in whose place" it must think, whose perspectives it must take into consideration, and without whom it never has the opportunity to operate at all.[106]

Arendt describes such a mode of political thinking as "representative." The judging political agent seeks "the liberation from one's own private interests." Arendt is clear, however, that this does not involve any kind of altruism or effacement of one's own particular identity or concerns: "this is a question neither of empathy, as though I tried to be or to feel like somebody else, nor of counting noses and joining a majority but of being and thinking in my own identity where actually I am not." She continues: "The more people's standpoints I have present in my mind while I am pondering a given issue, and the better I can imagine how I would think and feel if I were in their place, the stronger will be my

capacity for representative thinking and the more valid my final conclusions, my opinion." Such judgment is nothing less than a scrupulous and
self-critical process of considering the perspectives of others, anticipating
their reactions and their likely responses to various courses of action as a
prelude toward deciding how to act politically. I think it would be a mistake
to view such scrupulousness as being either exclusively moral and disin-
terested or exclusively strategic and instrumental. As we have seen, Arendt's
conception of politics is deeply pragmatic, and she believes that we ought
to think consequentially as political agents precisely because our own sense
of identity and dignity is bound up with the world that we share with
others.[107]

Such a conception of representative thinking is central to Camus as
well. Though it is never spelled out in philosophical terms, his writing is
marked by the sense that "nothing is true that compels me to make it
exclusive."[108] Camus comes closest to articulating the idea of representative
thinking when he writes, "All systems of morality are based on the idea
that an action has consequences that legitimize or cancel it. A mind imbued
with the absurd merely judges that those consequences must be considered
calmly. It is ready to pay up. In other words, there may be responsible
people, but there are not guilty ones."[109] Camus thus repudiates a politics
of expiation, rejecting the idea that the political universe can be divided
into camps of unadulterated virtue and irredeemable depravity. In insisting
that actions be considered "calmly," Camus upholds the need for moral
judgment while renouncing a posture of moral self-righteousness: "The
key words, the final secrets, are not in man's possession. But man nevertheless keeps the power to judge and to absolve."[110]

This model of judgment is exemplified in Camus's journalism and fiction. In the months immediately following the Liberation, Camus steadfastly supported the purge of Vichy collaborators, holding that "[we have]
chosen to assume the burden of human justice with all its terrible imperfections, careful only to correct them through a desperately maintained
sense of honesty."[111] This sense of honesty, which supported the power
to judge and to absolve, led him rather quickly to the conclusion that the
purge was hypocritical and unfair. Whereas many who had truly collab-
orated went unpunished, assuming positions of authority in postwar
France, others far less guilty received harsh sentencing and became the
objects of self-righteous public ridicule. Camus came to the conclusion
that such a purge was less an act of justice than a public ritual of mendacity
that allowed many to assuage their own guilty consciences by projecting
their guilt onto others. His writings on this subject beautifully display

representative thinking in action, as he considers the purge from the points of view of those who had sacrificed during the Resistance, those brought before the tribunal of justice, and those members of the French public for whom the purge would be a lesson in civic virtue or civic vice.[112] Though he rejected calls for blanket clemency, the process of his reflection and his eventual critical conclusion display that sobriety and lack of fanatical moral rigor characteristic of an "enlarged mentality." In Camus's case it is clear that he learned not only from a sensitive dialogue with himself but also from an equally sensitive public dialogue with François Mauriac; taking the other's position into account, he eventually came to see its rightness and to revise his own opinion.

A similar kind of ethical reflexivity is displayed by "the just assassins," the heroes of Camus's play of the same name, who scrupulously submit themselves to intense individual and collective soul-searching before undertaking to assassinate the Russian grand duke. These rebels retain the power to judge and to act, but their own deliberations reveal how important each believes the opinions of the others to be and how painful are the choices before them. In a moving scene, the grand duchess beseeches Kaliayev, now a prisoner, to acknowledge the private virtues of her deceased husband, who she claims was a kind man who "used to drink with" the poor peasants. Kaliayev does not deny the duke's private kindnesses; rather he ignores them as being of no relevance to the political injustices that the duke supported and symbolized. When he tells the duchess of the love binding his comrades, who share a commitment to justice, she replies that "I too loved—the man you killed." Kaliayev acknowledges the sincerity of the duchess's love for her husband, replying, "I know. That is why I forgive you for the wrongs that you and your kind have done me."[113] Kaliayev retains the capacity to absolve. While refusing to seek forgiveness and abjuring the Christian sense of guilt that the duchess wishes to induce, he nonetheless retains a sense of compassion and caring. Unlike his comrade Stepan, his heart is not hardened and his conscience not crippled. Maintaining till the end the justness of his violent act, he nonetheless treats his deed with great circumspection and modesty, and painfully acknowledges the sufferings it may have caused others.[114]

These examples show the rebel to be someone who is capable of acting decisively—even violently—but who is also capable of acknowledging his own limits, including most especially the limit represented by the other against whom he acts. This searching incorporation of the standpoint of others, even when those others are opponents, is the hallmark of Camus's political thinking. It shines forth in Camus's writings on Algeria, in which he avows that "if each individual, Arab or French, made an effort to think over his adversary's motives, at least the basis of a fruitful discussion would be clear."[115] But it is perhaps most evident in Camus's "The Unbeliever and Christians," originally an address presented at the Dominican Monastery of Latour-Maubourg in 1948. Here Camus admonishes the Catholic church for its complacent response to the rise of fascism, holding that "what the world expects of Christians is that Christians should speak out, loud and clear, and that they should voice their condemnation in such a way that never a doubt, never the slightest doubt, could rise in the heart of the simplest man." Yet if this message is rather unremarkable coming from a European leftist, the method of its delivery is remarkable indeed.

Camus begins by enunciating a set of principles. The first is his rejection of "lay pharisaism": "To me a lay pharisee is the person who pretends to believe that Christianity is an easy thing and asks of the Christian, on the basis of an external view of Christianity, more than he asks of himself." The second principle is his refusal to embrace "any absolute truth or any message. I shall never start from the supposition that Christian truth is illusory, but merely from the fact that I could not accept it." Camus goes on to say that he has learned much from "the dialogue between believer and unbeliever." Proceeding from a healthy respect for Christianity as well as a dissent from its creed, Camus then outlines his method, stating his third principle: "I shall not try to change anything that I think or anything that you think . . . in order to reach a reconciliation that would be agreeable to all. On the contrary, what I feel like telling you today is that the world needs real dialogue, that falsehood is just as much the opposite of dialogue as is silence, and that the only possible dialogue is the kind between people who remain what they are and speak their minds."[116] But how does refusing to change anyone's mind constitute a dialogue rather than simply talking past one's interlocutor? It is a dialogue because it seeks to reach "a reconciliation that would be agreeable to all" based on an honest airing of differences and an equally honest effort to find common ground through the airing of those differences. As an intellectual delivering his opinion on the political responsibilities of the Catholic church, Camus anticipates the differing concerns and commitments of his interlocutors, explicitly acknowledges these differences of perspective, and seeks to address the Church in terms of its own concerns and self-understandings while remaining true to *his* own. He thus abjures the moralism of the lay pharisee, who would condemn the Church and its Christianity for its political failings. Camus insists that "the world of today needs Christians who remain Christians" and who, precisely by virtue of their Christianity, might be persuaded to be more resolute and vocal in their opposition to human oppression than they had been in the recent past.

If Camus's political writing makes clear his commitment to an Arendtian conception of judgment as "representative thinking," the most vivid evocation of this theme in his writing is undeniably his novel *The Fall*. A psychologically complex first-person narrative in the vein of Dostoevsky's *Notes from Underground,* the novel is the story of Jean-Baptiste Clamence, a fallen jurist who insinuates himself into one-way conversation with the reader. A disingenuous cynic, Clamence announces that "his profession is double" and that he is a "judge-penitent." He then recounts his fall from righteousness and public esteem. He confesses that he was once "truly above reproach," championing the cause of justice and occupying "those supreme summits ... lofty places" in which he felt "above" others.[117] He recalls for his interlocutor his eventual awareness of his own self-righteousness and guilt, of the fact that "too many people," himself among them, "now climb onto the cross merely to be seen from a greater distance." In the course of his confession he allows that whereas he once stood as the beacon of innocence, he now knows "with certainty the guilt of all."[118] And yet this confession is not what it seems, for at the very moment at which Clamence confesses his frailty, he announces his true strategy as judge-penitent: "it is essential to begin by extending the condemnation to all, without distinction, in order to thin it out. ... The more I accuse myself, the more I have a right to judge you."[119] It becomes clear that Clamence is a nihilist, a poseur who seeks to dominate. Only his perspective matters, and he employs subtle strategies of disarming and negating others so as to master them. Piercing the hypocrisies of ordinary moral judgment, he acts only so as to realize the cynical project of judging others, whom he reduces to his own sense of guilt so as to exploit their weaknesses. The discourse of Clamence is the monologue; he uses language only to dominate others. In contrast to Kaliayev, he exhibits no concern for the viewpoints of others except insofar as he can manipulate them. Clamence demonstrates through his vices the importance of representative thinking.[120]

The Limits of Revolt and the Tragedy of Politics

For both Arendt and Camus politics is inherently fraught with difficulty and anxiety. It involves a ceaseless tension between ends and means, and is always threatened by the twin demons of political repression and public corruption, between too much enthusiasm and too little. Though both writers earnestly endorse an ethic of rebellion, they also appreciate the limits of politics, which is a risky and necessarily partial enterprise. Both acknowledge that the life of politics is far from idyllic and that the dream of total fulfillment attained through political means is a mistaken and dangerous one. Both see that political commitment entails deep personal sacrifices. For this reason neither offers their political principles as categorical imperatives. Insofar as they recognized the finitude of the human condition and the limits of all human options, both forswore the role of secular priest or prophet and refused to moralize about the choices people might make.[121] For Arendt and Camus political theories are hypotheses, which political agents are free to choose or reject and nonpolitical agents are free to ignore. Of course neither would deny that there are risks attached to dismissing an ethic of rebellion; but there are risks attached to adopting one as well.

The most obvious risk is the danger associated with intervening in the public realm. Arendt distinguishes between "the sheltered life in the household and the merciless exposure of the polis," observing that courage is thus a political virtue par excellence.[122] The point here is not that there is no suffering in private; it is that the public remonstrance of suffering calls attention to itself and so requires a special courage to confront the physical danger that attaches to identifying with a contestable cause. This point takes on added significance once we apply it to the contemporary world of revolutionary politics, public demonstrations, and civil disobedience that preoccupied Arendt. To become political is to threaten the convictions and complacency of others, calling forth often hostile reactions. It is to disturb the orderly routines of governance and often to risk imprisonment, deportation, and even death.

Political activism also involves psychological risk. One must identify oneself openly, come out for and against something, and expose one's opinions, allegiances, and actions to the "harsh light" of the public. To go public is to subject oneself to the judgments of others, risking censure, ridicule, social discrimination, and exclusion. Perhaps most frightening of all, it is to risk the embarrassing *indifference* of others to one's deeply felt concerns. Recall Arthur Koestler's "screamers," who were considered lunatics by citizens who simply could not believe the tales of Nazi atrocity. "Clearly we must suffer from some morbid obsession, whereas the others are healthy and normal. But . . . perhaps it is we, the screamers, who react in a sound and healthy way to the reality which surrounds us, whereas you are the neurotics who totter about in a screened phantasy world because you lack the faculty to face the facts."[123] The capacity to face the facts is surely quite scarcely exhibited in contemporary politics, and in-difference may well be the most pervasive reproach to the rebel in our world.

But the psychological risk of politics extends beyond the ways in which others might reprove or repress the rebel. It is not simply a question of obstacles to rebellion, but of the fact that success itself has its costs. As Camus writes in his *Notebooks,* "nothing is pure, nothing is pure—this is the cry that has poisoned our century."[124] The world is a painful one, and it is often necessary to become politically engaged. But such engagement is no less painful, for to act is to commit to consequential, even irreversible decisions. It is to insert oneself into a web of interactions without any guarantee that one's most noble deeds will not go astray. "From the moment he strikes, the rebel cuts the world in two."[125] And as fraught with unpredictability as is all political action, the ever-presence of violence enhances the risks of a "lacerating suffering," taking its toll on others and on the conscience of the rebel as well. "Ah!" Camus exclaims, "these are hours of doubt."[126]

Politics thus risks lacerating the very soul of the rebel. But the costs are not merely subjective or narrowly private. Political engagement cuts one off from normality, from security, from a certain kind of genuine pleasure. It is no accident that in all of Camus's political fiction and drama the rebel is severed from nature, especially from the sea. This is a major theme, for example, of *The Plague,* which Camus himself considered a novel about the problematics of separation and exile.[127] In *State of Siege* the Chorus speaks for the virtues of simplicity, the cycles of nature, the "fertile mother earth."[128] The oppression of the Plague separates them from these; "henceforth the sea is out of our reach."[129] But however much the rebel may be nourished by such simplicity and ordinary decency, he is not destined to share in and fully enjoy it. He stakes his claim in the realm of ideas like justice and pitches his battle on the harsher, riskier terrain of political conflict. There is fraternity here, and hope, but there is also solitude, estrangement, and pain.

The most vivid expression of this pain is the rebel's sacrifice of love. Victoria, in *State of Siege,* beseeches her beloved Diego to stay with her rather than give his life to the struggle against the Plague: "that's a man's idea of duty—one of those futile, preposterous crusades you men engage in as a pretext for evading the one struggle that is truly arduous, the one victory of which you could rightly be proud."[130] Throughout the play the Chorus supports Victoria, speaking for the earth and for beauty, for nature and love and against the insane sacrifices of politics:

Our curse on him! Our curse on all who forsake our bodies! And pity on us, most of all, who are forsaken and must endure year after year this world which men in their pride are ever aspiring to transform! Surely, since everything may not be saved, we should learn at least to safeguard the home where love is. . . . But no! Men go whoring after ideas, a man runs away from his mother, forsakes his love, and starts rushing upon adventure . . . a hunter of shadows or a lonely singer who invokes some impossible reunion under a silent sky.[131]

But Diego persists, and he defeats the Plague. "If I were alone, everything would be easy," he says. But he is not alone, and so, he declares, "I live for my city and for my age." And yet if the Plague perishes, so too does he. "I have burned myself out in the struggle," he confesses at the last. "I am no longer a man and it is right that I should die."[132]

Similarly, in *The Just Assassins* Kaliayev tries desperately to repress his love for Dora, clinging to political commitment, "to a love that's half frozen, because it's rooted in justice and reared in prison cells." As he tells her, "We don't belong to the world of men. We are the just ones. And outside there is warmth and light; but not for us, never for us! [*Averting her eyes*] Ah, pity on the just!"[133] In *The Plague,* too, Rieux is from the outset separated from his wife, his rebellion purchased at the price of celibacy and heartache. It is true that these rebels forge a "solidarity of chains" that advances the cause of justice and partially compensates for their personal sacrifices. But their commitment is nonetheless difficult and painful for themselves and their mates, something that is perhaps necessary but costly.

This cost comes out more clearly in Camus than it does in Arendt. But for both writers, though an ethic of revolt is virtuous, in it not unambiguous. Politics is no substitute for love, art, and the enjoyment of life. The limitations of rebellion raise other problems, about the treatment of gender and the valorization of a certain conception of family and the natural in Arendt and Camus, which I shall address in the final chapter. But however problematic their treatment of these issues might be, the point here is an important one. Although political rebellion answers to genuine human interests, it does not exhaust all such interests, nor is it even perfectly consistent with them all. This is for neither writer an excuse for political quiescence, but rather a warning against any Manichean or self-righteous attitude toward political engagement. This tension between rebellion and personal happiness must be endured, not resolved. It underscores once again the partial, limited, and provisional—that is, human—character of even the most justifiable political engagements. Though neither Arendt nor Camus was a political saint, their own political commitments, I believe, exemplify the virtues, limits, and difficulties inherent in a politics of rebellion. It is to these commitments that I now turn.

Chapter 6

SWIMMING AGAINST THE TIDE

Camus and Arendt saw totalitarianism as the supreme threat to human freedom. But they hardly took comfort from the politics of the Cold War that followed the end of World War II. It is worth recalling Arendt's observation that "it may even be that the true predicaments of our time will assume their authentic form—though not necessarily the cruelest—only when totalitarianism has become a thing of the past."[1] Writing forebodingly in 1951 about the likelihood of a third world war, Arendt suggested that "this moment of anticipation is like the calm that settles after all hopes have died."[2] If for many liberals the defeat of fascism marked the triumph of "Western freedom" and the "end of ideology," for both Arendt and Camus the dawning age seemed no more hospitable than the old to independent political thinking or acting.

Irving Howe expressed the mood of many dissenting intellectuals when he wrote, in 1954, that "the Zeitgeist presses down upon us with a greater insistence than at any other moment of the century. . . . established power and dominant intellectual tendencies have come together in a harmony [that] makes the temptations of conformism all the more acute."[3] Caught between the Scylla of authoritarian communism and the Charybdis of a moribund capitalism, the intellectual, "veering and tacking as history compels him," must "try to defend democracy with some realism while maintaining his independence from and opposition to the status quo."[4] In the Communist bloc such independence was rendered virtually impossible by the repressive powers of Stalinism although, as writers like Czeslaw Milosz and Václav Havel have reminded us, the forces of inertia and accommodation, as well as sheer delusion, operated here as well.[5] In the capitalist West such conformity also had its repressive supports, though it relied more heavily on a conservative mood sustained by a combination of economic growth and the professionalization of intellectual life.[6] The Cold War set up two superpowers defined in polar opposition to each other, each demanding allegiance to itself at the expense of the other. As Edward P. Thompson put it, "the rival ideologies of the Cold War disarmed those, on both sides, who might have put Europe back together."[7]

Such polar thinking was antithetical to the political sensibility that both Arendt and Camus sought to encourage. Forcing all opinion into the either/or of "pro-Communist" or "anti-Communist," the Cold War generated intellectual conformity and fear of any political agency outside of the confines of the bureaucratized and militarized states of the North Atlantic Treaty Organization (NATO) and the Warsaw Pact. Resting on a tense international system poised on the brink of superpower confrontation and nuclear annihilation, it was sustained by increasingly conservative domestic political systems that declared a monopoly on truth. Camus and Arendt each resisted this tendency. As Camus wrote, "Nothing is true that compels me to make it exclusive."[8]

Both writers refused the blackmail of "Western freedom." Though anti-Communist, they remained critical of Western liberalism as well. Despite their support of the constitutional liberties frequently associated with the West, liberties often imperiled by anti-Communist hysteria, both were alive to moments of political radicalism and experimentation, and sought to help sustain openings for such radicalism to flourish. In their resistance to the rhetoric of demonology and victimology purveyed by many liberals and radicals, their political writings display a sobriety that exemplifies their view of political judgment as representative thinking.

Their challenge to the logic of the Cold War has often gone unnoticed, and the writings of both thinkers have often been associated with liberal justifications of the West. This neglect is understandable, for neither's rebellion followed the typical path. As critics of communism and of Marxism more generally, neither writer felt at home within the ideological left. Perhaps more importantly, neither was aligned with the emerging ideology of Third World national liberation, which had captured the fancy of many Western Marxists despondent over the failure of revolutionary politics in Europe. As students of the failures of twentieth-century revolutionary politics, both saw this ideology as another version of that typically modern hubris which claims to have discerned the true direction of history. Both feared that the polarity *imperialist/anti-imperialist* was simply another invidious binary opposition destined to produce suffering, violence, and authoritarianism. Arendt's writings on Zionism and Palestine, and Camus's on Algeria, present remarkably similar critiques of this opposition. Whereas many commentators have either ignored these writings (in the case of Arendt) or dismissed them (in the case of Camus), I suggest that these writings epitomize what is most valuable in their political thinking— the idea of a self-limiting, moderate revolt and a principled conviction that political good and evil cannot be simplistically apportioned.

As both Arendt and Camus recognized, it is impossible to deduce specific political judgments or commitments from a political theory. It would thus be foolish to suggest that their similar theoretical visions converged on a single political strategy or affiliation. But it would be equally mistaken to ignore the extent to which their common revolt against the prevailing terms of Cold War discourse was rooted in the theoretical perspective they shared.

Beyond the Cold War

Camus, like many of his colleagues in the Resistance, sought to help create a radical politics in postwar France that was continuous with the wartime experience of resistance and fraternity. Indeed, as the editor of *Combat* and as the author of *The Stranger* and *The Myth of Sisyphus*—both published in 1942 during the Nazi Occupation—Camus seemed to be the incarnation of such resistance and fraternity.[9] The subtitle of *Combat* was *From Resistance to Revolution,* and from the eve of liberation onward Camus, through his journalism and his activism, attempted to navigate the difficult path of a "third way," an alternative to both American-style liberalism and Soviet-style communism. The agencies of this third way varied, but the effort to present a global alternative to the United States and the Soviet Union, and a local alternative to the visions of De Gaulle and Thorez, remained consistent. Like many resistants, on the eve of liberation in 1944 Camus supported the Mouvement de Liberation Nationale, the loosely organized federation of resistance movements that sought to sustain a radical politics after the war. As editor of *Combat* Camus spoke out forcefully on behalf of "tomorrow's liberty."[10] In August 1944 he announced the aims of the Resistance:

> We wish to realize without delay a true people's and worker's democracy . . . a Constitution under which freedom and justice recover all their guarantees, profound structural reforms without which a policy of freedom is a mockery, the pitiless destruction of trusts and of vested financial interests, the definition of a foreign policy based on honor and loyalty to all our allies without exception. In the present state of affairs this is a revolution; it is probable that it can be carried out in a calm and orderly fashion.[11]

Consistent with his anarcho-syndicalist leanings, Camus opposed concentrations of wealth and privilege and the bureaucratic work hierarchies characteristic of corporate enterprise. He thus supported currency reform, enterprise committees, and a redistribution of wealth. These reforms, which promised to empower ordinary citizens with bread and freedom, were seen by him as ways to alleviate much of the injustice of capitalism without producing the injustices of bureaucratic communism. In his writings during this period he frequently chastised "the bourgeoisie," but, as Parker points out, his scorn was really reserved for "la grande bourgeoisie," the upper strata of French society whose financial holdings he associated with political and economic corruption. Camus did not issue blanket calls for the socialization of private property, and his nuanced account of class stratification avoids the discourse of Manichean denunciation: "We shall call . . . justice a social state in which each individual receives every opportunity at the start, and in which the country's majority is not held in abject conditions by a privileged minority. And we shall call liberty a political climate in which the human being is respected for what he is as well as for what he expresses." Foreshadowing the arguments of *The Rebel*, Camus declared that he did not believe in "definitive revolutions. All human effort in history is relative."[12] In the sphere of economics, then, he supported a series of "radical reforms" that sought to alter property relations without abolishing small-scale private property.

He also fervently endorsed a fair and just purge of Nazi collaborators. His frequent calls for a "new Saint Just" in 1944–45 produced his now-famous exchange with François Mauriac, who called for clemency for collaborators, likening the purge to the Inquisition and observing sardonically that "there are traces of suppressed Christianity in the young masters of *Combat*."[13] Camus continued to defend the purge, replying that "[we have] chosen to assume the burden of human justice with all its terrible imperfections, careful only to correct them through a desperately maintained sense of honesty."[14] But by 1945 this honesty led Camus to the conclusion that the purges had been hypocritical and unfair, and that "a nation that fails in its purification is on the way to failing in its rejuvenation."[15] This was an important lesson in political judgment, one later incorporated into such works as *The Just Assassins* and *The Fall*.

Chastened by the course of postwar "revolutionary justice," Camus persisted in his effort to sustain a radical politics. He continued to criticize the economic policies of De Gaulle's provisional government for their timidity. And in August 1945 he came out with an editorial in *Combat* lamenting the dropping of the atom bomb on Hiroshima. "Mechanical civilization has just reached the last degree of savagery. It will be necessary to choose between collective suicide or the intelligent utilization of scientific conquests." Pleased by the imminent surrender of Japan, he refuses nonetheless "to draw from such grave news anything else but the decision to plead still more energetically in favor of a veritable international society."[16] Prefiguring *The Rebel*, he wonders whether the modern Prometheus will remain true to his genius or produce the prison of his own crimes. Camus worked valiantly as the editor of *Combat* to nourish the "hope for justice" which the Resistance represented. But as the spirit of resistance waned, and French politics was gradually normalized, ideological divisions between the resistance groups intensified, dashing idealistic hopes of radical reconstruction. Symptomatic of these divisions was the split within the editorial board of *Combat*, which led in 1947 to Camus's departure due in large part to his opposition to Gaullism.[17]

In 1948 and 1949 Camus supported the short-lived Rassemblement Démocratique Révolutionaire, the radical movement led by Jean-Paul Sartre and David Rousset, a Jewish ex-Trotskyist who had been interned in concentration camps under the Nazis. A left-wing group critical of both Stalinism and capitalism, the RDR's manifesto strenuously resisted the dualism of East and West:

> Europe is a battlefield for the two great enemy forces. For both sides she is prey and threat. Prey, because her disunion and her misery deliver her to every influence; threat because these influences divide her into two opposed camps and make her a reduced image of the conflict that divides the whole world. Since it is through the enslavement of Europe that each bloc attempts to defend itself, each looks for partisans and soldiers on our soil and stimulates by its actions the fears and counter-moves of the other. . . . Buffeted between the two forces, letting ourselves be maneuvered by one and by the other, we are divided by the cold war, and our division may cause war. Therefore, there is not one country of Europe, not one citizen of a European country who can escape the responsibility for war or peace.[18]

Seeking an alternative model of political radicalism, the RDR thus declared: "We believe that an association of free men who support revolutionary democracy is capable of giving new life to the principles of liberty and human dignity, by linking them to the struggle for a social revolution."[19]

During this period Camus also supported the abortive Crusade for World Federation, led by Gary Davis, an American who had renounced his citizenship as a symbolic gesture of protest against the world system of sovereign states. Camus's defense of Davis, printed in *Combat,* clearly articulates the sentiments of the RDR during this period. Rejecting the logic of the slogan "Better dead than red," Camus reproaches all those for whom there are only two alternatives—acquiescence in the Soviet domination of Europe or a single-minded anti-Communism that defines all challenges to liberalism as subversions of "the West": "I know that certain of those among you willingly accept the choice between hanging and the firing squad. That is their idea of human freedom. As for us, we are doing what we can to keep this choice from becoming inevitable. You are doing what is necessary to make this choice inevitable."[20] Throughout this period Camus sounded this theme of ethical responsibility in the face of the seeming inexorabilities of geopolitics. Refusing dualistic thinking, he encouraged creative efforts to find a "third way."

Perhaps Camus's most important political activity was his association with Groupes de Liaison Internationale, a precursor of Amnesty International that Camus had helped found in the autumn of 1948. The GLI, supported by such groups as the socialist trade union Force Ouvriere and the syndicalist paper *Révolution Prolétairienne,* worked to secure visas, apartments, and jobs for refugees from fascist and Stalinist repression, and its bulletin sought to publicize information about human rights violations.[21] The group's manifesto, drafted by Camus, declares its commitment to a dignity that is threatened "by totalitarian techniques . . . [and] at a lesser degree, it is true, by American worship of technology." It proclaims that "it is not a matter of adding more hatred to the world and to choose between two societies, even though we know that American society represents the lesser evil. We don't have to choose evil, even the lesser. . . . We have only to give a form to the protest of men against that which crushes them, with the single goal of holding on to what can be held, and with the simple hope of being on hand one day, workers in a necessary reconstruction."[22] The most significant aspect of the GLI was its internationalist character. The GLI was as an affiliate of the Europe-America groups (EAGS), an umbrella association organized by Dwight Macdonald, editor of the American independent left-wing journal *politics.* During the late 1940s Macdonald worked feverishly to create a transatlantic community of dissident intellectuals and activists. The EAG was central to this effort. The association's statement of purpose is notably Camusian. Commenting on the estrangement of intellectuals who feel isolation from "the great power blocs," "the mass parties," and each other, it declares:

> We want, above all, to show dissident Europeans that they are not alone, and that certain basic ideas of freedom and social equity remain for us common ground.... Our main emphasis is on free communication between American and European intellectuals—i.e., the creation of what Albert Camus calls a "community of dialogue." What we support in Europe today is not any specific program but the reexamination of political questions through controversy and discussion.[23]

Like GLI, the EAGs pledged themselves to provide material aid as well as books, magazines, and sources of communication for refugee intellectuals and activists. As Macdonald's notes indicate, the EAGs were modeled on Camus's conception of rebellion. Echoing *The Plague,* Macdonald's notes include frequent references to "fraternity." He writes that "Camus suggests they could be a kind of preaching brotherhood, committed to writing, talking (and I presume acting) to further their ideas in every possible context.... He also proposes an international weekly or monthly ... [which] would bind together the various groups, give them some sense of international fraternity and common interests."[24]

The thread that runs through these many activities was the idea of human dignity that played such an important role in Camus's theoretical writings. Yet such efforts were doomed to failure in a France hemmed in on one side by the Communist Party and on the other by the Gaullist forces of restoration. The demise of such efforts was finally sealed by the onset of the Korean War, which made the choice between the United States and the Soviet Union, "West" and "East," almost impossible to resist.[25] The intensifying Cold War, punctuated by the Korean conflict, divided the marginal and fragile coalition of left-wing forces seeking a third way. On the one hand many radicals followed the lead of Sartre, whose journal *Les Temps Modernes* adopted a policy of fellow-traveling support for communism tortuously combined with an effort to criticize Stalinism.[26] On the other hand many intellectuals followed the lead of the Congress for Cultural Freedom, enlisting as fellow-traveling liberals under the banner of a U.S.-led NATO.[27]

Camus resisted both of these alternatives. Locally he was a lukewarm supporter of the French Front Republicain coalition linking Pierre

Mendès-France of the Radical Party and Guy Mollet of the Socialists, which sought to present a vaguely social democratic alternative to Gaullism. But he was sharply critical of the coalition's inability to bring about either meaningful economic reform or a solution to France's colonial problems. In his column in *L'Express* he despaired of the coalition's failure to advance in the face of substantial popular support for Communist and right-wing parties, placing the weakness of French political reform in a global context.[28] He saw the choice between the Communist and capitalist extremes as a choice between death by hanging or by firing squad—two ways of extinguishing human freedom. Yet he refused to absolve French politicians and intellectuals of responsibility for accepting this polarization. Camus's criticisms of communism are well known, so much so that he is often portrayed, as we have seen, as an ideological liberal. As a journalist he was a withering critic of Stalinism and fellow-traveling leftism. *The Rebel*, his most important work of the period, is an extended attack on the metaphysic of revolution grounding the Communist project of proletarian radicalism. Camus did not mince words in denouncing the Communist crushing of East German workers in 1953, and he was equally vociferous in condemning the suppression of the Hungarian uprising in 1956.[29] In "Kadar Had His Day of Fear" he chastises the "bloody and monotonous rites" of Stalinism. "There is room for nothing in Stalinist culture," he asserts, "except for edifying sermons, colorless life, and the catechism of propaganda." Hungary, he contends, is "a counter-revolutionary state," and "Hungarian socialism is in prison or in exile today."[30]

In a published interview, "Socialism of the Gallows," he attacks the "generalized lie" of communism. Upbraiding the Soviet-sympathizing "camp of peace" which had supported the Stockholm Conference against nuclear weapons but remained silent about Soviet imperialism in Eastern Europe, he maintains that "no nation has a monopoly on peace." He also criticizes the "neutral" Third World nations of the Bandung Group, whose "realism" about world politics led them to avoid criticizing Kadar for fear of disturbing their Soviet allies. This interview sets forth clearly Camus's belief that "the attitude of those who insist on seeing nothing but doves in the East and vultures in the West" is blind and "nihilistic."[31] It also articulates Camus's own brand of independent leftism. As we shall see, Camus was an outspoken critic of French colonialism. But he was no less suspicious of ideologies of Third World "national liberation," whose denunciations of imperialism were complacent about the barbarities of many so-called revolutionaries, whether these occur in Budapest or Algiers.

Throughout this period Camus strenuously refused the false comfort of ideological slogans. While he supported the causes of peace and justice, he criticized movements for "peace" and "liberation" that too easily apportioned guilt and innocence and too blithely allowed utopian visions of future innocence to support a cynical politics of contemporary guilt.

Yet if Camus was a critic of communism, he remained equally critical of the Western accommodation to fascism. He energetically protested the admission of Spain into UNESCO and actively supported efforts to provide material aid to Spanish refugee dissidents and intellectuals (as well as their East European counterparts).[32] His 1948 essay "Why Spain?" clearly articulates the evenhanded criticism of East and West that he sought to sustain. Explaining why *State of Siege,* his play about totalitarianism, was set in Spain, he says that "the first weapons of totalitarian war were bathed in Spanish blood," and that the barbarities of communism in no way obviate those of anti-Communists:

> Anti-communism, whatever reasons there may be for embracing it (and I know some good ones), will never gain acceptance among us if it forgets the injustice that is going on with the complicity of our governments. I have stated as vigorously as I could what I thought of the Russian concentration camps. But they will not make me forget Dachau, Buchenwald, and the nameless agony of millions, nor the dreadful repression that decimated the Spanish Republic. Yes, despite the commiseration of our political leaders, all this must be denounced at one and the same time. And I cannot forgive that hideous plague in the West of Europe because it is also ravaging the East on a vaster scale.[33]

This resistance to the Manicheanism of the Cold War is even more clearly articulated in Camus's 1953 lecture "Bread and Freedom." Criticizing the ideological bifurcation of freedom and justice accepted by many on the left and right alike, he relates this artificial division to the dangerous global split between East and West, a "cynical dialectic which sets up injustice against enslavement while strengthening one by the other." Thus the critics of Spain's admission into UNESCO are reproached by anti-Communists who insist that because Poland has been admitted, Spain should be too—an "idiotic" yet effective argument serving only to harden the blocs and to multiply the Spains and Polands of the world:

> When anyone brings up the slave in the colonies and calls for justice, he is reminded of prisoners in Russian concentration camps, and vice versa. And if you protest the assassination in Prague of an opposition historian like Kalandra, two or three American Negroes are thrown in your face. In such a disgusting attempt at outbidding, one thing only does not change—the victim, who is

always the same. A single value is constantly outraged or prostituted—freedom—and then we notice that everywhere, together with freedom, justice is also profaned.[34]

Camus holds that the "infernal circle" of the Cold War can only be broken by affirming the unity of freedom and justice—by a politics, in other words, at odds with the dominant organizations of the day. It is a politics of opposition, an antipolitics not without constructive vision but defined primarily by its refusal to be co-opted by the polarities of the Cold War. This was not an easy project. The magnetic pull of anticommunism was strong and, as we shall see in his last writings on Algeria, it is not clear that Camus was fully able to resist it. But on the whole his writings exhibit a courageous refusal to choose between freedom and justice. An interviewer once asked Camus, "in the struggles dividing the world today, must we really be willing to forget all that is bad on one side to fight what is worse on the other?" He responded by referring to Richard Hilary's famous pronouncement during the Second World War: " 'We were fighting a lie in the name of a half-truth.' [Hilary] thought he was expressing a very pessimistic idea. But one may even have to fight a lie in the name of a quarter-truth. This is our situation at present. However the quarter-truth contained in Western society is called liberty."[35] Camus here refuses to forget all that is bad on one side. He acknowledges that the civil freedoms of liberal democracy are a necessary precondition of the justice that has always been sought by the left and that, in the world of the 1950s, the resistance to communism is a task of great importance. But he also recognizes that such resistance can be undertaken in good faith only on the basis of a steadfast critique of the injustices and moral indifference of Western capitalist societies.

Arendt too resisted the pull of Cold War divisions, holding to a vision of global reconstruction consistent with her concerns about human rights and political freedom. Unlike Camus, her writing was not nourished by sustained participation in radical politics. The German resistance to Nazism was almost nonexistent, something that troubled her deeply; and in any case, as a German-Jewish expatriate living in New York, she was far removed from the forefront of struggle.[36] This is not to minimize the importance of moments of intense activism. As we have seen, Arendt was profoundly affected by her experiences as a committed Zionist during the 1930s and 1940s.[37] But as she acknowledged on many occasions, her own engagement in politics was more as a writer and teacher than as an activist. In her postwar writings she articulated a position much like Camus's, based on a clear opposition to totalitarianism of the right and the left and on a sober assessment of the freezing of politics caused by the emergent Cold War.

This position is exemplified in "The Aftermath of Nazi Rule," a somber portrait of postwar German politics and society. Despairing the demoralization and irresponsibility of post-totalitarian society., Arendt is highly critical of the Allied reconstruction effort. Denazification, she argues, echoing Camus's critique of the French purge of collaborators, is a hypocritical and compromised endeavor leaving many former Nazis in positions of social and political authority. Economic reconstruction and privatization "meant handing over the factories and the control of economic life to those who, even if a little wrong about the ultimate consequences of Nazism, had been staunch supporters of the regime for all practical purposes"; wiping out even the minimal regulations passed under the Weimar Republic, and proceeding from a union movement destroyed by the Nazis, reconstruction was also detrimental to the standard of living of many Germans. And the newly instituted federal system of *Länder* (states) offered nothing but the shell of authentic local government.[38]

True to form, Arendt does not leap from this diagnosis to moralistic denunciations. Especially wary of anti-Americanism, she acknowledges that, sadly, "the Allied powers had very little choice." The only alternative, she avers, would have been "a revolution—the outbreak of the German people's spontaneous wrath" against former Nazis. Conceding that such a revolution might have been "uncontrolled and bloody," she suggests that "it would have followed better standards of justice than a paper procedure."[39] But she notes, apparently with some regret, that such a revolution did not come to pass because "this wrath does not exist today," a sad statement about the character of German society. Arendt here broaches the theme of revolutionary violence that we have already encountered in her more theoretical writings. Much like Camus, she remains skeptical of the curative powers of uncontrolled violence or political purgations. But she acknowledges that under some circumstances political violence is justifiable, both as a way of punishing evildoers and restoring justice and as a means of forging political solidarities.

That the essay does not explicitly broach any Cold War themes is precisely what is so notable about it. At the moment in which this essay was published West Germany was the frontline of the heightening Cold War. For nearly twelve months in 1948 and 1949 West Berliners had held out against the Soviet blockade. In 1948 *Der Monat,* a cultural monthly magazine, was set up under the sponsorship of the U.S. High Command to further the ideals of "Western freedom" in an emerging cultural combat between East and West. And in June 1950 the founding conference of the Congress for Cultural Freedom, bankrolled by the Central Intelligence Agency, was held in West Berlin, marking the formal beginning of a massive "counteroffensive" against communism.[40] While many Western liberals were celebrating the "freedom" of West Germany, Arendt bemoaned its conformity, regretting that a militarized state was being established instead of the "federated Europe" that alone might aid in the reconstruction of European politics as well as economics.

Arendt's other 1950s essays reveal a similar aversion to Cold War pieties. "The Ex-Communists," written in 1953, proceeds from a harsh critique of Whittaker Chambers to a scathing portrait of the ex-Communist, whose rabid anti-communism is governed by the same Manichean logic as the communism he once supported and now denounces. The ex-Communists, she says, are not former communists; they are "Communists turned upside down." Like the Communists, for them there are only saints and heretics. They exhibit the same contempt for allies as for opponents, the same confidence that the end will justify the means, the same faith in history. "Since they have divided the world into two, they can account for the disturbing variety and plurality of the world we all live in only by either discounting it as irrelevant altogether or by stating that it is due to lack of consistency and character." Arendt is revolted by this mentality. Alert to the inescapable pluralities of political life, she offers a vigorous defense of civil liberties and American constitutional government against American reactionaries like Chambers and Joseph McCarthy, whose anticommunism threatened the very freedom it purported to defend. As Arendt suggests, "if we became dragons ourselves, it would be of small interest which of the two dragons should eventually survive. The meaning of the fight would be lost."[41] Arendt's conclusion prefigures the radical republican criticisms of the Cold War to be found in her later *Crises of the Republic*:

> America, this republic, the democracy in which we are, is a living thing which cannot be contemplated or categorized, like the image of a thing which I can make; it cannot be fabricated. It is not and never will be perfect because the standard of perfection does not apply here. Dissent belongs to this living matter as much as consent does. The limitations on dissent are the Constitution and the Bill of Rights and no one else. If you try to "make America more American" or a model of a democracy according to any preconceived idea, you can only destroy it. Your methods, finally, are the justified methods of the police, and only of the police.[42]

Arendt, a refugee from Hitler, was frightened by the nativist spirit of McCarthyism. As someone deeply touched by the plight of stateless peoples she was particularly disturbed by the McCarran-Walters Act, which threatened to exclude or deport general categories of "alien subversives." Young-Bruehl has commented on the discrepancy between Arendt's "careful, reasonable public statements" about McCarthyism and the more passionate indignation expressed in her private correspondence, attributing it in part to her fear of the repercussions on her unnaturalized ex-Communist husband. Others have more harshly suggested that Arendt, both through commission and omission, gave succor to obsessive liberal anticommunism.[43] Yet during this period Arendt supported the National Committee for an Effective Congress, an anti-McCarthy group, and was part of an abortive effort to found a civil liberties journal called *Critic*.[44] More to the point, she consistently articulated a fear that freedom was threatened by the death struggle between communism and anticommunism. Though she was surely no partisan of communism and clearly discerned the tyranny that it had imposed in Eastern Europe, neither was she a partisan of postwar liberalism.

A sense of foreboding exercised a powerful hold on Arendt's thought during this period. "Dream and Nightmare" reports on the rise of "anti-Americanism" in Europe. Criticizing the Communist and fellow-traveling left, Arendt deplores this sentiment, insisting that U.S. assistance projects in Europe like the Marshall Plan are an important ingredient of postwar reconstruction. But she is equally critical of "certain current 'Americanistic' attitudes and ideologies in the United States."[45] Favoring a European confederation, she cautions that "Americanism" and "Europeanism" are both ideologies that oversimplify political reality and generate self-fulfilling tensions between the United States and Europe. "Europe and the Atom Bomb" continues this line of argument. Taking Europe to task for pretending "that the threat to our civilization comes to her from without, and that she herself is in danger from two outside powers, America and Russia, which are equally alien," Arendt criticizes European "anti-Americanism and neutralism." But this in no way makes her a celebrant of American power. To the contrary, she asserts, the appearance of atomic weapons means that "the whole political and moral vocabulary in which we are accustomed to discuss" war and peace has become "for all practical purposes meaningless." Atomic weapons threaten humankind and human posterity. They present a problem for civilization as a whole and implicate "the intimate connection between modern warfare and a technicalized society." There is only one viewpoint that is more sharply criticized than anti-Americanism, and that is "the conviction that it is better to be dead than to be a slave."[46] For Arendt the pressing concerns of human freedom and indeed human survival are best served by detaching them from the dualistic framework of Cold War thinking.[47]

Perhaps the clearest expression of this idea is Arendt's 1962 contribution to a *Partisan Review* exchange on the Cold War and the West. Asked by the editors to discuss whether the United States should support the forces of radical change or conservatism throughout the world, Arendt offers a critique of the Cold War itself. First, she avers that the conditions of modern warfare demonstrated in the First World War had rendered wars "politically, though not yet biologically, a matter of life and death." The destructiveness of modern conventional weaponry means that "all governments have lived on borrowed time" and that "only if we succeed in ruling out war from politics altogether, can we hope to achieve that minimum of stability and permanence without which no political life and no political change are possible."[48] Second, she maintains that awareness of the dangers of the nuclear age is foreclosed by the prevailing terms of political debate:

> To try and decide between "better dead than red" and "better red than dead" resembles nothing so much as trying to square the circle. For those who tell us better dead than red, forget that it is a very different matter to risk one's own life for the life and freedom of one's country and for posterity than to risk the very existence of the human species for the same purposes.... But this is not to say that its reversal has any more to recommend itself.... Within the framework of realities which we face, the slogan "better red than dead" can mean only the signing of one's own death sentence even before this sentence has been passed and decided upon.

Arendt maintains that no plausible answer can be decided "within the closed circle of this preposterous alternative," for within it both sides display a "reckless optimism"—"on one side, the readiness to count the losses in the tens and hundreds of millions ... on the other side, the readiness to forget the concentration—and extermination—camps and with them the terrible prospect of freedom vanishing from the earth forever."[49] Like Camus, she rejects the "cynical dialectic" that would force her to choose between hanging and the firing squad. Her remark about "the signing of one's own death sentence even before [it] has been passed and decided upon" recalls her critical comment on definitive knowledge of human nature in *The Human Condition*—that such knowledge would be like "jumping over our own shadows." Both remarks condemn a certitude of judgment that would foreclose our own agency and responsibility and would seal our doom by encouraging us to take refuge in a doctrine. Arendt prefers to stake her faith on the creativity of human beings.

She then undertakes a brief consideration of the failure of victory in World War II to lead to peace, as a consequence of which "the whole postwar period has been spent by the two major powers in defining their spheres of interest and in jockeying for position in the rapidly changing power structure of a world in turmoil." Arendt deplores this balance of mutual fright, going so far as to suggest that the bombings of Hiroshima and Nagasaki were an unnecessary precedent for and stimulus to a nuclear politics threatening the "extermination or wholesale slaughter of the civilian population."[50]

This view leads Arendt to her most important point. Anticipating *On Revolution,* she argues that the futile superpower confrontation has diverted attention from the more politically significant phenomenon of contemporary revolution. Arendt chastises both Marxism and liberalism for ignoring the "revolutionary spirit." Likening the American Bay of Pigs fiasco in Cuba to the 1956 Soviet suppression of the Hungarian uprising, Arendt criticizes the counterrevolutionary character of American foreign policy. She writes that if we understood "what it means when a poverty-stricken people in a backward country . . . is suddenly released from the obscurity of their farms and houses, permitted to show their misery and invited into the streets of the country's capital they never saw before," we would recognize that in the Third World the only alternative to Bolshevik-style revolution is republican revolution supported by a dynamic American policy of political and economic assistance.[51] For Arendt such revolutions, where ordinary citizens seize the streets and public spaces, represent moments of freedom to be prized and nurtured rather than suppressed or manipulated.

There is a short step from this argument to Arendt's criticisms of American foreign policy in *Crises of the Republic.* Published in 1972, at the height of anti–Vietnam War activism, this book presents Arendt's sharpest criticisms of American society. In "Lying in Politics," a review of *The Pentagon Papers,* she disparages the national security managers responsible for American foreign policy. Capable of calculation but possessing no common sense much less powers of judgment, these bureaucrats deceived themselves and the American public, all in the name of an unjust and unwise war in southeast Asia. Arendt also criticizes the more visionary "ideologists of the Cold War" whose "comprehensive ideology" was responsible for a situation where "sheer ignorance of all pertinent facts and deliberate neglect of postwar developments became the hallmark of established doctrine within the establishment."[52] For her, the Vietnam debacle epitomizes the lack of judgment and moderation characteristic of contemporary politics.

These themes are also sounded in "On Violence." Often read as a critique of left-wing politics, this essay offers a blistering attack on the celebration of revolutionary violence found in the writings of Jean-Paul Sartre and Frantz Fanon. Like Camus, Arendt has sympathy with revolutionaries struggling against colonial oppression. But also like him she refuses to lionize Third World revolutionaries. She is critical of Sartre's pronouncements likening national liberation movements to Marx's proletarian "universal class": "To think . . . that there is such a thing as a 'Unity of the Third World,' to which one could address the new slogan in the era of decolonization 'Natives of all underdeveloped countries unite!' (Sartre) is to repeat Marx's worst illusions on a greatly enlarged scale and with considerably less justification. The Third World is not a reality but an ideology."[53] Arendt of course would not deny that there is a Third World in the sense of a set of countries sharing certain postcolonial problems. But she does reject the effort to ideologize this reality, to offer a grand historical scheme in terms of which all postcolonial struggles make sense and all political agents can be deemed progressive or reactionary.[54] Like any grand ideology, Third Worldism grossly oversimplifies political reality, and it offers its proponents a false comfort about their own righteousness. The connection between such righteousness and an authoritarian attitude toward dissent and disagreement is not fortuitous.

But if Arendt criticizes the glorification of revolutionary violence she is equally harsh toward the deployment of violence in liberal democracies. Her essay begins by calling attention to "the obvious insanity" of nuclear deterrence and to the dangers of superpower politics in an era in which force is "the final arbiter in international affairs."[55] Citing Noam Chomsky's *American Power and the New Mandarins*, Arendt delivers a sweeping indictment of postwar American society:

> The Second World War was not followed by peace but by a cold-war and the establishment of the military-industrial-labor complex. To speak of "the priority of war-making potential as the principal structuring force in society," to maintain that "economic systems, political philosophies, and corpora juris serve and extend the war system, not vice versa," to conclude that "war itself is the basic social system, within which other secondary modes of social organization conflict or conspire"—all this sounds much more plausible than Engels' or Clausewitz's nineteenth century formulas.[56]

Arendt proceeds to defend student radicals for their courage in opposing such a system.[57] While criticizing some of the enthusiasms of the New Left, she admires the students' "sheer courage . . . astounding will to action, and . . . no less astounding confidence in the possibility of change."[58] The essays of *Crises* make clear that Arendt abhors the geopolitics of the Cold War, and that she believed that it had produced nothing less than a "constitutional crisis" of liberal politics, marginalizing dissent and closing off "all institutions that permitted the citizens' actual participation."[59]

Both Arendt and Camus criticized these disturbing effects of the Cold War on the politics of Western liberal democracies. Both saw that a more democratic politics could only thrive in a global environment less governed by mutual insecurity and fear and more hospitable to peaceful coexistence. They also saw that the dominant agencies of liberal politics—parties, trade unions, interest groups, intellectual elites—were at an impasse. Like C. Wright Mills, they believed that these agencies had been co-opted by and incorporated within a complacent consensus about the end of ideology, that they lived on more as Mannheimian ideological elements, obscuring the real situation in society, than as vital forces of a democratic politics.[60] Thus, although both celebrated the efforts of radical groups working at the margins of state-centered liberal politics, they also saw the importance and inspirational value of political conflicts at the peripheries of the superpower blocs—in Eastern Europe, northern Africa, and the Middle East.

Of particular significance to Arendt and Camus were the postcolonial conflicts in Palestine and Algeria. As a German Jew and a French-Algerian, respectively, they had deeply vested interests in the resolution of these conflicts. Both writers believed that such conflicts threatened to generate bloody civil wars and heighten international tensions. But they also believed that the peaceful settlement of such conflicts might presage a new form of confederational world politics. Here too both sought a third way between European postcolonial domination on the one hand and Third World revolutionary nationalism on the other.

Arendt's writings on Zionism and Camus's on Algeria beautifully illustrate the virtues of representative thinking. They also exemplify the profound risks attached to political commitment, as discussed in the previous chapter. Both writers experienced extraordinary pain and difficulty in their efforts to defend dialogue amidst the din of communal self-righteousness and hostile denunciation. Camus, already unnerved by the pervasive misreading of *The Rebel* as a form of liberal moralism, was traumatized by the bitter polemics that surrounded his 1950s interventions in the Algerian conflict. Condemned as a traitor by many French Algerians for his support for Arab rights, he was denounced as a hypocritical "accomplice of colonialism" by French leftists enamored with the cause of "the wretched of the earth."[61] Arendt experienced a similarly hostile response to her writings on Zionism, especially her book on Eichmann, which was met with virtually unanimous opposition among the American Jewish community, including the left-wing Jewish intellectual circles in which she traveled.[62] Both writers swam against the tide of conventional opinion in their efforts to refute simplistic attributions of innocence and guilt and to promote soul-searching within their own communities. The lack of fit between the moderation that they espoused and the dominant tendencies of contemporary politics caused them both no small degree of disconsolation, which was perhaps another source of the pervasive sense of exile that marks their works.

Camus and the Algerian Crisis

Camus's writings on Algeria have been harshly criticized for their moralism and naïveté.[63] As a French-Algerian, a *pied noir,* Camus felt caught in the middle of an explosive and savage conflict. Refusing to justify the barbarities of colonialism, he also resisted the call for Algerian national independence. This position was not without its difficulties. Nonetheless his writings on the Algerian crisis exemplify the strengths of his vision of politics—an emphasis on the relativity of justice and on the partiality, and the plurality, of political movements.

Michael Walzer has underscored these strengths in a brilliant essay on Camus's connectedness to the plight of French Algerians that rescues him from his harsh detractors.[64] It is true that for Camus this connectedness animated his deep concern for the fate of Algeria as well as his attunement to the complexities of the political conflict. Yet it is also true that Camus never felt himself to be wholly or unproblematically French or Algerian; his sense of self was too riven by ambivalence and estrangement to allow him such an unproblematic identity.[65] As a *pied noir* fully aware of this hybrid identity—part Algerian, part European—he defended a vision of coexistence informed by a universalistic conception of the human right to be free from torture, persecution, and murder, and of the political right to citizenship in autonomous political communities. In this respect my account differs from Walzer's, whose emphasis on Camus's particular attachments is not matched by attention to his universalist, humanist commitments. I think that Walzer is wrong when he writes, for example, that

"Camus would not have said . . . that French lives and Arab lives were of equal importance in his eyes. French lives, even *pied noir* lives, on the wrong side of history, meant more to him—just as Arab lives meant more to the intellectuals of the FLN."[66] As we shall see, the recurrent refrain of Camus's Algerian writings is that "we are condemned to live together" and "shall still have to go on living together forever on the same soil"[67]— the argument Camus presents in all of his writings in defense of a relative justice consistent with elementary human dignity. Certainly as a *pied noir* his own community and its culture mattered more to him than the community and culture of the Arabs. But it does not follow that French-Algerian *lives* mattered more, that he was any less pained by the suffering of Arab children than he was by the suffering of French children. It may be true that Arab lives mattered more to the Front de Libération Nationale (FLN), and that French lives mattered more to the Organisation de l'Armée Secrète (OAS), though in both cases it would be more accurate to say that *some* French and Arab lives were privileged—the lives of those who shared these groups' extreme objectives—while the rest were treated with equal contempt. But as a *pied noir* who honestly acknowledged his hybrid identity and refused to adopt a mythic, hyperinflated identity as a "true" Frenchman, Camus seemed genuinely caught in the middle; and as a writer he sought, without denying his irreducibly *pied noir* attachments, to occupy the no-man's land between the antagonists, the ground of a minimal common humanity that might support dialogue and mutual recognition.

Even his most severe critics acknowledge that Camus was a consistent and outspoken opponent of French colonialism.[68] This is clear in his earliest contributions as a journalist. His "Misere de la Kabylie," a series of eleven articles published in the *Alger-Républicain* in June 1939, documents in plain detail the suffering of Algerian Arabs, calling for land, educational, and political reforms in the name of justice for native Algerians.[69] Camus's writings during this period were influenced by the Blum-Violette Plan of 1937, an abortive attempt to effect gradual reforms of the French system of political representation so as to integrate Algerian Arabs as French citizens. Camus supported this general policy of assimilation, though his commitment to political *and* economic reform was more fervent than that of even the most enlightened metropolitan French politicians.[70]

As a writer for the *Alger-Républicain* Camus was a vocal critic of the repressiveness of the colonial regime. Challenging the persecution of Algerian nationalists, he declared that "the only way to wipe out Algerian nationalism is to eliminate the injustices that gave birth to it."[71] This text

encapsulates Camus's prewar position on Algeria, which sought to eliminate injustice and in so doing to undermine the force of Arab nationalism,
making some kind of coexistence between French and Arab possible. Camus continued this line of argument toward the war's end. One of the
first issues raised by *Combat* after the liberation was that of the French
empire. On 13 October 1944 Camus called for the granting of political
rights to indigenous peoples of French colonies, who had fought and died
as supporters of French democracy. In this editorial Camus acknowledged
the reactionary attitudes and widespread support for Vichy among the
colons and suggested that it was necessary to "reason away or reduce" their
resistance to reform. He insisted that any effort to retain the colonies
through force was doomed to failure: "No policy could be more blind.
We shall find no real support in the colonies until the moment we have
convinced them that their interests are ours and that we do not have two
policies: one that would give justice to the people of France and another
than would condone injustice with regard to the empire."[72]

In a subsequent editorial Camus chastised the French government for
failing to heed Arab demands for French political rights: "We had the
spectacle of an occupied nation (let us not indulge in idealism) dispossessed
of its territory, finally accepting the civilization of the conqueror and asking
to be completely integrated into it."[73] Though Camus still sought to make
real the French rhetoric about assimilation, he clearly refused any senti-
mentalizing of the colonial relationship. In recognizing the distinctive
concerns of French and Arab communities, and in advancing the cause of
coexistence between them, he vocally opposed a policy of continued political domination.

In March 1945 Arab nationalists demonstrated in Sétif, raising the
Algerian flag, and in the course of riots a number of European Algerians
were killed. The conservative French press responded by demanding immediate and uncompromising reprisals against Algerian nationalists, abetting a surge of *colon* violence that razed villages and took thousands of
Arab lives. In response Camus produced a six-part series in *Combat*, "Crise
en Algérie," ascribing the source of Arab radicalism to the failure of French
policies. Arab nationalism, Camus argued, was an authentic response to
these failures. French violence could only exacerbate an already unbearable
situation for the Arabs. The only appropriate response to Arab militancy
was political and economic reform that would incorporate Algerian Arabs
as citizens of France, organize genuine forms of local self-government,
and aid in the economic development of Algerian agriculture.[74]

By 1954 full-scale civil war had broken out in Algeria. The newly formed

Arab nationalist organization Front de Libération Nationale emphatically rejected any kind of reform, calling for the "restoration of the Algerian state, sovereign, democratic, and social, in the framework of Islamic principles."[75] An escalating cycle of violence and reprisals ensued, severely testing Camus's vision of assimilation. In response to this crisis Camus further developed his perspective on Algeria. Critical of both French colonialism and Arab nationalism, Camus believed the only responsible position was to seek "to disintoxicate minds and to calm fanaticisms." As he put it, social conflicts, if they cannot be eliminated, need at least to be "justified and elucidated" by humane values.[76]

This view is best summed up in Camus's 1958 preface to *Actuelles III,* the collection of his essays on the Algerian situation. He begins by stating that he opposes equally a continued policy of French colonial oppression and a policy of Algerian independence. But confronted with the ineffectiveness of a more moderate alternative, he has decided "to take no further part in the constant polemics that have had no result other than to harden the uncompromising points of view at loggerheads in Algeria and to split even wider a France already poisoned by hatreds and sects."[77] Lacking "the assurance that allows one to settle everything," Camus announces his disaffection from the prevailing political agencies and ideologies and his revulsion at the intransigence of French imperialists and Arab nationalists. Against the FLN and such left-wing French supporters as Sartre and Jeanson, Camus notes that Arab nationalist ends, and the terrorist means employed by the FLN to advance them, threaten French-Algerians, including his own family. "A reign of terror," he suggests, "changes the scale of values." Not denying the need for French justice for Arabs, Camus also announces his "natural solidarity" with the *pied noir* community and his hope "that it will survive at least and, by surviving, have a chance to show its fairness. If that is not honor and true justice, then I know of nothing that is of any use in this world."[78] Camus contends that is intellectually disingenuous and politically dangerous to claim to speak for national liberation and deny the rights of an entire community. Refusing to ideologize the conflict, he rejects essentialist claims about either nation, asserting the heterogeneity of both groups and the moral complexity of their antagonism. Echoing the arguments of *The Rebel,* he also refuses to identify the noble rebellious impulses of Algerian Arabs with the organization and tactics of the FLN.

Camus maintains that it is only from such a position that "we have the right and the duty" to criticize the injustice and the repression that the French have perpetrated against the Arabs. Camus is unambiguous here.

Terrorism and torture against Arabs is ethically unjustifiable and practically counterproductive, and censorship seeking to hide such repression is equally despicable: "The government's duty is not to suppress protests, even interested protests, against the criminal excesses of repression. Its duty is rather to suppress the excesses and to condemn them publicly."[79] But, he continues, "to be both useful and equitable, we must condemn with equal force and in no uncertain terms the terrorism applied by the FLN to French civilians and indeed, to an even greater degree, to Arab civilians." Camus insists that an awareness of injustices against Arabs in no way entails "a systematic indulgence toward those who indiscriminately slaughter Arab and French civilians without regard for age or sex." Citing the "just assassins" of 1905, and the more recent example of Gandhi, Camus holds that such slaughter debases the cause of Arab justice at the same time as it inflicts grievous harm on innocents.[80]

Just as Camus had refused the polarities of the Cold War, so too he refuses the polarities of French and Arab intransigence and mutual denial. Both extremes, he declares, must be condemned, and at the same time: "I have never failed to state . . . that these two condemnations could not be separated if we wanted to be effective." The failure of the protagonists to see this linkage is dangerous and irresponsible: "To justify himself, each relies on the other's crime. But that is a casuistry of blood, and it strikes me that an intellectual cannot become involved in it. . . . When violence answers violence in a growing frenzy that makes the simple language of reason impossible, the role of the intellectuals cannot be, as we read every day, to excuse from a distance one of the violences and condemn the other . . . [but] to strive for pacification so that reason will again have a chance.[81] Camus repudiates the intellectual and moral inflation of legitimate grievances into righteous and bitter accusations of original sin.[82] The question "is not how to die separately but how to live together." What he calls for above all else is some minimal mutual recognition among the combatants, a reciprocal acknowledgment of the authenticity, if not the legitimacy, of the claims of the other. This requires the French to "cease looking upon the mass of Arabs in Algeria as a nation of butchers" and requires the Arabs to "cease condemning the French in Algeria as a group." Both sides must abandon some of the worst stereotypes of the other and seek common ground.[83]

In issuing this call, Camus in no way ignores the depth of the hostilities or the authenticity of the competing claims and anxieties. He explicitly acknowledges the profound injustices of colonialism. But he also insists that nothing is to be gained, and much is to be lost, by considering all

French-Algerians to be colonizers pure and simple, tainted by an "original sin" and responsible for all of the problems of present-day Algeria: "I believe in a policy of reparation in Algeria rather than a policy of expiation. Problems must be seen in relation to the future, without endlessly going back over the errors of the past. And there will be no future that does not do justice at one and the same time to the two communities of Algeria."[84]

A policy of expiation presumes a Manichean account of contemporary history; it confidently identifies one side, whether Arab or French, with righteousness and the other with evil. It celebrates one side, seeks atonement from the other. It extends current animosities backward into the past, seeking from history a mythic account of a golden age of pastoral harmony or pioneer virtue that was disturbed by the other, and forward into the future, anticipating a day of reckoning in which all injustice and all antagonism will be eliminated. For Camus such an approach grossly oversimplifies political reality and is a recipe for continued resentment and reprisal. Both communities must disavow any nostalgia or myth of innocence; both must recognize their "reasonable culpability" (*The Rebel*) and act accordingly. Only by doing so, by acknowledging the claims of the other, can they secure any peace or justice for themselves.

Camus allows that "such a spirit of equity . . . seems alien to the reality of our history," in which, especially in the international arena, force usually holds sway. But he insists that such a spirit is necessary nonetheless. To that end he calls for "pacification" but not, contrary to his critics, a naive pacifism that remains nobly above the messy conflict. He writes:

> If it is true that in history . . . values do not survive unless they have been fought for, the fight alone is not enough to justify them. The fight itself must rather be justified, and elucidated, by those values. When fighting for your truth, you must take care not to kill it with the very arms you are using to defend it. . . . Knowing that, the intellectual has the role of distinguishing in each camp the respective limits of force and justice. That role is to clarify definitions in order to disintoxicate minds and to calm fanaticisms, even when this is against the current tendency.[85]

Camus argues that all justice is relative and all revolt must recognize a limit in itself. The identity of the *pied noir* community cannot be advanced by terrorizing Arabs and demanding fanatical commitment to a reactionary vision of a French Algeria as the price of admission into the community. And the identity of the Arab community cannot be advanced by antagonizing the French and terrorizing those civilians, Arab and French, who happen to stand in the way of a particular conception of revolutionary struggle. Camus observes that the cry for total justice shades off into a demand for injustice. It threatens to perpetuate a situation in which both sides suffer and neither achieves what it wants, much less what it needs. "The question," he writes, "is not how to die separately but rather how to live together."

In pressing that question Camus takes a resolutely pragmatic approach. His own view of the practical steps necessary to reach an answer can be traced in the essays on Algeria that he selected for inclusion in *Resistance, Rebellion, and Death*. In his 1955 "Letter to an Algerian Militant" Camus tells Aziz Kessous, an Arab socialist active in Algerian nationalist politics, that honest intellectuals must reconcile themselves to "taking one's stand in the no man's land between two armies and preaching amid the bullets that war is a deception and that bloodshed, if it sometimes makes history progress, makes it progress toward even greater barbarism and misery." Camus's suggestion here is neither naive nor optimistic. He does not imagine an easy peace, nor even any substantive consensus between the French and Arab communities. All that he endorses is "to leave room, however limited it may be, for the exchange of views that is still possible." The first step, then, is for French and Arab intellectuals to "put a stop to the attempt at outbidding each other." French and Arab intellectuals must criticize the absolutist claims on their respective sides.[86]

In his 1956 "Appeal for a Civilian Truce in Algeria," originally presented as a lecture to a mixed audience in Algiers, Camus outlines further measures, calling for a cessation of terrorism on both sides. More interesting than the substance of this call is the way in which it is articulated. Camus begins by protesting that "we don't want to get you to agree to anything politically. If we wanted to raise the problem on a political basis, we should run the risk of not getting the agreement that we need."[87] But as he proceeds it becomes clear that, true to form, it is not really politics that he abjures but the dominant political agencies and ideologies operative in the conflict. He wishes to avoid, at least initially, the more complicated programmatic positions that seem to have hardened into the unconditional demands of the two sides. What he seeks is a basis of agreement between Arabs and French that can be mutually and publicly recognized and that might lead to a more comprehensive political solution. Camus goes on to suggest that such a starting point may be "our love of our common soil, and our anguish." He hopes that from this point the opposing sides might come to see that "no cause justifies the deaths of the innocent."[88] Camus does not call for an immediate end to hostilities or even a cease-fire. Nor does he condemn those, particularly Arabs, who have taken up arms in order to advance their claims for justice. Rather he calls for a civilian truce, for a recognition that killing noncombatants is unacceptable. Such a truce would save human lives. It might also "prepare a climate more favorable to a discussion that will at last be reasonable." By beginning in a modest way, through some minimal agreement, it might be possible to take bolder, broader steps toward peace. Camus's remarks here indicate how he thought a realistic, humane politics might be constituted. He suggests that "if each individual, Arab or French, made an effort to think over his adversary's motives, at least the basis of a fruitful discussion would be clear." Repudiating any politics based on attributions of evil intent, he calls instead for a form of representative thinking, for a consideration of the perspective of the other. This does not mean that Camus saw such thinking as a means of eliminating differences. On the contrary, representative thinking presupposes those differences and seeks to reconcile them. The French and the Arabs can live together only "if they will take a few steps toward each other in an open confrontation. Then our differences ought to help us instead of dividing us. As for me, here as in every domain, I believe only in differences and not in uniformity."[89]

Camus calls for a concerted effort to give up the rancor and mistrust and seek to create a "climate for a healthy discussion that would not be spoiled by ridiculously uncompromising attitudes." In such a climate the grievances and concerns of the antagonistic communities would still exist. But instead of these being expressed through violent confrontation, "the various policies would have a hearing and each individual would again have the right to defend his own convictions and explain his difference."[90] Camus maintains that only if these differences can be explained is it possible to avoid carnage and mutual ruin.

This call—to stop acting out of anger and to start acting like civilized human beings, may seem quite unexceptional, a plea for simple human decency. And yet amid the din of self-righteous denunciations on both sides of the conflict, it was a brave initiative.[91] It fell, however, on deaf ears. Camus's appeal for a civilian truce was not heeded. Indeed his 1956 trip to Algeria was a disappointing failure, culminating in his being shouted down while making his appeal. As a consequence he fell silent on Algeria until 1958, when he wrote his last published essay, "Algeria 1958."[92] Its tone reflects both Camus's personal despair and the increasingly polarized and desperate state of affairs in Algeria. By that time any illusions about the possibility of French assimilation of the Algerian Arabs had been dashed. Camus is not so naive as to talk of assimilation. But while he acknowledges that "colonialism and its abuses" must be decisively repudiated, he adamantly opposes the FLN's call for national independence. He offers three reasons, all of which have a certain defensive and hollow ring. The first is that "there has never yet been an Algerian nation," that the Jews, Turks, Greeks, Italians, and Berbers "would have just as much right to claim the direction of that virtual nation" as would the Arabs. "At present the Arabs do not alone make up all of Algeria. The size and seniority of the French settlement," he asserts, "are enough to create a problem that cannot be compared to anything in history." The second reason is that "a purely Arab Algeria could not achieve the economic independence without which political independence is but a deception." The third reason is that Algerian nationalism is abetted by "the new Arab imperialism" of Gamal Abdel Nasser, which itself was manipulated by the Soviet Union to foment trouble in Africa and the Middle East so as "to encircle Europe on the south."[93]

There is an almost hysterical quality to these claims that is especially glaring in contrast to Camus's other writings on Algeria. The first claim is disingenuous, for in 1958 the Arabs made up more than 80 percent of the Algerian population. Camus himself, in his earlier writings, referred to the "Arab nation" in Algeria and to the "Algerian nation." The second claim is deceptive because it inexplicably implies that Algerian independence is inconsistent with programs of European and American foreign aid and economic development. And the third claim, whatever grains of truth it contains, almost rips the Algerian conflict out of its real historical context by interpreting it in Cold War terms. The Camusian words of Jules Roy, Camus's fellow *pied noir* and good friend, are a cogent rebuttal: "Why talk about the West when it is a question of the people I love? I proceed by instinct to the sea, like the rivers, and if my brother is attacked there is no need to invoke the West for me to go to his defense. Capital letters alarm me when it is a matter of expressing truths so brutal. Here in Algeria we do not receive someone in the name of human liberties. We say to him: 'Come in. Sit down.' And we do not fight in the name of the West."[94] It is ironic that in this last essay on Algeria Camus, who often wrote of the Mediterranean sky as an antidote to the "cold abstractions" of Europe, is almost overcome by European geopolitical abstractions. Roy's more balanced *The War in Algeria*, presented by its author as the position toward which Camus would probably have moved had he lived, is in this respect a much more compelling account.

Yet there remains a more generous reading of "Algeria 1958." Beyond the abstractions Camus is motivated by three real concerns. One was the fate of the French-Algerian community. Whatever its minority status, for

Camus it was an organic part of Algeria with rightful claims. Camus refused to believe that *pied noir* farmers and shopkeepers whose families had lived in Algeria for generations should have their political and economic rights curtailed, and their very existence jeopardized, by an Arab nationalist state. The second was the future of an Arab Algeria governed by the leadership produced by the FLN, which was likely to enact repressive policies and pursue economically unviable ones. Camus was convinced that an organization so inclined toward terrorism, and so intoxicated by its own violent strategies, had already demonstrated in practice its lack of democratic commitments. A state controlled by such an organization would hardly bring justice to the Arabs. The third was the unattractiveness of Nasserite pan-Arabism and Third World "neutralism" more generally, which for Camus was a pro-Soviet and undemocratic force in the world arena.[95] The subsequent historical record bears Camus out on much of this. Algerian independence did lead to the wholesale departure of the *pied noir* community from Algeria and the construction of an authoritarian Arab regime. And Third World nonaligned nations, though they have not abetted the "encirclement" of the West, have often been profoundly and cynically undemocratic in their domestic and foreign policies. The Algerian revolution, like the later revolution in Vietnam, may have offered liberation from colonial imperialism; but it can hardly be said to have offered succor to those seriously committed to democratic principles. It is in the light of these considerations that Camus's opposition to Algerian independence needs to be seen. Camus's call for a "New Algeria" might have been out of tune with the politics of its time, but in many ways it is a compelling plea.

Camus argues that the only regime that would do justice to all parts of the population would be "a federation based on institutions similar to those of the Swiss confederation, which make it possible for different nationalities to live in peace." Because the territories of the French and Arab populations overlap, "it is essential to associate without fusing together (since federation is to begin with the union of differences), not different territories, but communities with different personalities." Camus endorses the Lauriol Plan, "a regime of free association in which every Arab . . . will truly find the privileges of a free citizen."[96]

The Lauriol Plan envisioned a two-stage process of incorporating Algeria into the French republic. The first, transitional stage would involve the creation of a bicameral French parliament with a metropolitan section (representing all French of European descent, including the *pieds noirs*) and an Arab section. All exclusively metropolitan concerns would fall under the first section, all exclusively Arab concerns the second, and matters of common concern—taxation, budget, defense—would be decided by the two sections in concert. The second stage, "after the trial period necessary to a general reconciliation," would involve "the birth of a French federal structure that will create a true French Commonwealth." Here the structure of governmental authority would ascend from an Algerian regional assembly concerned with Algerian matters and incorporating all Algerians as citizens, to a unicameral federal Senate charged with managing the common affairs of the Commonwealth and electing a federal government. Camus comments on this plan that "contrary above all to the deep-rooted prejudices of the French Revolution, we should thus have sanctioned within the republic two equal but distinct categories of citizens. From one point of view, this would mark a sort of revolution against the regime of centralization and abstract individualism resulting from 1789, which, in so many ways, now deserves to be called '*Ancien Régime.*' "[97]

For Camus not only might this arrangement make justice possible in Algeria; it also prefigures "the European institutions that might come into existence in the future."[98] The Lauriol Plan's repudiation of the principle of unitary sovereignty, and its acknowledgment of multiple layers of genuine authority and political membership resonates with the localism and anarchism that was at the heart of Camus's political vision. Yet given the balance of forces in Algeria, France, and the world, the kind of creative, conciliatory politics of peace and justice envisioned by Camus had little chance of political success. The Lauriol Plan was doomed to failure by the furious pace of events. The national antagonisms were too great, the accumulated historical grievances and mistrust too powerful, and the political and moral resources of the French state too limited to realize such a confederal vision.

In this respect Camus's position was quixotic, pleading for morality at a time when war was the spirit of the day. Edward Said has argued that Camus's refusal of Arab nationalist claims was rooted in a Eurocentric perspective that is most clearly expressed in his fictional narratives, which "are connected to, and derive advantages from, earlier and more overtly imperial French narratives of Algeria."[99] Said, like Conor Cruise O'Brien, maintains that in Camus's fiction the Arab is the "other"—strange, often silent, always the object and never the subject of the story. The result of these deeply rooted stereotypes is that Camus was unable to see the Arab as a historical subject, unable to appreciate the force of Arab political claims. As Sprintzen puts it, although Camus was moved by the suffering of the Arabs and championed Arab rights long before it became fashionable among the French, "he could never sanction *their* demands for self-determination or for independence."[100]

There is much truth in this argument. Camus did think of Arabs as "they," as the other, and he thought of the *pied noir* community as "we," namely, a group that included himself. There can be no doubt that this identification imposed limits on his understanding of Arab experience and Arab political demands, just as there can be no doubt that as the conflict became more bitter it led him to oppose Algerian independence all the more strenuously. Yet it is hard to see this as an indictment of him. For he *was* a *pied noir* and not an Arab, and it is to be expected that his view of the Arabs would be colored by his own experience as a French-Algerian. In this light what is most remarkable is the extent to which he *was* able to recognize Arab demands for human rights and self-determination, though not for independence.

His refusal to accept Algerian independence may have been unrealistic given the uncompromising nationalism of the leading Arab forces. But his reasons for doing so were important and indeed compelling. The first was his idea that justice is relative and that political judgment requires representative thinking. He could recognize the claims of the Arabs, but never their absolute claims. Insofar as the demand for independence was a negation of the claims of the *pied noir* community, an attribution of objective, historical guilt to this community, it was a demand that Camus could not accept. This was especially so because he was a *pied noir;* to accept this would have meant accepting the negation of his own communal identity. But what is most meritorious about Camus's position is how far he was willing to go, not just in 1958 but in 1938, to recognize Arab claims. In spite of the undeniable limitations of his understanding of the Arabs, he was willing and able to be self-critical of, if not rise above, his *pied noir* identity, and to seek common ground with those who were his cultural others and yet at the same time his human brothers: "The road to human society passes through national society. National society can be preserved only by opening it up to a universal perspective."[101] But such a universal perspective cannot be premised on the privileging of certain nations at the expense of those deemed anachronistic, European, or otherwise essentially culpable and dispensable. Again we return to *The Rebel:* the problem is whether rebellion must result in mutual denunciation and oppression or whether, on the contrary, "without laying claim to an innocence that is impossible, it can discover the principle of reasonable culpability."[102] Many of Camus's critics have laid claim to such an impossible innocence; what they have demanded of him is that he think like an Arab instead of a French-Algerian, and that he denounce the *pied noir* community *tout court* and affirm the historical justice of the Arab nationalist cause in spite of the injustices it might institute.

The second reason for Camus's refusal of independence was his opposition to the principle of national sovereignty itself. Those who criticize Camus's position usually fail to acknowledge that what he supported was not a French empire but a French commonwealth or federation that granted genuine autonomy to the Arab community. And his opposition to national sovereignty cannot be attributed to his "narrow" *pied noir* commitments because this was a consistent refrain in his writings since the 1930s. It was not just the Arab that Camus expected to settle for less than absolute sovereignty; he expected the same of the Russians, the Germans, the British, and the French themselves, all in the name of a "veritable international society." At the heart of Camus's writings on Algeria lay the idea that linguistic, ethnic, and communal differences of the sort that plagued Algeria were endemic to human society and particularly explosive in the postcolonial world. Such differences, he believed, could either be the foundation of a healthy cultural pluralism or the source of great hostility and misery. A conciliatory, confederal settlement in Algeria, he believed, might indicate that "the future will have a meaning for the French, the Arabs, and the whole world."[103] Events proved that such a meaningful future was not to be.

Arendt on Zionism and Palestine

For Arendt, the demise of colonialism was not only a monumental fact of world politics but also a reality that profoundly challenged the ethical and political resources of her people. Raised as an assimilated German Jew, her sense of Jewish identity was heightened by the rise of Nazism and the Holocaust.[104] She saw that the postwar world offered opportunities for Jewish reconstruction at the same time as it posed great dangers. Arendt believed that in the wake of the Holocaust and the hundreds of thousands of Jewish refugees it produced, the resettlement of Jewish refugees was an urgent imperative. Thus the Zionist vision of a Jewish homeland in Palestine was more compelling than ever. But she was also highly critical of aspects of this vision. She deplored the prevalence of all-or-nothing thinking among Arabs *and* Jews in Palestine, asserting that antagonisms between Arabs and Jews could be resolved only by mutual recognition and coexistence, not by negating the identity or rights of one of the parties or seeking to transcend the antagonisms through a watery and abstract universalism. Consistent with the arguments of her more theoretical works, Arendt held that only such a policy of mutual recognition is consistent with the plurality of communities in the Middle East and with the need for worldly security experienced by all its inhabitants.

Arendt was well aware that such a policy threatened nationalistic myths on both sides. But as a Jew she was particularly disturbed by those Jewish myths that inhibited peaceful coexistence with the Arabs of Palestine. Perhaps the most powerful myth against which she revolted was the view that throughout history the Jews, in contrast to all other nations, "were not history-makers but history-sufferers, preserving a kind of eternal identity of goodness whose monotony was disturbed only by the equally monotonous chronicle of persecutions and pogroms."[105] Arendt believed that this view removed the problems of Jewish identity and suffering from history altogether, essentializing Jewish victimhood and denying "the Jewish part of responsibility for existing conditions." As she continues, such a view "not only cuts off Jewish history from European history and even from the rest of mankind; it ignores the role that European Jewry played in the construction and functioning of the national state; and thus it is reduced to the assumption, as arbitrary as it is absurd, that every Gentile living with Jews must become a conscious or subconscious Jew-hater."[106] Such an attitude produces political cynicism and undermines the possibility of envisioning historical solutions; and in so doing it encourages political irresponsibility.

In a remarkable 1946 essay, "The Moral of History," Arendt explicitly addressed this naïveté, which has rendered many Jews "unable to distinguish between friend and enemy, between compliment and insult." Maintaining that "the vitality of a nation . . . is measured in terms of the living remembrance of its history," she underlines the need to reappropriate Jewish history.[107] We are confronted, she says (paraphrasing Marx), with two choices. One possibility is that the dead weight of the past, and our unwitting decisions, can play havoc with us, so much "does unreason begin to function automatically when reason has abdicated to it." This is in fact one way of explaining the history that culminated in the destruction of European Jewry and the decimation of European civilization, a history wherein the "automatism of events" and the absence of any historical perspective acquitted its agents of responsibility and where "the terrible and bloody annihilation of individual Jews was preceded by the bloodless destruction of the Jewish people." Another possibility is that reason might take charge and Jews might begin to understand their past critically and to use such an understanding to create a better future. Such a path requires a willingness to assume political responsibility for one's condition, for "the moral of the history of the nineteenth century is the fact that men who were not ready to assume a responsible role in public affairs in the end were turned into mere beasts who could be used for anything before being led to the slaughter."[108] This responsibility, insists Arendt, is not unique to the Jewish people; nor is it absolved by the undeniable fact that they have historically been subjected to horrible persecution. Jews are, she says, "one group of people among other groups, all of which are involved in the business of this world . . . [who do] not simply cease to be coresponsible because . . . [they] became the victim of the world's injustice and cruelty."[109]

For Arendt the tragedy of Zionism is that it promised to represent a historical engagement with the world and yet failed to fulfill that promise. This tragic failure is epitomized for her by the career of Theodor Herzl, whose "lasting greatness lay in his very desire to do something about the Jewish question, his desire to act and to solve the problem in political terms," yet whose Zionism was fatally flawed from its inception. Crystallizing in the late nineteenth century as a response to anti-Semitic pogroms in Russia and Eastern Europe and the Dreyfus affair in France, Zionism was at once deeply political and sublimely antipolitical. It was political in its determination to solve the problem of anti-Semitism by establishing a Jewish state, and it pursued that end through organizational, diplomatic, economic, and ultimately military means. "The Zionist will to action, to come to grips with reality," was its greatest asset.[110] In this regard Arendt considered it infinitely superior to the "spurious doctrine . . . of assimilation," which would have the Jews abandon all their distinctive ethical and cultural characteristics in exchange for social acceptance and economic advancement. While assimilationists encouraged a parvenu strategy of social climbing, Zionists saw that Jews required a political solution to their problems, one based on national identity and collective action.[111]

And yet the rebellious political impulse of Zionism was undermined by the blindness of its nationalistic ideology. In this sense Arendt considered Zionism antipolitical. First, it was premised on a vision of history according to which anti-Semitism is the eternal and unchanging reality confronting the Jewish people, to be alleviated only by a flight from the Gentile world and the creation of a "new Zionist man" on virgin soil. This view, Arendt argues ironically, is derived from one of the worst features of German nationalism, the conception of the nation as an unchanging biological organism in a hostile world. It is also escapist because it supposes that there is a single solution to Jewish suffering, requiring a transcendence of the Diaspora and a reunification of the Jewish people in a new land of their own. Arendt declares that "the simple truth is that Jews will have to fight anti-Semitism everywhere or else be exterminated everywhere." Her point here is partly a narrowly pragmatic one, that Jewish suffering has many sources and sites and should be contested in all of its forms. Insofar as Jews make the creation of a state, with a territorially defined sovereignty, their focal preoccupation, they are liable to forget about what goes on elsewhere. But this point goes to a deeper issue as well, one that she continually returns to in her writings—the problematics of identity. Arendt is appalled by the idea that the condition of marginality and homelessness long imposed on the Jews should be turned into an injunction to flee, even if this injunction promises a safe haven. In part, I think, Arendt is troubled by the notion that the pluralism of the Diaspora should be surpassed. But she is also clearly disturbed by the suggestion that any state, through a policy of inclusion and exclusion, can definitively solve the problem of communal identity. In her view such a vision poses the problem much too simplistically.

She thus argues that Zionist ideology underwrote a strategy of "crackpot" realism, a "classic example of a policy hard-boiled enough to seem 'realistic,' but in reality completely utopian because it failed to take into account either one's own or the other party's relative strength." In Herzl's' weltanschauung "any segment of reality that could not be defined by anti-Semitism was not taken into account and any group that could not be definitely classed as anti-Semitic was not taken seriously as a political force."[112] Arendt believed that such dualistic thinking, in which everyone is either with us or against us, typifies ideological nationalism in its blindness to the pluralism of political identities. Such an outlook quite naturally justifies a strategy of political opportunism, as is manifest in Herzl's negotiations with the Ottoman and British empires and in the desperate dealings of some Zionist Revisionists with the Nazis in the early 1930s in order to facilitate the "transfer" and "emigration" of Jews to Palestine.[113] Arendt argues that instead of understanding Jewish problems in terms of imperialism, racism, and the crisis of European civilization as a whole, many Zionists have tended cynically to identify with imperialism as the agency through which Jewish problems can be solved.[114]

Arendt believes it tragic that political Zionism tends to make the establishment of a sovereign state the be-all and end-all of Jewish politics. Arendt argues that at the turn of the century "there was nothing absurd or wrong in a demand made by Jews for the same kind of emancipation and freedom" that had been attained by other oppressed European nationalities. It could not have been foreseen, she concedes, "that the whole structure of sovereign national states, great and small, would crumble within another fifty years under imperialist expansion and in the face of the new power situation." Yet she continues that Herzl's demand for a state "has been made utopian only by more recent Zionist policy—which did not ask for a state at a time when it might have been granted by everybody, but asked for one only when the whole concept of national sovereignty had become a mockery."[115] The Jewish quest for national statehood in the Middle East, then, could have no other consequence than the intrication of the Jewish people in the deepest entanglements of imperialist power politics, the identification of the Jews with the big powers, and, at best, a Balkanization of the region quite like that which caused the first two world wars.

Such an outlook is invidiously antipolitical in its blithe refusal to recognize the reality of the Arab population in Palestine. The vision of uniting "a land without a people with a people without a land" was, Arendt saw, a potent but dangerous myth fated to engender and exacerbate hostilities between Jews and Arabs, two peoples who had both suffered from imperialism. On the one hand it involved an almost Promethean quest to constitute a new Zionist man and a new Zionist polity virtually ex nihilo. In this respect Zionist ideology differed little from the equally grandiose design of Marxism, which similarly heralds the dawn of a new historical epoch, an end of history. On the other hand Zionism arrogantly ignored the recalcitrance of the world to its political aspirations, especially the resistance of the Arab inhabitants of Palestine, who were equally possessed of identity and subjectivity.

Arendt's critique of Zionism is unremitting, but not without appreciation for the historical context of Zionism and the genuine aspirations to which it gave expression. She thus pleads that "those who are dismayed at the spectacle of a national movement" whose idealism exhibited so little solidarity with other peoples equally aggrieved by imperialism "should in fairness consider how exceptionally difficult the conditions were for the Jews who, in contrast to other peoples, did not even possess the territory from which to start their fight for freedom."[116] Yet although Arendt never failed to note the challenging circumstances under which the Jews have operated, she consistently endorsed a strategic alternative to Herzelian Zionism, "to organize the Jewish people in order to negotiate on the basis of a great revolutionary movement. This would have meant an alliance with all progressive forces in Europe; it would certainly have involved great risks."[117] This outlook was embodied for Arendt in the career of

Bernard Lazare, the radical French Zionist and Dreyfusard, a contemporary of Herzl who sought to combat anti-Semitism (and injustice more generally) through a democratic alliance of oppressed nationalities and classes. Arendt characteristically offers little discussion of the plausibility of such a strategy, which serves mainly as a contrast to indicate how responsible agents might have arrested the movement toward world war through radical political activity in Central Europe.

Arendt was well aware, however, of the "break in tradition" caused by World War II and the Holocaust, which forced the Jewish people to confront unprecedented horrors and dramatically transformed Jewish consciousness. This awareness motivated her trenchant essay, "Zionism Reconsidered." The piece was written in October 1944, in the wake of the 1942 Biltmore program and the 1944 annual convention of the World Zionist Organization, which had affirmed that the creation of a Jewish state in Palestine would be the focal preoccupation of world Zionism. Arendt observes that "the Revisionist program, so long bitterly repudiated, has proved finally victorious." She views the convention's demand for a "free and democratic Jewish commonwealth . . . [which] shall embrace the whole of Palestine, undivided and undiminished," and its complete silence on the question of Arab rights, with foreboding. But she places these in the context of "the pressure of many injustices in Palestine and the terrible catastrophes in Europe," referring to the Holocaust as "the earthquake that has shaken the world in our time."[118]

Arendt notes that although the terroristic tactics of the revisionist Irgun and the Stern Gang are considered extreme, "the significant development lies in the unanimous adherence of all Zionist parties to the ultimate aim, the very discussion of which was still tabooed during the 1930s." Such unanimity, Arendt noted, is "an ominous phenomenon . . . [because] mass uniformity is not the result of agreement, but an expression of fanaticism and hysteria . . . [which] spreads like an infection into every related issue.[119] Arendt saw such unbreachable agreement on the necessity of Jewish statehood as profoundly at odds with the pluralistic character of politics and the creative powers of human initiative. It suppressed dissent and loyal opposition within the Jewish community. And it also placed Zionism on a collision course with political reality, establishing an agenda that could only be achieved at the behest of the imperial power of Great Britain and at the expense of the Arab people:

> Nationalism is bad enough when it trusts in nothing but the rude force of the nation. A nationalism that necessarily and admittedly depends upon the force

of a foreign nation is certainly worse. This is the threatened fate of Jewish nationalism and of the proposed Jewish State, surrounded inevitably by Arab states and Arab peoples. Even a Jewish majority in Palestine—nay, even a transfer of all Palestine Arabs, which is openly demanded by Revisionists— would not substantially change a situation in which Jews must either ask protection from an outside power against their neighbors or effect a working agreement with their neighbors.

She continues that a Jewish homeland can only be established "on the basis of a broad understanding that takes into account the whole region and the needs of all its peoples." Presenting representative thinking as the only alternative to the ideologization of the conflict, she warns that if Zionists ignore the realities of the Middle East they will become perceived as the tools and agents of foreign and hostile interests, and that "Jews who know their own history should be aware that such a state of affairs will inevitably lead to a new wave of Jew-hatred."[120]

This analysis is remarkably prescient. Arendt argues that the policy of sovereign statehood will engender Arab hostility and turn the prospective Jewish homeland into a beggar state dependent for its survival on foreign arms and the charity of Diaspora Jews. It will produce, she says, an elitist politics based upon the privileged position of fund-raising organizations, and a military mind-set incompatible with democratic politics. Her critique strikes an unmistakably Machiavellian note: "The erection of a Jewish state within an imperial sphere of interest may look like a very nice solution to some Zionists. . . . [but] in the long run, there is hardly any course imaginable that would be more dangerous, more in the style of an adventure . . . only folly could dictate a policy which trusts a distant imperial power for protection, while alienating the good will of neighbors."[121]

Like Camus she recognizes that the major European states can play a constructive role by encouraging "a broad understanding that takes into account the whole region and the needs of all of its peoples." But ultimately it is the Jewish and Arab peoples themselves that must work out an accommodation: "Either a bi-national Palestine state or a Jewish Commonwealth might conceivably have been the outcome of a working agreement with Arabs and other Mediterranean peoples. But to think that by putting the cart before the horse one can solve genuine conflicts between peoples is a fantastic assumption."[122] And, she insists, whatever modus vivendi is worked out between the parties, the only feasible political form of existence would be some form of federation that avoids the dangers of extreme centralization, tolerates national and religious differences, and provides a unifying framework for coexistence in place of the system of competitive nation-states characteristic of the age of imperialism.

Events only confirmed Arendt's sense of foreboding. "To Save the Jewish Homeland: There Is Still Time," written for the American Jewish Committee in May 1948, on the eve of the declaration of the State of Israel, documents the tumultuous events that eventually led to war, a situation where "not a single solution or proposition affecting the conflict is in sight that could be realized without enforcement by external authority."[123] Arendt notes the destructiveness brought on by Arab-Jewish guerrilla warfare. The Arab decision to evacuate whole cities and towns "declares more effectively than all proclamations the Arab refusal of any compromise." The Jewish community, in Palestine and the United States, is equally intransigent, having settled into a cynical consensus that

> the moment has now come to get everything or nothing, victory or death; Arab and Jewish claims are irreconcilable . . . the Arabs—all Arabs—are our enemies . . . only philistines believe in justice, and only *schlemiels* prefer truth and negotiation to propaganda and machine guns; Jewish experience in the last decades . . . has finally awakened us and taught us to look out for ourselves . . . we are ready to go down fighting, and we will consider anybody who stands in our way a traitor and anything done to hinder us a stab in the back.[124]

Arendt is aware of the roots of such a Jewish consensus. It would be foolish, she maintains, to deny the connection between it and the catastrophic suffering and displacement caused by the Holocaust as well as the callous indifference of most of the world to that suffering. The great danger of this situation is precisely "the semblance to common sense" that recent experience has lent to such cynical views. But for her it is because of the genuine importance of a Jewish homeland that such a Manichean mentality is so dangerous. "Beyond doubt," she maintains, "the center of Jewish politics today is constituted by the remnants of European Jewry . . . not only is all our practical activity concentrated upon them—even more important is the fact that our whole political outlook springs of necessity from their experiences, from our solidarity with them."[125]

It is in this light that events in Palestine strike her as insane, and the inclination of both parties to fight it out at any price as "nothing less than sheer irrationality." Arendt's discussion of this irrationality is marked by an unmistakable sense of vulnerability and despair, and it underscores her own deep and abiding identification with the project of Jewish settlement in Palestine, which she describes as "today the great hope and the great pride of Jews all over the world." Because of this the destruction of a

Jewish homeland would be a "tragedy" and "catastrophe . . . almost beyond imagining." And yet she is no more buoyant about the likely outcome of an Israeli victory, which "would find the unique possibilities and the unique achievements of Zionism in Palestine destroyed":

> The 'victorious' Jews would live surrounded by an entirely Arab population, secluded inside ever-threatened borders, absorbed with physical self-defense to a degree that would submerge all other interests and activities. The growth of Jewish culture would cease to be the concern of the whole people; social experiments would have to be discarded as impractical luxuries; political thought would center around military strategy; economic development would be determined exclusively by the needs of war.

She concludes that "under present circumstances, a Jewish state can only be erected at the price of the Jewish homeland."[126]

For this reason Arendt endorses the plan for United Nations trusteeship of Palestine briefly supported by President Truman and endorsed by Judah Magnes of Hebrew University and his associates in the Ihud Zionist group. Such a plan, she recognizes, would require far-sighted and decisive politico-military action on the part the United Nations under the leadership of the United States, establishing an effective set of sanctions and incentives to induce compliance on the part of the antagonists. And it would necessitate concessions on both sides. Along these lines she proposes the following: the immediate admission of Jewish refugees into Palestine and the United States, the former immigration to be "limited in terms of time and number," that is, undertaken in accordance with fair procedures for resettlement consistent with the rights of indigenous Arabs; Jewish-Arab social and economic cooperation along the lines of the Jordan Valley Authority project and designed to promote economic development for both communities; the elimination of all terrorist groups and the swift punishment of terrorist deeds, which, she adds "will be the only valid proof that the Jewish people in Palestine has recovered its sense of political reality and that the Zionist leadership is again responsible enough to be trusted" with representing it; and, finally, local self-government based on numerous "mixed Jewish-Arab municipal and rural councils."[127] Such measures "would postpone and possibly prevent partition of the country."[128]

Arendt's considers partition a piece of wishful thinking negated by political and geographical realities, which make it inevitable that an exclusively Jewish sovereignty be perceived as threatening to the Arab inhabitants of Palestine. Because of the social and demographic interdependencies between the Jewish and Arab communities, she argues that the idea of national sovereignty is a "mockery," a source of nationalistic illusions that can only engender communal conflict. She prefers Judah Magnes's proposal for a federated state based on a common government but grounded in "Jewish-Arab community councils, which would mean that the Jewish-Arab conflict would be resolved on the lowest and most promising level of proximity and neighborliness."[129] But, as she recognizes, either solution is outside of the realm of present political possibilities. This is what makes trusteeship, "whose chief aim is pacification and nothing more," imperative. It is, she avers, "not an ideal and not an eternal solution. But politics seldom offers ideal or eternal solutions." Like Camus's support for a civilian truce and the Lauriol Plan, Arendt calls for trusteeship as a first step toward the establishment of an enduring and just peace. Also like Camus, she recognizes that it is possible for the larger powers to play a constructive role in the fair settlement of civil and regional conflicts. Such measures might not offer grand or definitive solutions. But for her the only definitive solution in politics is death. Less terminal options now at least make possible the establishment of a framework for coexistence and more profound solutions later. As we have seen, rebellious politics envisions not the terminus of political divisions, but the flourishing and managing of such divisions.

This line of thinking is extended in Arendt's last major essay on Zionism, "Peace or Armistice in the Near East?" written in 1950 at the suggestion of Magnes, with whom she had developed a close collaboration. She begins by asserting that peace, unlike armistice, cannot be imposed by outside powers and can only be achieved by mutual recognition and mutual compromise on the part of the antagonists. She then proceeds to subject the "mutual refusal to take each other seriously" to a trenchant critique. Most Zionists, she contends, have never recognized the existence of the Arabs in Palestine, and in fact their greatest achievements, the kibbutzim and the Histadrut (Zionist labor movement) have been founded on an ideology of Jewish labor that excludes the Arabs economically and politically. Most Arabs, for their part, have been "inspired by the thought of *revanche*" and the pan-Arab myth of common hostility against Israel. In this light they have interpreted Zionism as a colonial enterprise and construed their own national self-determination in direct antagonism to the presence of Zionists in Palestine. Arendt criticizes this view, arguing that "the building of a Jewish National Home was not a colonial enterprise in which Europeans came to exploit foreign riches with the help and at the expense of native labor." Such a view misidentifies the true character of the exclusivism implicit within Zionist ideology. But it also fatefully dismisses the genuinely noble aspirations of Zionists wishing to flee oppression and build their own communal homeland, especially under the traumatic exigencies of the European genocide and displacement of the Jewish people. Both sides, Arab and Jew, confront each other with claims to absolute justice which exclude the other, claims "which are nationalistic because they make sense only in the closed framework of one's own people and history, and legalistic because they discount the concrete factors of the situation."[130]

Having exposed this senseless intransigence, Arendt identifies a hidden "non-nationalist tradition" in Jewish-Arab relations. She points to a number of historical moments in which negotiation and mutual accommodation seemed possible, fixing on the recent activities of Charles Malik, an Arab U.N. representative from Lebanon, and Judah Magnes. Her comment on their efforts has a peculiarly contemporary ring. Although they did not have mass support, "who knows what might have happened if their hesitating and tentative efforts had gotten a more sympathetic reception on the other side of the table?"[131]

Arendt seeks to break such a deadlock and, as a Jew, she does so by appealing to the *Jewish* non-nationalist tradition, seeking to give it strength by making explicit its accomplishments. What follows in the essay is a brief but penetrating discussion of the two basic values of this tradition— "the universality and predominance of learning and the passion for justice"—and its two most important historical embodiments in Palestine— the Hebrew University and the kibbutzim. These institutions, she argues, must be the moral and political foundation of a renaissance in Zionist culture and political strategy. Mutual accommodation with the Arab world, she declares, is the only alternative to the Balkanization of the Middle East, the degeneration of Zionism into a chauvinistic and tribalistic mentality, and a legacy of insecurity and war for future generations of Israelis and Arabs.

Toward a New Internationalism

There are similarities between Camus's writings on Algeria and Arendt's on Palestine. In both cases interest in these issues was driven by a deep sense of personal concern. Both writers were self-conscious members of ethnic groups, marginalized Europeans—Arendt a displaced Jew, Camus an "exiled" French-Algerian—seeking to justify a new role for European remnants in a postcolonial world. Each recognized the injustices of colonialism and the claims of indigenous Arab peoples; but each also insisted on the authenticity of the claims of their own national minority and believed that these claims made some kind of constructive participation on the part of outside powers imperative. Both opposed the nationalistic dreams of exclusive sovereignty harbored by many in their own ethnic communities; but they also opposed an ideology of anticolonial national liberation whose vilification of European minorities and myth of the virtuous unity of the native population were equally illusory.

Their experiences of marginality and ethnic attachment led them both to conclude that "honor and true justice" must accommodate the existence, indeed the flourishing, of particular loyalties. As witnesses to the crises of nationalism in this century both were especially attuned to the importance and persistence of national attachments, of the differences—in language, culture, history, and belief—between peoples that no universalism consistent with freedom could efface. As Camus put it, a universalism that has no room for the particular ignores the fact that "the two go together. The way to human society passes through national society." But, he continues, it is equally true that "national society can be preserved only by opening it up to a universal perspective."[132] Arendt shared this belief. "Fighters for freedom could be internationalists," she avers, "only if by that they meant that they were prepared to recognize the freedom of all nations; anti-national they could never be."[133] Such a belief underlay her admiration for those Jews who acted as "conscious pariahs" seeking to "weave the strands of their Jewish genius into the general texture of European life."

For Arendt such pariahdom is epitomized by Heinrich Heine, who saw the limits of Enlightenment universalism even as he recognized its accomplishments in ending enforced segregation and liberating underprivileged groups. Heine did not believe "that Jews could exist as 'pure human beings' outside the range of peoples and nations. . . . He knew that separate peoples are needed to focus the genius of poets and artists. . . . Just because he refused to give up his allegiance to a people of pariahs and schlemihls . . . he takes his place among the most uncompromising of Europe's fighters for freedom."[134]

Yet if Heine saw that the Enlightenment vision of an abstract humanity of "pure human beings," divested of all specific attachments, was an empty ideal, indeed a dangerous fiction, he also recognized that humans are not wholly embodied in and defined by their attachments. The truth of the Enlightenment is the idea that humans do have universal characteristics, that we are beings capable of reflexively judging, if not wholly transcend-

ing, our particular attachments. We are capable, in other words, of recognizing the other in ourselves, and ourselves in the other, even as we
also recognize what separates us. Heine thus sought neither to escape
Jewish culture nor to embrace it, but to interweave it with the threads of
the broader cultural world. This is what Arendt admired in him.

Such a healthy sense of particular identity, combined with an equally
healthy reflexivity and openness to criticism, is what marks the pariah.
Arendt's own career as a maverick Jewish intellectual epitomized this self-
reflexive identity, as is well illustrated in her famous exchange with Gershom Scholem over her Eichmann book. Chastised for a lack of connection
to and "love for the Jewish people," Arendt replied: "I have always regarded my Jewishness as one of the indisputable factual data of my life,
and I have never had the wish to change or disclaim facts of this kind.
There is such a thing as a basic gratitude for everything that is at it is; for
what has been *given* and was not, could not, be *made*; for things that are
physei and not *nomo*."[135] Echoing an ancient Greek distinction, this passage
also recalls her gloss on Jaspers's idea that "man is compelled to assent to
a Being which he has never created and to which he is essentially alien."[136]
Assent and estrangement—a paradoxical combination indeed. Arendt acknowledges that in many respects her identity is preformed by a history,
psychology, and biography over which she had little control. And yet this
identity is never entirely whole, self-sufficient, or compelling.

It does, she continues, render "certain types of behavior impossible"—
as a Jewish woman she feels an elementary connection to the Jewish people,
its history and its plight, a basic allegiance to Jewish existence. But it
would be a most egregious instance of what philosophers call the naturalistic fallacy to believe that this sense of connection can issue any definitive
prescriptions. Arendt suggests that such a belief is more often used to shut
off discussion when discussion is most needed. Declaring herself an independent, she accepts Jewish identity as a given that must be perpetually
open to reinterpretation and contestation. The pariah Jew is someone who
seeks to enrich his or her Jewishness by opening it up to divergent perspectives, someone who prizes its givenness and its otherness, who is both
at home and estranged in this identity. For Arendt this attitude is needed
by Jews in the midst of the traumas of Nazism and by all humans facing
the disempowering and dangerous world of the twentieth century: "only
within the framework of a people can a man live as a man among men,
without exhausting himself. And only when a people lives and functions
in consort with other peoples can it contribute to the establishment upon
earth of a commonly conditioned and commonly controlled humanity."[137]

For both Arendt and Camus this deep sense of the importance of otherness and the coexistence of peoples was rooted in a traumatic experience of marginality. But neither writer was motivated by purely personal or local concerns. Their shared commitment to federated settlements in a postcolonial world was also fueled by their understandings of the crises of imperialism that helped to produce totalitarianism, and of the remedies needed to prevent such catastrophes from recurring. Both saw that centralized nation-states were not hospitable agencies of human security or democratic political empowerment, and that any challenge to the principle of nation-state sovereignty must envision a new world order.

This conviction is clear in "Neither Victims Nor Executioners," where Camus proclaims that "we must minimize domestic politics. A crisis which tears the whole world apart must be met on a world scale." Pointing toward the confrontation of the superpowers and the assertions of colonial peoples in a postcolonial world, he concedes that "we are forced into fraternity—or complicity." The only solution to these global problems is "the mutual agreement of all parties," an "international democracy" based on a world parliament and an international legal code with "authority over national governments." Such a democracy could not "be united from above, by a single State more powerful than the others," but only from below, through a form of association consistent with more local forms of political authority.[138]

Camus's writings on Algeria, particularly on the Lauriol Plan, offer the most concrete account of how such an association might be organized. But perhaps the most vivid exposition of his vision of a universalism passing through nations is his 1937 essay "The New Mediterranean Culture." The purpose of this essay is to repudiate any connection between "the cause of Mediterranean regionalism" and fascism. Claiming only "a kind of nationalism of the sun," he rejects any Mediterranean nationalism. Nationalism, as an ideology, is for Camus a form of decadence. But its contrary is not a bland universalism; it is a robust and nonauthoritarian sense of particularity and of place. In contrast to fascist ideology, Camus believes that "there are no higher or lower cultures. There are cultures that are more or less true. All we want to do is help a country to express itself. Locally. Nothing more."[139]

Camus proceeds to defend the vision of a localist and ethnic internationalism based on the "historical facts." He suggests that sovereignty is contrary to true politics, that "it was not life that Rome took from Greece, but puerile, over-intellectualized abstractions . . . [which sacrifice] truth and greatness to a violence that has no soul." In contrast to this Caesarian vision of sovereignty, "our Country is not the abstraction that sends men off to be massacred, but a certain way of appreciating life which is shared by certain people, through which we can feel ourselves closer to someone from Genoa or Majorca than to someone form Normandy or Alsace. That is what the Mediterranean is—a certain smell or scent that we do not need to express: we all feel it through our skin."[140]

This sense of particular culture and place has nothing to do with a sense of superiority or any inclination toward conquest. It has everything to do with cultural specificity, with the ineradicable differences of language, cultural inflection, and perception that are given in human experience. "Politics are made for men," Camus insists, "and not men for politics." This does not mean that universal principles have no application. Rather, these principles have validity only insofar as they recognize and reflect a flourishing of cultural and national differences. And so just as Camus treasures Mediterranean culture, he is also able to understand how others will treasure the cultures to which they belong. The task, as he sees it, is to secure a world in which peoples and their cultures can coexist peacefully: "It is to this whole effort that men of the West must bind themselves. Within the framework of internationalism, the thing can be achieved. If each one of us within his own sphere, his country, his province agrees to work modestly, success is not far away."[141] Here again Camus articulates the vision of a robust, international civil society of engaged and responsible individuals working from the bottom up for human rights and the peaceful coexistence of peoples.

Arendt's similar concern can be traced back to her earliest writings. A major theme of *The Origins of Totalitarianism* is the crisis of nationalism in the twentieth century. One of Arendt's most important theses is the deep tension between nation and state in modern politics. Whereas in many parts of Western Europe nationalism was a "precious cement for binding together a centralized state and an atomized society,"[142] in other parts, where political centralization occurred much later, it functioned in a more malignant way. Concerned with the dynamics of nationalism on a European and global scale, Arendt argues that by the late nineteenth century the exclusivist aspects of nationalism and the parallel limits of the modern republican vision of the nation-state became more clear. One sign of these limits was the Dreyfus affair in France, in which the republicanism of Clemenceau inspired a noble but largely vain effort to stem the tide of national exclusivism and French anti-Semitism.[143] Another was the rise of pan-European Slavic and German movements fueled by chauvinistic and racist ideologies: "tribalism appeared as the nationalism of those peoples who had not participated in national emancipation and who had not achieved the sovereignty of the nation-state."[144] Such tribalism defied the boundaries of already constituted nation-states and challenged the liberal cosmopolitan vision of peaceful republican nation-states.

For Arendt these nationalistic antagonisms culminated in the outbreak of world war, and the limits of the nation-state were exposed even more vividly in its aftermath. In the penultimate chapter of *The Origins,* "The Decline of the Nation-State and the End of the Rights of Man," Arendt argues that the First World War underscored the contradiction between the nation-state and the modern principle of human rights. While the postwar settlements—the Versailles Treaty, the League of Nations, the Minority Treaties—sought to remedy the evils of national conflict, Arendt argues that these efforts were hopeless attempts to solve the problem without addressing its fundamental cause—the principle of national sovereignty itself: "No paradox of contemporary politics is filled with more poignant irony than the discrepancy between the efforts of well-meaning idealists who stubbornly insist on regarding as 'inalienable' those human rights, which are enjoyed only by citizens of the most prosperous and civilized countries, and the situation of the rightless themselves."[145] Arendt writes with great passion, no doubt informed by her own experience, about the mass denationalizations of Central Europeans following the war, the epidemic of displaced and stateless peoples. She points out that national laws of asylum and immigration exclude these peoples, that international law is unable to secure even the most basic rights for them, and indeed that its most powerful organ—Interpol—operates by controlling, regulating, and policing "aliens" in the name of legality. The only substitute for a home that is offered by the regime of nation-states is, Arendt allows, the internment camp.[146] Arendt's Burkean critique of the abstractions of natural rights theory is not intended to deny the principle of human rights, but to advance it by underscoring its necessarily communal and institutional character: "We are not born equal; we become equal as members of a group on the strength of our decision to guarantee ourselves mutually equal rights."[147]

As we have seen, at the heart of Arendt's political theory is the idea that as humans we share in the condition of natality and mortality, power and limit, and that this condition grounds our rights as human beings. But Arendt is also clear that these rights can only be secured through the agreements and commitments that are sustained by political agency itself. In this sense our rights are not natural but conventional, though they are based on certain natural facts of our condition. And they are not universal but always spatially and temporally limited, though because they are based on our universal capacities as reflexive beings they might always be expanded to become more universal in scope. Indeed Arendt, following Kant and her teacher Jaspers, sees such a cosmopolitanism as the unfinished project of the Enlightenment.

Highlighting the fragility of human rights, which is obscured by natural-law formulations, Arendt maintains that it may not be possible to secure these rights on a global scale. But she insists that only success in this effort can redeem the promise of "the dignity of our tradition": "human dignity needs a new guarantee which can be found only in a new political principle, in a new law on earth, whose validity this time must comprehend the whole of humanity while its power must remain strictly limited, rooted in and controlled by newly defined territorial units."[148] The idea of an authority that is universal in scope and yet limited in power strikes a paradoxical note in an age accustomed to equating political authority with the sovereignty of unitary states. And yet Arendt suggests that only a confederation of communities can secure human rights by countering the homogenizing and militarizing tendencies of modern politics.

The need for such a "new political principle" is a major concern of *Eichmann in Jerusalem*. Most commentators have focused on Arendt's treatment of Eichmann's banality and the complicity of Jewish victims, but the last quarter of the book deals in great detail with the legalities surrounding Eichmann's trial in Jerusalem. Arendt's central point here is that Eichmann's crime defies traditional standards of jurisprudence and poses fundamental challenges to the modern system of international law. The most basic is that whereas the traditional categories for handling war crimes—"acts of state" and "on superior orders"—consider these crimes as deviations from the general proscription against murder common to virtually all cultures, the Nazi genocide presents the case of "a state founded upon criminal principles." The policy itself presents a kind of criminality, with global aspirations, unanticipated by the relatively complacent standards of international law. Arendt then proceeds to an elaborate discussion of the postwar Nuremburg Charter and trials, which distinguished between "crimes against peace," "war crimes," and "crimes against humanity." Of these, Arendt observes, only the last was without precedent. Genocide is, she avers, "an attack upon human diversity as such, that is, upon a characteristic of the 'human status' without which the very words 'mankind' and 'humanity' would be devoid of meaning." Arendt thus reproaches the Jerusalem court for charging Eichmann only with war crimes against the Jewish people and not facing squarely the challenge posed by this new type of crime: "the supreme crime it [the court] was confronted with, the physical extermination of the Jewish people, was a crime against humanity, perpetrated upon the body of the Jewish people ... only the choice of the victims, not the nature of the crime, could be derived from the long history of Jew-hatred and anti-Semitism."[149]

Yet Arendt sees that the Israelis were hardly unique in their narrow interpretation of the problem of genocide. She thus criticizes those who challenged Israel's right to try Eichmann, maintaining that the trial, in spite of its limitations, was no different from the Successor trials held in Poland, Yugoslavia, and elsewhere to deal with crimes against nations. But she does lament that the opportunity to broach new legal principles was passed over. She observes that the Genocide Convention, adopted in 1948 by the General Assembly of the United Nations, provided that "persons charged with genocide ... shall be tried by a competent tribunal of the States in the territory of which the act was committed or by such international penal tribunal as may have jurisdiction."[150] Arendt argues that this convention has radical implications and that, in accordance with it, "the court should have either sought to establish an international tribunal or tried to reformulate the territorial principle in such a way that it applied to Israel." Regarding this latter option, Arendt holds that "no State of Israel would ever have come into being if the Jewish people had not created and maintained its own specific in-between space throughout the long centuries of dispersion, that is, prior to the seizure of its old territory."[151] The Jewish people, in other words, have until recently been a historical nation detached from any state or sovereignty; any right it may have to self-determination and international recognition presupposes concepts of international law at odds with the principles of national, territorially based sovereignty. As we have already seen in her writings on Zionism, Arendt thinks that the failure to articulate these concepts has been tragic for Jews and for world politics. She clearly believes that the "specific in-between spaces" in which national and ethnic groups exist, spaces often suppressed or marginalized by the principle of sovereignty, need to be opened up and protected, that their inhabitants need to be afforded the human rights that only forms of political empowerment can secure. In this respect the political experience of the Jews, a fractured and dispersed community existing in the interstices of modern political systems, is paradigmatic of the plight of many modern peoples and indeed of modern existence itself; in some ways all people are refugees of one identity or another, all strangers to others, and perhaps to themselves as well.[152] The problems and prospects presented by the crisis of world Jewry, centering on a Jewish homeland in Palestine, may forecast the prospects for a more civil and humane world politics. Rather than calling for a politics of exclusive domains, Arendt endorses one of multiple inclusions, where territorial residence and communal membership are connected in some ways but not congruent.[153] Arendt argues that if this issue is taken seriously, then there is no alternative to Karl Jaspers's proposal for some kind of "permanent international criminal court" and a powerful system of international institutions to support it: "if genocide is an actual possibility of the future, then no people on earth—least of all, of course, the Jewish people, in Israel or elsewhere—can feel reasonably sure of its continued existence without the help and protection of international law."[154]

This vision of international law is spelled out most clearly in her essay "Karl Jaspers: Citizen of the World?," perhaps Arendt's most lucid account of her thoroughly modern convictions. Addressing Jaspers's interest in the idea of world citizenship, she observes that "mankind, which for all preceding generations was no more than a concept or an ideal, has become something of an urgent reality." This need for some practical conception of mankind or humanity has been caused by the many technological, economic, and political interdependencies of modern global society. But, Arendt suggests, "at this moment the most potent symbol of the unity of mankind is the remote possibility that atomic weapons used by one country according to the political wisdom of a few might ultimately come to be the end of all human life on earth."[155]

Arendt considers such a "negative solidarity" the ultimate expression of modern powerlessness—people bound together as sufferers by their ever-present collective mortality. Yet she also suggests that this common fear and trembling might become the basis of a positive solidarity, a genuine "global responsibility." If that is to occur, "a process of mutual understanding and progressing self-clarification on a gigantic scale must take place." How might such understanding come about? Arendt argues that it cannot be on the basis of "a universal agreement upon one religion, one philosophy, or one form of government"; given the diversity of cultures in the world, such unity could only be achieved by the force of imposition, the basis, perhaps, of a global empire—one purchased at a bloody price—but hardly of a peaceful global community. She thus maintains that it must be based on some commitment to the idea of a universality in diversity. Along with the renunciation of sovereignty for the sake of a world-wide federated political structure, such an understanding would require "the renunciation, not of one's own tradition and national past, but of the binding authority which tradition and past have always claimed." Consistent with her conception of political judgment, Arendt calls for a new kind of reflexivity, requiring not the abandonment of particular attachments but the ability to incorporate into them the standpoints of the particular attachments of others. Such a "framework of universal mutual agreements" would be both the means and the end of global political community, and "political philosophy can hardly do more than describe and prescribe the new principle of political action."[156]

This vision of a truly global confederation of political communities is one upon which the writings of Arendt and Camus converge. Such a framework would serve to regulate differences, but never presume to abolish them. It would acknowledge the authority of local and regional forms of self-government and would override the centralizing and militarizing propensities of modern statist politics. In some respects this is an extraordinarily ambitious vision. But in other respects it is a modest one. For if it rejects the laissez-faire principle of national sovereignty, it also repudiates the invidiously utopian project of substantive global community. As Arendt writes, "Politics deals with men, nationals of many countries and heirs to many pasts; its laws are the positively established fences which hedge in, protect, and limit the space in which freedom is not a concept, but a living, political reality."[157]

For both writers the existing structures of national and international politics function less to protect than to darken, suffocate, and limit the spaces within which an authentic politics might live and thrive. And yet neither was without hope. One source of that hope was the dedication of human rights activists throughout the world, who offered material and moral support to the victims of political persecution and torture, acting on a commitment to human dignity and political freedom in the face of frustrating indifference and revolting cruelty.[158] Both writers counted themselves among such supporters—Camus in his activities with the Spanish Federation of Political Prisoners, GLI, and the EAGs, Arendt as a chairperson of Spanish Refugee Aid and a member of PEN and Amnesty International. Such activities epitomized an ethic of revolt, a refusal of human debasement. As Camus put it in imaginary dialogue with a fascist, "With your scornful smile you will ask me: what do you mean by saving man? And with all my being I shout to you that I mean not mutilating him and yet giving a chance to that justice that man alone can conceive."[159] In protesting against oppression, human rights activists issue a resounding "no" to the mutilation of people victimized by governments. Yet this protest involves a "yes" as well, that is, it attests, through its very resistance, to the positive value of human freedom. In demanding a halt to abuse the rebel "affirms that there are limits and also that he suspects—and wishes to preserve—the existence of certain things on this side of the borderline." Such modest acts of conscientious resistance, while they involve no grandiose ideological objectives or transformative projects, express the dignity of concrete human beings and recognize a "solidarity of chains" in which humans are irrevocably tied.[160] Indeed such praxis, which tends to be self-constituted outside of existing state and party structures, manifests in its own means the international civil society that is its end. Operating "across frontiers," challenging the symbolic and physical borders of nation-states, such human rights advocacy surpasses parochial identities and creates a modest, universalist discourse of human dignity and freedom. In this way it is not all that different from the more obviously political forms of radicalism—revolutionary struggles, worker insurgencies, civil rights campaigns and antiwar demonstrations—that also inspired Camus and Arendt. For both writers the problem of human freedom in the contemporary world is indissolubly a problem of local praxis *and* global concern. Only a consistent effort beginning at the local level might challenge entrenched and dangerous forms of centralized power. But unless this praxis acknowledges the global sources of political problems, it will be ineffectual and unsatisfying.

Here too we find a concern with equilibrating ends and means that is the hallmark of rebellious politics. The vision of civilian truces and confederal arrangements endorsed by both Arendt and Camus treats these forms of conflict resolution as steps in a process of regulating national and cultural differences. In one sense such steps can be seen as means toward the end of global harmony. But in another sense they are best viewed as processes that are necessary precisely because there can be no perfect global harmony. The most distinctive characteristic of these arrangements is their refusal to ideologize national conflicts and to codify violence as a way of resolving them and their equally sweeping refusal to wave such conflicts away by some ideological sleight of hand. In this respect the vision of confederation is a means that is also an end, a general framework within which some conflicts can be progressively mitigated and others might well emerge. But unlike the utopian visions of national sovereignty and world government, it incorporates within itself the means for articulating and resolving international differences in perpetuity, anticipating no terminus to their continued existence, but also sure that in the absence of some framework of genuine international civility the prospects for human security and freedom are greatly diminished.

Chapter 7

REBELLIOUS POLITICS RECONSIDERED

Arendt and Camus converged on a vision of a rebellious politics that speaks to many current concerns about the possibility of grounding political convictions and about the prospects for freedom at a time when the traditional agencies of mass democratic empowerment seem to have reached a dead end. And yet how relevant is this vision to our current predicament? How compelling is its understanding of human agency and politics?

In this chapter I shall explore some of the limits of the vision shared by Camus and Arendt. True to the spirit of my subjects, I do not mean to suggest that they should have been other than what they were, or that their writings would have been more valid or authentic had they been more socialist or feminist or "correct" in some other way. Indeed, one of their most appealing qualities is their brazen defiance of political correctness. Both were iconoclastic thinkers who refused the pious banalities served up by many on the right and the left. If they bequeathed nothing else, this spirit of refusal itself would be a worthy legacy. Nonetheless, if their refusals were beneficial, they also often had costs, and it is these shortcomings that I shall now explore.

Postmodern Perspectives

Postmodern writing, as Lyotard has said, is distinguished above all by its incredulity. Suspicious of modern science and philosophy and critical of the forms of power whose authority relies on them, postmodernism seeks to deconstruct and destabilize reigning conceptions of knowledge and politics. In the words of Michel Foucault, its design "is not the erecting of foundations: on the contrary, it disturbs what was previously considered immobile; it fragments what was thought unified; it shows the heterogeneity of what was imagined consistent with itself."[1] For postmodernists, modern philosophy seeks to mask the fragments and contingencies of social life by identifying something about the world that is essential, fixed, and foundational. The task of postmodern writing is thus to show that even the most longstanding and cherished beliefs, distinctions, and relations rest on wholly conventional foundations, and that such foundations are totalizing myths rather than absolute truths.

Foucault, certainly the most political of writers working within this idiom, has described his approach to politics as a type of "problematization." "The forms of totalization offered by politics are always, in fact, very limited. I am attempting, on the contrary . . . to open up problems that are as concrete and general as possible, problems that approach politics from behind and cut across societies on the diagonal."[2] This effort to problematize should be familiar from the work of Arendt and Camus. Like Foucault, both writers draw heavily on Nietzsche in order to produce "genealogies" of modern politics. Both suspect the kind of "general intellectual" who claims to speak with privilege for a universal historical agent, and both abjure grandiose ideological visions and a state-centered politics in favor or a more partial and localized "micro-politics." And like Foucault, both are inspired by those who exist at the political margins of normal society.

Yet where Foucault seeks always to deconstruct modern freedom, to "shatter the unity of man's being" and expose the "endlessly repeated play of dominations,"[3] both Arendt and Camus self-consciously and explicitly seek to *re*construct modern freedom as well. And despite their debt to Nietzsche, both also recognize that his thought does not offer much for constructive thinking about politics. Both are chastened humanists, but humanists nonetheless. Appreciating the absurdity of human existence and the tragic character of human agency, both remain robustly committed to the values of human empowerment and self-governance. As Arendt put it, "human dignity needs a new guarantee which can only be found in a new political principle."[4] This overriding concern with human dignity is not merely a matter of rhetoric or semantics. The value of living, breathing human beings, of their lives, freedom, and dignity, is unmistakable in the writings of Arendt and Camus. Both spoke out forcefully on behalf of human rights and the freedoms of civil society. Both, to be sure, recognized that such rights and freedoms were themselves imperfect and partial. Indeed it is precisely because of the limits and partialities of all politics that they favored decentralized, revisable forms of democratic praxis. Like Foucault, both writers were deeply attuned to the discordances and ambiguities of political life, and to the limits of even the best political commitments and arrangements. But both were also aware of the importance of concordances in politics, of the need for some kind of free and decent normality that would not suppress difference but which would give it expression, however imperfectly.[5]

Camus and Arendt differ from Foucault, as well as from the postmodern idiom more generally, in their forthright use of the language of right, freedom, and truth, and in their insistence that all forms of normality and power are not equally repressive, and that some universal norms of freedom are indispensable.[6] A number of recent works have made the case for an "agonistic democracy" inspired by the postmodern writing of Nietzsche and Foucault.[7] There is much of interest in this argument; it would be foolish to deny that there are pluralistic themes developed by postmodern writers, and tendentious to deny that creative thinking about democracy has been inspired by them. Yet in the end it seems to me that the ethical agnosticism characteristic of postmodernism renders its democratic commitments highly suspect. Camus was surely correct when he refused to dismiss Nietzsche. And yet the effort to mine Nietzsche's rabidly antiegalitarian corpus, or to labor over Foucault's cryptic remarks about Vietnamese boat people, in search of a democratic theory would seem to have sharply diminishing returns. Why not look instead to thinkers, like Arendt and Camus, whose egalitarian political convictions make them more appropriate sources of a "postmodern" democratic theory? Although they share Foucault's Nietzschean sensibility, they join it with explicit support for distinctively modern forms of rebellious political agency. In this respect their views are closer to those of Charles Taylor, who insists, against indiscriminate critics and apologists alike, that "modernity needs to be saved from its most unconditional supporters."[8] Like Taylor, both writers seek to incorporate postmodern insights without prematurely pronouncing the dusk of modernity.

And yet though Arendt and Camus anticipate much that is valuable in postmodern writing, there are definite limits to their deconstructive spirit. As we have seen, both of them reject essentialist conceptions of human nature. Having experienced the human transformations wrought by to-

talitarianism, they appreciated the variability of human conduct and resisted the idea that human nature is preformed. This appreciation grounds
their shared commitment to a rebellious politics that recognizes that there
are no ontologically privileged forms of human authority, and that to be
human is to construct and to challenge forms of life. Neither writer,
however, is able to carry this insight to its proper conclusion. Both—in
different ways, and in spite of their best insights—fail to problematize
important, and contestable, aspects of human existence.

Many commentators have noted that Arendt's most rigid categorial
distinctions—between labor, work, and action, the social and the political,
violence and power—cannot be sustained in the sweeping way they are
often presented.[9] Indeed Arendt herself often departs from them in discussing actual political phenomena like contemporary revolutions or the
Jewish-Arab conflict in Palestine. Nonetheless, however charitably we may
wish to interpret these distinctions, there is no denying their often essentialist character. This seems particularly true of her understanding of "the
private." Arendt's purpose in formulating her distinction between public
and private is clearly to present a nonreductive conception of a public life
where people could articulate their interests in a discursive fashion and
act on them in a concerted manner—a counter to the individualism so
prominent in modern society. Yet ironically, although this distinction was
intended to advance a conception of freedom, Arendt's characterization
of "the private" seems to allow, if not explicitly require, the insulation of
gender questions from the question of freedom.

Feminist critics of Arendt have fixed upon two troubling aspects of her
conceptualization. The first is Arendt's frank admission that in the ancient
world, where the public sphere was properly distinguished from the private, citizenship was established on the basis of servility within the household. In discussing these matters, Arendt candidly acknowledges the
subordination of women and slaves and yet treats the principle that establishes this subordination, if not the subordination itself, as exemplary.
I think it a serious error to see Arendt as waxing nostalgic for the ancient
world. Whatever the limits of her discussion, she seems to seek, in
Nietzsche's words, "a past from which we may spring rather than that
from which we seem to have derived."[10] Many of her historical comparisons, particularly in *The Human Condition* and *On Revolution,* are designed
less to represent events as they occurred than to present counterfactuals
that subvert our unreflective preconceptions about our current politics. If
this is true, then her treatment of the Greek *oikos,* though disturbing, is
not decisive, for she is very much aware that she is not practicing con-

ventional history and thus is not offering us the Greek world as a model so much as a spur to creative action. On this score the worst that can be said of Arendt is that in her mythical treatment of the Greek *polis* she is silent about the private indignities that supported Greek civic life. This silence is disheartening. But it does not constitute an endorsement. Unfortunately, however, Arendt's treatment of labor and necessity presents deeper conceptual problems.

Arendt consistently identifies nature with necessity, body, production, and reproduction. For her, the activities of production and reproduction are immanent rather than historical, mute rather than discursive.[11] Arendt emphasizes the narrative character of action, but suggests that the cyclical character of corporeal existence provides little about which to speak.[12] In short, she consistently treats certain activities—those historically associated with women's work—as less than fully human. Her high valuation of praxis seems to rest on this treatment. Although there is no reason to infer that Arendt seeks to justify the subordination of women, there can be no doubt that her conceptual schema serves to insulate certain concerns from the rebellious politics that she does seek to justify. Had Arendt been more true to her own anti-essentialism, she might have recognized that all human activities are meaningful, practical, and historical, and that the capacity to begin anew—to act as an historical agent— that she so prized is implicated in everything that human beings think and do. Such a recognition would not require us to abandon Arendt's insights about the limits of human praxis and the impossibility of transforming everything about ourselves. But the limits of human power are more malleable than Arendt's schema suggests, and there is no justification for her conceptual treatment of nature and labor as prepolitical or beyond contestation. Indeed, much of twentieth-century politics has concerned itself precisely with the ways in which women have contested—politicized—the treatment of such seemingly natural activities as sex, conception, and childbirth. Movements in support of birth control, abortion rights, and public support for child care have brought these issues to public awareness, empowering women and shifting the boundaries of public and private. Women, true to the spirit but not the letter of Arendt's theory, have made their interests actionable.[13]

A similar criticism can be made of Camus, who also often speaks of nature in an unreflective way. Camus treats rebellion as a naturalistic impulse—a rejection of injustice and a "passionate affirmation" of justice that seems rooted in the conditions of human existence. A rebellion that remains true to itself thus remains true to nature, the sun, sky, and landscape—it remains true to, and recognizes, human finitude in an expansive and inclusive natural universe. But here we encounter two problems with Camus's "nature." The first is that his writings often privilege an essentialist conception of nature. Contrary to the absurdist character of his general philosophy, Camus frequently treats nature not simply as a source of human limit and possibility but as a source of *comfort*. This attitude is expressed rather benignly in *The Plague,* in the communion between Rieux and Tarrou while they are bathing in the ocean. More problematic is the conclusion to *The Rebel,* where Camus appeals to "an irrepressible demand of human nature, of which the Mediterranean, where the intelligence is intimately related to the blinding light of the sun, guards the secret."[14] In passages like these Camus counterposes the Mediterranean and Europe, nature and history, revolt and revolution. Both the explanation of political troubles—Europe, German historical thinking—and the source of their solution—the Mediterranean coast—seem too easy. This is a powerful motif in Camus's writings, traceable to his earliest youthful musings about Algeria. Perhaps, as David Sprintzen has suggested, the impact of the motif can be most clearly seen in Camus's fictional treatments of Algeria, where his powerful identification with a particular *pied noir* version of the Mediterranean meant that "subtly but perhaps not surprisingly the surrounding Arab world finds itself situated beyond the horizons of his vision."[15]

This sentimental vision of the Mediterranean is an important lacuna in Camus's writing, but I believe it is mitigated by his strong naturalistic tendencies. If there are moments when he seems to counterpose nature and history, the main burden of *The Rebel* is to show the mutual dependence of nature and history, of human revolt and political revolution. Far from underwriting a retreat from history and politics, Camus's writings on ethics and politics consistently explore the possibilities and limits of political engagement while recognizing that the human condition is irredeemably social, and that human contact with the nonhuman is never unmediated and unproblematic. In *The Stranger,* for example, when Meursealt becomes virtually identical with the scorching sun, the result is murder, an act abhorrent to human society. It is true that Meursault is not guilty in the way that the prosecution argues. But Camus leaves no doubt that he is responsible nonetheless. In *The Myth of Sisyphus* Camus does not deny that there are wrong acts. But "a mind imbued with the absurd," he maintains, judges these wrongs "calmly." The murder scene in *The Stranger* illustrates that nature has a dark side, that it can offer no ultimate solace.

The temptation to quit history and identify with nature is futile. Humans are thus condemned to their own artifice.[16]

But if the privileging of the Mediterranean is arguably marginal to Camus's explicitly political thinking, the same cannot be said of his gender imagery. In Camus's concern with the majesty and limits of human revolt, as powerful as the figure of the Mediterranean or the sea is the figure of woman. And if rebellion finds its inspiration in and takes its nourishment from nature, from the sea, it finds its reproach in woman. In Camus's writing there is not a single female rebel or hero.[17] Women play a crucial role in his thinking, just as women—especially his mother—played a crucial role in his own life.[18] But in every case woman stands for stability, nurturance, happiness, the private—for comfort and safety. The characters of Caesonia in *Caligula,* Victoria in *State of Siege,* and Dora in *The Just Assassins* refuse the rebellious logic of their male partners, admonishing them in the name of intimacy and simple love. The female Chorus in *State of Siege,* chastising Diego for refusing love, clearly articulates this distinctively feminine perspective:

> Our curse on him! Our curse on all who forsake their bodies! And pity on us ... who are foresaken and must endure year after year this world in which men in their pride are ever aspiring to transform! Surely, since everything may not be saved, we should learn at least to safeguard the home where love is. ... But no! Men go whoring after ideas, a man runs away from his mother, foresakes his love, and starts rushing upon adventure ... a hunter of shadows or a lonely singer who invokes some impossible reunion under a silent sky.[19]

Diego, maintaining his right to rebel, rebukes the Chorus and its message; but he accepts the dualism upon which its criticism rests. For Camus women represent embodiment and intimacy. And revolt, a difficult and lacerating choice, seems a distinctly transcendent, courageous, *male* activity. The consistent and indeed quite compelling remonstrances of the women in his drama indicate that Camus was deeply aware of the tragic costs and limits of rebelliousness. The voices of the women tell us something that Camus believed important. But he also leaves no doubt that the quest for an impossible reunion under a silent sky is an urgent ethical imperative, that men with integrity will forsake their bodies and their women in the name of justice. This conception of politics seems to reserve little space for the participation of women and, more important, associates woman with the distinctively private and unpolitical sphere of family and love. A similar motif can also be discerned in "The Myth of Sisyphus," where two of Camus's hero types, Don Juan and the Conqueror, are also distinctively male.[20] It would seem that for Camus an ethic of rebellion transcends the private but does not challenge it; it surpasses women but does not include them or recast their plight.[21]

An alternative reading of these texts might underscore their ironic posture. On this view the reproach articulated to the (male) rebel represents a call for a more sensitive revolt, for some integration of love and justice, a recognition of the limits of political commitment and the futility of inflated ideological aspirations. The Chorus's lament of having to "endure year after year this world which men in their pride are ever aspiring to transform" recalls Camus's proclamation in *The Rebel:* "The astonishing history evoked here is the history of European pride."[22] Both texts seek to rebuke a political arrogance that is so carried away with itself that it is blind to the sufferings of others. It is suggestive that the character most paralleling Diego in his fixation with justice is Casado, the self-righteous, legalistic, and cold judge of Cadiz, and that it is Casado's wife who, disgusted with her husband, utters: "I spit on your law! I have on my side the right of lovers not to be parted, the right of the criminal to be forgiven, the right of every penitent to recover his good name. . . for justice—do you hear, Casado?—is on the side of the sufferers, the afflicted, those who live by hope alone."[23] Here the language of justice and the language of compassion are combined, in the words of a wife and mother whose concern for her daughter compels her to ignore her husband's command, "Keep silent, woman!" and leads her to articulate a principled political stand.

This moment in Camus's drama is anomalous, for Camus never draws from it the conclusions that his own ethic of revolt would seem to require. What it suggests is a general conception of rebelliousness that is open to the claims of *all* of "the afflicted," contesting a plurality of oppressions in politics, economics, *and* gender relations, yet privileging none of these. *State of Siege* recalls Camus's controversial statement regarding Algeria: "I believe in justice, but I will defend my mother before justice."[24] But it suggests that, as Michael Walzer has put it, instead of maintaining an uncomfortable antinomy of love and justice Camus "might better have . . . [said] simply that a justice without room for love would be itself unjust."[25] Camus might also have added that a love without justice would be less than love. In other words, without effacing the tragic tension between the demands of the intimate and personal and the demands of public life and universal principle, Camus might have articulated this tension in a less essentialist way, refusing to privilege any particular conception of love, body, or woman, and indeed opening even these up to forms of resistance.

In sum, though Arendt and Camus present a conception of politics in accord with much current postmodern writing, and indeed offer a democratic vision of rebellious politics from which current postmodernists can learn, they also have something to learn from this more recent idiom of political theory. As many commentators have noted, postmodern writing is largely a product of the New Left and the "new social movements" that it spawned in the 1960s. Whatever the limits of this genre, its great contribution has been to challenge what have long been taken to be givens of social and political life, particularly in those areas, like gender and sexuality, that have long been considered beyond human artifice.[26] Both Arendt and Camus were driven by a similar suspicion, but their writings fail to raise important questions, particularly in regard to gender, race, and sexuality. The spirited support of plurality and difference in their writings is an important contribution; indeed it serves as a remonstrance to those activists for whom a single essentialist conception of nature, femininity, sexuality or race functions as an absolute criterion of political virtue or vice.[27] When efforts to politicize sexuality or race produce rigid orthodoxies or organizations claiming a monopoly on righteousness, they threaten to undermine the very liberation that they seek. For there is no single way to be straight or gay, black or Hispanic, and no reason to expect members of oppressed groups to fall lockstep in line behind a single agenda. Both Arendt and Camus had good reason, derived from their own experience, to fear such expectations. Yet their rebellious spirit needs to be extended so as to incorporate issues and constituencies about which they thought little.

Theory and Practice

In one sense, then, Arendt and Camus were perhaps insufficiently Nietzschean, having failed adequately to question their own assumptions about nature and gender. Yet in their suspicion of the epistemological claims of political theory they were perhaps too Nietzschean. Placing great emphasis on the innovative capacities of human agency, both Arendt and Camus forswore the Hegelian-Marxist conception of praxis, the idea that through reason humans can grasp the conditions under which they live, see them as the products of human activity, and then consciously work to transform them.[28] The classic statement of this conception is in *The German Ideology*:

> History . . . [is] a material result: a sum of productive forces, a historically created relation of individuals to nature and to one another, which is handed down to each generation from its predecessor; a mass of productive forces, capital funds and conditions, which, on the one hand, is indeed modified by the new generation, but also on the other prescribes for it conditions of life and gives it a definite development, a special character. It shows that circumstances make men just as much as men make circumstances.[29]

Marx's main concerns are encapsulated in this materialist conception of history: human praxis as the transformation of given materials by individual and collective subjects; the importance of a scientific understanding of the materials of society; historical evolution as the progressive development of human powers; and the ideal of a communist society which "for the first time consciously treats all natural premises as the creatures of hitherto existing men, strips them of their natural character and subjugates them to the power of united individuals."[30]

Arendt and Camus resolutely reject this Hegelian vision of human history as the reappropriation of essential human powers. Criticizing the naive belief in a solution to "the riddle of history," both associate this view with a Promethean exaltation of human mastery and subjugation that is blind to the limits of human power. Emphasizing the importance of otherness, they support an anarchistic conception of agency that does not seek to bring the world under human control. Yet although this conception offsets some of the more heroic assumptions of Marxism about "the power of united individuals," the dismissal of a materialist conception of praxis has a number of unfortunate consequences.

The first is a voluntaristic understanding of human agency. Both Camus and Arendt viewed human action as a worldly phenomenon, encumbered by constraints and concerned with practical consequences. Yet the materialist and pragmatist elements in the conception of the human condition shared by Arendt and Camus are often marginalized by an existentialist view of human agency as spontaneous performance and self-creation that is at odds with any kind of pragmatism or materialism. Although both underscore the importance of unacknowledged limits to and unintended consequences of human action, neither offers a robust account of what Anthony Giddens calls "the constitution of society."[31] Deeply attuned to the often tragic character of human agency, in some ways both writers perceived human history more as Machiavelli's *fortuna* than as a socially caused and, at least in retrospect, rationally discernible process. Writing in the wake of world war, totalitarianism, and genocide, both were profoundly aware of discontinuities in history and of the bankruptcy of the nineteenth-century faith in progress. They rightly dismissed that aspect of Hegelian-Marxian philosophical anthropology that posits a unitary subject (mankind) whose identity is estranged and ultimately recovered through a progressive, redemptive, and unilinear historical process eventuating in human emancipation.

And yet this revolt against historicism does not require us to abandon the genuine insight of the Hegelian-Marxist tradition—that humans make history, in however discontinuous and fragmented a fashion, under definite conditions not of their own choosing. Humans are historical creatures who construct, in complex and often unintended ways, social worlds of meaning and power, and who through their continued interaction sustain or change these social worlds. Arendt and Camus, in their effort to rescue a conception of human agency from deterministic philosophies of history, give short shrift to these questions of social causality.[32] In this respect they miss a rich tradition of inquiry into the constitution of society. I am thinking here of the sociological tradition founded by Emile Durkheim, Georg Simmel, and Max Weber, but also of what Perry Anderson has called the tradition of Western Marxism.[33] Such writers as Antonio Gramsci, Karl Korsch, and George Lukacs sought to articulate conceptions of social causality that avoided the mistakes of the mechanistic naturalism associated with more dogmatic versions of Marxism. Sartre's *Critique of Dialectical Reason,* a book that in many ways responds to the criticisms of Marxism articulated by Camus, similarly takes up these concerns.[34] Contemporary social theorists like Alain Touraine, Pierre Bourdieu, and Jürgen Habermas have continued this tradition, developing a conception of human agency that disavows a "philosophy of the subject" but retains the core insight of the Hegelian-Marxist idea of praxis—that humans are enabled and constrained by historically evolved social structures which it is possible to understand and consciously change.[35] Anthony Giddens and Roy Bhaskar have both neatly captured this insight in their conception of the duality of structure and agency. In their view human agents are always constrained and enabled by preexisting social structures which are themselves understood recursively as the media and outcomes of purposive individual and collective activity.[36] This view, though inspired by certain aspects of Marxist philosophy, in no way requires a commitment to a philosophy of history or a belief in the primacy of class.[37] Such a view is not without its own problems. But it more adequately expresses the importance of unintended consequences and the material reality of the social world, which it is possible to understand rationally and refashion even if it is not possible to subjugate it to the demands of a homogeneous, unitary collective subject.

The voluntarism often expressed by Arendt and Camus is accompanied by a suspicion of theoretical discourse that is well summed up in Nietzsche's observation that "as soon as philosophy begins to believe in itself it always creates the world in its own image; it cannot do otherwise. Philosophy is this tyrannical drive itself."[38] This skepticism is evident in Camus's association of science with a quest for certainty that "founders in metaphor," a futile urge to apprehend and conquer the world that "bumps into walls that defy its assaults."[39] It is also evident in Arendt's insistence that "the modes of thought and communication that deal with truth, if seen from the political perspective, are necessarily domineering and thus anti-political," that "truth carries within itself an element of coercion."[40] Both authors rightly reject the totalizing vision associated with modern ideologies, which purport to offer a privileged reading of the entirety of human history. They rightly question any perspective that denies the intersubjective character of society and the indeterminacy of human history. Underscoring the importance of human initiative, both writers focus on the agent as a center of ethical responsibility, suspicious of social theories whose concern with question of causality might obscure the importance of the agent. They thus celebrate the operation of judgment and common sense, casting doubt on the claims of any theory purporting to speak with epistemic authority about the world of opinion.[41] But by counterposing judgment to theory, and contingency to determination, Arendt and Camus sadly miss the opportunity to rethink the possibility of a critical theory of politics and society. In this regard they compare unfavorably with writers like those associated with the Frankfurt school, who identified many of the same problems connected with a faith in science yet also sought to defend the critical role of social science in enhancing human freedom.[42]

The subject of critical theory is a complex one, but I think it is clear that contemporary theorists working in this idiom are committed to certain beliefs which Arendt and Camus might profitably have considered. As postpositivists, they believe that all forms of science are interpretive and socially constructed. Such an understanding of scientific reasoning and its fallibility refuses to equate scientific knowledge with the foundationalist claims about it often made by positivist philosophers and scientific socialists. Untroubled by the reliance of science on metaphor and on the contextualized judgments of scientists, postpositivist philosophers nonetheless acknowledge that specific standards of evidence and argument peculiar to modern science provide it with a cognitive authority in its explanatory claims about the world.[43] Critical theorists also believe that aspects of the social world, in particular sources of human oppression, often remain unacknowledged by social agents, and that a critical social science might analyze such conditions and bring them and the possibilities for changing them to public awareness.[44]

This vision of a critical social science does not imply that theorists can diagnose the movement of history or offer blueprints for social reconstruction. Nor does it imply that reason can fully apprehend the world, rendering it entirely transparent and subjecting it absolutely to human purposes. As Camus wrote: "All the knowledge in the earth will give me nothing to assure me that the world is mine."[45] And yet if reason cannot live up to its grandest conceits, is still possible to for it to assume a more modest role, seeking not conquest but simply a way to identify the realities of our condition so that we can more intelligently and freely grapple with them.[46] Obviously Arendt and Camus were not wholly averse to such a conception. As I have argued, their own writings are best understood as modest proposals about the primary elements of the human condition and their normative significance. Both rejected the unmediated unity of theory and practice—the idea that theory could be both an absolutely accurate representation of the world and the consciousness of freedom itself, the unproblematic voice of the oppressed—a view whose most influential proponent was Marx.[47] But both clearly presented theoretical accounts that they hoped would inform a reorientation of political thinking and practice. Yet in spite of this hope their works lack a rich conception of the constructive possibilities of theoretical discourse. Revolting against prevailing forms of scientism, Camus and Arendt sought refuge in existence itself, countering the hegemony of truths imposed on a recalcitrant world by valorizing rebellious spirit and unadorned action.

Thus it is not surprising that although they offer important insights into the human condition, their vision of a rebellious politics is not embedded in a consistent social theory. Both writers offer penetrating criticisms of modern society, but neither presents or even draws upon a systematic social scientific theory, a weakness that is particularly pronounced in their understanding of the contemporary state. Neither took much interest in political economy, and absent from their writings is any sustained treatment of the problems of postindustrial capitalism or the welfare state. Again in contrast to the Frankfurt school, although both writers were sensitive to the banalities of modern mass society, neither offers any systematic account of the sources or significance of mass culture or, like Habermas, any theory of the tendencies to crisis of the welfare state.[48]

This lack of theoretical rigor carried over into their historical vision. Although Arendt and Camus celebrated the unpredictable emergence of rebellious political agencies, neither writer devotes any sustained attention to the likely sources of political radicalism or specifies the historical agents whose praxis might further democratize political life. This neglect is no doubt due largely to their justified aversion to the Marxian "labor metaphysic" and its faith in the historical mission of the proletariat. But there is no reason to equate the causal analysis of sources of oppression and resistance with the limited kinds of monocausal analysis they associate with Marxism; indeed there is no reason even to equate Marxism with such monocausal analysis.[49] Arendt and Camus may have acutely perceived its weaknesses, but they failed to recognize the richness of Marxism as a political tradition. Both ignore the efforts of twentieth-century Marxists— and here Rosa Luxemburg was less unusual than Arendt allows—to rethink historical materialism and reconsider the kinds of pedagogical and coalitional politics required by a vital socialist movement.[50] Both writers, in short, ignore the problem of what Gramsci called *hegemony*—how to understand the sources of political quiescence and mobilize and organize oppressed social groups so as to effectively challenge their oppression and constructively create a freer society. Although the concept of hegemony has its own complicated and far-from-innocent genealogy, it identifies a problem—the means of coordinating diverse insurgent constituencies and the forms of organization appropriate to a mass democratic politics—that seems crucial to any realistic vision of public freedom in the modern world.[51]

Yet before leaping too quickly to the mistaken conclusion that Arendt and Camus ought to have been neo-Marxists, it is important to keep in mind what the Marxian unity of theory and practice had produced at mid-century. If a less voluntaristic conception of human agency than that offered by Arendt and Camus may have been called for, it is also true that the Hegelian conception of a unified, rational subject, even as modified by Gramsci, is hardly more satisfactory. As we have come to appreciate, all such unities are artificial and fragile, all such totalizations partial and provisional. The aspiration to organize all oppressed groups beneath a single banner under the leadership of a historically privileged, uniquely revolutionary force is the residue of a long-gone era—an age with grand aspirations and genuine achievements, to be sure, but one still wedded to a theology in spite of itself—the deification of man. And the issue here is not simply the problem of vanguardism, for it plagues even the most resolutely democratic hegemonic politics; it is the impossibility of producing anything like the substantive unity that the vision of hegemony imagines. Once one abandons a philosophy of history, one must recognize that freedom and oppression, justice and injustice, good and evil, are not faced off against one another in any neat or simple way. To the contrary, they interpenetrate each other in often complex ways, producing strange compounds and startling reversals. Similarly, it is no longer possible to speak of progress and reaction as if these terms have anything more than a pragmatic meaning. For history does not have a single meaning and does not move along a single continuum; and what is good in one respect may often turn out to be harmful in others. In this regard the Nietzschean insights of Arendt and Camus into the ambiguous character of human agency and the recalcitrance of the world to human purposes are extremely valuable. And their sharing of an exaggerated epistemological skepticism is certainly understandable given the foundationalist claims to knowledge being advanced at the time by orthodox Marxism, positivism, and techn-ocratic social science. These discourses all shared a faith in the ability of instrumental action to link benign intention with scientific truth that can only be judged naive in the light of twentieth-century events. It is not hard to understand the revulsion of writers like Arendt and Camus at such a faith.

Although both writers were perhaps too ready to sever the links between theory and practice, their suspicion of the political claims of theory is understandable in light of the ethical insensitivity displayed by scientific socialism and positivist liberalism. Both thinkers rightly insist that human choices cannot be deduced from explanatory theories, that there is an inevitable contingency to human identity, and that ethical conduct is pri-marily a matter of the self-reflective and intersubjective praxis of complex agents and not a matter of sovereign subjects "correctly" discerning reality. Both see that there is a disjunction between fact and value that no theory can efface. Theory might provide guideposts of ethical conduct, but it can offer us neither categorical imperatives nor historical guarantees. Arendt and Camus avoid social science, even "critical" social science,[52] largely because they reject the project of a theory of objective social interests capable of fixing political identities and charting likely historical outcomes. In arguing that all individual and collective human subjects are diverse and fragmented agents whose identities are defined by their differences to others, they maintain that all politics, even the most hegemonic, is het-erogeneous and provisional.

This vision of a rebellious politics in many ways presents a truer con-ception of the sources and operations of political radicalism than that offered by theories, like Marxism, whose historical framework anticipates a moment of collective unity, historical rupture, and radical transformation. Whereas such approaches are bolstered by a faith, however implicit, in the prospects for unified mass collective agency, the vision of rebellious politics frankly acknowledges and indeed embraces the unanticipated, partial, and provisional character of any kind of democratic empowerment. Who can doubt that this vision best captures the most dramatic political episodes of our time—the pockets of underground resistance to Nazi and Stalinist forms of totalitarianism, the American civil rights movement, the contemporary movements for ecology, peace, and human rights, and the toppling of communism in Central Europe? And yet its lack of emphasis on questions of causality is a serious weakness nonetheless. In spite of the undeniable travesties of freedom generated by modern social science in its various political guises, it would be a mistake to dismiss social scientific inquiry as a possible agency of illumination, and hence of freedom as well.

The State and Revolution

This dismissal of causal inquiry is most damaging to the conception of political change offered by Arendt and Camus. According to both writers, humans possess capacities for creative agency that are best exemplified in revolutionary situations and can be nourished only by quasi-anarchist forms of local democratic community that are driven "from below." And yet though they support the project of democratic empowerment, both lack a richly strategic conception of power and a theory of the state whose alteration they seek.[53]

There is in both writers the basis for such a theory, for neither thoroughly abjures strategic considerations. As I have argued, whereas Arendt seems to polarize power and violence, and Camus seems to polarize revolt and revolution, both recognize the inextricability of ends and means in politics and acknowledge the need for institutional embodiments of rebellious impulses. Nonetheless, although in theory both reject false dualisms, their actual discussions lean heavily on the side of agency at the expense of structure. Both tend to treat political agency—the exercise of political powers—as expressive or performative more than as strategic, as refusing and breaking free of existing constraints rather than as shaped by the conditions under which it emerges. While seeing the need to equilibrate ends and means in politics, both also tend to privilege spontaneity over organization—thus the importance of fleeting revolutionary moments for

Arendt, of anarcho-syndicalist experiments for Camus. Though both writers are animated by a deeply rooted and well-founded aversion to the modern state and its principle of sovereignty, neither offers any deep understanding of the state, and both sidestep some of the most difficult issues posed by its awesome power.

Both writers present an indiscriminate conception of the modern state that is well summed up in Camus's assertion that "the evil of our times can be defined by its effects rather than by its causes. That evil is the State, whether a police state or a bureaucratic state. Its proliferation in all countries under cover of the most varied ideological pretexts . . . make[s] of the State a mortal danger for everything that is best in each of us. From this point of view, contemporary political society, in any form, is despicable."[54] Such antipathy toward the state is understandable given the extraordinary violence and displacement witnessed by both writers. Nonetheless, there is something obviously exaggerated about a political perspective that so easily dismisses all contemporary forms of state as despicable. Absent from the writings of Camus and Arendt is a sense that the modern state is both a dangerous concentration of force and an indispensable means of social coordination and public law. Both writers ignore the complex causes of the increasing role of the state in a postindustrial society.[55] The bureaucratic features of the modern state, in other words, are not so easily dismissed or condemned, even if they do warrant severe criticism for inhibiting more democratic forms of political activity.

Missing from both writers is an appreciation of the genuinely ambiguous character of the modern state, particularly in its capacity as an agency of social welfare. If on the one hand it is bureaucratic and disempowering, on the other hand it has functioned, haltingly and partially, as a primary source of justice. Although both Arendt and Camus understand the deleterious effects of capitalism on human security and freedom, and support alternative, more moderate forms of property, neither was deeply concerned with the kinds of public policies necessary to bring such alternatives about. On more than one occasion, it is true, Camus referred favorably to the welfare state, and clearly he supported most of the social democratic policies of the postwar French Socialists; but this support was lukewarm in contrast to his passionate identification with anarcho-syndicalist movements.[56] Arendt, on the other hand, retained an apparently indiscriminate aversion to the interventionist state.[57] Neither writer appreciated sufficiently the extent to which the welfare state is the outcome of a rebellious politics itself animated by the causes of social and economic justice. Virtually every form of state intervention in social life, from labor policy and entitlements to social and environmental regulation, can be seen as the product of intense political resistance to corporate power on the part of aggrieved and disenfranchised social groups. It is true that modern state agencies often co-opt such resistance and become ossified and self-perpetuating organizations. But some such agencies of justice seem indispensable under the complex conditions of modernity. Instead of viewing them as corruptive forces, it should be at least conceptually possible to imagine scenarios in which they can be seen as genuine repositories of a rebellious politics.[58]

Arendt and Camus are no more appreciative of the institutions of representative government. Although both writers underscore the importance of limits in politics and rebel against authoritarian revolutionary doctrines, neither has much that is positive to say about parliamentary government or political parties. Suspicious of the corrupting effects of political organizations, both place extraordinary emphasis on the unpredictable and spontaneous character of rebellious political agency.[59] While both writers rightly refuse to reduce political agency to its social or political conditions, they often imply that popular radicalism is entirely self-generated and self-constituted, and give insufficient attention to the problems of political mobilization and leadership. No matter how important one considers political participation and self-governance to be, the facts of social life in contemporary postindustrial societies seem to indicate that many kinds of political radicalism require organization and planning, and even those that arise more spontaneously require definite organizational form and leadership. Even council forms of democracy have involved elaborate preparation and coordination; and the more extensive such forms, the more such planning and coordination are necessary in order to handle the range of interests they encompass.[60]

If this is true, then it is also true that a fully adequate conception of political radicalism must offer some account of the constructive role of political parties as instrumentalities of political pedagogy, interest aggregation, and political representation. As products respectively of the German Weimar and French Fourth republics, Arendt and Camus were attuned to the corrupting possibilities of parliamentary government and partisan politics, which tend to produce entrenched systems of political privilege and freeze more local and spontaneous forms of political participation. It is well and good to offer a vision of a rebellious politics that is far richer than electoral politics. But it hardly follows that political parties are dispensable as intermediaries between democratic citizens and political authorities.[61]

The celebration of councils and soviets to be found in the writings of Camus and Arendt is almost blind to the limits of these forms of self-government and to the strengths of parliamentary institutions. Since both writers clearly abjure the Leninist vision of smashing the state and radically transforming society, it is ironic that in some ways their view of councils echoes the Bolshevik notion of dual power as it is found in Lenin's most radical writings of the revolutionary period, such as *The State and Revolution*. Like Lenin, Arendt and Camus see parliamentarism as a sclerotic and corrupt form of government best replaced by spontaneous forms of local participation and direct democracy. Both writers, of course, reject the conceptions of vanguard party and total revolution espoused by the Bolsheviks, and thus for both of them such revolutionary forms of government must always remain true to their rebellious impulses, recognizing and respecting their own limits. In other words, despite their admiration of the institutions of the revolutionary council system, Arendt and Camus reject the abuses to which they have often given rise. But, crucially, both fail to see how the virtues of the council system—spontaneity, direct democracy, extraordinarily high levels of participation, and the absence of a professional political stratum—are integrally linked to its vices—transitory existence, instability, and lack of an effective system of national interest representation. Council forms of politics have much to recommend them. In the absence of more enduring forms of authority, however, they are notoriously tumultuous, ineffective, and insufficient to guarantee a stable democratic system of civil and political rights. The failures of soviets and councils cannot simply be attributed to the misapprehension and exploitation of them by doctrinaire revolutionaries, for these institutions have their own very definite failings.

Ironically, this important point, lost on two penetrating critics of twentieth-century Marxism, has been emphasized by many democratic Marxists, perhaps most clearly in the later writings of Nicos Poulantzas. Criticizing the model of revolutionary dual power based on a soviet system of compulsory mandate and instant recall, Poulantzas asserts that democratic liberties require a representative national assembly elected by universal suffrage in a secret ballot. "Historically," he maintains, "every experience of direct democracy at the base which has not been tied to the maintenance of representative democracy for a certain period has failed"; soviets, he insists, have "always and everywhere been accompanied by the suppression of the plurality of parties, and then the suppression of political and formal liberties."[62] As Arendt acknowledged, council forms of revolutionary democracy result not from the machinations of revolutionary elites but the crisis of legitimacy and "loss of power" of constituted authorities. "Revolutionaries are those who know when power is lying in the street and when they can pick it up."[63] But, as Poulantzas recognized, such a complete loss of power is a dangerous thing, for when power is lying about in the street, it can be picked up by anybody. Not only are there no guarantees that democratic forms of power will be constituted; in contemporary society there are powerful financial and geopolitical pressures toward centralized, bureaucratic forms of power. If so, then any political praxis that envisions a revolutionary situation in which it can simply sidestep the problem of the state is doomed to be haunted by authoritarianism.[64]

On the other hand, the effort to practice soviet or council forms of democracy in the absence of a breakdown of political authority risks being ineffective in challenging the centralizing and disempowering institutions of the contemporary state and economy. Although purely local and ad hoc forms of political activism may engender a healthy sense of empowerment, and may successfully address matters of local concern, unless these efforts acquire a more coordinated and disciplined form they will probably remain powerless to address more global concerns, whether these be questions of economic justice, environmental regulation, or war and peace. Democratic socialists like Poulantzas have maintained that while any genuine democratization of society must rely upon popular initiatives and forms of direct, rank-and-file democracy, it must also seek "a sweeping transformation of the State itself."

The rebellious politics endorsed by Arendt and Camus here seems undermined by its anarchist leanings, either being insufficient to challenge forms of entrenched power or requiring a dangerous breakdown of political authority while remaining ill-prepared to fill the vacuum that will invariably ensue. In neither case does it seem able to sustain the rebellious, democratic impulses that drive it. Poulantzas seems to offer a more adequate formulation of this problem. Rejecting the idea that there is a simple choice—either liberal parliamentarism or rank-and-file democracy—he declares that "the essential problem...must be posed in a different way: how is it possible radically to transform the State in such a manner that the extension and deepening of political freedoms and the institutions of representative democracy (which were also a conquest of the popular masses) are combined with the unfurling of forms of direct democracy and the mushrooming of self-management bodies?"[65] Such an approach shares with Camus and Arendt a deep suspicion of all forms of statism; but it insists on the ethical and strategic inextricability of local democracy and a social democratic state with representative institutions. What Arendt and Camus both seem to ignore is that if rebellious politics is to be more than a self-actualizing and self-consuming phenomenon, then it must challenge and seek to reshape, however cautiously and imperfectly, existing political institutions. A viable radical politics, however rebellious and alive to the partiality of political movements and organizations, must constructively engage the state rather than simply oppose it or sidestep it through local forms of resistance. It must deepen rather than dismiss the institutions of representative democracy, in the name of current liberties and those yet to be won.

And yet such constructive engagement always threatens to overwhelm and constrain rebellion; here again we confront the dilemmas of ends and means that so concerned Arendt and Camus. Some kinds of means may be necessary if political rebellion is to have any enduring effect; but there is also the danger that such effectiveness may be purchased at the price of freedom itself. The socialist tradition, particularly Marxism, has long been preoccupied with means, discipline, and organization, with identifying "nodal points" or "strategic heights," with concentrating political force, and with developing a counterhegemony. Historical materialism since Marx has prided itself on its being realistic rather than utopian, strategic rather than ethical.[66] Yet its realism has often been morally oblique, and its strategic thinking has often been blind to less visible or less global forms of oppression, to unimagined sources of political radicalism and unanticipated sources of tyranny. The strategic orientation of socialist political thought even at its most democratic, as exemplified in Poulantzas's arguments, is an important counterweight to utopian visions of direct democracy and the abolition of the state. But it needs to be complimented by the vigorously rebellious impulses celebrated by Arendt and Camus. For these writers understood that there is a reservoir of unanticipated energy that escapes even the most provident of strategies.

The strategic weaknesses of rebellious politics weigh heavily in thinking about global questions of social and political transformation. How ought global economic justice be achieved? How can the property relations of capitalism be restructured? Such questions are no doubt important ones. But when we acknowledge that Arendt and Camus do not offer their perspectives as strategies of transformation, such weaknesses become less decisive. We can then see these lacunae less as failures to answer questions that these writers pose than as silences regarding questions of strategic transformation that their writings *refuse* to pose. A generous reading would allow that in a world too preoccupied with strategies, organizations, and hegemonies, Arendt and Camus above all seek to loosen things up. Both emphasize the presentness of rebellion, its rootedness in the here and now, in order to counter models of politics whose fixation on past conditions or imagined futures distract us from what is truly within our reach—the modest results that can be achieved through our own unmediated concerted efforts. As Camus put it: "the doctrines that explain everything to me also debilitate me at the same time. They relieve me of the weight of my own life."[67] Such a relaxation of political forces and concerns may not help us to resolve all of our world's problems, but it offers a healthy antidote to the frozen politics of a world still locked into the ideological and organizational rigidities of nineteenth-century class politics. The power of this rebellious vision can perhaps best be demonstrated by likening it to the more current discourse of civil society in Central Europe.

Rebellious Politics and Civil Society

Certainly the most exciting and momentous political developments since the end of World War II have been the Central European revolutions of 1989. Revolting against the vestiges of Stalinist totalitarianism, democrats throughout the region have raised the banner of "civil society against the state."[68] Rejecting communism and pushing far beyond the bounds of political reform, these activists claim to speak for a "new Europe" and to presage a new, confederational world order beyond the superpower bloc system. This model of politics has striking affinities with the vision offered by Arendt and Camus.[69]

The Central European democrats have long abjured prevailing forms and strategies of political opposition, whether revolutionary or reformist. Cutting against the grain of normal politics, they have exemplified and indeed personified what Václav Havel has called "a new model of behavior": "don't get involved in diffuse general ideological polemics with the center, to whom numerous concrete causes are always being sacrificed; fight 'only' for those concrete causes, and be prepared to fight for them unswervingly, to the end." As Havel describes this model of conduct, resistance to oppression is deeply moral, but instead of directly challenging the state, it seeks to fashion "an island of freedom in an ocean of something that thought of itself as immensely free but in fact was not."[70] Such a project is informed by the values of human freedom and dignity. But though ethically inspired and often requiring the rebel to be a voice in the wilderness, it is also a political project deeply concerned with the consequences of behavior. Havel indicates that he has no faith in history or humanity but, like Camus, he does have a certain modest faith in man.

As he writes: "even a purely moral act that has no hope of any immediate and visible political effect can gradually and indirectly, over time, gain in political significance."[71] Such moral acts have the force of example; manifesting something in the individual that reaches beyond himself, they strike a common chord among those who suffer a common oppression and share a common fate.

This "new model of conduct" is insistently rebellious. Like Arendt and Camus, its proponents maintain that humans are never exhausted by their oppressive conditions, that they possess capacities to resist indignity and reconstitute community that can neither be written off nor saddled by a political ideology. A clear statement of this belief is Havel's 1975 "Letter to Dr. Gustav Husák," in which he warned the Czech dictator:

> Life may be subjected to a prolonged and thorough process of violation, enfeeblement and anesthesia. Yet, in the end, it cannot be permanently halted. Albeit quietly, covertly, and slowly, it nevertheless goes on. Though it be estranged from itself a thousand times, it always manages in some way to recuperate; however violently ravished, it always survives, in the end, the power which ravished it.... If life cannot be destroyed for good, neither, then, can history be brought entirely to a halt. A secret streamlet trickles on beneath the heavy lid of inertia and pseudoevents, slowly and inconspicuously undercutting it. It may be a long process, but one day it must happen: the lid will no longer hold and will start to crack.[72]

Echoing Camus's view that acceptance of the status quo signals "a mood of absolute Utopia insofar as it assumes the 'freezing' of history," Havel rejects the idea that all possibilities for change have been foreclosed.[73] To the contrary, he avows that human freedom has a way of restoring itself in unexpected ways. In his 1978 essay "The Power of the Powerless" he hales a rebelliousness rooted in "the human predisposition to truth" and residing in a "hidden sphere ... where the potential for communication exists." In a passage that recalls Arendt's comments on natality, he holds that "this power does not participate in any direct struggle for power; rather it makes its influence felt in the obscure arena of being itself."[74] Such a capacity, in other words, is latent in all of human interaction, all of social being itself; it is a possibility waiting to be realized. Similar recourse to the recalcitrance of human freedom can be found in the writings of George Konrad, who appeals to the "authority of the spirit" against the conformism demanded by the state, and Adam Michnik, who declares that "solidarity provides a shelter for spiritual homelessness; it is the declaration of war against human solitude in the face of the communist Leviathan."[75]

Joined with this appeal to the rebellious spirit is a vision of an antistatist politics driven by self-constituted and self-limiting political agents, associations of individuals confident in their capacity for creative opposition and profoundly aware of their own limits. Havel, reflecting on the Prague Spring of 1968, recalls the "genuine civic-mindedness" of the normally quiescent populace, noting that this experience revealed the unsuspected, latent political potentialities of civil society: "That week showed how helpless military power is when confronted by an opponent unlike any that power has been trained to confront; it showed how hard it is to govern a country in which, though it may not defend itself militarily, all the civil structures simply turn their backs on the aggressors."[76] This conception of civil resistance is also articulated, in a somewhat different vein, in George Konrad's model of "antipolitics," which "neither supports nor opposes governments; it is something different. Its people are fine right where they are; they form a network that keeps watch on political power, exerting pressure on the basis of their cultural and moral stature alone, not through any electoral legitimacy. That is their right and their obligation, but above all their self-defense."[77]

For both Havel and Konrad rebellion emerges less from conventional forms of political organization than from the social networks of ordinary life, from the "hidden spaces" and "islands of freedom" to be found in civil society.[78] It is here, in the course of daily life, that conscientious individuals constitute themselves as historical agents, more or less spontaneously organizing voluntary associations that are independent of the state and seek "social defense" against its imperatives. Perhaps the most politically sophisticated version of such a self-constituted radicalism is that of Adam Michnik, one of the leaders of the Polish intellectual group KOR (Worker's Defense Committee), later a key Solidarity adviser and politician and currently a leader of the Polish democratic movement. In "A New Evolutionism," an influential 1976 essay on political strategy, Michnik, like Havel, concludes that "the lesson of Czechoslovakia is that change is possible and that it has its limits." He insists that "an unceasing struggle for reform and evolution that seeks an expansion of civil liberties and human rights is the only course East European dissidents can take," and asserts that it is important to retain "a sense of reality and moderation." The central problem as he defines it is to determine "the area of permissible political maneuver . . . the sphere of possible compromise" with the communist regime. "The new evolutionism" seeks to alter the character of this regime without organizing any frontal challenge to its power or to the power of the Soviet-led Warsaw Pact. Rejecting the dualism of reform and revolution, Michnik endorses an evolution whose driving force is the autonomous political praxis of civil society: "a program for evolution ought to be addressed to an independent public, not to totalitarian power. Such a program should give directives to the people on how to behave, not to the powers on how to reform themselves. Nothing instructs the authorities better than pressure from below. . . . The democratic opposition must formulate its own political goals and only then, with these goals in hand, reach political compromises."[79] Michnik thus maintains that political rebellion ought to be self-constituted, organized through voluntary associations and oriented not toward the state but toward itself. This self-reflexivity relates both to the organization and to the tactics of the opposition. It requires a healthy sense of confidence in the ability of the opposition to effect change through its own activities, without relying upon the agencies of the state, and an equally healthy sense of the limits of its power, foresight, and righteousness. And so Michnik also insists that the opposition be self-limiting as well as self-constituting. Its "directives to the people on how to behave" are thus modest and tolerant, though impassioned.

This conception of self-limitation is most clearly developed in his 1979 essay "Maggots and Angels." Advocating what Arendt calls representative thinking, Michnik chastises those oppositionists who refuse any compromise with the regime and condemn all who "collaborate" with it in any way as "maggots." Declaring "I do not favor excessive moral rigor," he refuses "an exaggerated cult of clean hands." He cautions Solidarity against self-righteousness, urging that people open their eyes to "the complexity of the whole picture."[80] Exploring the range of political alternatives available to those opposed to the regime, he admits that although he has stood with those who have directly challenged authority, "I have also attempted to understand those who acted differently and to respect their choices."[81] This is not a brief for ethical relativism, but a defense of political sobriety. Michnik's words here echo those of Camus in his "The Unbeliever and the Christians" and "Letter to an Algerian Militant":

> We live and will live among people who think otherwise. We must learn to live with them and teach them to live with us. We must learn the difficult art of compromise, without which authentic pluralism will not be possible . . . only then will we manage to confront totalitarian power with dignity. . . . Bless those times when one can sign protest letters as well as publish books or direct films.

But we know that often one has to choose. And I have no easy formula for such choices. I envy anyone who knows such a formula. But I am a little afraid of them as well. . . . It is sectarian nonsense to throw all those who think and act differently into that capacious sack labelled "maggots." It can be done only by someone who believes that he has discovered the sole moral and correct road to sovereignty and democracy. I well know this type of "truth bearer" from history. And that is why I am afraid.[82]

According to this view, political opposition needs to be self-limiting in two senses. First, it must remain true to its own ethical impulses, refusing to sacrifice integrity to expediency. Like Camus's "just assassins," the self-limiting activist must be ceaselessly scrupulous and self-critical. Second, activists must remain sensitive to the limits imposed by the political balance of forces, avoiding a decisive confrontation with a regime capable of crushing them at great human and political cost. Jacek Kuron, another influential Polish democrat, starkly posed this question: "Is it possible to set limits to the movement's dynamic? Not only is it possible, it is necessary; but the only way of achieving this would be to define a programme of action which would allow the movement to develop without losing sight of its limits."[83] This sensitivity was the distinguishing characteristic of Solidarity as a movement. As Alain Touraine wrote in 1983, "The movement is self-limiting in the sense that, against a background of radical aspirations, it is prepared to adopt strategies involving compromise with the authorities. . . . The movement always adopts and modifies the limits which are imposed on it, always acting within its capacities . . . [but its] aim was to promote a self-limiting struggle which would avoid the catastrophes which had befallen Hungary and Czechoslovakia."[84]

The politics of civil society in Central Europe on the eve of democratic revolution seemed to exemplify all that is attractive in the vision of rebellious politics articulated by Arendt and Camus. Revolting against the experience of totalitarianism and animated by the ideals of human dignity, solidarity, and self-determination, the democrats of the region remained attuned to the problem of equilibrating means and ends. Aware of the ethical and practical dangers of political violence, steering between the Scylla of ineffectiveness and the Charybdis of civil war, they supported a vigorous yet self-limiting praxis, a radical yet "relative revolution" that pioneered new forms of nonviolent resistance. Confronting authoritarian states that repressed all organized forms of political opposition, they sought to create islands of freedom amid the ossified structures of authoritarian communism.[85] Calling themselves "Dialogue," "Civic Forum," "Solidarity," and "Democratic Forum," they seemed to incarnate the "solidarity of chains" of which Camus wrote.[86]

Most important, these democrats, positioned between East and West, sought to navigate between the jagged edges of the frozen geopolitics of the Cold War, creatively pursuing a third way between capitalism and communism. Sadly, the vision of rebellious politics foundered after World War II, marginalized, co-opted, and eventually overwhelmed by the widening polarization between East and West. A striking feature of the politics of civil society that is still under way in Central Europe is its bringing to life the ideas of Arendt and Camus under the dramatic circumstances of the demise of the Cold War. These new circumstances provide the occasion to reconsider the fruitfulness of a vision that was tragically foreclosed but that seems to have made a remarkable reappearance. Camus's call for an international democracy built "from the ground up, so as to shape a living society inside a dying society" and Arendt's plea for a "new guarantee" for human dignity beyond the principle of sovereignty seem visionary when viewed against the backdrop of the extraordinary forms of global and regional cooperation regarding human rights and the environment that are currently being contemplated as a result of the breakup of the Soviet empire.

Many such forms of cooperation have involved diplomacy and interstate negotiation. But many important forms of cooperation have been unofficial. European Nuclear Disarmament (END), the various Green movements and parties, and even less formalized networks and activists, have all sprung into existence from below, as it were, challenging the right of existing states to speak in the name of their citizens. Such groups have prefigured in their very structure the post–Cold War world they have sought. Perhaps the most innovative and promising of these groups is the Helsinki Citizens Assembly. An outgrowth of the international links forged between East European dissidents and West European peace activists after the Helsinki Accords of 1975, the Assembly, established in 1990, seeks to nurture the international civil society that promoted a "détente from below" throughout the 1980s. As Mary Kaldor, writing in 1988, described this politics, "It is not addressed to governments except in so far as they are asked to guarantee freedom of travel and freedom of assembly so that citizens's groups can meet and communicate. It is a strategy of dialogue, an attempt to change society through the actions of citizens rather than governments . . . in short, to create a new political culture. In such a situation, the behaviour of governments either changes or becomes less and less relevant."[87]

The Citizens's Assembly seeks to continue this process, "whereby citizens may not only exercise public oversight over governments but also find imaginative ways of loosening ossified positions" under the new post-Cold War conditions. As its Prague Appeal of 1990 states, "Overcoming the division of Europe is the job above all of civil society, of citizens acting together in self-organized associations, movements, institutions, initiatives and clubs across national boundaries."[88]

Taking a more worldly view of things, recoiling not simply from communism but from the modern hubris that it represented, the democrats of European civil society, East and West, echo Arendt and Camus in their insistence on a more careful politics, one that promotes dialogue rather than silence and is respectful of individual rights, national and regional cultures, and the environment.[89] Soberly recognizing the limits of their politics, they seek proximate, flexible institutions that might serve as vehicles for their resistance to domination. The praxis of groups like the Helsinki Citizens' Assembly exemplifies the model of politics presented by Camus's Dr. Rieux and by Arendt's revolutionary elites. It is a self-constituted rebellion by those, delegated and appointed by no one, who have taken responsibility for their future upon themselves. While they are clearly concerned with the consequences of their actions, such concern is focused on what they can do *now* and on how their empowerment enables them to act with dignity. For them the agency is not quite its own reward; but neither is it viewed in merely instrumental terms. Instead, it is a means that is also an end. Mary Kaldor describes such a politics:

> So what kind of organization are we? ... We are not a representative of civil society; we are a part of civil society. If we were representative of civil society we would be no different from a parliament. ... In fact, we don't represent anyone except the movements and institutions in which we are involved. In many cases, we represent no one but ourselves. And our power rests not on whom we represent but in what we do—in what we say, in our ideas, in our quest for truth, in the projects we undertake. It rests on our energy and commitment.[90]

Such a politics has proven itself enormously potent in challenging Soviet-style Marxism and Cold War liberalism, both of which have long relied upon fatuous claims to represent the interests of their respective citizens. And yet here too the vision of rebellious politics comes up against its own limitations. As the Central Europeans are currently learning, freedom presents difficult and painful choices; it furnishes, as James Madison put it, the oxygen upon which faction feeds. It thus requires authoritative institutions of conflict resolution and public order. Although a rebellious politics has demonstrated its effectiveness in generating grass-roots political power and creating a vital network of democratic activists across frontiers, it is not clear that such a politics, centered in civil society, can be equally effective in fashioning stable democratic economic and political institutions.[91] Stability would seem to require forms of institutional design and social discipline perhaps more demanding—and more frustrating—than the voluntary associations envisioned by Arendt and Camus and constituted by the citizens of European civil society. Ex-dissident Havel, now the president of Czechoslovakia, has acknowledged this problem:

> It turns out that no matter how difficult it is to bring down a totalitarian system, it is even more difficult to build a new and better system from its ruins. Since we have entered the world of high politics, we have realized that in this world one has to take account of various interests, of various ambitions, of the balance of power represented by different groupings.... Thus a person in the world of high politics is forced to behave diplomatically, to maneuver. Simply, we now find ourselves in a different arena... and have a totally different kind of responsibility from when we were in opposition.[92]

Havel maintains that "this fact cannot change the essence of our efforts and ideals"; but he concedes that "the forms and ways in which these ideals are being implemented may have to be modified." Such modification requires, in other words, the forms and ways of representative government—partisan competition, regular multiparty elections, the formation of a government, legislative politics, and the institution of bureaucratically administered public policies. A rebellious politics is not necessarily hostile to these forms and ways. But neither is it particularly attuned to them. Rather, it is concerned with more direct, spontaneous, and unofficial (if not anti-official) activities.

In the post-Communist societies of Central Europe, then, a rebellious politics of civil society seems clearly insufficient. Meanwhile in the West, although such a politics deserves much credit for having challenged Cold War pieties, protested the arms race, and most of all for having supported East European dissidents, it lacks the advantage of having successfully challenged a repressive state. It thus risks being diluted by the "repressive tolerance" of liberal democratic society.[93] Here too rebelliousness confronts the limits of its power—how to organize a politics that is both democratic in its agencies and effective in challenging the national and global structures of domination associated with the centralized state and the corporate economy. In the West, of course, this problem has not reached the crisis proportions it has in the East. In some ways this is a blessing, for Western democrats operate in a much less hostile and perilous environment; unlike their Eastern counterparts, they need not fear the prospect of imminent reversion to authoritarianism or nationalist fanaticism. On the other hand, the instability of Central Europe also presents a fluidity unmatched in the West, where there seem fewer openings for genuine political and economic experimentation. Western leaders have demonstrated unparalleled rhetorical enthusiasm for the discourse of democracy as it has reemerged in the East, but they have shown little interest in such democracy in their own societies. Although the problems of capitalism mount in the West, there is little evidence of serious questioning of liberal institutions much less of an insurgent politics. This complacency is the source of much legitimate despair among those seriously committed to democracy and social justice. And though this despair is more pronounced in the West, it is not confined there; for as the great liberal celebration moves eastward it carries in tow the values and practices of a capitalist market society that threatens a democratic civil society just as potently—and certainly as efficiently—as did the former Communist regimes.[94]

On both sides of the former Cold War divide, then, the politics of civil society confronts deep problems. Though it has played an important role in ending the balance of terror, and has inspired democratic theorists and activists no longer satisfied with more traditional modes of liberal democratic and socialist politics, it has failed, so far, to supplant the problems of modern politics or transcend its state and market-centered agencies. But should this failure be surprising? Did such a politics ever promise to remake the world? We may not have entered upon a new epoch, and it may well be that the new politics of civil society has much to learn from older forms of political radicalism, most notably from the politics of democratic socialism. But whatever its limits, it is absurd to assert that the politics of civil society represents a "loss of nerve," a "full retreat" from "the traditional role of the Western left as a critic of capitalism."[95] It is true that it represents an abandonment of the left's fixation on capitalism in favor of a broader, more inclusive concern with the democratization of all areas of social life. It is also true that it breaks with the "traditional" left's preoccupation with the transformation of the state. But this is neither a retreat nor a loss of nerve. It is a courageous and innovative move beyond the confines of traditional class politics at a time when that form of politics has proven itself stale, perhaps anachronistic, and certainly lacking in either popular appeal or the political power it seeks. And though this politics is most certainly novel, it is not quite as novel as its critics and perhaps some its defenders seem to think. For, as I have attempted to document, it is rooted in a vision developed by an earlier generation of radical intellectuals whose struggle against totalitarianism moved them beyond liberalism and socialism, a generation inspired by "the lost treasure" of even earlier experiments in anarchist and council self-government.

The vision of rebellious politics articulated by Arendt and Camus has much to offer contemporary democrats. In a world overcome with relativism, banality, and political cynicism—features mirrored in many current academic fashions—it insists that human beings do have a nature, that our condition offers us limits and opportunities, and that it is within our power to constitute forms of political community within which we may experience a sense of individual and collective dignity. In a world in which politics has largely been reduced to the manipulation of media images, ritualized performances of partisan competition, and bureaucratic administration, it appeals to the unanticipated and unthought possibilities latent within the present, and imagines new "spaces for public freedom" that defy the conventional logic of modern politics. Abetting a revitalization of political energies, it nonetheless emphasizes the tragic dilemmas and sacrifices of politics, and cautions a healthy skepticism of any politics that claims to embody all that is noble and good. In a world riven with proliferating ethnic, national, racial, and gender conflicts, it is this suspicion of political commitments when they become ideologies, this spirit of tolerance—this insistence on representative thinking—that is perhaps the most important contribution the vision of rebellious politics can offer. As we think what we are doing—to use Arendt's famous phrase—we must always be aware of those others with whom we are doing it and those others whom we are doing it *to*. In the Middle East, in southern Africa, in Yugoslavia, in the former republics of the Soviet Union, indeed in the inner cities of the United States, this is a most valuable lesson. The realm of politics is a realm of limits, a realm of the relative; as Camus saw, "pure and unadulterated virtue is homicidal."[96]

In these respects a rebellious politics recommends itself to us. And yet it too has its limits. Intent on rescuing the rebellious impulse from the many modern agencies that have misappropriated and corrupted it, the vision of rebellious politics often too easily dismisses important strategic concerns, and too readily dispenses with what are indispensable agencies of modern politics. Camus's thoughts here are apposite: "Does the end justify the means? That is possible. But what will justify the end? To that question, which historical thought leaves pending, rebellion replies: the means." A democratic politics must never allow its means to overwhelm the end of human freedom. But it also must employ means sufficient to pursue that end. Such calculations can never be rendered a priori. But I believe it is fair to suggest that a rebellious politics requires as its complement a more institutional kind of politics, one suspicious of but not wholly averse to political organization and state power, and committed to using state power to reform social, economic, and political structures of domination. It requires, in other words, a social democratic politics, based among other things on a vigorous labor movement, social democratic parties, and a state committed to social justice.[97]

Both a rebellious politics and a more conventional social democratic politics have much to recommend themselves. Although they share a commitment to certain general universalist and democratic values, these kinds of politics are not the same; indeed, there are serious tensions between them regarding styles of activism, organizational forms, and the purposes of politics itself. And yet I find it impossible to choose between them. As a political theorist and as someone committed to democratic values I am less than fully satisfied with such ambivalence. There are powerful pressures for closure, for stating one's position for or against, for taking sides, built into our intellectual life and into our politics. And yet if the writings of Arendt and Camus teach us anything, it is that sometimes such pressures ought to be resisted. There are times when a clear "yes" or "no" may be called for; but there are also times, far more frequent, when such exclamations will not do, and when a more subtle consideration of possibilities is required. We could do worse than to heed Camus's words: "In the difficult times we face, what more can I hope for than the power to exclude nothing and to learn to weave from strands of black and white one rope tautened to the breaking point?"[98]

Ambiguity is the stuff of life. The most valuable lesson of a rebellious politics may be that the effort definitively and exclusively to choose a single vision of democratic politics is futile. Perhaps the most that political theory can hope to accomplish is to bring alternative approaches to democracy into contact with one another, to foster their disagreements, and to work to achieve some always tenuous, always provisional, mutual understanding. Hopefully this effort will inform, and perhaps even inspire, people whose own spirit inclines them to refuse the indignities of our world. But in any case the fostering of such argument will at least allow us to retain our own sense of integrity. For it is no longer possible to believe that we can place the mind in the service of a single cause or that a single version of the truth about the world will set us free. Democratic politics requires convictions and organizational commitments. But it also requires rebels, of the mind and of the spirit, who are courageous enough to unsettle convictions and commitments and to insist that if we truly prefer human freedom and dignity, we must be willing to live with our imperfections and with our differences.

Abbreviations

by Hannah Arendt

BPF   *Between Past and Future: Eight Exercises in Political Thought*. Middlesex: Penguin, 1977.

CR   *Crises of the Republic*. New York: Harcourt, Brace, Jovanovich, 1972.

EJ   *Eichmann in Jerusalem: A Report on the Banality of Evil*. Middlesex: Penguin, 1977.

HC   *The Human Condition*. Chicago: University of Chicago Press, 1958.

JP   *The Jew as Pariah*. Edited by Ron H. Feldman. New York: Grove Press, 1978.

LKPP   *Lectures on Kant's Political Philosophy*. Edited by Ronald Beiner. Chicago: University of Chicago Press, 1982.

LM   *The Life of the Mind*. New York: Harcourt, Brace, Jovanovich, 1978.

MDT   *Men in Dark Times*. New York: Harcourt, Brace, Jovanovich, 1968.

OR   *On Revolution*. Middlesex: Penguin, 1977.

OT   *The Origins of Totalitarianism*. Rev. ed. New York: Harcourt, Brace, Jovanovich, 1973.

by Albert Camus

BHR   *Between Hell and Reason: Essays from the Resistance Newspaper "Combat," 1944–47*. Translated by Alexandre de Gramont. Hanover: Wesleyan University Press, 1991.

CTOP   *Caligula and Three Other Plays*. Translated by Stuart Gilbert. New York: Knopf, 1958.

F   *The Fall*. Translated by Justin O'Brien. New York: Knopf, 1956.

LCE   *Lyrical and Critical Essays*. Edited by Philip Thody. Translated by Ellen Conroy Kennedy. New York: Knopf, 1968.

MS   *The Myth of Sisyphus and Other Essays*. Translated by Justin O'Brien. New York: Knopf, 1955.

N1   *Notebooks, 1935–1942*. Translated by Philip Thody. New York: Knopf, 1963.

N2   *Notebooks, 1942–1951*. Translated by Justin O'Brien. New York: Knopf, 1966.

Pl   *The Plague*. Translated by Stuart Gilbert. New York: Modern Library, 1948.

Po   *The Possessed: A Play in Three Parts*. Translated by Justin O'Brien. New York: Knopf, 1960.

R   *The Rebel: An Essay on Man In Revolt*. Translated by Anthony Bower. New York: Random House, 1956.

RRD   *Resistance, Rebellion, and Death*. Translated by Justin O'Brien. New York: Knopf, 1960.

S   *The Stranger*. Translated by Stuart Gilbert. New York: Random House, 1946.

Notes

Introduction

1. Charles Taylor, *Sources of the Self: The Making of the Modern Identity* (Cambridge, Mass.: Harvard University Press, 1989), p. x.
2. This last question is posed by Camus in "Pessimism and Courage," *RRD,* p. 58.
3. See Francis Fukuyama, "The End of History?" *National Interest,* no. 16 (Summer 1989): 3–18.
4. Friedrich Nietzsche, *Untimely Meditations,* quoted in Mark Warren, *Nietzsche and Political Thought* (Cambridge, Mass.: MIT Press, 1988), p. 86.
5. C. Wright Mills, *The Sociological Imagination* (Oxford: Oxford University Press, 1959), p. 166.
6. See Imre Lakatos and Alan Musgrave, eds., *Criticism and the Growth of Knowledge* (Cambridge: Cambridge University Press, 1970), and Harold I. Brown, *Perception, Theory, Commitment: The New Philosophy of Science* (Chicago: University of Chicago Press, 1977).
7. Richard Rorty, *Philosophy and the Mirror of Nature* (Princeton: Princeton University Press, 1978) and *Consequences of Pragmatism* (Minneapolis: University of Minnesota Press, 1982).
8. See Peter Dews, *Logics of Disintergration: Post-Structuralist Thought and the Claims of Critical Theory* (London: Verso, 1987).
9. Jean-François Lyotard, *The Postmodern Condition: A Report on Knowledge* (Minneapolis: University of Minnesota Press, 1984), p. xxiii–xxiv.
10. See Don Herzog, *Without Foundations: Justification in Political Theory* (Ithaca: Cornell University Press, 1985).
11. See Ian Shapiro, *The Evolution of Rights in Liberal Theory* (Cambridge: Cambridge University Press, 1986).
12. Judith Shklar, *Ordinary Vices* (Cambridge, Mass.: Harvard University Press, 1985) and *The Faces of Injustice* (New Haven: Yale University Press, 1990).

13. John Rawls, "Justice: Political, Not Metaphysical," *Philosophy and Public Affairs* 14, no. 3 (1985). Bruce Ackerman similarly disavows any "foundationalist" commitment in his interesting *We the People* (Cambridge, Mass.: Harvard University Press, 1991).

14. Richard Rorty, "Postmodern Bourgeois Liberalism," in Robert Hollinger, ed., *Hermeneutics and Praxis* (South Bend, Ind.: University of Notre Dame Press, 1985).

15. Richard Rorty, *Contingency, Irony, Solidarity* (Cambridge: Cambridge University Press, 1989), p. 198.

16. This point is made with particular sharpness by Terry Eagleton in "Defending the Free World," in Ralph Miliband and Leo Panitch, eds., *The Socialist Register 1990: The Retreat of the Intellectuals* (London: Merlin Press, 1990). Unfortunately Eagleton does not subject his own Marxism to the same withering scrutiny that he rightly bestows upon Rorty's liberalism. See also Sheldon S. Wolin, "Democracy in the Discourse of Postmodernism," *Social Research* 57, no. 1 (Spring 1990), and Thomas McCarthy, "Private Irony and Public Decency: Richard Rorty's New Pragmatism," *Critical Inquiry* 16, no. 2 (Winter 1990).

17. See Ian Shapiro, *Political Criticism* (Berkeley and Los Angeles: University of California Press, 1990), pp. 207–30.

18. Alasdair MacIntyre, *After Virtue* (South Bend, Ind.: University of Notre Dame Press, 1981) and *Whose Justice? Which Rationality?* (South Bend, Ind.: University of Notre Dame Press, 1988).

19. Allan Bloom, *The Closing of the American Mind* (New York: Simon and Schuster, 1987).

20. See Perry Anderson, *Considerations on Western Marxism* (London: Verso, 1976) and *In The Tracks of Historical Materialism* (Chicago: University of Chicago Press, 1982).

21. See Jeffrey C. Isaac, "One Step Sideways, One Step Backwards: Postmarxism and Its Critics," *Theory, Culture, and Society* (forthcoming, 1992).

22. Alasdair MacIntyre, *Marxism and Christianity* (South Bend, Ind.: University of Notre Dame Press, 1968).

23. See Mary Kaldor, *The Baroque Arsenal* (New York: Hill and Wang, 1981). On the sorry state of contemporary politics, see "Democratic Vistas: A Statement for the Democratic Left," *Dissent,* Fall 1991.

24. Ian Shapiro, *Political Criticism* (Berkeley and Los Angeles: University of California Press, 1990), p. 14.

25. Rorty, *Contingency,* pp. 73–141.

26. Edmund Burke, *Reflections on the Revolution in France* (Middlesex: Penguin, 1984), p. 171.

27. Jacques Derrida, "Racism's Last Word," *Critical Inquiry* 12 (1985). See also Thomas McCarthy, "The Politics of the Ineffible: Derrida's Deconstruction," *Philosophical Forum* 21, nos. 1–2 (Fall-Winter 1989–1990). For a more favorable view, see Christopher Norris, *What's Wrong with Postmodernism: Critical Theory and the Ends of Philosophy* (Baltimore: Johns Hopkins University Press, 1990).

28. Norman Jacobson, *Pride and Solace: The Functions and Limits of Political Theory* (Berkeley and Los Angeles: University of California Press, 1978).

29. Camus, "Pessimism and Courage," in *RRD,* p. 58.
30. See James D. Wilkinson, *The Intellectual Resistance in Europe* (Cambridge, Mass.: Harvard University Press, 1981).
31. There are some notable exceptions here: Judith Shklar, *After Utopia: The Decline of Political Faith* (Princeton: Princeton University Press, 1957); George Kateb, *Utopia and its Enemies* (New York: Free Press, 1963); Michael Walzer, *The Company of Critics: Social Criticism and Political Commitment in the Twentieth Century* (New York: Basic Books, 1988); and Jean Bethke Elshtain, *Women and War* (New York: Basic Books, 1987).
32. See John Gunnell, *Political Theory: Tradition and Interpretation* (Boston: Winthrop, 1979).
33. See Theodor W. Adorno, "After Auschwitz," in *Negative Dialectics* (New York: Continuum, 1973), pp. 361–65.
34. Michel Foucault, "Truth and Power," in *Power/Knowledge: Selected Interviews and Other Writings, 1972–1977* (New York: Pantheon, 1980), pp. 125–33.
35. Michael Walzer, *Interpretation and Social Criticism* (Cambridge, Mass.: Harvard University Press, 1987), and *The Company of Critics,* pp. 3–28. I have criticized aspects of Walzer's view in my review of *The Company,* in *The American Political Science Review* 83, no. 2 (June 1989).
36. See Kerry Whiteside, *Merleau-Ponty and the Foundation of an Existential Politics* (Princeton: Princeton University Press, 1988), and Mary G. Dietz, *Between the Human and the Divine: The Political Thought of Simone Weil* (Totowa, N.J.: Rowman and Littlefield, 1988).
37. Camus, *N2,* p. 119, 215. See also p. 216: "Mounier advises me in *Esprit* to give up politics since I have no head for it (this is indeed obvious) and to be satisfied with the quite noble role, which would be so charmingly appropriate to me, of sounding the alarm. But what is a political mind? Reading *Esprit* doesn't tell me. As to the 'noble' role of sounding the alarm, it would require a spotless conscience. And the only vocation I feel in myself is telling consciences that they are not spotless and reasons why they lack something."
38. Arendt, "French Existentialism," *Nation,* February 23, 1946:226–28.
39. Arendt, "Civil Disobedience," in *Crises of the Republic* (New York: Harcourt Brace, 1972), p. 64.
40. Camus, "On Sartre's *Le Mur* and Other Stories," in *LCE,* p. 205.
41. Camus, "Letter to Roland Barthes on *The Plague*," in *LCE,* p. 339.
42. Elisabeth Young-Bruehl, *Hannah Arendt: For Love of the World* (New Haven: Yale University Press, 1978), pp. 216, 281. In accounting for Arendt's historical concerns I have relied heavily on Young-Bruehl's superb biography.
43. See Stephen J. Whitfield, *A Critical American: The Politics of Dwight Macdonald* (Hamden, Conn.: Archon, 1984), p. 89.
44. My understanding of the importance of this network has been deepened immeasurably by Gregory Sumner, "Europe-America: The Transatlantic Intellectual Community of *politics* Magazine, 1944–1949" (Ph.D. diss., Indiana University, 1992).
45. Arendt, "French Existentialism." p. 226.

Chapter One: Humanity at Zero Hour

1. This text is taken from the transcription of the speech made by Nichola Chiaromante and included in his "Albert Camus: In Memorium," in Germain Bree, ed., *Camus: A Collection of Critical Essays* (Englewood Cliifs, N.J.: Prentice Hall, 1962), pp. 14–15.
2. Ibid., p. 12.
3. See Judith Shklar, *After Utopia: The Decline of Political Faith* (Princeton: Princeton University Press, 1958), esp. pp. 164–217.
4. Sheldon Wolin, *Politics and Vision* (Boston: Little, Brown, 1960), p. 8.
5. For criticisms, see Quentin Skinner, "Meaning and Understanding in the History of Ideas," *History and Theory* 8 (1969), and John Gunnell, *Political Theory: Tradition and Interpretation* (Boston: Winthrop, 1978).
6. On this theme see Maurice Mandelbaum, *History, Man, and Reason: A Study in Nineteenth Century Thought* (Baltimore: Johns Hopkins University Press, 1971). The classic contemporary statement of this theme was Pierre-Joseph Proudhon, *General Idea of the Revolution in the Nineteenth Century* (New York: Haskell House, 1923), esp. pp. 13–19.
7. For an interesting account see Isaiah Berlin, "Joesph de Maistre and the Origins of Fascism." *New York Review of Books,* September 27, 1990. See also Albert O. Hirshmann, *The Rhetoric of Reaction* (Cambridge, Mass.: Harvard University Press, 1991).
8. Albert Camus, "Nobel Prize Address, Stockholm, December 10, 1957," reprinted as epigraph to David Sprintzen, *Camus: A Critical Examination* (Philadelphia: Temple University Press, 1988), viii. There are striking parallels between the address and Camus's Columbia speech.
9. Quoted in Ken Coates, "The Peace Movement and Socialism," *New Left Review* 145 (May–June 1984), p. 90.
10. Raymond Aron, *The Century of Total War* (Boston: Beacon Press, 1955).
11. See Paul Johnson, *Modern Times: The World from the Twenties to the Eighties* (New York: Harper, 1983), pp. 1–48; C. S. Nichols, ed., *Power: A Political History of the Twentieth Century* (New York: Oxford University Press, 1990), pp. 56–87; Jack J. Roth, ed., *World War One: A Turning Point in History* (New York: Knopf, 1967); Arno J. Mayer, *Politics and Diplomacy of Peacemaking: Containment and Counterrevolution at Versailles, 1918–1919* (New York: Vintage, 1969).
12. See Nichols, ed., *Power,* pp. 90–125, and Raul Hilberg, *The Destruction of European Jewry* (Chicago: Quadrangle, 1961).
13. See Paul Fussell, "Precision Bombing Will Win the War," in his *Wartime: Understanding and Behavior During the Second World War* (Oxford: Oxford University Press, 1989), pp. 13–19.
14. See Coates, "The Peace Movement and Socialism," pp. 90–91.
15. See Fussell, *Wartime,* pp. 115–29, 180–95. As George Orwell put it, "Mass-suggestion is a science of the last twenty years, and we do not yet know how successful it will be." "Review: Russia Under Soviet Rule," in *The Collected Essays, Journalism, and Letters of George Orwell,* ed. Sonia Orwell and Ian Angus (New York: Harcourt, 1968), vol. 1, p. 381.
16. Edmund Wilson, *Europe Without Baedecker* (New York: 1947), quoted in Greg

Sumner, "Radical Criticism For a Time of Troubles" (Unpublished manuscript, Department of History, Indiana University), p. 36.

17. Quoted in Sumner, "Radical Criticism," p. 36.

18. George Orwell, "Review: Beggar My Neighbor," in *Collected Essays*, vol. 2, p. 314.

19. Quoted in Sumner, "Radical Criticism," p. 7.

20. Simone Weil, "Words and War," *Politics*, March 1946:70.

21. As Raymond Aron put it: "Since, under a July sun, bourgeois Europe entered into the century of total war, men have lost control of their history and have been dragged along by the contradictory promptings of techniques and passions.... How far will we be dragged by chain reactions of violence?" Aron, *The Century of Total War*, p. 55.

22. George Orwell, "Notes on the Way," in *The Collected Essays*, vol. 2, p. 15.

23. Walter Benjamin, "Theses on the Philosophy of History," in *Illuminations*, ed. Hannah Arendt (New York: Schocken,1969), p. 257.

24. Ibid., p. 258.

25. Ibid., p. 257.

26. Benjamin must have been aware of the parallel between this image and that offered by Marx and Engels in the *Manifesto:* "Modern bourgeois society ... is like the sorcerer, who is no longer able to control the powers of the nether world whom he has called up by his spells." Robert C. Tucker, ed., *The Marx-Engels Reader* (New York: Norton, 1972), p. 340.

27. Arthur Koestler, "The Fraternity of Pessimists," in *The Yogi and the Commissar and Other Essays* (New York: Macmillan, 1946), pp. 103–4. See also Max Horkheimer and Theodor Adorno: "Mankind, instead of entering into a truly human condition, is sinking into a new kind of barbarism." *Dialectic of Enlightenment* (New York: Continuum, 1988), p. xii.

28. See Hannah Arendt's comment on the Jews in "The Jew as Pariah," in *JP*, p. 90.

29. Elisabeth Young-Bruehl, *Hannah Arendt: For Love of the World* (New Haven: Yale University Press, 1978), pp. 69–74, 99–110. The biographical sketch of Arendt that follows is taken largely from Young-Bruehl's indispensable account. See also Dagmar Barnow, *Visible Spaces: Hannah Arendt and the German-Jewish Experience* (Baltimore: Johns Hopkins University Press, 1990).

30. Arendt, "We Refugees," in *JP*, p. 56.

31. *JP*, p. 64.

32. *JP*, p. 56.

33. Arendt, "The Jew As Pariah," in *JP*, p. 90.

34. Quoted in Young-Bruehl, *Hannah Arendt*, pp. 184–85.

35. See Arendt, "Understanding and Politics," *Partisan Review* 20, no. 4 (July-August 1953), pp. 377–92.

36. Arendt, *OT*, pp. vi-vii.

37. She writes of totalitarianism that "its unprecedentedness cannot be comprehended through the usual categories of political thought," and its crimes "cannot be judged by traditional moral standards or punished within the legal framework of our civilization." Arendt, "Tradition and the Modern Age," in *BPF*, p. 26.

38. Arendt, "Organized Guilt and Universal Responsibility," in *JP*, pp. 235–36.

39. See Norman Jacobson, *Pride and Solace* (Berkeley and Los Angeles: University of California Press, 1978).

40. See Patrick McCarthy, *Camus* (New York: Random House, 1982), pp. 71–96, and Herbert Lottman, *Albert Camus: A Biography* (New York: Doubleday, 1979), pp. 97–187.

41. See McCarthy, *Camus,* pp. 88–96, and Lottman, *Albert Camus,* pp. 156–70.

42. "Why Spain?" in *RRD,* pp. 78–79.

43. Camus, *N1,* p. 48.

44. *N1,* pp. 139–42.

45. Quoted in Lottman, *Albert Camus,* p. 225. *Le Soir Républicain* was the evening edition of *Alger Républicain.*

46. Camus, *N1* p. 143.

47. This pervasive theme of Camus's literature is pronounced in his notebook entries in 1943, during a period of prolonged separation from his wife, when he appears to have first sketched the outlines of *The Plague.* Camus, *N2,* pp. 42–58.

48. Camus, "Letters to a German Friend," in *RRD,* p. 29. A similar text can also be found in Camus's 1943 entry to his *N1,* p. 90.

49. Camus, "Pessimism and Courage," in *RRD,* pp. 58–9.

50. Camus, *R,* pp. 3–4.

51. The idea of the extreme or "limit situation" was central to the philosophy of Karl Jaspers, an important influence on both writers. See Elisabeth Young-Bruehl, *Karl Jaspers's Philosophy of Freedom* (New Haven: Yale University Press, 1981), pp. 20–22; and Karl Jaspers, "Limit Situations," in Edith Ehrlich et al., eds., *Karl Jaspers: Basic Philosophical Writings* (Athens, Ohio: Ohio University Press, 1986), pp. 96–103.

52. Alan Megill, *Prophets of Extremity: Nietzsche, Heidegger, Foucault, Derrida* (Berkeley and Los Angeles: University of California Press, 1985), pp. 347–48.

53. See Young-Bruehl, *Hannah Arendt,* pp. 199–48, 173–81. A more detailed account is David S. Wyman, *The Abandonment of the Jews: America and the Holocaust, 1941–1945* (New York: Pantheon, 1984), pp. 84–103.

54. See Emmett Parker, *Albert Camus: The Artist in the Arena* (Madison: University of Wisconsin Press, 1965), pp. 46–69.

55. For the original text see René Char, *Leaves of Hypnos* (New York: Grossman Publishers, 1973), p. 62.

56. Arendt, *BPF,* pp. 3–4. See Char: "Archiduc confides in me that he discovered his truth when he espoused the Resistance. Until then he was an actor of his life, irreverent and suspicious. Insincerity poisoned him. A sterile gloominess had gradually laid its pall upon him. Now he loves, he expends himself, he's involved, he goes naked, he provokes. I much appreciate this alchemist." *Leaves of Hypnos,* p. 30.

57. A propos Arendt's own work with Youth Aliyah, it is also worth noting her comment, "One is tempted to recommend the story [of Danish efforts to rescue Jews from the Nazis] as required reading in political science for all students who wish to learn something about the enormous power potential inherent in non-violent action and in resistance to an opponent possessing vastly superior means of violence." *EJ,* pp. 171–75. Arendt insists that the Danes's active, principled, *open* resistance to the Nazis is a model of political conduct in the contemporary world.

58. Camus, "The Night of Truth," in *RRD,* pp. 38–39. On the occupation and re-

sistance in France, see Germain Bree and George Bernauer, eds., *Defeat and Beyond: An Anthology of French Wartime Writing, 1940–1945* (New York: Pantheon, 1970).
59. *RRD*, p. 39.
60. Camus, "The Blood of Freedom," in *RRD*, pp. 36–37. Camus, like many of his colleagues in the Resistance, was disturbed by the normalization of the Resistance experience in postwar France. In a memorium for René Leynaud, one of those colleagues who had not survived, Camus wrote, "But now he is forever silent. And some who are not worthy speak of the honor that was identified with him." "The Flesh," in *RRD*, p. 44. This also recalls the death of Diego and the return of the rulers of Cadiz at the close of *State of Siege*: "The blood of those you call the just ones still glistens on the walls—and what are those fine fellows up to? Giving each other medals!" *State of Siege*, in *CTOP*, p. 231.
61. Arendt, *OT*, p. 479.
62. In his "Letters to a German Friend" Camus writes, "Man is the force which ultimately cancels all tyrants and gods. He is the force of evidence." *RRD*, p. 14.
63. Char, *Leaves of Hypnos*, p. 189.

Chapter Two: Totalitarianism and the Intoxication of Power

1. Particularly important here was the normalization of postwar West Germany and the tendency to limit the term *totalitarianism* to the Soviet Union, thus cementing the NATO alliance. On this, see Geoffrey Hartmann, ed., *Bitburg in Moral and Political Perspective* (Bloomington: Indiana University Press, 1986), and Jurgen Habermas, *The New Conservatism* (Cambridge, Mass.: MIT Press, 1990).
2. Benjamin Barber, "Conceptual Foundations of Totalitarianism," in Carl J. Friedrich, Michael Curtis, and Benjamin R. Barber, *Totalitarianism in Perspective: Three Views* (New York: Praeger, 1969), pp. 4–5.
3. Ibid., p. 37. See also Robert Burrowes, "Totalitarianism: The Revised Standard Version," *World Politics* 21, no. 2 (January 1969).
4. Herbert J. Spiro, "Totalitarianism," in David L. Sills, ed., *International Encyclopedia of the Social Sciences,* vol.16 (New York: Macmillan, 1968), p. 112.
5. Herbert J. Spiro and Benjamin R. Barber, "Counter-Ideological Uses of 'Totalitarianism,'" *Politics and Society* 1, no. 1 (November 1970). See also Robert Booth Fowler, *Believing Skeptics: American Political Intellectuals, 1945–1964* (Westport, Conn.: Greenwood Press, 1978), especially pp. 3–37.
6. Hans Mommsen, "The Concept of Totalitarian Dictatorship vs. The Comparative Theory of Fascism: The Case of National Socialism," in Ernest A. Menze, ed., *Totalitarianism Reconsidered* (New York: Kennikat Books, 1981), p. 153.
7. Ibid., pp. 165–66.
8. Spiro and Barber, "Counter-Ideological Uses," p. 21.
9. Karl Dietrich Bracher, "The Disputed Concept of Totalitarianism," in Menze, ed., *Totalitarianism Reconsidered*, p. 13.
10. Gentile wrote that the totalitarian state embodied "the whole will, thought, and feeling of the nation," quoted in Michael Curtis, "Retreat from Totalitarianism," in Friedrich, Curtis, and Barber, *Totalitarianism in Perspective*, p. 59. Mussolini is quoted in Juan J. Linz, "Totalitarian and Authoritarian Regimes," in Fred I.

Greenstein and Nelson W. Polsby, eds., *Handbook of Political Science: Macropolitical Theory,* vol. 3 (Reading, Mass.: Addison-Wesley, 1975), p. 127. See also the discussion in Stephen J. Whitfield's *Into the Dark: Hannah Arendt and Totalitarianism* (Philadelphia: Temple University Press, 1980), esp. pp. 8–11.

11. See Antonio Gramsci, "The Modern Prince," in *Selections from the Prison Notebooks,* ed. Geoffrey Nowell Smith and Quentin Hoare (New York: International Publishers, 1971).

12. See the essays by Bracher, "Disputed Concept," and Linz, "Totalitarian and Authoritarian Regimes." See also Martin Greiffenhagen, "The Concept of Totalitarianism in Political Theory," in Menze, ed., *Totalitarianism Reconsidered.*

13. See Bernard Crick, "On Rereading *The Origins of Totalitarianism,*" in Melvyn A. Hill, ed., *Hannah Arendt: The Recovery of the Public World* (New York: St. Martin's, 1979), pp. 28–29.

14. Hans Kohn, "Communist and Fascist Dictatorship: A Comparative Study," in Guy Stanton Ford, ed., *Dictatorship in the Modern World* (Minneapolis, 1935), and Sigmund Neumann, *Permanent Revolution: The Total State in a World at War* (New York: Harper, 1942).

15. Elie Halévy, "The Era of Tyrannies," in *The Era of Tyrannies* (New York: New York University Press, 1966).

16. Quoted in Robert Colquhoun, *Raymond Aron,* vol. 1, *The Philosopher in History, 1905–1955* (Beverly Hills, Calif.: Sage, 1986), p. 111.

17. The most influential of these works included Franz Borkenau, *The Totalitarian Enemy* (London: Faber and Faber, 1940); Karl Mannheim, *Man and Society in an Age of Reconstruction* (New York: Harcourt Brace, 1940); Emil Lederer, *State of the Masses: The Threat of a Classless Society* (New York: Norton, 1940); Guenther Reimann, *The Myth of the Total State* (New York: Morrow, 1941); James Burnham, *The Managerial Revolution* (Bloomington: Indiana University Press, 1941); Ernst Fraenkel, *The Dual State: A Contribution to the Theory of Dictatorship* (London: Oxford University Press, 1941); Ludwig von Mises, *Omnipotent Government: The Rise of the Total State and Total War* (New Haven: Yale University Press, 1944), and Friedrich von Hayek, *The Road to Serfdom* (Chicago: University of Chicago Press, 1944). In a class by themselves are the writings of Hermann Rauschning, the former Nazi who published a steady stream of books denouncing Nazism and highlighting its similarities with Stalinism. See especially *The Revolution of Nihilism: Warning to the West* (New York: Alliance Books, 1939) and *The Beast from the Abyss* (London: Heinmann, 1941).

18. On these writers see Michael Walzer, *The Company of Critics: Social Criticism and Political Commitment in the Twentieth Century* (New York: Basic Books, 1988).

19. Herbert Marcuse, "The Struggle Against Liberalism in the Totalitarian View of the State," reprinted in *Negations* (Boston: Beacon Press, 1968); Max Horkheimer, "The Authoritarian State," reprinted in Andrew Arato and Eike Gebhardt, eds., *The Essential Frankfurt School Reader* (New York: Urizen, 1978); Friedrich Pollock, "State Capitalism: Its Limits and Possibilities," reprinted in Arato and Gebhardt, eds., *Frankfurt School Reader,* p. 93; Franz Neumann, *Behemoth: The Structure and Practice of National Socialism* (London: Oxford University Press, 1942). On the efforts of the Frankfurt school see Martin Jay's seminal *The Dialectical Imagination* (Boston: Little, Brown, 1973).

20. Leon Trotsky, *The Revolution Betrayed* (New York: Doubleday, 1937), p. 278.
21. This essay is discussed in Dwight Macdonald, "The Root Is Man," *politics*, April and July 1946: 97–115, 194–214. For a fascinating critique of Trotsky's ambivalences, see Claude Lefort, "The Contradiction of Trotsky," in his *The Political Forms of Modern Society*, ed. John B. Thompson (Cambridge, Mass.: MIT Press, 1986).
22. Max Schactman, *The Bureaucratic Revolution: The Rise of the Stalinist State* (New York: Donald Press, 1962). On Schactman see Maurice Isserman, *If I Had a Hammer: The Death of the Old Left and the Birth of the New* (New York: Basic Books, 1987), pp. 35–124, and Alan Wald, *The New York Intellectuals: The Rise and Decline of the Anti-Stalinist Left from the 1930s to the 1980s* (Chapel Hill: University of North Carolina Press, 1987).
23. See Victor Serge, *Russia Twenty Years After* (New York: Hillman-Curl, 1937). See also Anton Ciliga, *The Russian Enigma* (London: Labour Book Service, 1940), first published in Paris in 1938, a moving account of its author's experience of political repression in the Soviet Union.
24. Rudolph Hilferding, "State Capitalism or Totalitarian State Economy," *Modern Review* 1 (1947): 597–605.
25. André Liebich, "Marxism and Totalitarianism: Rudolph Hilferding and the Mensheviks," *Dissent*, Spring 1987:239, 223.
26. George Orwell, "Wells, Hitler, and the World State," *Horizon*, August 1941, reprinted in *The Collected Essays, Journalism, and Letters of George Orwell*, vol. 2, *My Country Right or Left, 1940–1943*, ed. Sonia Orwell and Ian Angus (New York: Harcourt, 1968), p. 142.
27. George Orwell, "Inside the Whale," in *A Collection of Essays* (New York: Harcourt Brace Jovanovich, 1970), p. 249.
28. George Orwell, "Review: *Power: A New Social Analysis,* by Betrand Russell," *Adelphi*, January 1939, reprinted in *The Collected Essays, Journalism, and Letters of George Orwell*, vol. 1, *An Age Like This, 1920–1940*, ed. Sonia Orwell and Ian Angus (New York: Harcourt, 1968), p. 376.
29. George Orwell, "Review: *Russia under Soviet Rule,* by N. de Basily," *Peace News*, January 1939, reprinted in Orwell, *The Collected Essays*, vol. 1., pp. 380–81.
30. Francis Bacon, *The New Organon*, ed. Fulton H. Anderson (Indianapolis, In.: Bobbs-Merril, 1960), p. 39.
31. Arendt, *OT,* pp. 458–59.
32. See Rainer C. Baum, "Holocaust: Moral Indifference as *the* Form of Modern Evil," in Alan Rosenberg and Gerald E. Myers, eds., *Echoes from the Holocaust: Philosophical Reflections on a Dark Time* (Philadelphia: Temple University Press, 1988), and Zygmunt Bauman, *Modernity and the Holocaust* (Ithaca, N.Y.: Cornell University Press, 1989), esp. pp. 169–208.
33. Arthur Koestler, "On Disbelieving Atrocities," reprinted in *The Yogi and the Commissar* (New York: Macmillan, 1945), pp. 88–89.
34. Ibid., p. 89.
35. Camus, *R,* p. 3.
36. Arendt, *OT,* pp. 458–59.
37. *OT,* p. 438.
38. *OT,* pp. 437–38.

39. *OT*, p. 440.
40. *OT*, p. 411.
41. *OT*, p. 454.
42. *OT*, p. 441.
43. For a useful comparative perspective see Frank Chalk and Kurt Jonassohn, *The History and Sociology of Genocide* (New Haven: Yale University Press, 1990).
44. Arendt, *EJ*, p. 153.
45. *EJ*, pp. 196–97.
46. *EJ*, p. 269.
47. *EJ*, pp. 287–89. See Elisabeth Young-Bruehl's discussion in *Hannah Arendt: For Love of the World* (New Haven: Yale University Press, 1982), pp. 367–78.
48. Camus, *R*, pp. 182–83.
49. *R*, p. 184.
50. *R*, p. 185.
51. *R*, pp. 238–40.
52. Camus, "Letter to Roland Barthes on *The Plague*," in *LCE*, p. 339.
53. Camus, *Pl*, pp. 155–58.
54. Camus, *Caligula*, in *CTOP*, p. 29.
55. *CTOP*, pp. 20–21.
56. Camus, *State of Siege*, in *CTOP*, p. 163.
57. *CTOP*, pp. 165–69.
58. *CTOP*, pp. 170–73.
59. George Orwell, *1984* (New York: Signet, 1983), pp. 216–17.
60. As Orwell's O'Brien says, "The two aims of the Party are to conquer the whole surface of the earth and to extinguish once and for all the possibility of independent thought." *1984*, p. 159.
61. For a good summary see Linz, "Totalitarian and Authoritarian Regimes."
62. Orwell's O'Brien again puts this clearly: "The command of the old despotisms was 'Thou shalt not'...Our command is 'Thou art.'" *1984*, p. 211.
63. On this aspect of Hobbes's thought see Sheldon Wolin, *Politics and Vision* (Boston: Little, Brown, 1960).
64. Camus, *R*, pp. 239–40, 284.
65. Camus, *Caligula*, in *CTOP*, p. 72.
66. Camus, *State of Siege*, in *CTOP*, p. 216.
67. *CTOP*, p. 186.
68. Orwell, *1984*, pp. 46–48, 64.
69. Arthur Koestler, "The Initiates," in Richard Crossman, ed., *The God That Failed* (New York: Harper, 1950), pp. 39–42.
70. Arendt, *EJ*, p. 85. See also Berel Lang, "Language and Genocide," in Rosenberg and Myers, eds., *Echoes*, p. 341–64.
71. Arendt, *EJ*, p. 49. Camus too observes that "the language peculiar to totalitarian doctrines is always a scholastic or administrative language." *R*, p. 283.
72. Arendt, "The Crisis in Culture," in *BPF*, p. 220.
73. Arendt, *HC*, p. 178.
74. See Edith Wyschogrod, "Concentration Camps and the End of the Life-World," in Rosenberg and Myers, eds., *Echoes*, pp. 327–40.
75. Camus, *R*, p. 239. Note the parallel between this point and Arendt's comments

on friendship in "On Humanity in Dark Times," in particular her contrast between the French Revolutionary notion of general *fraternité* and Lessing's notion of friendship as a relationship "which is as selective as compassion is egalitarian." *MDT,* pp. 12, 24–25.

76. Arendt, *OT,* p. 475.
77. *OT,* p. 477.
78. See Waldemar Gurian, "Totalitarianism as Political Religion," in Carl J. Friedrich, ed., *Totalitarianism* (New York: Grosset and Dunlap, 1964).
79. As Claude Lefort has put it, totalitarian ideology represents the attempt "to close the social space in on itself from the imaginary centre of its institution, to make being and appearance coincide here and now." "Outline of the Genesis of Ideology in Modern Societies," in Lefort, *The Political Forms,* p. 220.
80. Camus, *R,* pp. 3–5.
81. *R,* p. 237.
82. *R,* p. 237.
83. Camus, *State of Siege,* in *CTOP,* p. 180.
84. Arendt, *OT,* pp. 462–64.
85. *OT,* p. 457.
86. Camus, *R,* p. 185.
87. Arendt, *OT,* pp. 380–87.
88. *OT,* p. 385.
89. Orwell, *1984,* p. 205. Czeslaw Milosz's *The Captive Mind* (New York: Vintage, 1981) originally published in 1951, the same year as Arendt's *The Origins of Totalitarianism* and Camus's *The Rebel,* is a vivid account of the mechanisms of ideological delusion.
90. Orwell, *1984,* pp. 148–49.
91. Arthur Koestler, *Darkness At Noon* (New York: Time, 1962), pp. 75, 152, 156, 167.
92. See Stephen F. Cohen, *Bukharin and the Bolshevik Revolution* (Oxford: Oxford University Press, 1976).
93. Burrowes, "Totalitarianism," p. 280.
94. Whitfield, *Into The Dark,* p. 51.
95. See Isaac Deutscher, "*1984*—The Mysticism of Cruelty," in Irving Howe, ed., *Orwell's Nineteen Eighty-Four: Text, Sources, Criticism* (New York: Harcourt, 1963), and Raymond Williams, *George Orwell* (New York: Columbia University Press, 1981).
96. See Roland Barthes, "*La Peste*: Annales d'une épidémie ou roman de la solitude," *Club,* February 1955:4–6; Francis Jeanson, "Albert Camus, ou L'âme révoltée," *Les Temps Modernes,* no. 79 (May 1952): 270–90; and Jean-Paul Sartre, "Réponse à Albert Camus," *Les Temps Modernes,* no. 89 (August 1952): pp. 334–53, reprinted in *Situations* (New York: Braziller, 1965).
97. Deutscher, "*1984*," p. 201.
98. In a more literary vein, Phillip Lopate has recently insisted that the Holocaust was but one of many human atrocities, comparable to various other historical episodes. The rejoinder of Yehuda Baeur, the renowned scholar of the Nazi genocide, is apt: "Lopate's problem is that he demands—rightly—to make comparisons and then does not compare at all. He simply throws into the pot distinct cases of diverse

peoples in different circumstances, as though all these cases were parallels to the Holocaust. They were not." See Phillip Lopate, "Resistance to the Holocaust," and Yehuda Baeur, "Don't Resist," in *Tikkun*, May–June 1989:55–67.

99. Arendt, *OT*, pp. 437, 453.

100. *OT*, pp. 445–46.

101. See Mary Hesse, *The Structure of Scientific Inference* (Berkeley and Los Angeles: University of California Press, 1974).

102. The footnotes to *Origins* alone make clear that Arendt in no way dismissed conventional historical and scientific accounts of totalitarianism.

103. Elie Wiesel, *A Jew Today* (New York: Random House, 1978), pp. 197–98.

104. Arendt, *OT*, pp. 437, 411.

105. This is most explicitly addressed in Arendt, *EJ*, pp. 253–98.

106. Mark Krispin Miller, "The Fate of *1984*," in Irving Howe, ed., *1984 Revisited* (New York: Mentor, 1984), p. 27.

107. Carl J. Freidrich and Zbigniew K. Brzezinski, *Totalitarian Dictatorship and Autocracy* (Cambridge, Mass.: Harvard University Press, 1956), Jean-François Revel, *The Totalitarian Temptation* (New York: Doubleday, 1977), and Jeane Kirkpatrick, *Dictatorships and Double Standards* (New York: Harper, 1980).

108. Camus, *R*, pp. 132, 248.

109. Camus, *Pl*, p. 5.

110. Camus, *State of Siege*, in *CTOP*, pp. 227–28.

111. *CTOP*, p. 230.

112. Camus, "Why Spain?" in *RRD*, pp. 78–79.

113. Camus, *Pl*, p. 278.

114. Arendt, *OT*, p. 460.

115. *OT*, p. 267.

116. *OT*, p. xxvii.

117. *OT*, p. 269.

118. *OT*, p. ix.

Chapter Three: The Ambiguities of Humanism

1. Camus, *R*, pp. 177–87.

2. Quoted in Elisabeth Young-Bruehl, *Hannah Arendt: For Love of the World* (New Haven: Yale University Press, 1982), p. 279.

3. See especially Friedrich Nietzsche, *The Birth of Tragedy and The Genealogy of Morals*, trans. Francis Golffing (New York: Doubleday, 1956); Martin Heidegger, "Letter On Humanism," in Martin Heidegger, *Basic Writings*, ed. David Farrell Krell (New York: Harper & Row, 1976); and Heidegger, *The Question Concerning Technology and Other Essays*, trans. William Lovitt (New York: Harper & Row, 1977).

4. Martin Heidegger, "The Age of the World Picture," in *Concerning Technology*, p. 133.

5. See Leo Strauss, *Natural Right and History* (Chicago: University of Chicago Press, 1965); Eric Voegelin, *The New Science of Politics* (Chicago: University of Chicago

Press, 1987); and Max Horkheimer and Theodor Adorno, *Dialectic of Enlightenment* (New York: Continuum, 1974).

6. William E. Connolly, *Political Theory and Modernity* (Oxford: Blackwell, 1988), p. 2. On the theme of self-assertion, see Hans Blumenberg, *The Legitimacy of the Modern Age* (Cambridge, Mass.: MIT Press, 1985), esp. pp. 137–44.

7. In this regard their writings have affinities with more contemporary works like Blumenberg's *The Legitimacy of the Modern Age* and Jürgen Habermas's *The Philosophical Discourse of Modernity* (Cambridge, Mass.: MIT Press, 1987), which also seek to reappropriate a modern self-consciousness appropriately divested of illusions about the ability wholly to "take charge of the world."

8. See Alan Megill, *Prophets of Extremity: Nietzsche, Heidegger, Foucault, Derrida* (Berkeley and Los Angeles: University of California Press, 1985), for a discussion of the apocalyptic cast of the writings of Nietzsche and Heidegger.

9. See Richard Wolin, *The Politics of Being: The Political Thought of Martin Heidegger* (New York: Columbia University Press, 1990).

10. In this respect there are affinities with the recent writings of Luc Ferry and Alain Renaut, especially *Heidegger and Modernity* (Chicago: University of Chicago Press, 1990) and *French Philosophy of the Sixties: An Essay on Antihumanism* (Amherst: University of Massachusetts Press, 1990).

11. Arendt, *BPF,* pp. 26–27.

12. Eric Voegelin, "The Origins of Totalitarianism," *Review of Politics* 15, no. 1 (January 1953): 75.

13. Arendt, "A Reply," *Review of Politics* 15, no. 1 (January 1953): 80–81. It is likely that Arendt had scholars like Voegelin—as well as Heidegger—in mind when she wrote, "We are still surrounded by intellectuals and so-called scholars, not only in Germany, who, instead of speaking of Hitler, Auschwitz, genocide, and 'extermination' as a policy of permanent depopulation, prefer, according to their inspiration and taste, to refer to Plato, Luther, Hegel, Nietzsche, or to Heidegger, Junger, or Stefan George, in order to dress up the horrible gutter-born phenomenon with the language of the humanities and the history of ideas." Arendt, "Martin Heidegger at Eighty," in Michael Murray, ed., *Heidegger and Modern Philosophy: Critical Essays* (New Haven: Yale University Press, 1978), p. 302. Arendt also criticizes Voegelin in *The Origins of Totalitarianism,* dismissing his claim that totalitarianism is an inevitable outgrowth of modern scientific thinking (pp. 346–47).

14. Francis Jeanson, "Albert Camus, Ou L'Ame Revoltée," *Les Temps Modernes,* no. 79 (May 1952): 2076–77.

15. Camus, "Lettre au Directeur des *Temps Modernes,*" *Les Temps Modernes,* no. 80 (August 1952): 321–22.

16. Martin Heidegger, "The Age of the World Picture," in *Concerning Technology,* p. 116. The metaphor of psychic subsoil is taken from David Sprintzen, *Camus: A Critical Examination* (Philadelphia: Temple University Press, 1988).

17. Camus, *R,* p. 11. See Nietzsche, *The Genealogy of Morals:* "Nothing was ever bought more dearly than the small portion of human reason and freedom that is now our pride" (p. 250).

18. *R,* pp. 26–27. Camus did not believe that rebellion was either a prevalent activity

or the subject of sustained philosophical reflection in the ancient world, but his discussion of the revolt of Spartacus indicates that he certainly acknowledged the existence of sporadic uprisings. See *R*, pp. 108–11.

19. *R*, p. 28. See Nietzsche, *The Birth of Tragedy*, on "the thoroughly sane" Greeks and their gods: "Whoever approaches the Olympians with a different religion in his heart, seeking moral elevation, sanctity, spirituality, loving-kindness, will presumably be forced to turn away from them in ill-humored disappointment. Nothing in these deities reminds us of asceticism, high intellect, or duty; we are confronted by luxuriant, triumphant existence, which deifies the good and the bad indifferently" (p. 29).

20. Camus writes that "rebellion. . . can only be imagined in terms of opposition to someone. The only thing that gives meaning to human protest is the idea of a personal god who has created, and is therefore responsible for, everything. And so we can say, without being paradoxical, that in the Western world the history of rebellion is inseparable from the history of Christianity" (*R*, p. 28).

21. Quoted in Sprintzen, *Camus*, p. 8. For affinities between Camus's sense of the absurd and Augustine's sensibility in *The City of God*, see for example Augustine's observation regarding the randomness of life: "It would be intelligible if there were only some consistency in the seeming senselessness of these arrangements. . . . The whole arrangement makes God's judgments all the more inscrutable and His ways unsearchable." *The City of God*, bk. 20, chap. 2 (New York: Image Books, 1958), pp. 485–86.

22. *R*, 32–35; Sprintzen, *Camus*, p. 7. Possibly the most vivid embodiment of this in Camus's fiction is the character of Father Paneloux in *The Plague*, who declares to the citizens of Oran that "from the dawn of recorded history the scourge of God has humbled the proud of heart and laid low those who hardened themselves against him. Ponder this well, my friends, and fall on your knees. . . . This same pestilence which is slaying you works for your good and points your path . . . towards deliverance" (pp. 87, 90). It is worth noting that Paneloux is a complex and sincere man, whose viewpoint is in no way ridiculed in the text, even if Doctor Rieux, the hero, eloquently refutes it (pp. 115–18); indeed, as the course of events unfolds he exhibits exemplary compassion.

23. Camus, "Metaphysique Chrétienne et Néoplatonism," quoted in Sprintzen, *Camus*, p. 6; see Nietzsche on the "profound sickness" of Christianity, which is a "libel on life," *The Birth of Tragedy*, pp. 10–11. See also Nietzsche, *Beyond Good and Evil*, trans. R. J. Hollingdale (Middlesex: Penguin, 1973), p. 57: "The Christian faith is from the beginning sacrifice; sacrifice of all freedom, all pride, all self-confidence of the spirit, at the same time enslavement and self-mockery, self-mutilation."

24. Camus, *R*, pp. 34–5, 26.

25. Quoted in Habermas, *Philosophical Discourse*, p. 16.

26. R, pp. 102–3. For the similar views of Michel Foucault, see his *Discipline and Punish* (New York: Pantheon, 1977).

27. See Jean-François Lyotard, *The Postmodern Condition: A Report on Knowledge* (Minneapolis: University of Minnesota Press, 1984), pp. xxiii-xxiv.

28. Camus, *Caligula*, in *CTOP*, p. 43.

29. Camus writes that "Rousseau pushes to its limits the theory of the social contract to be found in Hobbes. *The Social Contract* amplifies and dogmatically explains

the new religion whose god is reason, confused with nature, and whose representative on earth, in place of the king, is the people considered as an expression of the general will." *R*, p. 115. For similar accounts, see François Furet and Mona Ozouf, eds., *A Critical History of the French Revolution*, trans. Arthur Goldhammer (Cambridge, Mass.: Harvard University Press, 1989), and Claude Lefort, "Interpreting Revolution within the French Revolution," in *Democracy and Political Theory*, (Minneapolis: University of Minnesota Press, 1988), pp. 89–114.

30. Camus, *R*, p. 132.
31. *R*, p. 120. See Foucault: "In a society like that of the seventeenth century, the King's body wasn't a metaphor, but a political reality. Its physical presence was necessary for the functioning of the monarchy. [The Republic, one and indivisible, is] a formula that was imposed against the Girondins and the idea of American-style federalism.... It's the body of the society which becomes the new principle in the nineteenth century. It is this social body which needs to be protected, in a quasi-medical sense." "Body/Power," in Michel Foucault, *Power/Knowledge: Selected Interviews and Other Writings, 1972–1977*, ed. Colin Gordon (New York: Pantheon, 1980), p. 55.
32. See Zygmunt Bauman, *Legislators and Interpreters: On Modernity, Postmodernity, and Intellectuals* (Ithaca: Cornell University Press, 1987).
33. See "Encounter With Albert Camus," in Camus, *LCE*: "The evil geniuses of contemporary Europe bore the label of philosopher: they are Hegel, Marx, and Nietzsche.... I place [Nietzsche] infinitely higher than the two others" (p. 354).
34. See Peter Euben, ed., *Greek Tragedy and Political Theory* (Berkeley and Los Angeles: University of California Press, 1986), and Peter Euben, *The Tragedy of Political Theory: The Road Not Taken* (Princeton: Princeton University Press, 1990).
35. The distinction between the *vita contemplativa* and the *vita activa* can be found in Heidegger's "Science and Reflection," in *Concerning Technology*, p. 166.
36. As John Gunnell has pointed out, there are problems with the way in which Arendt delineates "the tradition" of Western political thought. These are somewhat mitigated by an awareness of the purpose that motivates Arendt's historical generalizations—the desire less to provide a nuanced account of intellectual history than to sketch out certain main lines of political thought in the light of the "break in history" signaled by totalitarianism. See Gunnell, *Political Theory: Tradition and Interpretation* (Boston: Winthrop, 1979).
37. Arendt, *HC*, p. 225. Arendt acknowledges the genuinely political intentions of Plato and Aristotle (pp. 33–37), and although she is highly critical of both of them, she obviously draws heavily from Aristotle's conceptions of language, citizenship, and political community. See especially *HC*, pp. 22–38.
38. On this fear of contingency, see Benjamin Barber, *The Conquest of Politics: Liberal Philosophy in Democratic Times* (Princeton: Princeton University Press, 1988).
39. See Joanna Vecchiarelli Scott, " 'A Detour through Pietism': Hannah Arendt on St. Augustine's Philosophy of Freedom," *Polity* 20, no. 3 (Spring 1988), and Patrick Boyle, "Elusive Neighborliness: Hannah Arendt's Interpretation of Saint Augustine," in James W. Bernaeur, ed., *Amor Mundi: Explorations in the Faith and Thought of Hannah Arendt* (Dordrecht: Martinus Nijhoff, 1987).
40. Arendt, *HC*, pp. 10–11.
41. Of such free will Arendt writes: "In the deadly conflict with worldly desires and

intentions from which will-power was supposed to liberate the self, the most willing seemed able to achieve was oppression. Because of the will's impotence, its inca- pacity to generate genuine power, its constant defeat in the struggle with the self, in which the power of the I-can exhausted itself, the will-to-power turned at once into the will-to-oppression. I can only hint here at the fatal consequences for political theory of this equation of freedom with the human capacity to will; it was one of the causes why even today we almost automatically equate power with oppression or, at least, with rule over others." *BPF*, p. 162.

42. *BPF*, p. 167.

43. See Jürgen Habermas, *The Philosophical Discourse of Modernity*, pp. 294–326, on the need to replace a philosophy of the subject with a philosophy of intersubjec- tivity.

44. In making this claim Arendt is not denying the fact that Christian philosophy and theology supported the organization of the church—a worldly institution, to be sure. Nor is she rendering a judgment about Christian social practice so much as about the logic of Christian theology. What she denies is that Christian *metaphysical beliefs* are consistent with the values of free citizenship as she understands these, not that Christians can be worldly political agents. Christopher Lasch argues that Christian metaphysics can be the basis of a robust practice of citizenship in his *The True and Only Heaven: Progress and Its Critics* (New York: Norton, 1991), pp. 226–95.

45. Arendt, *HC*, pp. 53–55. See Claude Lefort, "The Death of Immortality?" in his *Democracy and Political Theory*, pp. 265–68.

46. This Machiavellian insight is most clearly expressed in her response to the charge leveled against her criticisms of Zionism by Gershom Scholem—that she did not love her people. First, she insists, "I have never in my life loved any people or collective. . . . I indeed love only my friends and the only kind of love I know of and believe in is the love of persons." More important, she continues, "Generally speaking, the role of the 'heart' in politics seems to me altogether questionable. . . . We both know . . . how often these emotions are used in order to conceal factual truth." "Eichmann in Jerusalem: An Exchange of Letters Between Gershom Scho- lem and Hannah Arendt," in Arendt, *JP*, p. 247. Arendt's Machiavellian critique of Christianity, and of political "goodness," can be found in *HC*, pp. 77–78, and *OR*, pp. 79–84. Arendt's views on this subject have generated much criticism. The most powerful critique is provided by George Kateb, for whom Arendt's Machia- vellianism seems to compromise any kind of principled political ethic. See his *Hannah Arendt: Politics, Conscience, Evil* (Totowa: Rowman & Allanheld, 1983). For Arendt the road to heavenly salvation may well be secured by good intentions, but the road to earthly hell is most certainly paved with them. A politics based on love is both disingenuous, pretending to foist on the public realm a value necessarily intimate, and dangerous in its indifference to the problem of consequences. This theme will be taken up below, where I draw parallels between Arendt and Camus and Reinhold Niebuhr's *Moral Man and Immoral Society* (New York: Scrib- ners,1932).

47. Camus, *R*, p. 21.

48. A similar account is presented in Charles Taylor, *Sources of the Self: The Making of the Modern Identity* (Cambridge, Mass.: Harvard University Press, 1989), pp. 127– 58.

49. "Homelessness is coming to be the destiny of the world. . . . What Marx recognized in an essential and significant sense, though derived from Hegel, as the estrangement of man has its roots in the homelessness of modern man." Martin Heidegger, "Letter on Humanism," in *Basic Writings,* ed. David Farrell Krell (New York: Harper and Row, 1977), p. 219.

50. Arendt, *HC,* p. 254, 228. As Heidegger writes in "The Age of the World Picture": "The whole of modern metaphysics taken together, Nietzsche included, maintains itself within the interpretation of what is to be and of truth that was prepared by Descartes. . . . Man frees himself from the bonds of the Middle Ages in freeing himself to himself. . . . Man becomes that being upon which all that is, is grounded as regards the manner of its Being and its truth. Man becomes the relational center of that which is as such." *Concerning Technology,* pp. 127–28.

51. See Arendt, *OT,* pp. 139–47, for a penetrating discussion of Hobbes's absolutism and its distinctively modern character. The connection between modern sovereignty and humanism is also developed in Connolly's discussion of Hobbes, Rousseau, and Hegel in *Political Theory and Modernity,* pp. 16–115, and in Blumenberg's discussion of Carl Scmitt in *The Legitimacy of the Modern Age,* pp. 89–102.

52. Max Weber, "Politics as a Vocation," in H. H. Gerth and C. Wright Mills, eds., *From Max Weber: Essays in Sociology* (New York: Oxford University Press, 1946), pp. 77–78.

53. As Arendt remarks: "As long as we believe that we deal with ends and means in the political realm, we shall not be able to prevent anybody's using all means to pursue recognized ends." *HC,* p. 229.

54. Arendt, "On Violence," in *CR,* 1972, p. 106.

55. Arendt, *OR,* pp. 76–81.

56. Arendt, "On Humanity in Dark Times," in *MDT,* p. 27. See Nietzsche: "May we not say that ethics has never lost its reek of blood and torture—not even in Kant, whose categorical imperative smacks of cruelty?" *The Genealogy of Morals,* p. 197.

57. See Jürgen Habermas, *Moral Consciousness and Communicative Action* (Cambridge, Mass.: MIT Press, 1990). As Seyla Benhabib writes: "Kantian ethics is monological, for it proceeds from the standpoint of the rational person, defined in such a way that differences among concrete selves become quite irrelevant. . . . [It assumes] that the solitary moral thinker can define a relevant moral content for all." In *Critique, Norm, Utopia: A Study of the Foundations of Critical Theory* (New York: Columbia University Press, 1986), p. 300. See also her essay "The Generalized and the Concrete Other," in Seyla Benhabib and Drucilla Cornell, ed., *Feminism as Critique* (Oxford: Blackwell, 1987).

58. Karl Marx, *Capital,* vol. 1 (New York: International Publishers, 1967), pp. 78–79.

59. Friedrich Nietzsche, *Untimely Meditations,* quoted in Mark Warren, *Nietzsche and Political Thought,* (Cambridge, Mass.: MIT Press, 1988), p. 86. Recall Father Paneloux's speech in *The Plague,* quoted in note 18 above.

60. Camus, *R,* p. 134. In spite of their shared view of Hegel, it is worth noting the distance between Camus and Nietzsche on this score. Nietzsche, in almost Burkean tones, describes the French Revolution as "that gruesome . . . superfluous farce" and writes of its reactionary denouement: "What a blessing, what a release from a burden becoming intolerable, the appearance of an unconditional commander is

for this herd-animal European, the effect produced by the appearance of Napoleon is the latest great witness—the history of the effect of Napoleon is almost the history of the higher happiness this entire century has attained in its most valuable men and moments." *Beyond Good and Evil,* pp. 49, 103. In this context Nietzsche also praises Julius Caesar and Caesare Borgia.

61. *R,* p. 142. It is worth noting that both Arendt and Camus, like many of their contemporaries, focused on Hegel's philosophy of history rather than his explicit political theory in *The Philosophy of Right,* in which he defends a vision of civil society and *sittlichkeit* ("concrete ethics") that many contemporary theorists have drawn upon. It is also worth noting that most contemporaries dwell on his political writings to the exclusion of the philosophy of history in which they were embedded. See Charles Taylor, *Hegel and Modern Society* (Cambridge, Mass.: Cambridge University Press, 1979), and Steven B. Smith, *Hegel's Critique of Liberalism: Rights in Context* (Chicago: University of Chicago Press, 1989).

62. "The owl of Minerva owl spreads its wings only with the fall of dusk." G. W. F. Hegel, *Philosophy of Right,* trans. T. M. Knox (London: Oxford University Press, 1967), p. 13.

63. Arendt, *OR,* pp. 51–52.

64. G. W. F. Hegel, *The Phenomenology of Mind,* trans. J. B. Baille (New York: Harper Colophon, 1967), pp. 76, 89–90.

65. Arendt, *OR,* p. 54. See Arendt's essay "The Concept of History: Ancient and Modern," in *BPF,* pp. 41–90, for an elaborate discussion of this.

66. Arendt, *OT,* pp. 460–79.

67. See, for example, Arendt, *LM,* part 2, *Willing,* pp. 149–58, for a discussion German idealism's "rainbow bridge" of "personified concepts."

68. See George Lukacs, *History and Class Consciousness* (Cambridge, Mass.: MIT Press, 1971); Jean-Paul Sartre, *The Communists and the Peace* (New York: George Brazilier, 1968); and Maurice Merleau-Ponty, *Humanism and Terror* (Boston: Beacon Press, 1969). Merleau-Ponty's later *Adventures of the Dialectic* (Evanston, Ill.: Northwestern University Press, 1973) is a superb critique of the faith in history to which he himself had earlier subscribed.

69. Arendt, *OR,* p. 54. In this respect the views of Arendt and Camus are similar to the critique of "identity reason" developed by members of the Frankfurt school. See Max Horkheimer and Theodor Adorno, *Dialectic of Enlightenment* (New York: Continuum, 1988); Theodor Adorno, *Negative Dialectics* (London, 1973); and Peter Dews, *Logics of Disintegration: Post-Structuralist Thought and the Claims of Critical Theory* (London: Verso, 1987). On this point there are also, ironically, affinities with the criticisms leveled against Marxist "humanism" and "historicism" by the French Communist philosopher Louis Althusser in *Reading Capital* (London: New Left Books, 1970).

70. Karl Marx, "Theses on Feuerbach," in Robert C. Tucker, ed. *The Marx-Engels Reader,* 1st ed. (New York: Norton,1972), p. 109.

71. Arendt, "The Concept of History: Ancient and Modern," in *BPF,* pp. 77–78.

72. Ronald Beiner rightly notes that Arendt's work, like Merleau-Ponty's *Humanism and Terror,* seeks to understand the tragedies of totalitarianism. But he fails to note that Arendt's approach, especially her view of judgment, was directed against the view of historical understanding—of deriving political conscience from his-

torical consciousness—that Merleau-Ponty's book epitomized. See Beiner, "Interpretive Essay," in Arendt, *LKPP*, p. 100.
73. Arendt, *HC*, p. 106.
74. *HC*, p. 108, 111.
75. *HC*, p. 116.
76. See Bikhu Parekh, "Hannah Arendt's Critique of Marx," in Melvyn A. Hill, ed., *Hannah Arendt: The Recovery of the Public World* (New York: St. Martin's, 1979).
77. As Arendt writes of Marx's legacy in *On Revolution*: "Thus the role of revolution was no longer to liberate men from the oppression of their fellow men, let alone to found freedom, but to liberate the life process of society from the fetters of scarcity so that it could swell into a stream of abundance. Not freedom but abundance became now the aim of revolution," p. 64.
78. See the following: G. A. Cohen, *Karl Marx's Theory of History: A Defense* (Princeton: Princeton University Press, 1978); Andrew Levine, *Arguing for Socialism* (London: Routledge & Kegan Paul, 1985); Jean Cohen, *Class and Civil Society* (Amherst: University of Massachusetts Press, 1982); Ernesto Laclau and Chantal Mouffe, *Hegemony and Socialist Strategy: Toward a Radical Democratic Politics* (London: Verso, 1985); and Jürgen Habermas, *Communication and the Evolution of Society* (Boston: Beacon Press, 1979).
79. Karl Marx and Friedrich Engels, "Manifesto of the Communist Party," in Tucker, ed., *Marx-Engels Reader*, p. 338.
80. See Norman Geras, "The Controversy about Marx and Justice." *New Left Review*, no. 50 (March–April 1985).
81. Arendt's appreciation for Marx is not often noticed. See her comments at the outset of her chapter on labor in *The Human Condition*, where she acknowledges "the great wealth of Marxian ideas and insights" and, distinguishing herself from "professional anti-Marxists," quotes Benjamin Constant's statement, "Certainly, I shall avoid the company of detractors of a great man" (p. 79). See also her remark in an essay on Jewish history about Karl Marx, who "wrote *Das Kapital*, a book which in its fanatical zeal for justice, carried on the Jewish tradition much more efficaciously than all the success of the 'chosen man of the chosen race' [Disraeli]." Arendt, "The Moral of History" in *JP*, p. 110.
82. See Arendt, "The Moral of History," *JP*, p. 110.
83. Arendt, *HC*, p. 104.
84. See Steven Lukes, *Marxism and Morality* (Oxford: Oxford University Press, 1985).
85. Karl Marx, *The German Ideology*, in Tucker, ed., *The Marx-Engels Reader*, p. 124. See Carmen Sirianni, "Power and Production in a Classless Society: A Critical Analysis of the Utopian Dimensions of Marxist Theory," *Socialist Review*, no. 59 (September–October 1981), and Jeffrey Isaac, *Power and Marxist Theory: A Realist View* (Ithaca: Cornell University Press, 1987), pp. 219–31.
86. Arendt, *HC*, p. 131.
87. An exception would be the final paragraph of Marx's fragment "The Power of Money in Bourgeois Society," where he allows that even in a fully emancipated society one's love might not produce love in return, and people would experience what he calls "misfortune." "The Economic and Philosophic Manuscripts of 1844," in Tucker, ed., *Marx-Engels Reader*, p. 83. It is unfortunate that Marx never integrated this tragic insight into his view of history.

88. Camus, *R*, p. 192. This recalls Nietzsche's comment on modern socialism: "In this way a goal seems to have entered the development of mankind: at any rate, the belief in progress towards the ideal is the only form in which a goal in history is thought of today. In summa: one has transferred the arrival of the 'kingdom of God' into the future, in human form—but fundamentally one has held fast to the belief in the old ideal." *The Will to Power*, trans.. Walter Kaufmann and R. J. Hollingdale (New York: Vintage, 1968), p. 186. See also Nancy S. Love, *Marx, Nietzsche, and Modernity* (New York: Columbia University Press, 1986), chap. 5.

89. See Simone Weil, *Oppression and Liberty*, trans. Arthur Wills and John Petrie (Amherst: University of Massachusetts Press, 1958). For a treatment of this theme in Weil, see Mary G. Dietz, *Between the Human and the Divine: The Political Thought of Simone Weil* (Totowa: Rowman and Littlefield, 1988). Camus was profoundly influenced by the work of Weil, which he helped to get posthumously published in his capacity as editor at Gallimard after the war. See Fred Rosen, "Marxism, Mysticism, and Liberty: The Influence of Simone Weil on Albert Camus," *Political Theory* 7, no. 3 (August 1979). Camus's suspicion of Marx's "scientific messianism" is also influenced by the writing of Georges Sorel. As he inscribes in his *Notebooks*: "The idea of progress which infects all working-class movements is a *bourgeois* idea developed in the eighteenth century. 'Our whole effort must be to prevent bourgeois ideas from poisoning the rising class: this is why we can never do enough to break every link between the people and eighteenth-century literature.' (*Illusion du Progres* . . .)." *N1*, p. 67.

90. Camus, *R*, p. 192. Camus's argument here parallels the writings of Leszek Kolokowski, particularly his essays "The Opiate of the Demiurge" and "Determinism and Responsibility," in his *Marxism and Beyond* (London, 1969).

91. *R*, p. 207.

92. *R*, p. 188.

93. *R*, pp. 200–201.

94. *R*, p. 207.

95. *R*, pp. 226, 234, 226.

96. *R*, p. 230.

97. Arendt, *OT*, p. xxxii. These remarks underscore Arendt's argument, in the body of the text, that "at the moment of Lenin's death the roads were still open" (pp. 319–23). The best account of this is Stephen F. Cohen, *Bukharin and the Bolshevik Revolution* (Oxford: Oxford University Press, 1976). See also Cohen, "Bolshevism and Stalinism," in Robert C. Tucker, ed., *Stalinism* (New York: Norton, 1977).

98. Young-Bruehl reports that Hilferding was connected with Hannah's mother Martha Arendt through their common socialist associates, and that in 1929 he solicited Hannah's review of Mannheim's *Ideology and Utopia* for his journal, *Die Gesellschaft*. According to Young-Bruehl, this began an acquaintanceship that continued in France after the rise of Hitler and ended abruptly in 1941 when Hilferding was turned over to the Nazis by Vichy and was shot. *Hannah Arendt*, pp. 83, 159.

99. Arendt, *OT*, p. 152.

100. *OT*, pp. 263–66.

101. *OT*, p. 319.

102. See Carmen Sirianni, *Workers Control and Socialist Democracy: The Soviet Experience* (London: Verso, 1982).

103. Arendt, "The Ex-Communists," *Commonweal,* no. 57 (March 20, 1953): 597.

104. Arendt, "Rosa Luxemburg, 1871–1919," in *MDT,* p. 50.

105. Walter Benjamin, "Theses on the Philosophy of History," in his *Illuminations,* ed. Hannah Arendt (New York: Schocken, 1969), p. 258.

106. See Rosa Luxemburg, "The Russian Revolution," in Mary-Alice Waters, ed., *Rosa Luxemburg Speaks* (New York: Pathfinder Press, 1970). Luxemburg's insistence that "the only way to rebirth is the school of public life itself, the most unlimited, the broadest democracy and public opinion" (p. 395) clearly prefigures Arendt's notion of public space and political freedom.

107. Arendt, "Rosa Luxemburg," in *MDT,* p. 43.

108. See Shlomo Avineri, "Toward a Socialist Theory of Nationalism," *Dissent,* Fall 1990:447–57.

109. *MDT,* p. 36.

110. Camus, *R,* pp. 234–35.

111. For Trotsky's view, see "The German Catastrophe," in Irving Howe, ed., *The Basic Writings of Trotsky* (New York: Schocken Books, 1976), pp. 257–67. For a recent account of the interplay between geopolitical pressures and revolutionary politics, see Theda Skocpol, *States and Social Revolutions* (Cambridge: Cambridge University Press, 1979).

112. Camus, *R,* p. 244–45.

113. Nietzsche, *The Will To Power,* pp. 18, 30.

114. Camus, *MS,* pp. 10, 5.

115. This phrase comes from Raymond Aron, *The Century of Total War* (Boston: Beacon, 1955).

116. Camus, "Letters to a German Friend," in *RRD,* pp. 27–30.

117. Camus, *R,* pp. 36–45. Camus's psychological novel *The Fall* is a brilliant deconstruction of the "presumptuous alliance of freedom and virtue." Yet Camus seems equally revolted by the dripping cynicism that attends this deconstruction. For a similar, though more positive account of Sade, see Connolly, *Political Theory,* pp. 72–85.

118. *R,* pp. 47–8, 49, 50, 51–2. The famous murder scene in Camus's novella *The Stranger,* in which Merseault is "transfixed" by the harsh light of the sun, can be read as a depiction of the dangers of such an apocalyptic naturalism. See Sprintzen, *Camus,* pp. 36–38.

119. Nancy L. Rosenblum, *Another Liberalism: Romanticism and the Reconstruction of Liberal Thought* (Cambridge, Mass.: Harvard University Press, 1987), provides a more favorable account of the positive contribution of romanticism to liberalism. See also Taylor, *Sources of the Self,* pp. 305–92.

120. I owe this insight to Jean Elshtain. For an interesting discussion of this polarity of progress and nostalgia, see Christopher Lasch, *The True and Only Heaven: Progress and Its Critics* (New York: Norton, 1990), especially pp. 82–119.

121. Camus, *R,* pp. 97–99.

122. Yet Camus also insists that true art cannot come from a total subversion of the world, but rather from a combination of rejection and consent; there must be

something of value in the world for there to be authentic creation: "The only real formalism is silence." *R,* pp. 268–72.

123. *R,* pp. 95, 93, 95, 94.

124. Camus, *S,* 1946. The best commentary on this work is Jean-Paul Sartre, "An Explication of *The Stranger,*" reprinted in Germain Brée, ed., *Camus: A Collection of Critical Essays* (Englewood Cliffs, N.J.: Prentice-Hall, 1962). See also Sprintzen, *Camus,* pp. 23–41.

125. Camus, *R,* p. 10.

126. Arendt, *OT,* pp. 330–31. See Robert Wohl, *The Generation of 1914* (Cambridge, Mass.: Harvard University Press, 1979), and Megill, *Prophets,* pp. 110–16.

127. *OT,* p. 334.

128. *OT,* p. 334–35.

129. See Arendt's critical remarks on Heidegger, whose metaphysical flirtation with Nazism derived, in her view, from the fact that he "had read instead of Hitler's *Mein Kampf* the writings of the Italian futurists. . . . There is no doubt that these writings make more interesting reading, but the point of the matter is that Heidegger, like so many other German intellectuals, Nazis and anti-Nazis, of his generation never read *Mein Kampf.* This misunderstanding of what it was all about is inconsiderable when compared with the much more decisive 'error' that consisted in not only ignoring the most relevant 'literature' but in escaping from the reality of the Gestapo cellars and the torture-hells of the early concentration camps into ostensibly more significant regions." See "Martin Heidegger at Eighty," p. 302. As Victor Farías has incontrovertibly demonstrated, Heidegger hardly evaded the barbarities of Nazism, but rather helped, as a loyal member of the Nazi Party, to bring them into the German university system. See his *Heidegger and Nazism* (Philadelphia: Temple University Press, 1989). Arendt must have known about at least some of this. Yet in her public comments she never let on. let on. Her relationship with Heidegger—their early love affair, the resumption of their personal relationship after the war—certainly constitutes one of the most enigmatic unions in intellectual history, especially given Arendt's Jewishness and Heidegger's Nazi leanings. See Young-Bruehl, *Hannah Arendt,* esp. pp. 50–69, 246–48.

130. Camus, *R,* p. 70.

131. Arendt, *BPF,* pp. 30–31.

132. *BPF,* pp. 31, 35.

133. "Somebody who wills gives orders to something in him that obeys. . . . The strangest aspect of this multiple phenomenon we call 'Will' is that we have but one word for it, and especially only one word for the fact that *we are in every given case at the same time those who issues the orders and those who obey them*; insofar as we obey, we experience the feelings of coercion, urging, pressing, resisting, which usually begin to manifest themselves immediately after the act of willing; insofar however . . . as we are in command . . . we experience a sensation of pleasure, and this all the more strongly as we are used to overcoming the dichotomy through the notion of the I, the Ego, and this in such a way that we take the obedience in ourselves for granted and therefore identify willing and performing, willing and acting." Arendt, *LM,* part 2, *Willing,* p. 161. See Nietzsche, *Beyond Good and Evil,* no. 19, pp. 29–31.

134. See William E. Connolly, *Politics and Ambiguity* (Madison: University of Wisconsin Press, 1987), and *Political Theory and Modernity* (Oxford: Basil Blackwell, 1988), on Nietzsche and dissonance. For a recent effort to link Arendt with this approach, see B. Honig, "Arendt, Identity, and Difference." *Political Theory* 16, no. 1 (February 1988).

135. Arendt, *LM*, part 2, *Willing*, 170–71.

136. See Arendt, *HC*, pp. 117, 172, 203–4, 245, and "On Violence," in *CR*, pp. 170–71.

137. Martin Heidegger, "The Word of Nietzsche: 'God is Dead,'" in *Concerning Technology*, p. 95–96.

138. Ibid., p. 108.

139. Camus, *MS*, p. 41, 45–7.

140. Nietzsche, *The Gay Science*, quoted in Arendt, *LM*, part 2, *Willing*, p. 166. Camus's account of the Sisyphus myth appears in *MS*, pp. 88–91.

141. *MS*, p. 50.

142. See Camus, "Reflections on the Guillotine," in *RRD*, pp. 173–234.

143. Nietzsche, *The Genealogy of Morals*, p. 208. James Miller, "Carnivals of Atrocity: Foucault, Nietzsche, Cruelty," *Political Theory* 18, no. 3 (August 1990), is a brilliant discussion of the rhetorical glorification of cruelty in Nietzsche and his heirs.

144. Camus, *MS*, pp. 66–67. This text bears the traces of the cult of heroism popular in France at the time and best developed in the novels of André Malraux. See H. Stuart Hughes, *The Obstructed Path: French Social Thought in the Years of Desperation, 1930–1960* (New York: Harper, 1966), pp. 102–52.

145. Camus, "Letter to Roland Barthes on The Plague," in *LCE*, p. 339. Camus also insists on this in his response to Jeanson, asserting that "no reader, except for your review, would think of denying that if there is an evolution from *The Stranger* to *The Plague*, it consists in consciousness of solidarity and participation." "Lettre au Directeur du Temps Modernes," p. 321.

146. Camus, *R*, pp. 65, 70.

147. "This magnificent consent, born of abundance and fulness of spirit, is the unreserved affirmation of human imperfection and suffering, of evil and murder, of all that is problematic and strange in our existence." *R*, pp. 71, 72.

148. *R*, pp. 73, 75. In this light it is worth recalling Camus's famous 1957 Nobel address, an eloquent statement of the intellectual responsibilities of the artist: "I cannot live as a person without my art. And yet I have never set that art above everything else. It is essential to me, on the contrary, because it excludes no one and allows me to live, just as I am, on a footing with all . . . the writer's function is not without arduous duties. By definition, he cannot serve today those who make history; he must serve those who are subject to it. . . . No one of us is great enough for such a vocation. Yet in all the circumstances of his life, the writer can recapture the feeling of a living community that will justify him." Reprinted in Sprintzen, *Camus*, pp. vii–ix. On the motif of aestheticism deriving from Nietzsche, see Megill, *Prophets of Extremity*.

149. Camus, *R*, p. 75–77.

150. *R*, p. 77.

151. *R*, p. 78.

152. Camus, preface to *CTOP*, pp. v–vi.
153. Camus, *N2*, p. 59. See also Camus's comment, "The situation Socrates faced is analogous to our own. There was evil in men's souls because there were contradictions in communication.... We too have our sophists and call for a Socrates, since it was Socrates' task to attempt the cure of souls by the search for a dictionary. If the words justice, goodness, beauty have no meaning, then men can tear one another to pieces." *LCE*, p. 213.
154. On Arendt, see Gunnell, *Political Theory*. On Camus, see Conor Cruise O'Brien, *Albert Camus of Europe and North Africa* (New York: Viking, 1970), and Germain Brée, *Camus and Sartre* (New York: Dell, 1972).
155. Arendt thus quotes Nietzsche's observation that German philosophy "is the most fundamental form of... homesickness there has ever been: the longing for the best that has ever existed; at last one longs back for that place in which alone one can be at home: the *Greek* world!" *LM, Willing*, p. 157. But she immediately proceeds to distance herself from this impulse.
156. Quoted in Sprintzen, *Camus*, p. xiii.
157. Arendt, *LM*, pp. 157–58.
158. Quoted in Sprintzen, *Camus*, p. 41.
159. I believe that both Arendt and Camus would agree with Christopher Lasch, who argues that nostalgia, in its "dream of childlike simplicity and security," is the "ideological twin" of the modern faith in human progress, presenting an equally simplified view of history. See *The True and Only Heaven*, p. 83.
160. Camus, *R*, p. 22. See my "On Rebellion and Revolution: Albert Camus's *The Rebel* Reconsidered," *Dissent*, Summer 1989.

Chapter Four: Revolt and the Foundations of Politics

1. Camus, *N2*, p. 109.
2. See Jean-François Lyotard, *The Postmodern Condition* (Minneapolis: University of Minnesota Press, 1984).
3. Richard Rorty, *Contingency, Irony and Solidarity* (Cambridge: Cambridge University Press, 1989).
4. Camus, "The Almond Trees," in *LCE*, pp. 135–36.
5. Arendt, "Tradition and the Modern Age," in *BPF*, pp. 28–29.
6. Arendt, "On Humanity in Dark Times: Thoughts about Lessing," in *MDT*, pp. 10–11.
7. See James Miller, "The Pathos of Novelty: Hannah Arendt's Image of Freedom in the Modern World," in Melvyn A. Hill, ed., *Hannah Arendt: The Recovery of the Public World* (New York: St. Martins, 1979).
8. Joseph Margolis, *Pragmatism Without Foundations: Reconciling Realism and Relativism* (Oxford: Basil Blackwell, 1986), p. 38.
9. See Richard Rorty, *Philosophy and the Mirror of Nature* (Princeton: Princeton University Press, 1979).
10. Margolis, *Pragmatism*, p. 48.
11. Margolis writes that theoretical judgments must be alive to "the openness, plurality, and profound sense of contingency with which they ought to be regarded."

Ibid., p. 55. A similar argument is made by Ian Shapiro, *Political Criticism* (Berkeley and Los Angeles: University of California Press, 1990).

12. See Ian Shapiro, "Gross Concepts in Political Argument," *Political Theory* 17, no. 1 (February 1989): 51–76.

13. Eric Voegelin, "The Origins of Totalitarianism," *Review of Politics* 15, no. 1 (January 1953): 74–75.

14. Arendt, "A Reply," *Review of Politics* 15, no. 1 (January 1953): 83–84.

15. Margolis, *Pragmatism,* p. 38.

16. Arendt, *HC,* pp. 9–10.

17. *HC,* p. 10–11.

18. *HC,* p. 11.

19. Camus, *R,* p. 189. See Arendt, "What Is Existenz Philosophy?" *Partisan Review* 13 (Winter 1946): pp. 51–52, for Arendt's similar invocation of Jaspers.

20. Camus, *MS,* pp. 11, 15.

21. *MS,* p. 21.

22. Camus, *R,* p. 10. In his essay "The Minotaur, or Stop at Oran," Camus writes of the "temptation to identify oneself with those stones, to melt into that burning and impassive universe that defies history and its ferments. That is doubtless futile." *LCE,* p. 130. The rock is also a recurrent metaphor for irresponsibility in Sartre. See his "Existentialism Is a Humanism," in Walter Kaufman, ed., *Existentialism From Dostoievski to Sartre,* rev. ed. (New York: New American Library, 1975), p. 361, and his portrait of the anti-Semite in *Anti-Semite and Jew* (New York: Schocken, 1965), pp. 18–19, 27.

23. For a more recent exposition of the view that we cannot dispense with "some conception of a shared human nature as a set of shared potentialities," see Stuart Hampshire, *Innocence and Experience* (Cambridge, Mass.: Harvard University Press, 1989), pp. 30–32.

24. Arendt, *HC,* p. 5. Whether these are activities, distinct spheres of social life, or analytical dimensions of any human activity is unclear in Arendt's various formulations. It is also unclear how these relate to other human properties, like thought and reason, which Arendt notes but chooses to ignore. For a penetrating discussion see Margaret Canovan, "The Contradictions of Hannah Arendt's Political Thought," *Political Theory* 6, no. 1 (February 1978).

25. Arendt, *HC,* p. 7.

26. Arendt, "What Is Existenz Philosophy?" p. 37.

27. Arendt, *HC,* p. 157.

28. Arendt, "What is Existenz Philosophy?" p. 37.

29. Ibid., p. 9.

30. Ibid., pp. 24–28.

31. Ibid., p. 7.

32. Ibid., p. 8.

33. On this point see Richard Bernstein, *Praxis and Action* (Philadelphia: University of Pennsylvania Press, 1974) and *Beyond Objectivism and Relativism* (Philadelphia: University of Pennsylvania Press, 1983).

34. See Jürgen Habermas, *The Philosophical Discourse of Modernity* (Cambridge, Mass.: MIT Press, 1987), pp. 294–326.

35. Arendt, *HC,* p. 184. See Anthony Giddens, *New Rules of Sociological Method* (New

York: Basic Books, 1976), for a cogent account of the problem of unintended consequences.

36. *HC,* p. 191.
37. Arendt, "What Is Existenz Philosophy?" pp. 51, 53.
38. Ibid., pp. 55–56.
39. Arendt, *HC,* p. 26–7.
40. *HC,* p. 32.
41. *HC,* p. 246.
42. See especially Arendt, *OT,* pp. 290–302, and "Civil Disobedience," in *CR,* pp. 82–102.
43. Arendt, *HC,* pp. 201–05.
44. Here I have found particularly helpful Paul Ricoeur, "Action, Story, and History: On Re-Reading *The Human Condition,*" *Salmagundi,* no. 60 (Spring-Summer 1983), and Martin Levin, "On *Animal Laborans* and *Homo Politicus* in Hannah Arendt: A Note," *Political Theory* 7, no. 4 (November 1979).
45. Arendt, *HC,* p. 177.
46. Ibid., pp. 182, 179. See James T. Knaeur, "Motive and Goal in Hannah Arendt's Concept of Political Action," *American Political Science Review* 74 (1980).
47. Arendt, *HC,* p. 185.
48. See also Simone de Beauvoir, *The Ethics of Ambiguity* (New York: Citadel Press, 1976), esp. pp. 96–154.
49. *MS,* p. 50.
50. See, for example, her observation regarding the rise of anti-Semitism in *The Origins of Totalitarianism*: "The general weakening of political factors, for two decades having brought about a situation in which reality and appearance, political reality and theatrical performance could easily parody each other, now enabled them to become the representatives of a nebulous international society in which national prejudices no longer seemed valid" (p. 53). The same point is also made in an essay on Stefan Zweig: "For fifty years ... political representation had become a kind of theatrical performance, sometimes an operetta, of varying quality." "Portrait of a Period," in Arendt, *JP.*
51. Arendt, "Thoughts on Politics and Revolution," in *CR,* pp. 201–3, 227–28. For a different perspective see George McKenna, "Bannisterless Politics: Hannah Arendt and Her Children," *History of Political Thought* 5, no. 2 (Summer 1984).
52. Camus, *R,* p. 22.
53. Camus, "Prometheus in the Underworld," in *LCE,* p. 139, 142.
54. Camus, "On Jean Grenier's *Les Isles,*" in *LCE,* p. 328.
55. See Kate Soper, *Humanism and Anti-Humanism* (LaSalle, Ill.: Open Court Books, 1986), p. 22.
56. In his "Letters to a German Friend" Camus insists that "man is that force which ultimately cancels all tyrants and gods. He is the force of evidence." *RRD,* pp. 28–29.
57. Camus, *MS,* p. 5.
58. *MS,* p. 12.
59. The words of Roquentin in Jean-Paul Sartre's *Nausea* (New York: New Directions, 1964). Cf. Camus: "Man is nothing in himself. He is but an infinite chance. But he is

infinitely responsible for that chance.... No one can say that he has reached the limit of man." *N2*, p. 118. In *The Ethics of Ambiguity*, p. 129, de Beauvoir associates absurdity, which she distinguishes from ambiguity, with pointlessness. This was a common charge leveled against Camus by his left-wing existentialist critics.

60. Camus, *MS*, p. 16.

61. *MS*, p. 7.

62. Camus, *R*, p. 6.

63. *R*, pp. 13, 16.

64. The literature that considers both Camus and Sartre under the heading *existentialist* is immense. Symptomatic is Walter Kaufmann's *Existentialism From Dostoevsky to Sartre*. Although Arendt displays great sympathy toward Camus, she too makes this mistake. See Arendt, "French Existentialism," *The Nation*, February 23, 1946, pp. 226–28, especially her claim that both Sartre and Camus "deny the possibility of a genuine fellowship between men."

65. *R*, p. 22.

66. Camus, "On Sartre's *Le Mur and Other Stories*," in *LCE*, p. 205.

67. Albert Camus, "On Jean-Paul Sartre's *La Nauseé*," in *LCE*, p. 201. Note the similarities between Camus's criticism of Sartre and Arendt's agreement with Jaspers, against Heidegger, that "Existenz itself is never isolated." See note 38 above.

68. *LCE*, p. 346. Camus also brings out these differences with Sartre in his spirited defense of existentialism against the harangues of conservative philosophy. See Camus, "Pessimism and Courage," in *RRD*. This rejection of existentialist individualism is a point of deep convergence with Arendt.

69. *R*, p. 281. See Camus's description of the condition of the Oranis in *The Plague*: "No longer were there individual destinies; only a collective destiny, made of plague and the emotions shared by all. Strongest of these emotions was the sense of exile and of deprivation, with all the cross-currents of revolt and fear set up by these" (p. 151).

70. See Kerry Whiteside, *Merleau-Ponty and the Foundation of an Existential Politics* (Princeton: Princeton University Press, 1988), and William L. McBride, *Sartre's Political Theory* (Bloomington: Indiana University Press, 1991).

71. Camus, *R*, p. 281.

72. Sprintzen, *Camus*, p. 133.

73. Quoted in Ibid., p. 242.

74. William E. Connolly's defense of "agonistic respect" develops many similar concerns. See his *Identity/Difference: Democratic Negotiations of Political Paradox* (Ithaca: Cornell University Press, 1991).

75. Burton Zweibach, *The Common Life: Ambiguity, Agreement, and the Structure of Morals* (Philadelphia: Temple University Press, 1988), p. 203.

76. Camus *R*, p. 283–4. See also Camus's account of the silence imposed on Oran by the plague, and the rebellious effort to sustain dialogue in its face. *Pl*, p. 69.

77. Camus, preface to *CTOP*, p. vii. See also the comment on the lesson of this play in his notebooks: "The whole misfortune of men comes from the fact that they don't use simple speech.... From this point of view, Socrates is the one who is right, against Jesus and Nietzsche. Progress and true nobility lie in the dialogue from man to man and not in the Gospel, a monologue dictated from the top of

a solitary mountain. That's where I stand. What balances the absurd is the community of men fighting against it. And if we choose to serve that community, we choose to serve the dialogue carried to the absurd against any policy of falsehood or of silence. That's the way one is free with others." *N2,* pp. 125–26.

78. Richard Bernstein, *Beyond Objectivism and Relativism,* p. 231.

79. *MS,* pp. 14–15.

80. On the varieties of democratic speech, see Benjamin Barber, *Strong Democracy* (Berkeley and Los Angeles: University of California Press, 1984), and Iris Marion Young, "Impartiality and the Civic Public: Some Implications of Feminist Critiques of Moral and Political Theory," in Seyla Benhabib and Drucilla Cornell, ed., *Feminism as Critique* (Minneapolis: University of Minneapolis Press, 1986), pp. 67–76.

81. Christopher Lasch, *The True and Only Heaven: Progress and Its Critics* (New York: Norton, 1990), pp. 120–67.

82. Arendt, *OR,* p. 19.

83. Camus, *R,* p. 11.

84. See Anthony Giddens, *The Constitution of Society* (Berkeley and Los Angeles: University of California Press, 1984). Arendt offers a similar formulation in "Civil Disobedience," in *CR,* pp. 88–90.

85. Arendt enthusiastically quotes Jefferson's reaction to Shays's Rebellion: "God forbid we should ever be twenty years without such a rebellion." *OR,* p. 233. This is consistent with her support for the principle of "augmentation" and political change that she believes at least implicit in the United States Constitution. *OR,* pp. 201–3. Arendt also quotes Jefferson's famous aphorism that "the tree of liberty must be refreshed from time to time with the blood of patriots and tyrants. It is its natural manure," p. 233. Martial virtue was no doubt an important ideal of early republicanism. For an exchange on the significance of this for Arendt, see George Kateb, "Death and Politics: Hannah Arendt's Reflections on the American Constitution," and Fred Dallmayr, "Public or Private Freedom? Response to Kateb," in *Social Research* 54, no. 3 (Autumn 1987).

86. This view is shared by many commentators on the right *and* the left. The most influential liberal proponent is Germain Brée, in *Camus and Sartre: Crisis and Commitment* (New York: Delacorte Press, 1972), pp. 156–233. See also Philip Thody, *Albert Camus: A Study of His Work* (New York: Grove Press, 1957), pp. 37, 72–73, and *Albert Camus* (New York: St. Martins, 1989), p. 67. On the left, the most influential proponent is Jean-Paul Sartre, in "Réponse à Albert Camus," *Les Temps Modernes,* no. 80 (August 1952): 334–53. Francis Jeanson initiated this charge in his harsh review of *The Rebel,* "Albert Camus, ou L'Ame Révoltée," *Les Temps Modernes,* no. 79 (May 1952): pp. 2070–90. Camus then answered with his famous "Lettre au Directeur des Temps Modernes," *Les Temps Modernes,* no. 80 (August 1952): 317–33, prompting Sartre to respond. Only Sartre's contribution to this debate has been translated into English, in his *Situations* (New York: George Braziller, 1965), pp. 71–104. This at least in part explains why his view has been adopted by English-speaking commentators. See Mark Poster, *Existential Marxism in Postwar France* (Princeton: Princeton University Press, 1975); Ronald Aronson, *Jean-Paul Sartre: Philosophy in the World* (London: Verso, 1980), and Fred Hirsch, *The French New Left* (Boston: South End Press, 1981). For criticism,

✓

see my "On Rebellion and Revolution: Albert Camus's *The Rebel* Reconsidered," *Dissent* (Summer 1989): 376–84.

87. Camus, *R*, p. 249.
88. *R*, p. 248–49.
89. Camus, *Pl*, p. 231.
90. Camus, *R*, p. 250.
91. *R*, p. 288. See Arthur Koestler, *The Yogi and the Commisar* (New York: Macmillan, 1946). If Koestler gravitates toward the yogi, then Maurice Merleau-Ponty, in his 1947 *Humanism and Terror* (Boston: Beacon Press, 1969), gravitates toward the commisar. Camus was personally engaged in the intense dispute between these writers. See Camus, *N2*, pp. 141–46, 166.
92. *R*, p. 290.
93. *R*, p. 289.
94. *R*, pp. 290–91.
95. *R*, p. 292.
96. Camus's account here draws from Boris Savinkov, *Memoirs of a Terrorist* (New York: Albert and Charles Boni, 1931), pp. 71–117.
97. Camus, *The Just Assassins,* in *CTOP*, p. 259–60.
98. See Camus: "Virtue cannot separate itself from reality without becoming a principle of evil. Nor can it identify itself completely with reality without denying itself." *R*, 296. Camus also illustrates the dangers of a messianic virtue in *The Possessed,* a dramatization of Dostoevsky's novel of the same name.
99. In *Utopia and Its Enemies* (New York: Free Press, 1963), George Kateb argues that Camus puts forward the unrealistic principle that violence is only justifiable when a life is given for a life. Kateb rightly insists that such a principle both is a recipe for the sacrificial self-destruction of any revolutionary movement and leads to the dangerous conclusion that "the stain of blood can be wiped clean by more blood" (pp. 38–40). I think, however, that Camus needs to be read less stringently. He nowhere articulates such a principle, and indeed the argument of *The Rebel* is that any such categorical principles are dangerous. Kaliayev embodies not a principle but an attitude, namely, that violence is a "desperate exception" (*R*, p. 282). On this point see also Fred H. Willhoite, Jr., *Beyond Nihilism: Albert Camus's Contribution to Political Thought* (Baton Rouge: Louisiana State University Press, 1968), pp. 156–60.
100. "Défense de "L'Homme Révolté," in *Oeuvres Complètes II* (Paris: Gallimard, Bibliothèque de la Pléiade, Gallimard, 1965), ed. Roger Quilliot and L. Faucon, quoted in Sprintzen, *Camus,* p. 189.
101. George Kateb brings out these themes in "Arendt and Representative Democracy" *Salmagundi*, no. 60 (Spring-Summer 1983).
102. Miller, "The Pathos of Novelty," p. 183.
103. Arendt, *OR*, p. 39.
104. *OR*, p. 183.
105. Arendt, *OR*, p. 212.
106. *OR*, p. 159.
107. *OR*, p. 126.
108. Arendt, *OR*, p. 19.
109. *OR*, p. 11.

110. *OR*, p. 20. See Nietzsche: "How much blood and horror lies behind all 'good' things?" *The Genealogy of Morals*, p. 194.

111. Arendt, *OR*, p. 19.

112. Arendt, "On Violence," in *CR*, p. 142. See also *HC*, pp. 200–202.

113. *CR*, pp. 143, 145, 106.

114. *CR*, pp. 145–46.

115. *CR*, p. 148.

116. *CR*, pp. 150–51.

117. *CR*, pp. 150–51.

118. Camus, *R*, p. 292.

119. *R*, pp. 169, 293.

120. See Camus's essay "Reflections on the Guillotine," in *RRD*, pp. 176–77, originally published along with Arthur Koestler's "Reflections on Hanging" in *Réflexions sur la piene Capitale* (Paris: Calmann-Levy, 1957). Camus's harsh position immediately after the war, in which he called for another Saint-Just to purge liberated France, was challenged by François Mauriac, causing Camus to temper his position and eventually reverse it and champion a more "lucid" and "charitable" view of the requirements of postwar reconstruction. See Emmett Parker, *Albert Camus: The Artist in the Arena* (Madison: University of Wisconsin Press, 1965), pp. 83–96, and Willhoite, *Beyond Nihilism*, pp. 153–55.

121. Arendt, *EJ*. On Eichmann's execution, see pp. 250–52, 277–79. On the hypocrisy of the prosecution, see pp. 3–20. See also Jeffrey Isaac, "At the Margins: Jewish Identity and Politics in the Thought of Hannah Arendt," *Tikkun* (January-February 1990).

122. *EJ*, p. 265.

123. Reinhold Niebuhr, *Moral Man and Immoral Society* (New York: Scribners, 1932), pp. 171, 170.

124. Ibid., p. 199.

125. *OR*, p. 232.

126. Camus, *R*, p. 249.

127. *R*, p. 292.

Chapter Five: Rebellion and Democratic Politics

1. Arendt, "On Hannah Arendt," in Melvyn Hill, ed., *Hannah Arendt: The Recovery of the Public World* (New York: St. Martin's Press, 1979), pp. 333–36.

2. Camus, "*On a Philosophy of Expression, by Brice Parain,*" in *LCE*, p. 240.

3. Martin Jay, "Hannah Arendt," *Partisan Review* 45, no. 3 (1978): 353, 355, 364.

4. James Miller, *Democracy Is in the Streets: From Port Huron to the Siege of Chicago* (New York: Simon and Schuster, 1987), pp. 50–52, 143–148. Miller notes that Tom Hayden's heroes were Albert Camus and James Dean—both idealistic rebels who flouted convention (p. 41).

5. McKenna further argues that for Arendt "the important thing was to strike a pose," a nihilism that he also associates with the New Left. See "Bannisterless Politics: Hannah Arendt and Her Children," *History of Political Thought* 5, no. 2 (Summer 1984): 346.

6. Arendt, "On Humanity in Dark Times," in *MDT,* p. 27.

7. On the "democratic ethos," see Ian Shapiro, *Political Criticism* (Berkeley and Los Angeles: University of California Press, 1990), pp. 265–298.

8. Arendt, "Walter Benjamin: 1892–1940," in *MDT,* pp. 205–206.

9. See Stephen Holmes, *Benjamin Constant and the Making of Modern Liberalism* (New Haven: Yale University Press, 1984); Nancy Rosenblum, *Another Liberalism* (Cambridge, Mass.: Harvard University Press, 1987); George Armstrong Kelly, "Parnassian Liberalism in Nineteenth Century France: Tocqueville, Renan, Flaubert," *History of Political Thought* 8, no. 3 (Winter 1987); Larry Siedentop, "French Liberalism," in Alan Ryan, ed., *The Idea of Freedom: Essays in Honor of Isaiah Berlin* (Oxford: Oxford University Press, 1979), and Judith Shklar, *Ordinary Vices* (Cambridge, Mass.: Harvard University Press, 1984). For a review of this literature, see Don Herzog, "Up toward Liberalism," *Dissent* (Summer 1989). On possessive individualism, see C. B. Macpherson, *The Political Theory of Possessive Individualism* (Oxford: Oxford University Press, 1962).

10. In his *Notebooks (N1,* p. 197), Camus quotes Tocqueville's aphorism that "it is always a great crime to deprive a people of its liberty on the pretext that it is using it wrongly." In later entries he transcribes two interesting texts from Constant, whom he describes as "a prophet": "In order to live in peace one has to take almost as much trouble as one would to govern the world" (*N2,* p. 172); and, underscoring the dangers of ideological absolutism, "One must study men's woes but count among these woes the ideas they have of the means of combatting them" (*N2,* p. 244).

11. Arendt, *OT.* See the appendix, "Ideology and Terror," for the influence of Montesquieu; Tocqueville is quoted only once, but the text itself makes clear his influence: he criticizes "absolutist systems which represent all the events of history as depending upon the great first causes linked by the chain of fatality, and which, as it were, suppress men from the history of the human race" (p. 345); on Clemencau, see *OT,* pp. 100, 113.

12. See Max Weber, "Politics as a Vocation," in H. H. Gerth and C. Wright Mills, eds., *From Max Weber: Essays in Sociology* (Oxford: Oxford University Press, 1949), on Weber's critique of an "ethic of ultimate ends." It is worth noting the friendship and intellectual kinship between Arendt's teacher, Karl Jaspers, and Weber. See Jaspers's "Max Weber," in *Karl Jaspers: Basic Philosophical Writings,* ed. Edith Ehrlich et al. (Athens, Ohio: Ohio University Press, 1986), pp. 478–93.

13. See Arthur M. Schlesinger, Jr., *The Vital Center* (New York, 1950). For a critical account of Schlesinger's Cold War liberalism see Michael Wreszin, "Arthur Schlesinger, Jr., Scholar-Activist in Cold War America: 1946–1956," *Salmagundi,* nos. 63–64 (Spring-Summer 1984).

14. Quoted in Robert Colquhoun, *Raymond Aron: The Philosopher in History 1905– 1955* (Beverley Hills, Calif.: Sage, 1986), p. 284. As Aron writes: "A political doctrine is and must be a philosophy of the real and not just a question of morality. ... Certainty and total conviction [are] unattainable" (pp. 79–80). See also his remark that "the man who no longer expects miraculous changes either from a revolution or an economic plan is not obliged to resign himself to the unjustifiable.

It is because he likes individual human beings, participates in living communities and respects the truth, that he refuses to surrender his soul to an abstract ideal of humanity, a tyrannical party and an absurd scholasticism" (p. 479). See James D. Wilkinson, "Jean-Paul Sartre and Raymond Aron," *Salmagundi,* nos. 70–71 (Spring-Summer 1986).

15. See Colquhon, *Raymond Aron,* pp. 365–488, esp. 453–88.

16. Rosa Luxemburg, "The Russian Revolution," in *Rosa Luxemburg Speaks,* ed. Mary-Alice Waters (New York: Pathfinder, 1970), pp. 389–91. Arendt quotes this in *OR,* pp. 327–28, Camus in *N2,* pp. 192–93.

17. Arendt, "Rosa Luxemburg, 1971–1919," in *MDT,* p. 52. Luxemburg was clearly one of Arendt's heroes. As Arendt writes: "her commitment to revolution was primarily a moral matter, and this meant that she remained passionately engaged in public life and civil affairs, in the destinies of the world. Her involvement with European politics outside the immediate interests of the working class, and hence completely beyond the horizon of all Marxists, appears most convincingly in her repeated insistence on a 'republican program' for the German and Russian parties" (p. 51). For Luxemburg's views on the importance of revolutionary spontaneity, see her famous 1906 pamphlet, "The Mass Strike, the Political Party and the Trade Unions," in *Rosa Luxemburg Speaks,* pp. 153–219. A critical account of this text is provided in Ernesto Laclau and Chantal Mouffe, *Hegemony and Socialist Strategy* (London: Verso, 1985).

18. See Svetozar Stojanovic, *In Search of Democracy in Socialism: History and Party Consciousness* (New York: Prometheus, 1981).

19. Arendt notes that revolution "was no more an article of faith with her than Marxism," and that "she was not an orthodox Marxist, so little orthodox indeed that it might be doubted that she was a Marxist at all." "Rosa Luxemburg," in *MDT,* p. 38. But this claim, however near to the truth, is merely an example of Arendt's penchant for provocation.

20. Many have considered Dewey a "technocratic" liberal, but Robert Westerbrooks's masterful *John Dewey and American Democracy* (Ithaca: Cornell University Press, 1991) effectively demolishes this view. See also Alfonso J. Damico, "Impractical America," *Political Theory* 14, no. 1 (February 1986), and Richard Bernstein, "One Step Forward, Two Steps Backward: Richard Rorty on Liberal Democracy and Philosophy," *Political Theory* 15, no. 4 (November 1987).

21. On affinities between pragmatism and Continental philosophy, see Richard Bernstein, *Praxis and Action* (Philadelphia: University of Pennsylvania Press, 1974), and Richard Rorty, *The Consequences of Pragmatism* (Minneapolis: University of Minnesota Press, 1982).

22. See Leon Trotsky, *Their Morals and Ours* (New York: Pioneer Publishers, 1942).

23. Quoted in Steven Lukes, *Marxism and Morality* (Oxford: Oxford University Press, 1985), p. 120.

24. Dewey maintained that "with the idea of the liberation of mankind as the end-in-view, there would be an examination of all means that are likely to attain this end without any fixed preconceptions as to what they must be, and that every suggested means would be weighed and judged on the express ground of the consequences it is likely to produce." Quoted in Lukes, *Marxism and Morality,* p. 121. Arendt develops a similar critique of Marxism, attacking Trotsky's famous dictum that

"you cannot make an omelette without breaking eggs," in her "The Ex-Communists," *Commonweal*, March 20, 1953:596–97.

25. John Dewey, *The Public and Its Problems* (Chicago: Swallow Press, 1927), p. 21.
26. Ibid., pp. 110–42.
27. Ibid., pp. 147–48.
28. Ibid., p. 148.
29. Arendt, *HC*, p. 146.
30. Dewey, *The Public*, p. 152.
31. Ibid., p. 203.
32. Ibid., pp. 202–3.
33. Reinhold Niebuhr, from a neo-orthodox Christian perspective, picks up on the optimism of Dewey in *Moral Man*, esp. pp. xi-xxv.
34. Dewey, *The Public*, pp. 213, 216–17.
35. John Dewey, *John Dewey's Impressions of Soviet Russia and the Revolutionary World: Mexico—China—Turkey 1929*, ed. William W. Brickman (New York: Teachers College, Columbia University, 1964), pp. 49, 61.
36. My argument here is indebted to Peter T. Manicas's "John Dewey: Anarchism and the Political State," *Transactions of the Charles S. Pierce Society* 15 (Spring 1982).
37. Quoted in Daniel Guerin, *Anarchism* (New York: Monthly Review Press, 1970), p. 43.
38. Quoted in Martin Buber, *Paths in Utopia* (Boston: Beacon Press, 1958), p. 43.
39. Arendt, "On Violence," p. 139; *OR*, p. 30.
40. Camus, *N2*, p. 266.
41. Camus, *R*, p. 297–98.
42. Ibid., p. 299.
43. See especially *N2*, pp. 176–82.
44. Camus, "The New Mediterranean Culture," in *LCE*, p. 197.
45. Arendt, *OR*, pp. 256–57. Arendt's account here parallels Emma Goldman's anarchist critique of Bolshevism in *My Further Disillusionment in Russia* (Garden City, N.Y.: Doubleday, 1924), pp. 144–78.
46. Ibid., pp. 248–49, 261.
47. Ibid., pp. 263–64.
48. Ibid., p. 264.
49. See Arendt, *OT*, especially the chapter "The Decline of the Nation-State and the Rights of Man," pp. 267–302; and *EJ*, pp. 234–98, where Arendt criticizes the absence of international juridical institutions capable of regulating and judging "law-abiding" conduct in a "criminal state."
50. Arendt, *OR*, p. 266.
51. Ibid., p. 267.
52. Ibid., p. 264–65.
53. Arendt, *HC*, pp. 212–14.
54. Ibid., p. 217.
55. Ibid., pp. 33, 41.
56. See Canovan, "The Contradictions of Hannah Arendt," *Political Theory* 6, no. 1 (February 1978). Less sympathetic is Sheldon Wolin's "Hannah Arendt: Democracy and the Political," *Salmagundi*, no. 60 (Summer 1983).
57. Arendt, *OR*, p. 271.

58. Here I would underscore the observation of George Kateb: "Arendt is clear that when she speaks of the masses she is not endorsing the views of those who deplore the spread of education and leisure to the hitherto excluded, and who lament the overall equality of condition in modern society.... She succeeds in not being reactionary. I doubt, however, that she is free of a certain coldness, or remoteness, that resembles condescension." *Hannah Arendt,* p. 72. It is worth emphasizing that one searches Arendt's writings in vain for any traces of the kind of conservatism that one finds in, say, Ortega y Gasset's *The Revolt of the Masses.* On this point, see Eugene E. Leach, "'Just Human Atoms Massed Together': The Evolution of Mass Society Theory from Ortega y Gasset to Riesman and Mills," *Mid-America* 71, no. 1 (January 1989): 36–39.

59. Arendt, *OR,* p. 268.

60. Ibid., pp. 32–33; *OT,* p. 467; "Civil Disobedience," in *CR,* p. 79.

61. Arendt, *OR,* p. 269.

62. Ibid., p. 275. This metaphor, which resurfaces in Alasdair MacIntyre's *After Virtue,* was used frequently by Resistance-generation intellectuals such as Koestler, Camus, Macdonald, and Buber.

63. Ibid., p. 276, 279.

64. Ibid., p. 277.

65. Ibid., pp. 279–80.

66. Ibid., p. 277.

67. Ibid., pp. 263, 264, 267.

68. Arendt, "Thoughts on Politics and Revolution," in *CR,* p. 232.

69. See Arendt, "Civil Disobedience" and "Thoughts on Politics and Revolution," in *CR.* For a similar way of thinking about American politics, see Harry C. Boyte, *The Backyard Revolution: Understanding the New Citizen Movement* (Philadelphia: Temple University Press, 1980), and Sara M. Evans and Harry C. Boyte, *Free Spaces: The Sources of Democratic Change in America* (New York: Harper and Row, 1986).

70. This view was largely shared by social democratic critics. Michael Harrington said of Camus, "Positively, he could find nothing more than a romantic syndicalism to counterpose against his own corrosive skepticism. He died as he lived, a victim." *The Accidental Century* (New York: Macmillan), p. 169. See also Irving Howe, "Albert Camus: The Life of Dialogue," *Dissent* (Spring 1961): 210–13.

71. Camus, "Letter to Roland Barthes on *The Plague,*" in *LCE,* p. 340.

72. Camus writes, "The complaints because my books do not bring out the political aspect. Translation: they want me to feature parties. But I feature only individuals, opposed to the State machine, because I know what I am saying," *N2,* p. 183.

73. Camus, *Pl,* p. 177.

74. Ibid., p. 197.

75. Camus, "Neither Victims nor Executioners," *politics* (July-August 1947): 144.

76. Ibid., p. 145. Camus's argument here bears the traces of the thinking of two other European radicals with whom he was associated. See European [pseudonym for Andrea Cafi], "Violence and Sociability," *politics* (January 1947), and Nicola Chiaromante, "Remarks on Justice," *politics* (May-June 1947).

77. Claude Lefort, "Politics and Human Rights," in *The Political Forms of Modern Society* (Cambridge, Mass.; MIT Press, 1986), pp. 258–72, at p. 266.

78. Arendt, "On Hannah Arendt," p. 335.
79. See especially Hannah Pitkin's "Justice: On Relating Public and Private," *Political Theory* 9 (August 1981). See also Mildred Bakan, "Hannah Arendt's Concepts of Labor and Work," and Bikhu Parekh, "Hannah Arendt's Critique of Marx," in Melvyn Hill, ed., *Hannah Arendt: The Recovery of the Public World* (New York: St. Martin's Press, 1979); Richard Bernstein, "Rethinking the Social and the Political," in his *Philosophical Profiles* (Philadelphia: University of Pennsylvania Press, 1986); and Joseph M. Schwartz, "Arendt's Politics: The Elusive Search for Substance," *Praxis International* 9, nos. 1 and 2 (April and July 1989).
80. Arendt, *HC,* p. 215.
81. Ibid., p. 219.
82. Ibid., pp. 216, 218.
83. See V. I. Lenin, "What Is to Be Done?" in Robert C. Tucker, ed., *The Lenin Anthology* (New York: Norton, 1977), and Antonio Gramsci, "The Modern Prince," in *Selections from the Prison Notebooks,* ed. Geoffrey Nowell Smith and Quentin Hoare (New York: International Publishers, 1971).
84. Arendt, *OR,* p. 273.
85. Camus, "The Wrong Side and the Right Side," in *LCE,* p. 8.
86. Arendt, *OR,* pp. 64–119. This is at least in part the rationale behind Arendt's notorious essay "Reflections on Little Rock," *Dissent* 6, no. 1 (Winter 1959), in which she construed the efforts of black parents to enter their children in white schools as an attempt at social and economic advancement rather than as political empowerment. See Young-Bruehl, *Hannah Arendt,* pp. 308–18.
87. Arendt, *HC,* p. 219.
88. Arendt, *OR,* pp. 273–75.
89. Quoted in Arendt, "On Hannah Arendt," p. 322. See also Albrecht Wellmer's similar criticism (p. 325).
90. Arendt, "On Hannah Arendt," p. 316.
91. Ibid., pp. 317–18.
92. Arendt, *HC,* p. 219.
93. Arendt, "To Save the Jewish Homeland: There Is Still Time," in *JP,* p. 185.
94. It is worth noting that it was common among Zionists to refer to Jewish pioneers in Palestine as an elite. See Buber, *Paths in Utopia,* p. 143–45. Michael Walzer comments critically on this in his "Martin Buber's Search for Zion," in *The Company of Critics: Social Criticism and Political Commitment in the Twentieth Century* (New York: Basic Books, 1988).
95. "To Save the Jewish Homeland," in *JP,* p. 186.
96. Arendt, "Peace or Armistice in the Near East?" in *JP,* pp. 212–14.
97. Arendt, "Thoughts on Politics and Revolution," in *CR,* p. 216–17.
98. Buber, *Paths,* p. 137.
99. Camus, "Kadar Had His Day of Fear," in *RRD,* p. 164.
100. Camus, "Bread and Freedom," in *RRD,* p. 90.
101. Ibid., pp. 89, 91, 94.
102. Ibid., p. 96.
103. Arendt, *OR,* p. 264.
104. The literature on this subject is immense. See especially Ronald Beiner, "Interpretive Essay: Hannah Arendt on Judging," postscript to Arendt, *LKPP.* See

also Richard J. Bernstein, *From Objectivism to Relativism: Science, Hermeneutics, Praxis* (Philadelphia: University of Pennsylvania Press, 1983), pp. 207–23, and Benjamin Barber, *The Conquest of Politics: Liberal Philosophy in Democratic Times* (Princeton: Princeton University Press, 1988). For more critical accounts see Seyla Benhabib, "Judgment and the Moral Foundations of Politics in Arendt's Thought," *Political Theory* 16, no. 1 (February 1988), and Patrick Riley, "Hannah Arendt on Kant, Truth and Politics," *Political Studies* 35 (1987).

105. These texts come from Arendt's earliest essay on the subject, "Understanding and Politics," *Partisan Review* 20, no. 4 (July-August 1953), pp. 391–92.
106. Arendt, "The Crisis in Culture," in *BPF*, pp. 220–21.
107. This view of judgment is clearly in the vein of much so-called neo-Kantian writing about *verstehen* or sympathetic understanding. It has particularly striking affinities with Karl Mannheim's *Ideology and Utopia* (New York: Harcourt Brace and World, 1936), which Arendt reviewed as a young German scholar in 1930. See Young-Bruehl, *Hannah Arendt*, pp. 83–84. See especially Mannheim's argument in support of "an integration of many mutually complementary points of view into a comprehensive whole" (p. 149). For a similar view see Jürgen Habermas, *Moral Consciousness and Communicative Action* (Cambridge, Mass.: MIT Press, 1990). See also Seyla Benhabib, "The Generalized and the Concrete Other," and Iris Marion Young, "Impartiality and the Civic Public," in Seyla Benhabib and Drucilla Cornell, eds., *Feminism as Critique* (Oxford: Blackwell, 1987).
108. Camus, "Return to Tipasa," in *LCE*, p. 165.
109. Camus, *MS*, p. 50.
110. Camus, "Roger Martin du Gard," in *LCE*, p. 286.
111. Quoted in Emmett Parker, *Albert Camus: The Artist in the Arena* (Madison: University of Wisconsin Press, 1965), p. 84.
112. See Camus, *BHR*, pp. 66–82, 93–95, 100–115, and *RRD*, pp. 33–55.
113. Camus, *The Just Assassins*, in *CTOP*, pp. 288–90.
114. On the theme of modesty in Camus see Nicola Chiaromonte, "Albert Camus and Moderation," *Partisan Review* 15, no. 10 (October 1948).
115. Camus, "Appeal for a Civilian Truce," in *RRD*, p. 135.
116. Camus, "The Unbeliever and Christians," in *RRD*, pp. 70–71. See also *BHR*, pp. 97–99.
117. Camus, *F*, pp. 10, 19, 23.
118. Ibid., pp. 110, 114.
119. Ibid., pp. 131, 140.
120. It seems quite clear that Clamence at least in part represents the "grim philanthropists" of the existentialist left, especially Sartre. Camus seems to consider his pathology symptomatic of righteous humanism. It is also clear that in some ways Clamence is Camus, who never sought to separate himself from the maladies that he diagnosed. See Sprintzen, *Camus*, pp. 202–17, and Herbert Lottman, *Albert Camus: A Biography* (New York: Doubleday, 1979), pp. 589–94.
121. Arendt once responded to a student's question about how she would instruct him by objecting, "No. I wouldn't instruct you, and I would think that this would be presumptuous of me. I think that you should be instructed when you sit together with your peers around a table and exchange opinions.... And I think

that every other road of the theoretician who tells his students what to think and how to act is . . . my God! These are adults! We are not in the nursery!" Arendt, "On Hannah Arendt," p. 310. Camus, when asked how he handled his status as a "master" of "the new generation," laughed and then replied, "A master, already! But I don't claim to teach anybody! . . . What are the young people looking for? Certainties. I haven't many to offer them. . . . Those who trust me know that I will never lie to them. As to the young people who ask others to think for them, we must say 'No' to them in the clearest possible terms." Camus, "Encounter with Albert Camus," in *LCE*, p. 352.

122. Arendt, *HC*, pp. 35–36.
123. Arthur Koestler, "On Disbelieving Atrocities," in *The Yogi and the Commissar and Other Essays* (New York: Macmillan, 1946), p. 89.
124. Camus, *N2*, p. 159.
125. Camus, *R*, p. 281.
126. Camus, *N2*, p. 160.
127. See Ibid., pp. 48–57.
128. Camus, *State of Siege*, in *CTOP*, p. 144.
129. Ibid., p. 170.
130. Ibid., p. 198.
131. Ibid., p. 239.
132. Ibid., p. 228.
133. *The Just Assassins*, in *CTOP*, p. 272.

Chapter Six: Swimming Against the Tide

1. Arendt, *OT*, p. 460.
2. Ibid., p. vii.
3. Irving Howe, "This Age of Conformity," *Partisan Review* (January-February 1954), pp. 8, 10–11.
4. Irving Howe, "Our Country and Our Culture: A Symposium," *Partisan Review* 19, no. 5 (September-October 1952), p. 577.
5. Czeslaw Milosz, *The Captive Mind* (New York: Vintage, 1981), and Vaclav Havel, "The Power of the Powerless," in *Living in Truth* (London: Faber and Faber, 1987).
6. See C. Wright Mills, *The Sociological Imagination* (London: Oxford University Press, 1956), and Russell Jacoby, *The Last Intellectuals* (New York: Basic Books, 1987). As Edward Thompson observed, "The Natopolitan intellectual was disabled by self-distrust no less than the Stalinist intellectual was disabled by fear of reverting to bourgeois modes of thought. The very fact of an intellectual espousing any public cause (unless as a career politician) was enough to touch off suspicion. . . . In Natopolitan culture today, no swearword is more devastating than 'romantic,' just as the 'utopian' or 'idealist' is the butt of Stalinist abuse." Edward P. Thompson, "Outside the Whale," in *The Poverty of Theory and Other Essays* (New York: Monthly Review Press, 1978), p. 230.
7. Edward P. Thompson, *Beyond the Cold War* (New York: Pantheon, 1982), p. 160.
8. Camus, "Return to Tipasa," in *LCE*, p. 165.

9. See James D. Wilkinson, *The Intellectual Resistance in Europe* (Cambridge, Mass.: Harvard University Press, 1981), pp. 96–100. Much of my discussion is informed by this superb study.

10. Camus, "The Blood of Freedom," in *RRD*, p. 37. See also the essays collected in *BHR*, as well as Alexandre de Gramont's useful introduction.

11. Quoted in Emmett Parker, *Albert Camus: The Artist in the Arena* (Madison: University of Wisconsin Press, 1965), p. 74.

12. Ibid., pp. 90, 76–80.

13. Quoted in Patrick McCarthy, *Camus* (New York: Random House, 1982), p. 214.

14. Quoted in Parker, *Camus*, p. 84.

15. Quoted in Parker, *Camus*, p. 94.

16. Herbert R. Lottman, *Albert Camus: A Biography* (New York: Doubleday, 1979), p. 382.

17. See Lottman, *Albert Camus*, pp. 370–83.

18. "Manifesto," reprinted in *politics* (Winter 1948): 35–36.

19. Quoted in Wilkinson, *The Intellectual Resistance*, pp. 101–02. See also Mark Poster, *Existential Marxism in Postwar France* (Princeton: Princeton University Press, 1975), pp. 139–44.

20. Quoted in Parker, *Albert Camus*, p. 116.

21. McCarthy, *Camus*, pp. 240–42.

22. Quoted in Lottman, *Albert Camus*, pp. 485, 478. Lottman also discusses Camus's extensive activity on behalf of the anti-Franco Spanish Federation of Political Prisoners.

23. Quoted in Gregory D. Sumner, "Window on the First New Left: Dwight Macdonald's *politics* Magazine, 1944–49" (Ph.D. diss., Indiana University, 1992), pp. 313–14.

24. Quoted in Ibid., p. 312.

25. See Poster, *Existential Marxism*, pp. 161–65.

26. Ibid., pp. 161–94, and James Miller, *History and Human Existence* (Berkeley and Los Angeles: University of California Press, 1979), pp. 165–73. Sartre's most notorious work of this genre was *The Communists and the Peace* (New York: George Braziller, 1968), the first installment of which was published in *Les Temps Modernes* in July 1952, a month before Sartre's famous exchange with Camus over *The Rebel*.

27. See Peter Coleman, *The Liberal Conspiracy: The Congress for Cultural Freedom and the Struggle for the Mind of Postwar Europe* (New York: Free Press, 1989), and Christopher Lasch, "The Cultural Cold War: A Short History of the Congress for Cultural Freedom," in his *The Agony of the American Left* (New York: Vintage, 1969), pp. 61–114.

28. Quoted in Parker, *Albert Camus*, p. 155.

29. Ibid., p. 145.

30. Camus, *RRD*, pp. 165, 158.

31. Ibid., p. 167.

32. See Lottman, *Albert Camus*, pp. 529, 542; McCarthy, *Camus*, p. 241.

33. Camus, "Why Spain?" in *RRD*, p. 79.

34. Camus, "Bread and Freedom," in *RRD*, pp. 92–93.

35. Camus, "The Wager of Our Generation," in *RRD*, p. 248.

36. On the complicity of German society see Arendt's 1945 essay "Organized Guilt

and Universal Responsibility," in *JP*, pp. 228–34, and "The Aftermath of Nazi Rule: Report from Germany," *Commentary* 10 (October 1950): 344, 348–49.

37. Elisabeth Young-Bruehl, *Hannah Arendt: For Love of the World* (New Haven: Yale University Press, 1982). On Youth Aliyah, see pp. 120–140, on the Jewish Army, see pp. 173–79.

38. Arendt, "The Aftermath," pp. 347, 349, 352.

39. Ibid., p. 349.

40. A useful albeit uncritical account of these events is Peter Coleman's *The Liberal Conspiracy*. Oblivious to the Leninist overtones, for example, he quotes Nicolas Nabokov declaring, "Out of this Congress we must build an organization for war. ...We must see to it that it calls on all figures, all fighting organizations, and all methods of fighting, with a view to action. If we do not, we will sooner or later all be hanged. The hour has long struck" (p. 29).

41. Arendt, "The Ex-Communists," *Commonweal*, March 20, 1953:596.

42. Ibid., p. 599.

43. Alexander Bloom asserts that in *The Origins* "Arendt provided the material which anti-Communists awaited," that her analysis "became the philosophical cement which firmly set" Cold War liberalism. *Prodigal Sons: The New York Intellectuals and Their World* (Oxford: Oxford University Press, 1986), pp. 219–20. See also Alan M. Wald, *New York Intellectuals* (Durham: University of North Carolina Press, 1987).

44. Young-Bruehl, *Hannah Arendt*, p. 287. It is worth recalling Arendt's quotation of Benjamin Constant in discussing Marx in *The Human Condition*: "Certainly, I shall avoid the company of detractors of a great man. If I happen to agree with them on a single point I grow suspicious of myself; and in order to console myself for having seemed to be of their opinion. . . . I feel I must disavow and keep these false friends away from me as much as I can" (p. 79). In 1951 these words took no small degree of courage.

45. Arendt, "Dream and Nightmare," *Commonweal*, September 10, 1954:553.

46. Ibid., pp. 578–80.

47. See also Karl Jaspers's influential *The Future of Mankind* (Chicago: University of Chicago Press, 1961), published in book form in Germany in 1958.

48. Arendt, "The Cold War and the West: An Exchange," *Partisan Review* 29 (Winter 1962): 11–12.

49. Ibid., pp. 12–13.

50. Ibid., pp. 13–14.

51. Ibid., p. 19.

52. Arendt, "Lying in Politics," in *CR*, pp. 39–40. For a similar analysis, see Richard J. Barnet, *Intervention and Revolution* (New York: New American Library, 1968) and *The Roots of War* (New York: Atheneum, 1972).

53. Arendt, "On Violence," in *CR*, p. 173.

54. Arendt's comments here recall the cynical recollections of Camus's Clamence: "I had a specialty: noble cases . . . it was enough for me to sniff the slightest scent of victim on a defendant for me to swing into action. And what action! A real tornado! My heart was on my sleeve. You would really have thought that justice slept with me every night. I am sure you would have admired the rightness of my tone. . . I was on the right side; that was enough to satisfy my conscience. . . I have never

felt comfortable except in lofty places. Even in the details of my life I needed to feel *above*." Camus, *F*, pp. 17–18, 23.

55. Arendt, "On Violence," pp. 105–7.

56. Ibid., p. 111. Note the similarity between these observations and C. Wright Mills's 1956 *The Power Elite* (London: Oxford University Press, 1956). See also Seymour Melman, *Pentagon Capitalism: The Political Economy of War* (New York: McGraw Hill, 1970).

57. Ibid., p. 116.

58. Ibid., p. 118.

59. Arendt, "Civil Disobedience," in Ibid., p. 89.

60. See Mills, *The Power Elite*, as well as his *The Sociological Imagination* (London: Oxford University Press, 1959).

61. These words, and others more hurtful, are by Sartre in his famous preface to Frantz Fanon's *The Wretched of the Earth* (New York: Grove Press, 1968), pp. 24–25, the text in which Sartre pronounced that "to shoot down a European is to kill two birds with one stone, to destroy an oppressor and the man he oppresses at the same time" (p. 22). A more sympathetic and subtle account is in Albert Memmi's *Colonizer and Colonized* (New York: Orion Press, 1965). See McCarthy, *Camus*, pp. 268–302, and Lottman, *Albert Camus*, pp. 600–606.

62. The pages of *Partisan Review* and *Commentary* contained many attacks on Arendt's thesis about Eichmann's banality and her criticisms of Zionism more generally. See especially Norman Podhoretz, "Hannah Arendt on Eichmann: A Study in the Perversity of Brilliance," *Commentary* (September 1963), pp. 201–208. For discussion see Leon Botstein, "Liberating the Pariah: Politics, Jews, and Hannah Arendt," *Salmagundi*, no. 60 (Spring-Summer 1983), and my "At the Margins: Hannah Arendt on Jewish Politics and Identity," *Tikkun* (September 1989).

63. See Conor Cruise O'Brien, *Albert Camus: Of Europe and Africa* (New York: Viking, 1970), and Edward Said, "Narrative, Geography, and Interpretation," *New Left Review* 180 (March-April 1990). McCarthy substantially shares this view in *Camus*, pp. 268–302. See also David L. Schalk, *War and the Ivory Tower: Algeria and Vietnam* (New York and Oxford: Oxford University Press, 1991), pp. 62–71.

64. Michael Walzer, "Albert Camus's Algerian War," in *The Company of Critics: Social Criticism and Political Commitment in the Twentieth Century* (New York: Basic Books, 1988).

65. On the ambiguities of Camus's identity see David Sprintzen, *Camus: A Critical Examination* (Philadelphia: Temple University Press, 1988), pp. 9–13, 273–280.

66. Walzer, *The Company of Critics*, p. 146.

67. Camus, *RRD*, pp. 127, 130.

68. Schalk notes that even Amar Ouzegane, a leader of the Front de Libération Nationale and a political antagonist, praised Camus's "exceptional qualities of lucidity and courage" and his receptivity to the Arab population (p. 62).

69. See Parker, *Albert Camus*, pp. 3–24.

70. On the policy of assimilation, see David C. Gordon, *The Passing of French Algeria* (London: Oxford University Press, 1966), pp. 4–48.

71. Quoted in Parker, *Albert Camus*, pp. 36–7.

72. Ibid., p. 98–99.

73. Ibid., p. 99.

74. Ibid., pp. 101–102.
75. Gordon, *The Passing*, p. 55.
76. Camus, "Preface to Algerian Reports," in *RRD*, p. 121.
77. Ibid., pp. 111–12.
78. Ibid., pp. 113–14.
79. Ibid., p. 115.
80. Ibid., p. 115.
81. Ibid., p. 116.
82. "As soon as man, through lack of character, takes refuge in a doctrine, as soon as crime reasons about itself, it multiplies like reason itself." Camus, *R*, p. 3.
83. Camus, "Preface to Algerian Reports," pp. 117–18.
84. Ibid., p. 120.
85. Ibid., p. 121.
86. Camus, "Letter to an Algerian Militant," in *RRD*, pp. 128–29.
87. Camus, "Appeal for a Civilian Truce," in *RRD*, pp. 132–33.
88. Ibid., p. 134.
89. Ibid., pp. 135–36.
90. Ibid., p. 138.
91. It would be a mistake, though, to imply that Camus stood as the lone voice of reason. There were others, like Jean-Marie Domenach and those associated with the left-wing Catholic journal *Esprit*, who were equally critical of extremism on the part of French and Arabs, yet more vocal and active in criticizing French policy in the late 1950s than was Camus. See Schalk, *War and the Ivory Tower*, pp. 72–97.
92. Camus did break his silence in a letter defending himself from a critic who accused him of hypocrisy for condemning repression in Hungary while refusing to "state plainly" his position on Algeria. Camus replied that "any effort to assimilate the Algerian question to the Hungarian comes up against a historical fact—a fact one may regret but which is a fact nevertheless. There was not in Hungary, installed for more than a century, more than a million Russians (of whom 80 per cent are ordinary folk) whose lives, whose rights (and not merely privileges) the Hungarian revolution menaced. The Hungarian problem is simple; the Hungarians must be given back their liberty. The Algerian problem is different: there, it is necessary to assure the liberties of the two peoples of the country." *Encounter* 45 (July 1957): 68.
93. Camus, "Algeria 1958," in *RRD*, pp. 145–46. Camus's second claim relies heavily on Germaine Tillion, *Algeria: The Realities* (New York: Knopf, 1958), who argues that massive foreign assistance would be necessary to help lift Algeria out of its terrible poverty.
94. Jules Roy, *The War in Algeria* (New York: Grove Press, 1961), p. 125.
95. Here Camus was thinking as much of Third World indifference to the plight of the nations of Eastern Europe as he was about Algeria itself. See his criticisms of the Bandung Conference in "Socialism of the Gallows," in *RRD*, p. 166.
96. Camus, "Algeria 1958," in *RRD*, pp. 148–49.
97. Ibid., pp. 150–51.
98. Ibid., p. 151.
99. Said, "Narrative, Geography, Interpretation," p. 87.

100. Sprintzen, *Camus,* p. 279.
101. Camus, *RRD,* p. 118.
102. Camus, *R,* p. 11.
103. Camus, "Preface to Algeria Reports," in *RRD,* p. 118.
104. See Dagmar Barnow, *Visible Spaces: Hannah Arendt and the German-Jewish Experience* (Baltimore: Johns Hopkins University Press, 1990).
105. Arendt, "Jewish History, Revised," in *JP,* p. 96.
106. Arendt, "Zionism Reconsidered," in *JP,* p. 147. On this theme see David Biale, *Power and Powerlessness in Jewish History* (New York: Schocken, 1986).
107. Arendt, "The Moral of History," in *JP,* pp. 107–8.
108. Ibid., pp. 109–110.
109. Arendt, *OT,* p. 6.
110. Arendt, "The Jewish State: Fifty Years After—Where Have Herzl's Politics Led?" in *JP,* pp. 166, 170.
111. Arendt, "The Jew as Pariah: A Hidden Tradition," in *JP,* p. 76.
112. Arendt, "The Jewish State," pp. 175, 174, 171.
113. See Arendt, *EJ,* pp. 58–61.
114. In this regard they compare unfavorably with her hero, Bernard Lazare, who "took his place as a conscious Jew, fighting for justice in general but for the Jewish people in particular." Arendt, "Herzl and Lazare," in *JP,* p. 126.
115. Ibid., p. 173.
116. Arendt, "Zionism Reconsidered," *JP,* p. 152.
117. Ibid., pp. 152–53.
118. Ibid., pp. 131, 160.
119. Arendt, "To Save the Jewish Homeland: There is Still Time," in *JP,* p. 182.
120. Arendt, "Zionism Reconsidered," p. 133.
121. Ibid., p. 162.
122. Ibid., p. 162.
123. Arendt, "To Save the Jewish Homeland," p. 179.
124. Ibid., p. 181.
125. Ibid., p. 175.
126. Ibid., p. 188.
127. In this passage Arendt focuses her criticism on Jewish terrorism, though elsewhere she acknowledged the reciprocity of terrorism between Jews and Arabs. On the role of terror during the 1947–49 period, see Benny Morris, *The Birth of the Palestinian Refugee Problem, 1947–1949* (Cambridge: Cambridge University Press, 1987), and the exchange among Norman Finkelstein, Nur Masalha, and Morris, "Debate on the 1948 Exodus," in *Journal of Palestine Studies* 21, no. 1 (Autumn 1991): 66–114.
128. Arendt, "To Save the Jewish Homeland," pp. 190–91.
129. Ibid., p. 191. On the vision of Magnes and Ihud, see two 1947 volumes: Martin Buber, Judah Magnes, and Ernst Simon, eds., *Towards Union in Palestine* (Westport, Conn.: Greenwood Press, 1972), and Judah Magnes and Martin Buber, *Arab-Jewish Unity* (Westport, Conn.: Hyperion Press, 1976). See also Arthur A. Goren, ed., *Dissenter in Zion: From the Writings of Judah L. Magnes* (Cambridge, Mass.: Harvard University Press, 1982). For a critical discussion, see Michael Walzer, "Martin Buber's Search for Zion," in *The Company of Critics,* pp. 64–79.

130. Arendt, "Peace or Armistice in the Near East?" in *JP*, pp. 199, 205, 201.

131. Ibid., p. 210. This recalls Camus's words in his "Letter to an Algerian Militant": "If you Arab democrats fail in your work of pacification, the activity of us French liberals will be doomed to failure in advance. And if we falter in our duty, your poor words will be swept away in the wind and flames of a pitiless war." *RRD*, p. 130. Mark A. Heller and Sari Nusseibeh's recent *No Trumpets, No Drums: A Two-State Settlement of the Israeli-Palestinian Conflict* (New York: Hill and Wang, 1991), is a careful and compelling plea for such mutual recognition between Israelis and Palestinians.

132. Camus, "Preface to Algerian Reports," p. 118. On recent statements of this theme se also Günter Grass, *Two States—One Nation?* (New York: Harcourt Brace Jovanovich, 1990), and Adam Michnik, "Nationalism," *Social Research* 58, no. 4 (Winter 1991).

133. Arendt, "Herzl and Lazare," p. 129.

134. Arendt, "The Jew as Pariah," p. 75.

135. "Eichmann in Jerusalem: An Exchange of Letters Between Gershom Scholem and Hannah Arendt," in *JP*, p. 246.

136. Arendt, "What is Existenz Philosophy?" *Partisan Review* 37 (Winter 1946): 37.

137. *JP*, p. 90.

138. Camus, "Neither Victims nor Executioners," *politics* (July-August 1947): 144–47.

139. Camus, "The New Mediterranean Culture," in *LCE*, pp. 190–91.

140. Ibid., pp. 193, 191. Camus's *Notebooks* bear the inscription, "The principle of law is that of the State. Roman principle that 1789 reintroduced into the world through force and against the right. We must return to the Greek principle, which is autonomy." *N2*, p. 266. Compare Camus's account of love of country with Emma Goldman's "Patriotism: A Menace to Liberty," in her *Anarchism and Other Essays* (New York: Dover, 1969), pp. 127–28.

141. Camus, *LCE*, p. 197.

142. Arendt, *OT*, p. 231.

143. Ibid., pp. 89–120.

144. Ibid., p. 227.

145. Ibid., p. 279.

146. Ibid., pp. 284–86.

147. Ibid., p. 301.

148. Ibid., p. ix.

149. Arendt, *EJ*, pp. 255, 268–69.

150. Ibid., p. 262.

151. Ibid., p. 263.

152. This last idea is developed in Julia Kristeva's wonderful *Strangers to Ourselves* (New York: Columbia University Press, 1991), which links the experience of migrants in Europe to the experience of modernity.

153. Jean Elshtain's *Women and War* (New York: Basic Books, 1987), clearly inspired by both Arendt and Camus, provides an excellent discussion of this theme, esp. pp. 226–258. A similar position, inspired by postmodern writing, is suggested in William E. Connolly, *Identity/Difference: Democratic Negotiations of Political Paradox* (Ithaca: Cornell University Press, 1991), pp. 36–63, and Stephen K.

White, *Political Theory and Postmodernism* (Cambridge: Cambridge University Press, 1991), pp. 105–113.

154. Arendt, *EJ*, pp. 270–73.

155. Arendt, "Karl Jaspers: Citizen of the World?" in *MDT*, pp. 82–83. Cf. Arendt's pessimistic observation in her 1945 essay "Organized Guilt and Universal Responsibility": "Our fathers' enchantment with humanity was of a sort which not only light-mindedly ignored the national question; what is far worse, it did not even conceive of the terror of the idea of humanity and of the Judeo-Christian faith in the unitary origin of the human race. . . . For the very idea of humanity, when purged of all sentimentality, has the very serious consequence that in one form or another men must assume responsibility for all crimes committed by men and that all nations share the onus of evil committed by all others. Shame at being human is the purely individual and still nonpolitical expression of this insight. . . . How great a burden mankind is for man," *JP*, pp. 234–35. This essay influenced Dwight Macdonald's essay "The Responsibility of Peoples," *politics* (March 1945).

156. Arendt, "Karl Jaspers," p. 93. Not only Arendt's argument but her very language prefigures the recent arguments by Jürgen Habermas in favor of a self-critical, "post-traditional" national identity in Germany. See his *The New Conservatism* (Cambridge, Mass.: MIT Press, 1989), pp. 232–34, 249–67.

157. Ibid., pp. 81–82.

158. Lawrence Weschler's *A Miracle, A Universe: Settling Accounts with Torturers* (New York: Pantheon, 1990), a moving and penetrating discussion of human rights advocacy, is clearly inspired by Arendt.

159. Camus, "Letters to a German Friend," in *RRD*, pp. 28–29.

160. Camus *R*, p. 13.

Chapter 7: Rebellious Politics Reconsidered

1. Michel Foucault, "Nietzsche, Genealogy, History," in *The Foucault Reader*, ed. Paul Rabinow (New York: Panthon, 1984), p. 82.

2. Michel Foucault, "Politics and Ethics: An Interview," in *The Foucault Reader*, pp. 376–76.

3. Foucault, "Nietzsche, Genealogy, History," pp. 85–87.

4. Arendt, *OT*, p. ix.

5. The language of discordance and concordance here is drawn from William E. Connolly, *Political Theory and Modernity* (Oxford: Blackwell, 1988).

6. "Schematically, we can formulate the traditional question of political philosophy in the following terms: how is the discourse of truth, or quite simply philosophy as that discourse which par excellence is concerned with truth, able to fix limits to the rights of power? . . . My problem is rather this: what rules of right are implemented by the relations of power in the production of discourse of truth?" Michel Foucault, "Two Lectures," in *Power/Knowledge* (New York: Pantheon, 1980), p. 93. See also Foucault's remark in "Nietzsche, Genealogy, History": "Genealogy, however, seeks to reestablish the various systems of subjection: not the anticipatory power of meaning, but the hazardous play of dominations" (p. 83). For criticism of Foucault's reluctance to employ normative language, see

Nancy Fraser, *Unruly Practices: Power, Discourse, and Gender in Contemporary Social Theory* (Minneapolis: University of Minnesota Press, 1989), pp. 17–68. It is worth noting that Foucault was moving toward a rapprochement with aspects of liberal humanism when he died. See the essays collected in his *Philosophy, Politics, Culture* (London: Routledge, 1990).

7. See William E. Connolly, *Identity/Difference: Democratic Negotiations of Political Paradox* (Ithaca: Cornell University Press, 1991), and B. Honig, *All That Is Generally Forbidden: Politics and Virtue from the Perspective of Virtu* (Ithaca: Cornell University Press, forthcoming). Honig innovatively draws on Arendt but in the end emphasizes her deficiencies from a Nietzschean perspective. See also Stephen K. White, *Political Theory and Postmodernism* (Cambridge: Cambridge University University Press, 1991).

8. Charles Taylor, *Sources of the Self: The Making of the Modern Identity* (Cambridge, Mass.: Harvard University Press, 1989), p. xi.

9. See Margaret Canovan, "The Contradictions of Hannah Arendt's Political Thought," *Political Theory* 6, no. 1 (February 1978).

10. Friedrich Nietzsche, *The Use and Abuse of History* (Indianapolis: Bobbs Merrill, 1957).

11. Arendt, *HC*, pp. 96–98.

12. Simone de Beauvoir offers a very similar account of the private sphere of women's work in *The Second Sex* (New York: Knopf, 1953), though she is explicitly critical of women's lack of "transcendence" of nature and body.

13. A similar argument can be found in B. Honig, "Toward an Agonistic Feminism: Hannah Arendt and the Politics of Identity," in Judith Butler and Joan W. Scott, *Feminists Theorize the Political* (London: Routledge, forthcoming).

14. Camus, *R*, p. 300. He continues: "Thrown into the unworthy melting-pot of Europe, deprived of beauty and friendship, we Mediterraneans, the proudest of races, live always by the same light. In the depths of the European night, solar thought, the civilization facing two ways awaits its dawn."

15. David Sprintzen, *Camus: A Critical Examination* (Philadelphia: Temple University Press, 1988), p. 275.

16. See ibid., pp. 36–38.

17. There is a possible exception here—Dora in "The Just Assassins," who, unlike the other women in Camus's fiction, is a political agent, a coequal of Kaliayev and the other men. But even Dora manifests characteristically "feminine" traits and concerns.

18. See Patrick McCarthy, *Camus* (New York: Random House, 1982), pp. 10–15. As Camus remarks in the preface to his *Lyrical and Critical Essays*, "I shall still place at the center of this work the admirable silence of a mother and one man's effort to rediscover a justice or a love to match this silence … a man's work is nothing but this slow trek to rediscover, through the detours of art, those two or three great and simple images in whose presence the heart first opened" (pp. 16–17).

19. Camus, *State of Siege*, in *CTOP*, p. 229.

20. See Camus, *MS*, pp. 51–68. As H. Stuart Hughes has observed, the cult of heroism was an important genre of 1930s French literature, whose most famous contributors included André Malraux, Roger Martin du Gard, and Antoine de Saint-

Exupéry. See *The Obstructed Path: French Social Thought in the Years of Desparation, 1930–1960* (New York: Harper, 1966), pp. 102–52.

21. There is one partial exception to this. Camus's play *The Misunderstanding*, or *Cross-Purposes*, is all about how the absence of dialogue among family members leads to death and despair. Here political concerns reach directly into the domestic realm, though Camus fails to draw any conclusions that speak directly to the operation of power in this realm.

22. Camus, *R*, p. 11.

23. Camus, *Caligula*, in *CTOP*, p. 192.

24. Quoted in Michael Walzer, "Albert Camus's Algerian War," in his *The Company of Critics: Social Criticism and Political Commitment in the Twentieth Century* (New York: Basic Books, 1988), p. 145.

25. Ibid., p. 138.

26. See Jeffrey C. Isaac, "Why Postmodernism Still Matters," *Tikkun* 4, no. 4 (July/August 1989): 118–22.

27. Honig, "Toward an Agonistic Feminism" presents an excellent Arendtian critique of this essentialist possibility within feminism. Se also Shane Phelan, "The Jargon of Authenticity," *Philosophy and Social Criticism* 16, no. 1 (1990).

28. See Richard J. Berstein, *Praxis and Action* (Philadelphia: University of Pennsylvania Press, 1974); Jürgen Habermas, "Toward a Reconstruction of Historical Materialism," in *Communication and the Evolution of Society* (Boston: Beacon Press, 1979); and "Excursis on the Obselescence of the Production Paradigm," in *The Philosophical Discourse of Modernity* (Cambridge, Mass.: MIT Press, 1987).

29. Karl Marx and Friedrich Engels, "The German Ideology," in Robert C. Tucker, ed., *The Marx-Engels Reader* (New York: Norton, 1972), pp. 128–29.

30. Ibid., p. 157.

31. Anthony Giddens, *The Constitution of Society* (Berkeley and Los Angeles: University of California Press, 1984).

32. This point is made by Sprintzen, *Camus*, pp. 276–78.

33. See Perry Anderson, *Considerations on Western Marxism* (London: Verso, 1976). On the sociological tradition, see C. Wright Mills, *The Sociological Imagination* (London: Oxford University Press, 1959), and Anthony Giddens, *New Rules of Sociological Method* (New York: Basic Books, 1976).

34. Jean-Paul Sartre, *Critique of Dialectical Reason* (London: New Left Books, 1976) and *The Search for Method* (London: Metheun, 1964).

35. See Alain Touraine, *The Self-Production of Society* (Chicago: University of Chicago Press, 1977); Pierre Bourdieu, *Outline of a Theory of Practice* (Cambridge: Cambridge University Press, 1977); and Jürgen Habermas, *Communication and the Evolution of Society* (Boston: Beacon Press, 1979).

36. Giddens, *New Rules*, and Roy Bhaskar, *The Possibility of Naturalism: A Philosophical Critique of the Contemporary Human Sciences* (Brighton: Harvester, 1979).

37. See Jeffrey C. Isaac, "Realism and Reality: Some Realistic Reconsiderations," *Journal for the Theory of Social Behaviour* 20, no. 1 (March 1990), esp. pp. 22–27.

38. Quoted in Benjamin Barber, *The Conquest of Politics: Liberal Philosophy in Democratic Times* (Princeton: Princeton University Press, 1988), p. vi. For a slightly different rendition, see Friedrich Nietzsche, *Beyond Good and Evil* (Middlesex: Penguin, 1973), p. 21.

39. Camus, *MS,* pp. 15-16.
40. See especially Arendt, "Truth and Politics," in *BPF,* pp. 239-41.
41. See also Benjamin Barber, *The Conquest of Politics,* pp. 3-21, 193-211.
42. See Martin Jay, *The Dialectical Imagination* (Boston: Beacon, 1963), and Seyla Benhabib, *Critique, Norm, Utopia: A Study of the Foundations of Critical Theory* (New York: Columbia, 1986).
43. See Joseph Margolis, *Pragmatism Without Foundations: Reconciling Realism and Relativism* (Oxford: Blackwell, 1986); Richard Bernstein, *Beyond Objectivism and Relativism* (Philadelphia: University of Pennsylvania Press, 1983); Harold I. Brown, *Perception, Theory, Commitment: The New Philosophy of Science* (Chicago: University of Chicago Press, 1977); and Roy Bhaskar, *Scientific Realism and Human Emancipation* (London: Verso, 1986), pp. 1-102.
44. See Theodor Adorno, ed., *The Positivist Dispute in German Sociology* (New York: Harper, 1971), and Jürgen Habermas, *Knowledge and Human Interests* (Boston: Beacon Press,1973).
45. Camus, *MS,* p. 15.
46. See Ian Shapiro, *Political Criticism* (Berkeley and Los Angeles: University of California Press, 1990), and Brian Fay, *Critical Social Science* (Ithaca: Cornell University Press, 1987).
47. See especially Marx's "Contribution to the Critique of Hegel's *Philosophy of Right:* Introduction," where he writes, "Will theoretical needs be directly practical needs? It is not enough that thought should seek to realize itself; reality must also strive towards thought." Tucker, ed., *Marx-Engels Reader,* p. 19. Arendt observes, "If we really believe ... that plurality rules the earth, then I think one has got to modify this notion of the unity of theory and practice to such an extent that it will be unrecognizable for those who tried their hand at it before." Hannah Arendt, "On Hannah Arendt," in Melvyn A. Hill, *Hannah Arendt: The Recovery of the Public World* (New York: St. Martin's, 1979), p. 305. Yet Arendt's rejection of the belief "that there is any direct influence of theory on action" leaves open the possibility of mediated relationships between them.
48. See Max Horkheimer and Theodor Adorno, "The Culture Industry: Enlightenment as Mass Deception," in *Dialectic of Enlightenment* (New York: Continuum, 1988), pp. 120-67; Hebert Marcuse, *One-Dimensional Man* (Boston: Beacon Press); Jürgen Habermas, *Legitimation Crisis* (Boston: Beacon Press, 1975) and "The New Obscurity: The Crisis of the Welfare State and the Exhaustion of Utopian Energies," in *The New Conservatism* (Cambridge, Mass.: MIT Press, 1989).
49. See Jeffrey C. Isaac, *Power and Marxist Theory: A Realist View* (Ithaca: Cornell University Press, 1987), Part II, and "One Step Sideways, One Step Backwards: Postmarxism and Its Critics," in *Theory, Culture, and Society* (forthcoming).
50. See Ralph Miliband, *Marxism and Politics* (Oxford: Oxford University Press, 1977), and James Miller, *History and Human Existence: From Marx to Merleau-Ponty* (Berkeley and Los Angeles: University of California Press, 1979).
51. See Ernesto Laclau and Chantal Mouffe, *Hegemony and Socialist Strategy: Towards a Radical Democratic Politics* (London: Verso, 1985).
52. See Brian Fay, *Critical Social Science* (Ithaca: Cornell University Press, 1987).
53. This argument is made by Jürgen Habermas in "Hannah Arendt: On the Communications Concept of Power," in *Philosophical-Political Profiles* (Cambridge,

Mass.: MIT Press, 1983). The criticisms of Camus made by Sartre and his associates also make this point, though in an exaggerated way.

54. Camus, "Why Spain?" in *RRD*, p. 78.

55. See James O'Connor, *The Fiscal Crisis of the State* (New York: St. Martin's, 1973); Alan Wolfe, *The Limits of Legitimacy* (New York: Free Press, 1977); and Claus Offe, *Contradictions of the Welfare State* (Cambridge, Mass.: MIT Press, 1984).

56. See Camus's favorable reference to the Scandinavian integration of "the most fruitful form of trade unionism" with a powerful state, in *R*, p. 298. See also his 1944 comment in *Combat*: "For France we want a collectivist economy and a liberal political structure." Quoted in Emmett Parker, *Albert Camus: The Artist in the Arena* (Madison: University of Wisconsin Press, 1965), p. 88. See Camus, *BHR*, pp. 57–64, 78–80, for his critical support for the French Socialist Party.

57. The most glaring and disturbing example is Arendt's 1959 essay "Reflections on Little Rock," where her distinction between the social and the political is deployed to criticize federal government "interference" in "social" racial discrimination in the South. *Dissent* 6, no. 1 (Winter 1959). See also the responses of her critics, David Spitz and Melvin Tumin, in *Dissent* 6, no. 2 (Spring 1959).

58. See, for example, Richard Cloward and Frances Fox Piven, *Poor Peoples' Movements* (New York: Pantheon, 1977).

59. Here again we can discern the influence of Rosa Luxemburg, especially her 1906 essay "The Mass Strike, The Political Party, and the Trade Unions," in *Rosa Luxemburg Speaks* (New York: Pathfinder Press, 1970). See also Laclau and Mouffe, *Hegemony and Socialist Strategy*, pp. 8–14.

60. Some of these questions are sensitively explored in Carmen Sirianni's *Worker's Control and Socialist Democracy: The Soviet Experience* (London: Verso, 1982).

61. These comments are influenced by the writings of Robert Dahl, especially his *Dilemmas of Pluralist Democracy* (New Haven: Yale University Press, 1982), and *Democracy and Its Critics* (New Haven: Yale University Press, 1989).

62. Nicos Poulantzas, "The State and the Transition to Socialism," *Socialist Review* 8, no. 2 (March–April 1978): 20–21.

63. Arendt, "Thoughts on Politics and Revolution," in *CR*, p. 206.

64. See Theda Skocpol, *States and Social Revolutions* (Cambridge: Cambridge University Press, 1978), and Ralph Miliband, *Marxism and Politics* (Oxford: Oxford University Press, 1977).

65. Nicos Poulantzas, *State, Power, Socialism* (London: Verso, 1978), p. 196.

66. This hard-headed anti-utopianism is of course only one dimension of Marxism, although it is an important one. For a recent example, see Ellen Wood, *The Retreat from Class* (London: Verso, 1985).

67. Camus, *MS*, p. 41.

68. See Timothy Garton Ash, *The Magic Lantern* (New York: Knopf, 1990); John Keane, ed., *Civil Society and the State* (London: Verso, 1986); John Keane, *Democracy and Civil Society* (London: Verso, 1986); and Andrew Arato and Jean Cohen, "Civil Society, History, and Socialism: Reply to John Keane," *Praxis International* 9, nos. 1 and 2 (April and July 1989).

69. In what follows I will treat the most influential Central Europeans—Václav Havel, Adam Michnik, George Konrad—as if they share a common political perspective, though it is also important to recognize differences of attitude and political strategy.

See Timothy Garton Ash, *The Uses of Adversity: Essays on the Fate of Central Europe* (New York: Vintage, 1990), esp. pp. 179–213, and Jeffrey C. Goldfarb, *Beyond Glasnost: The Post-Totalitarian Mind* (Chicago: University of Chicago Press, 1989).

70. Václav Havel, *Disturbing the Peace* (New York: Knopf, 1990), pp. 83, 79.

71. Ibid., p. 115. Compare this remark with Dwight Macdonald's hope, expressed in his draft Statement of Purpose for the Europe-America Groups, that such efforts "would set in motion all kinds of actions which it is impossible to plan or foresee in advance." This text was made available to me by Gregory Sumner.

72. Václav Havel, "Letter to Dr. Gustav Husák, General Secretary of the Czechoslovak Communist Party," in *Living in Truth* (London: Faber & Faber, 1987), pp. 27–28.

73. Camus, "Neither Victims nor Executioners." *politics,* July-August 1947:144.

74. Havel, "The Power of the Powerless," in *Living in Truth,* pp. 57–58.

75. George Konrad, *Antipolitics* (New York: Harcourt, 1984), p. 224; Adam Michnik, "Conversation in the Citadel," in *Letters from Prison* (Berkeley and Los Angeles: University of California Press, 1985), p. 327. Konrad's appeal to "the authority of the spirit" recalls Thoreau's essay "On Civil Disobedience," which sharply distinguishes between morality, which regards people's souls, and politics, which treats people as objects and concerns itself with their bodies.

76. Havel, *Disturbing the Peace,* p. 109.

77. Konrad, *Antipolitics,* p. 231.

78. This valorization of society over the state recalls the writings of such early modern revolutionary republicans as Thomas Paine, William Godwin, and Thomas Jefferson, thinkers highly praised by Arendt.

79. Adam Michnik, "A New Evolutionism," in *Letters from Prison,* pp. 139–45.

80. Adam Michnik, "Maggots and Angels," in *Letters from Prison,* pp. 176–77.

81. Ibid., p. 182. See also Adam Michnik, "Why You Are Not Signing," in *Letters from Prison,* pp. 3–15.

82. Michnik, "Maggots and Angels," pp. 190–91.

83. KOR news-sheet, quoted in Alain Touraine et al., *Solidarity: Poland 1980–1981* (Cambridge: Cambridge University Press, 1983), p. 75.

84. Ibid., pp. 64, 74. See also Jadwiga Staniszkis, *Poland's Self-Limiting Revolution,* (Princeton: Princeton University Press, 1984).

85. In *On Revolution,* Arendt refers to the "spaces of freedom" as "islands in a sea or oases in a desert" (p. 275).

86. See, for example, Ferenc Miszlivetz, " 'Dialogue'—and What Is Behind It," *Across Frontiers* (Summer 1989): pp. 30–33. *Across Frontiers* is a superb source for the pamphlet literature of civil society in Central Europe.

87. Mary Kaldor, introduction to Mary Kaldor, Gerard Holden, and Richard Falk, eds., *The New Detente* (London and Tokyo: Verso and United Nations University, 1989), p. 15.

88. Quoted in "Address by Václav Havel to the Helsinki Citizens' Assembly Opening Session," *East European Reporter* 4, no. 4 (Spring-Summer 1991): 72–73.

89. See Havel: "I favour 'anti-political politics,' that is politics not as the technology of power and manipulation, of cybernetic rule over humans or as the art of the useful, but politics as one of the ways of seeking and achieving meaningful lives, of protecting them and serving them. I favour politics as practical morality, as

service to the truth, as essentially human and humanly measured care for our fellow humans." Václav Havel, "Politics and Conscience," in *Living in Truth,* p. 155. It is worth noting the Arendtian inspiration of Jonathan Schell's sensational *The Fate of the Earth* (New York: Knopf, 1982), esp. pp. 118–78, a book that galvanized Western peace movements and helped undermine the logic of the Cold War and crack the bloc system. On the connections between the peace movements and the emergence of Central European civil society, see Mary Kaldor, Gerard Holden, and Richard Falk, eds., *The New Detente* (London: Verso, 1989).

90. Mary Kaldor, "Speech to the Closing Session of the Helsinki Citizens' Assembly," in Mary Kaldor, ed., *Europe from Below: An East-West Dialogue* (London: Verso, 1991), p. 215.

91. For some early warning signals, see Adam Michnik, "After the Revolution," *New Republic,* July 2, 1990; George Konrad, "Ethics and Politics," *Dissent,* Fall 1990; and Timothy Garton Ash, "Eastern Europe: Après le Deluge, Nous." *The New York Review of Books,* August 16, 1990.

92. Havel, "Helsinki Citizens' Assembly," 74–75.

93. See Herbert Marcuse, "Repressive Tolerance," in Robert Paul Wolff, Barrington Moore, and Herbert Marcuse, *A Critique of Pure Tolerance* (Boston: Beacon Press, 1969).

94. See Ralph Dahrendorf, "Threats To Civil Society, East and West," *Harper's* (July 1990): 24–27; Robert A. Dahl, "Social Reality and 'Free Markets,' " *Dissent* (Spring 1990): 225–28.

95. Ellen Meiksins Wood, "The Uses and Abuses of Civil Society," in Ralph Miliband and Leo Panitch, ed., *Socialist Register 1990: The Retreat of the Intellectuals* (London: Merlin Press, 1990), pp. 80, 60.

96. Camus, *R,* p. 297

97. See Michael Harrington, *Socialism: Past and Future* (New York: Arcade, 1989), and Jeffrey Isaac, "Socialism and Its Discontents," *Tikkun* 5, no. 2 (March-April 1990): 99–102. See also Andrew Arato and Jean Cohen, "Social Movements, Civil Society, and the Problem of Sovereignty," *Praxis International* 4, no. 3 (October 1984).

98. Camus, "Return to Tipasa," in *LCE,* p. 169.

Index

Absolutism, 138, 171, 200; Camus on, 128–31

Absurdity, 92–95, 98–99, 110, 118–20, 222, and surrealism, 94–95

Action, political, 114, 132, 141, 169; Arendt on, 111–18; consequences of, 116–17, 173–76, 193; and Dewey, 145; local, 225, 226; and Luxemburg, 144. *See also* Politics

Adams, John, 152–53

Adorno, Theodor, 69, 70

Algeria, 186, 232; and Camus, 193–206, 219; independence for, 201–2, 205–6; and Palestine, 216–17

Alger-Républicain, 31, 155

Amnesty International, 182, 225

Anarchism, 148–49, 204, 236

Anderson, Perry, 237

Anthropocentrism, 103

Anti-Americanism, 189–90; Arendt on, 187

Anticommunism, 188; Camus on, 186

Anti-Semitism, 48, 66, 208, 212, 220, 223

Arab-Jewish conflicts, 213. *See also* Palestine; Zionism

Arabs: Arendt on, 210–11; Camus on, 195, 204–6. *See also* Algeria; Palestine; *Pied noir*

Arendt, Hannah, 2, 11; biographical sketch of, 27–30, 34; classicism of, 14–15, 102; historical vision of, 240; influences, 33; political activities of, 186–94, 206–16; view of Camus, 16–17; works: "Aftermath of Nazi Rule, The," 187; *Between Past and Future*, 34, 88, 104; "Civil Disobedience," 16; "Cold War and the West, The," 190n.48; *Crises in the Republic*, 188, 191, 193; "Crisis in Courage, The," 168; *Critic* (journal),

189; "Dream and Nightmare," 189; *Eichmann in Jerusalem*, 47–48, 194, 218, 222–23; "Europe and the Atom Bomb," 189; "Ex-Communists, The," 188; "French Existentialism," 289n.64; *Human Condition, The*, 54, 71, 76, 78, 88, 104, 147, 152, 190, 230; and Christianity, 77; and labor movements, 159, 163; and Marx, 83; and Nietzsche, 97; and power, 111; "Karl Jaspers: Citizen of the World?," 224; *Life of the Mind, The*, 96–97, 104; "Lying in Politics," 191; "Moral of History, The," 207; "On Hannah Arendt," 309n.47; "On Humanity in Dark Times," 272n.75; *On Revolution*, 104, 160, 164, 165, 191, 230; influences, 142; and power, 133; and republics, 131–32; *On Violence*, 97, 135, 192; "Organized Guilt and Universal Responsibility," 30, 306n.155; *Origins of Totalitarianism, The*, 29–30, 32, 46, 57, 62, 104, 133, 220, 221; and action, 117; criticism of, 60; and faith in history, 82; influences, 142; and nihilism, 95–96; and roots of totalitarianism, 66–67; and Stalin, 87–88; and Voegelin, 71–72; and World War I, 88; "Peace or Armistice in the Middle East?," 215–16; "Portrait of a Period," 288n.50; "Reflections on Little Rock," 297n.86, 310n.57; "Thoughts on Politics and Revolution," 164; "To Save the Jewish Homeland: There Is Still Time," 213; "Tradition and the Modern Age," 96; "We Refugees," 28; "Zionism Reconsidered," 211

Aristotle, 52, 76, 112, 121

Aron, Raymond, 24, 40, 143

Capitalism, 64, 78; Arendt's criticisms of, 158–59; Camus's criticisms of, 158–59

Capital punishment, 99, 137

Catholic church, 171–72

Central Europe. *See* Eastern Europe

Central Intelligence Agency (CIA), 188

Chambers, Whittaker, 188

Char, René, 34

Chiaromante, Nicola, 17, 22

Chomsky, Noam, 192

Christianity: Arendt on, 76–78; Camus on, 73–74, 171–72

Civil disobedience, 156

Civil society, 156, 220, 248–58. *See also* Community

Cold War, 12, 14, 64, 65, 67, 177–94, 253; Arendt on, 186–94; Camus on, 185–86; and the Korean War, 183

Communication, 114, 123–24, 147, 157

Communism, 1, 3, 6, 7, 40, 85, 184

Communist Manifesto (Marx and Engels), 267n.26

Communist Popular Front, 30, 31

Communitarianism, 5–6, 124–25

Community, 99, 125, 146, 147, 164. *See also* Civil society

Concentration camps, 43–44, 45–51, 61–62; Soviet, 49

Confederational government, 151, 156, 222, 225, 226. *See also* Council system of government

Congress for Cultural Freedom, 183, 188

Connolly, William, 69

Constant, Benjamin, 142, 281n.81

Council system of government, 149–50, 152, 165, 245–46. *See also* Confederational government

Critical theory, 8–10, 238–39

Crusade for World Federation, 182

Dadaism, 94

Danish resistance efforts, 154, 268n.57

Darkness at Noon (Koestler), 59–60, 128

Davis, Gary, 182

Death camps. *See* Concentration camps

Democracy, 140–76, 257–58; Arendt on, 149–56; Camus on, 156–57; in Eastern Europe, 6, 7; international, 157; and judgment, 166–72; and political economy, 158–66; radical, 142–58

Derrida, Jacques, 4, 10

Deutscher, Isaac, 60, 61

Dewey, John, 145–48, 150

Dialogue, political, 123–24, 171, 183, 254

Diaspora, Jewish, 209, 212

Dictatorships and Double Standards (Kirkpatrick), 64

Domenach, Jean-Marie, 303n.91

Dreyfuss Affair, 220

Dualism, East-West, 181–82

Durkheim, Emile, 237

Eastern Europe, 7, 10, 248, 250

Economism, 158–59, 160

Eichmann, Adolf, 47–48, 54, 137, 151. *See also* Arendt, Hannah, works: *Eichmann in Jerusalem*

Elites (political), 152, 153, 154

Engels, Friedrich, 162

Enlightenment, 43–44, 74–75, 163, 217–18

Essentialism, 106–8, 109, 145

Ethical foundations, 106–110

Ethical requirement, 125, 238

"Ethic of efficacy," 79

Ethic of revolt, 125–39, 173, 225, 234

Europe-America Groups (EAGs), 182–83, 225

European Nuclear Disarmament (END), 253

Existentialism, 16, 32–33, 121, 140–41

Express, L', 184

Fainsod, Merle, 87

Fanon, Frantz, 192

Farias, Victor, 284n.129

Imperialism, 179
Intellectuals, 13–14, 75–76, 95–96
Internationalism, 216–26; Arendt's view
 of, 220–26; Camus's vision of, 219–
 20, 225–26
International law, 221, 223, 224
Interpol, 221
Irgun, 211
Isonomy, 114, 149

Jacobinism, 142
Jacobson, Norman, 11
Jaspers, Karl, 27, 33, 109, 114, 218,
 222, 224
Jay, Martin, 141
Jeanson, Francis, 60, 72, 156, 197
Jefferson, Thomas, 149, 290n.85
Jewish-Arab relations, 216, 230
Jewish history, 207–8
Jewish homeland. *See* Zionism; Feder-
 ated settlements
Jordan Valley Authority, 214
Judgment: Arendt on, 167–69; Camus
 on, 169–72; political, 166–72
Junger, Ernest, 40
Justice, 129, 166, 185, 234

Kafka, Franz, 33
Kaldor, Mary, 253–54
Kant, Emmanuel, 79–80, 114, 135,
 141, 168, 222
Kateb, George, 278n.46, 291n.99,
 296n.58
Kautsky, Karl, 89
Kibbutzim, 163–64, 215
Kierkegaard, Søren, 33, 96
Koestler, Arthur, 27, 41, 44–45, 53,
 173
Kohn, Hans, 40
Konrad, George, 249, 310n.69
Korean War, 183–84
Korsch, Karl, 237
Kropotkin, Peter, 148
Kundera, Milan, 1, 2
Kuron, Jacek, 252

Labor movements: Arendt's treatment
 of, 159–65; Camus on, 165–66; Eu-
 ropean, 158
Language, 8, 112, 113, 116, 124, 125;
 Arendt on, 54–55; Camus on, 52–
 53; subversion of, 52–55
Lasch, Christopher, 125
Lauriol Plan (Algeria), 203–4, 215, 219
Lazare, Bernard, 211
Lederer, Emil, 40–41
Lefort, Claude, 158, 273n.79
Lenin, V. I., 87–88, 128, 245; Arendt's
 opinion of, 88–90
Leviathan (Hobbes), 79
Liberalism, 4–5, 38, 241; and action,
 117; continental, 142; lexicon of,
 144–45; Western, 178, 255–56
Liebich, Andre, 42
Liebknecht, Karl, 90
Ligue contre l'antisemitisme, 34
Local governments. *See* Confederational
 government
Localist internationalism, 219–220
Loneliness, 55–56
Lopate, Phillip, 273n.98
Love, 174–75, 234, 281n.87
Lukacs, George, 82, 112, 237
Luxemburg, Rosa, 23, 143–44, 166,
 240; Arendt's essay on, 89–90
Lyotard, Jean-François, 14, 76, 105,
 227

McCarran-Walters Act, 189
McCarthy, Joseph, 188–89
McCarthy, Mary, 17
Macdonald, Dwight, 17, 24, 25, 182–
 83
Machiavelli, Niccolò, 77–78
MacIntyre, Alasdair, 5, 6, 8
Macpherson, C. B., 162
Madison, James, 254
Magnes, Judah, 214–16
Mannheim, Karl, 40–41
Marcel, Gabriel, 65
Marcuse, Herbert, 41
Margolis, Joseph, 106–7
Marx, Karl, 76, 82–86, 96, 112, 165,